Microsoft® IIS 5 Administration

Gerry O'Brien

A Division of Macmillan USA
201 West 103rd St., Indianapolis, Indiana, 46290 USA

Microsoft® IIS 5 Administration

International Standard Book Number: 0-672-31964-0

Library of Congress Catalog Card Number: 00-102227

Printed in the United States of America

First Printing: September 2000

03   02   01   00   4   3   2   1

Trademarks

Warning and Disclaimer

EXECUTIVE EDITOR
Chris Denny

ACQUISITIONS EDITOR
Neil Rowe

DEVELOPMENT EDITOR
Kevin Howard

MANAGING EDITOR
Charlotte Clapp

PROJECT EDITOR
Paul Schneider

COPY EDITOR
Mary Ellen Stephenson

INDEXER
Sheila Schroeder

PROOFREADER
Katherin Bidwell

TECHNICAL EDITOR
Emmett Dulaney

TEAM COORDINATOR
Meggo Barthlow

INTERIOR DESIGNER
Anne Jones

COVER DESIGNER
Aren Howell

COPYWRITER
Eric Borgert

LAYOUT TECHNICIANS
Ayanna Lacey
Heather Hiatt Miller
Stacey Richwine-DeRome

Overview

Contents

About the Authors

Gerry O'Brien has been working with IIS 5.0 since the Windows 2000 beta program. He has administered IIS and developed front-end interfaces for back-end data sources using VBScript and Active Server Pages for a WAN environment using Windows NT along with Routing and Remote Access using PPTP and Virtual Private Networking for secure data transfer, email gateways, and intranet usage. He has been using Windows 2000 Server and Professional in a production environment in his own company, a VAR that provides hardware and software implementations, consulting, sales, and software development.

Dylan B. DeAnda, MCSE, works as a Windows NT/2000 systems engineer for Loudcloud, Inc. (www.loudcloud.com) as well as a Web technologies consultant. He has worked extensively with IIS 3.0, 4.0, and 5.0; Microsoft's Site Server 3.0 Commerce Edition; and Windows 2000 Active Directory. Dylan has served as an instructor for Microsoft Certified Systems Engineer courses in Hawaii.

Dedication

I would like to dedicate this book to the members of my family.

To my wife, Dianne, for her enduring patience and understanding when I spent night after night looking at a computer keyboard and monitor instead of taking her out to a movie or to dinner. I couldn't have done it without your love and support. I love you. Thanks.

To my mother-in-law, Grace. You never complained when I offered a quick thank you for the meal you prepared and then disappeared to the computer room.

To my parents for their support and encouragement and providing me the opportunity to achieve the knowledge I have.

Last, but certainly not least, to my seven-year-old son Brandon. At about 85% completion of the book, my energy level and interest was dwindling somewhat, not to mention that the weather was getting a little nicer too. When I thought I couldn't sit in front of the keyboard another night, he provided the inspiration I needed to get back at it.

We were having dinner one night, and he said that he was sorry he had to finish eating so fast but he had some work to do that evening. When my wife asked him what work he had to do, he said that a friend at his school wanted a book written about Pokémon. He said he would make $100 dollars for the project, and he only had a year to complete it so he had to get right to work on it.

I guess maybe they do look up to their parents sometimes. That was all the boost I needed to meet my last deadline. Thank you, Brandon, I owe you big time, buddy. I love you—Dad.

Acknowledgments

For the most part, when I read a computer book, I rarely look at the page that contains the legal mumbo jumbo and the names of the people who work behind the scenes to make the publication possible.

Writing a book myself has made me realize that there are more than just one or two people responsible for the completion of a book project. The authoring is actually the smallest part of the entire process. For that reason, I would like to acknowledge all of those who made this book a reality.

From the start, my first contact for writing at Sams was with Karen Opal. Many thanks to you Karen for the opportunity and passing my name on to the appropriate people. Neil Rowe, my Acquisitions Editor for having faith in my abilities, thank you for this opportunity as well. I know it must be tough to take on a new author and I appreciate it sincerely. Paul Schneider for his coordination and patience during author review. It made things much easier for me for sure.

Kevin Howard, development editor, thanks for your excellent insight and input. It's hard to keep track of your target audience sometimes when you get involved in a chapter's contents. You brought me back on track.

The editing team responsible for this book was just phenomenal. My high school English teacher would have loved you, Mary Ellen. She may have been disappointed that I couldn't remember all of her teachings but you offered the reminders where they were needed. Thanks.

Emmett Dulaney, technical editor, awesome input. It makes it so much easier when the feedback is as good as you provided for technical accuracy and content. You can work with a product for many years and still not touch every aspect of it. You are very knowledgeable, and your input was greatly appreciated.

These are the names of those I dealt with on a regular basis during the project. I know that there are others involved in layout and design work, indexing, and printing. Such a huge team for one book. Thanks to all of you as well.

Tell Us What You Think!

As the reader of this book, *you* are our most important critic and commentator. We value your opinion and want to know what we're doing right, what we could do better, what areas you'd like to see us publish in, and any other words of wisdom you're willing to pass our way.

As an Associate Publisher for Sams, I welcome your comments. You can fax, email, or write me directly to let me know what you did or didn't like about this book—as well as what we can do to make our books stronger.

Please note that I cannot help you with technical problems related to the topic of this book, and that due to the high volume of mail I receive, I might not be able to reply to every message.

When you write, please be sure to include this book's title and author as well as your name and phone or fax number. I will carefully review your comments and share them with the author and editors who worked on the book.

Fax: 317-581-4770

Email: adv_prog@mcp.com

Mail: Bradley Jones
          Associate Publisher
          Sams Publishing
          201 West 103rd Street
          Indianapolis, IN 46290 USA

Introduction

Welcome to the Internet Information Server 5.0 book in the Sams Professional Series. This title is aimed at providing the intermediate-to-advanced user with the skills and information necessary to get the best performance and security from Microsoft's latest Web server software for the Windows 2000 platforms.

In this book you will find information that pertains to IIS running on Windows 2000 Server. In version 4.0 of Windows NT, Microsoft provided the IIS product for the Server operating system, while offering the Windows NT Workstation users Personal Web Server. This has changed with IIS 5.0, which now runs on both platforms. Windows 2000 Professional still has the 10-user connection limit that existed in NT Workstation, but IIS 5.0 offers much better security and performance than PWS did. Although we are targeting the Server OS, you will find that many concepts in this book apply to IIS 5.0 on Windows 2000 Professional as well.

As we go through the examples and discussions in the book, we will mention the areas that are different or specific to the Windows 2000 Professional installation of IIS.

I am assuming that, if you are reading this book as an intended user, you will already have IIS installed, or are capable of installing it. For the most part, IIS is installed by default when you install the Windows 2000 Server operating system but not with Windows 2000 Professional.

I hope you enjoy reading this book and find the information presented to be of use to you and your organization in the day-to-day task of administering Internet Information Server 5.0.

Management

PART
I

IN THIS PART

Internet Information Server 5.0 Features

IN THIS CHAPTER

Internet Information Server 5.0 has been enhanced with some new features while maintaining the features that were present in earlier versions of IIS.

This chapter will serve as an introduction to the features of IIS 5.0. Each of them will be covered in detail in the respective chapters relating to the subject area.

Introduction to New Features in IIS 5.0

Microsoft, like any other software company, continuously improves its products. The same goes for Internet Information Server. Whether improvements are made for security reasons, to enhance performance, or in response to customer feedback, the end user is the one who wins.

The changes that are made to a software product reflect customer feedback and input from within Microsoft itself. Microsoft does indeed use its own products, and it has also set up usability labs for testing purposes.

You will find that IIS 5.0 contains most, if not all, of the features that were available in IIS 4.0, but Microsoft has also added the new features that will be introduced here and explained throughout the book. You may or may not have a use for some of the new features included with IIS 5.0, but being aware of what they are and how to use them will benefit you as an IIS administrator.

The added features in security can help you to take advantage of the latest in encryption technologies and authentication methods using client- and server-side certificates. Financial institutions will appreciate the use of Server Gated Cryptography (SGC) for dealing with 128-bit encrypted transactions on the export side.

Administration and performance issues have been addressed as well with IIS 5.0 as you will see later in the book.

This chapter will introduce you to these new features and describe what they offer to you, the IIS administrator.

Security

It seems that security concerns are a top priority, or *the* top priority, when it comes to computers connected to the Internet. The "crackers," or to use today's more common term, "hackers," have concentrated their efforts lately on Microsoft's operating systems and Internet-related software. IIS 5.0 adds some newer capabilities along with existing features to help thwart attacks by hackers and ensure data security.

Secure Sockets Layer (SSL)

One of the ways IIS 5.0 helps to ensure data security is through the use of Secure Sockets Layer (SSL) version 3.0 and Transport Layer Security protocols. These provide a method of transferring data between client and server in a secure manner and also allow the client to be verified by the server before the user logs on.

Another feature is the use of client certificates. These can be used by programmers in ASP applications and ISAPI for tracking users who visit the site. Client certificates can also be used in conjunction with user accounts on the system, allowing the administrator to map the user accounts to the certificates. This provides a way of controlling access to resources on the server.

Server Gated Cryptography (SGC)

SGC is a great new feature for use on your Web server if you are looking into e-commerce or financial transactions over the Internet. As an extension of SSL, it allows the use of export versions of IIS to use 128-bit encryption or standard 40-bit encryption. This reduces the need for multiple versions of IIS.

Although SGC is integrated into IIS 5.0, you are still required to use a special SGC certificate to use it.

For more information on SGC, visit Microsoft's Web site at
`http://www.microsoft.com/security/tech/sgc`.

Digest Authentication

Another new feature added to IIS is Digest Authentication. By implementing this feature, administrators can authenticate users securely across firewalls and proxy servers.

For those of you who are familiar with Anonymous, HTTP Basic, and NT Challenge/Response authentication, you'll be happy to know that these still exist in IIS 5.0.

IP and Domain Name Restrictions

If you've had or have a mail server connected to the Internet, you might have run across the embarrassing or frustrating situation of being used as a relay for spammers and hackers. IIS 5.0 can help prevent users with known IP addresses and/or Internet domain names from gaining unauthorized access to your server by allowing you to specify the appropriate information in a restriction list.

Take note that you must know the IP address of the domain that you want to restrict. This feature is not automatic, and you must administer it for it to be effective.

Fortezza

Newly added in IIS 5.0, Fortezza is a U.S. Government security standard. It complies with the Defense Message System security architecture and provides message authentication, integrity, and confidentiality through a cryptographic mechanism. It can also be used for access control to systems and components.

Kerberos v5

Windows 2000 implements this authentication protocol, allowing you to pass credentials among connected computers running Windows. IIS 5.0 has the Kerberos v5 protocol integrated into it.

Certificate Storage

Storage of your IIS certificates is now integrated with the Windows CryptoAPI Storage. You can use the Windows Certificate Manager to back up, store, and configure your certificates.

Security Wizards

If trying to administer the security of your IIS server seems like a daunting or difficult task, take heart. Microsoft has provided security wizards to help make your job a little easier.

One thing that IIS 5.0 brings to the server is the capability to set access permissions on virtual directories and even on files. Using the Permissions Wizard, this task is simplified, and the wizard can also update your NTFS permissions to reflect these changes.

You can create certificate requests and manage certificates easier with the Web Server Certificate Wizard.

If you are dealing with certification authorities, you can manage your certificate trust lists (CTLs) with the CTL Wizard.

Administration

IIS 5.0 offers a fair number of new administration features as well. We will list them here and give a brief description of them. You will be using them later in the book.

Centralized Administration

For those of you who are coming to IIS 5.0 from version 4.0, you will be familiar with the Microsoft Management Console (MMC). For those who are not familiar with MMC, it is a common administrative console that uses snap-ins to provide an interface to various services and components.

By using the IIS snap-in in MMC, you can administer other IIS servers from your own workstation running Windows 2000 Professional or from a Windows 2000 Server. This prevents the need to administer the IIS service at the server in which it is installed.

Restarting IIS

In the past, when you made significant changes to your IIS configuration, or applications faltered, you had to reboot the server. With IIS 5.0, you can now restart IIS without needing to do a reboot.

You can restart the server from the MMC snap-in or from the command line. These steps will be outlined later in the book.

Backup and Restore

Have you ever made changes to your IIS configuration, tested it, and had it crash? Well, IIS 5.0 offers you the ability to back up your configuration and then later restore it, should you find the need to.

Process Accounting

With the increased use of CGI and ASP scripting on servers, it's nice to have a way of determining how these scripts are affecting performance if at all.

Process Accounting is new in IIS 5.0 and provides this capability by allowing you to view CPU resources being used by individual Web sites on your server.

Process Throttling

After you have determined the performance hits of Web sites or scripts using Process Accounting, you can set up limits on CPU utilization for out-of-process applications.

This style of throttling will place a limit on the amount of CPU time that an application can use but not a limit on the network bandwidth. Network bandwidth throttling is covered in Chapter 11, "Performance Tuning."

Custom Error Messages

IIS 5.0 offers improved error message customization, allowing you to send more informative messages to the clients when errors occur.

A great feature for ASP developers, it provides detailed error processing capabilities. This is implemented through the use of the 500-100.asp custom error messages. ASP developers can use these messages or create their own.

Remote Administration

As a hotly debated and talked about topic, Remote Administration has earned its own chapter in this book. You will find this information in Chapter 15, "Remote Administration." We will look at the capabilities that IIS introduces, allowing you to administer your server from almost any Web browser on any platform.

Terminal Services

This feature is actually a part of the Windows 2000 Server. By implementing this in the operating system, you can now run 32-bit applications on the server from any correctly configured client that would not normally support such an application.

What does this have to do with IIS? Well, it actually falls under the Remote Administration umbrella by allowing you to remotely administer your IIS server as if you were sitting in front of the server itself.

Programmability

With server-side scripting, ASP, and XML taking the development community by storm, it would only make sense to add programming features into Microsoft's premier Web platform.

Active Server Pages

Almost all IIS administrators are familiar with the term Active Server Pages (ASP) by now. At least you had better be. IIS 4.0 offered support for ASP, and version 5.0 continues that.

ASP allows your developers and Web authors to create dynamic, browser-independent Web sites by running applications and scripting on the server instead of the client.

Your developers don't need to use CGI or ISAPI but instead can embed VBScript or Jscript code right into the HTML page. Developers also gain complete access to the HTTP response and request streams.

Another major advantage of ASP is database connectivity.

New ASP Features

ASP in version 5.0 of IIS has added some new features such as

- Flow control capabilities for redirecting requests
- Performance enhanced objects
- Error handling

You will also find other new features explained in Chapters 16, "Active Server Pages," and 17, "Installable ASP Components," on ASP and its installable components.

Application Protection

IIS offers you the ability to run your applications in different processes. By default, IIS runs your applications in a pooled process that is separate from the IIS process itself. This is similar to running the application out-of-process.

You can also run mission-critical applications in their own process where they will not interfere with, or be interfered by, other applications.

ADSI 2.0

Developers can now extend ADSI by adding custom objects, methods, and properties to the provider. This will give you more flexibility in site configuration, should you decide that you need this customization.

Support for Internet Standards

What good is an Internet server if it doesn't support the standards of the Internet? Not much, really. IIS 5.0 has built-in support for the existing Internet standards.

Supported Standards

IIS is compliant with the HTTP 1.1 standard. This means that it supports the PUT and DELETE methods, custom error messages, and custom HTTP headers.

Multiple Sites

In previous versions of IIS, you needed to have an IP address assigned for each virtual Web site that you hosted on your server. IIS 5.0 allows you to create and serve multiple Web sites with one IP address. (This nice feature helps to lower your costs in not requiring you to lease multiple IPs from your ISP.)

Web Distributed Authoring and Versioning (WebDAV)

This feature allows authors to manipulate files on the Web server remotely over an HTTP connection. What this means is that you can copy, delete, or modify files using a Web browser interface or Windows 2000's Network Places, or from Microsoft Office 2000 to WebDAV directories on the server.

WebDAV also allows you to deal with version control of files by providing locking capabilities that enable multiple users to see the same file but only one authorized person to modify that file.

WebDAV also uses the security features of IIS and the Windows 2000's NTFS file system.

SMTP and NNTP Services

IIS 5.0 can work with these two services on the Internet or on an intranet. This offers you the ability to host a news group server with IIS using the NNTP protocol. An NNTP server provides the capability to provide discussion groups on your internal network or WAN, or over the Internet.

The SMTP service can be used to send and receive SMTP mail to users on the Internet or on your intranet. These mail messages can take the form of responses to clients that are connecting to your Web sites, or they can be used to send administrative alerts to Web administrators.

> **NOTE**
>
> The NNTP service included with IIS 5.0 is not intended to be used as push/pull news feed server for your organization. It is meant to be used as an intranet discussion forum.

Platform for Internet Content Selection Ratings (PICS)

This feature of IIS 5.0 allows you to set ratings for each of your Web sites in the event that they are required, (such as, to indicate adult content).

FTP Restart

Another welcome addition to IIS 5.0 is the FTP Restart feature that allows for FTP download resumes when a transfer is interrupted. This prevents the need for the client or user to restart the download from the beginning.

HTTP Compression

If your server and clients are compression-enabled, you can achieve faster page transfers thanks to this HTTP Compression.

Static files can be compressed and cached for quicker access, and IIS can perform compression of dynamically generated pages on demand.

Summary

This chapter has introduced you to a fair number of new features that have been added to or modified in IIS 5.0. These additions and extensions to IIS enhance the performance, security, and manageability of IIS 5.0. Each feature that has been introduced here will be covered in more detail in the chapters throughout *Administering IIS*.

Web Site Management

IN THIS CHAPTER

I think you will agree with me when I say that we have come a long way since our first Web page. I can remember rushing the design and layout just to get my home page posted on that Web server for the entire connected world to see. Most people had the same idea, which was why we saw a lot of "Under Construction" notices.

Back then, my Web pages were hosted by my ISP. I had, and still have, 5MB of disk space on the ISP's server for a personal Web page. Most of that is dedicated to Visual Basic.

But, as we look at the scenario of having an ISP host a Web site, what is the one thing that is missing from the picture? The ability to manage the site the way we want.

As is the case with most ISPs, the servers are all UNIX based with a surprising number of Linux servers as well. There are companies on the Net that provide Web-hosting services, for reasonable prices as well, based on UNIX, NetWare, or Windows NT technologies. Some provide FrontPage Server extensions offering the ability to create your Web site from home or office and publish and maintain it on the ISPs' servers.

All of this is great for the individual user or SOHO (Small Office, Home Office) that only need a simple Web site or even one or two pages. You're reading this book because you are an IIS administrator for a company with the responsibility of creating and maintaining whole, complete Web sites that likely take up more hard drive space than the average user's applications do.

Tweaking performance, enhancing security, and providing a good return on your invested dollar and time are prime goals in the minds of IIS administrators.

This chapter deals with managing your IIS 5.0 server for Web, FTP, SMTP, and NNTP services. You will find information in this chapter that will help you get the most from IIS 5.0.

Introducing IIS 5.0 Web Site Management Capabilities

To help you do a better job of managing your Web site, you can take advantage of the management features of IIS 5.0. Not only can you manage your home directory, but you can also create and manage virtual directories with relative ease. Virtual directories enable you to publish your Web site from any directory on the computer even if it is not listed in the home directory.

Your management of IIS 5.0 will start with the use of the Microsoft Management Console (MMC).

Figure 2.1 shows MMC's Internet Information Services Snap-In, which is used for administrative purposes.

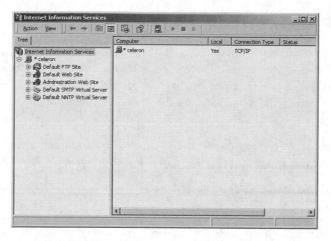

FIGURE 2.1

The Internet Information Services Snap-In is the central point of administration for IIS.

Authoring Tools

Although IIS 5.0 doesn't include any authoring tools to design Web pages with, it enables you to host pages that have been created by various methods. One of the most popular for Microsoft shops is the FrontPage application.

Now in version 2000, Microsoft FrontPage is included with Microsoft Office 2000 Premium Edition. This Web-authoring tool gives you WYSIWYG authoring capabilities and, of course, integrates very well with IIS 5.0.

Another nice feature of FrontPage, and one of the main reasons that I like to use it, is the capability to create and maintain a Web site remotely if you have the FrontPage Server Extensions installed and the appropriate permissions set. FrontPage provides various views for looking at the structure and layout of your Web site.

Of course, FrontPage and text editors are not the only tools available for authoring Web pages. With IIS, it doesn't matter what your favorite tool is—this Web server will host them all for you.

Alternative options include other tools in the Microsoft Office Suite of applications. You can publish your word processing documents, spreadsheets, presentations, and even Access databases to the Internet by using the conversion and export features of these applications.

Whatever tool you decide to use, take heart in knowing that IIS 5.0 will serve them up for you.

Using ASP to Manage Sites

Active Server Pages might bring to mind dynamic Web pages or data access capabilities. The functionality of ASP is implemented by the use of scripting. You can use VBScript, which is a subset of the Visual Basic programming language, or JScript, which is based on Sun Microsystems Java development language, for this scripting. (Don't confuse JScript with JavaScript.)

ASP uses two types of scripts: server-side and client-side. As you might expect, server-side scripts run on the server, whereas client-side scripts run on the client's Web browser.

> **NOTE**
>
> Although not every browser supports VBScript on the client side, you don't have to learn JScript just to cover every browser type. You can use VBScript on the server side and generate platform-independent scripts that forward only HTML to clients. This reduces the need for multiple versions of a page.

I certainly cannot teach you all there is to know about ASP in a chapter or two in this book; the topic requires a complete book of its own. I can, however, show you enough to let you use ASP for the administration tasks that I am talking about.

Scripts that run on the server are placed in the HTML code of the page and are surrounded by the opening and closing tags <%> and </%>. Also, you must specify the scripting language at the top of the page, before any other element, as in Listing 2.1.

LISTING 2.1 Simple ASP Page (9640Font.asp)

```
<%@ LANGUAGE=VBScript %>
<HTML>
<HEAD>
<TITLE>Page Title</TITLE>
</HEAD>
<BODY>
<% Dim i
      For i = 1 to 5
%>

<FONT SIZE=<% =i %>>
<CENTER>Font Size Example
<% Next %>

</BODY>
</HTML>
```

Listing 2.1 depicts a small code snippet that uses the basic HTML code for a page with a little ASP code in VBScript that will increase the font size from 1 to 5.

Although ASP is a great tool for data access and the other features mentioned previously, (we'll see some examples later in Chapter 16, "Active Server Pages"), you can also use it for Web server management tasks.

One of the nicest features I have come across in most Web sites is a navigation bar that remains consistent across pages. Microsoft FrontPage provides this feature in the themes that come with the FrontPage product. If you are creating your pages using a text editor, you can still implement this feature rather simply using ASP or frames. I will show you the ASP implementation here.

The first step is to create a Web page that contains the HTML for the navigation bar. Next create each of your main HTML pages and use ASP's #include directive to include the navigation bar file into your pages. ASP does this with one line:

```
<!-- #include file="navbar.stm" -->
```

Listings 2.2, 2.3, and 2.4 illustrate three brief sample pages that are simple in design. Copy and paste the code into your favorite HTML editor to see how the pages function.

The first page, navbar.stm, shown in Listing 2.2, is an actual HTML page with the extension of .stm. The extension informs your ASP code that the page is an #include file.

LISTING 2.2 Navigation Bar for Home Page (navbar.stm)

```
<html>

<head>
<title>Navigation Bar Page</title>
</head>

<body>

<table border="1" width="100%" cellspacing="0" cellpadding="0">
  <tr>
    <td width="33%" align="center"><a href="home.asp">Home</a></td>
    <td width="34%" align="center"><a href="contact.asp">Contact</a></td>
  </tr>
</table>

</body>

</html>
```

Listing 2.3 contains your home page, home.asp, which would be the starting point of the Web site. Note the use of the script tag at the start of the document.

LISTING 2.3   The Home Page That Will Use the #include Files (home.asp)

```
<%@ LANGUAGE=VBScript %>
<html>

<head>
<title>Home Page</title>
</head>

<body>
<!-- #include file="navbar.stm" -->
<h1 align="center"><b>This is the Home Page</b></h1>
<hr>

<p>
This is the body of the page.<p>
<BR><BR>
This navigation bar is at the bottom as well.
<!-- #include file="navbar.stm" -->
</body>

</html>
```

The last page, contact.asp, shown in Listing 2.4, simply shows how you can have one file included in multiple pages by simply using the #include directive. Neither the home page nor contact.asp contains the actual HTML code for the navigation bar. This is a great time-saver.

LISTING 2.4   Contacts Page Code with Two #include Directives (contact.asp)

```
<%@ LANGUAGE=VBScript %>
<html>

<head>
<title>Contacts Page</title>
</head>

<body>
<!-- #include file="navbar.stm" -->
<h1 align="center">This is our contact page!</h1>
<hr>
```

```
<p>Gerry O'Brien - <a
href="mailto:gkcomput@nbnet.nb.ca">gkcomput@nbnet.nb.ca</a></p>
<p>Macmillan Publishing USA - <a
href="http://www.mcp.com">http://www.mcp.com</a></p>
<p> </p>
<p align="center"> </p>
<!-- #include file="navbar.stm" -->
</body>

</html>
```

Note that the filename must contain the full path of the file if it is not in the same directory as the HTML file using it. It is also good practice to name your #include files with the .inc or .stm extension.

CAUTION

When dealing with ASP pages and code, you must remember to give each page that contains any ASP code an extension of .asp. If you fail to do this, IIS will not process the code.

NOTE

While you have one of the ASP pages displayed in your browser, use your browser's source viewing capabilities and compare the source code displayed in the notepad window with the code that you used to create the page. You will notice that no ASP code is displayed. This is a nice little feature that prevents the client from stealing your code or seeing how your pages are created.

You can use ASP to redirect users to the correct URL if you have made changes to the Web site that have rendered existing URLs broken. The following line accomplishes this:

```
<% Response.Redirect (new url) %>
```

ASP also contains the Browser Capabilities component. Using this component, you can activate features specific to each browser that visits your site. (In order to use this feature, you should be familiar with using COM components. Information is available in most ASP tutorials.)

Directories

Web sites are stored in directories. This is a rather blunt statement, but it says all there is to say about the structure of a Web site. Most Web administrators will set up a logical directory structure that makes sense from their perspectives. Usually, there are subdirectories under the main or home directory for images, scripts, #include files, and so on.

As far as IIS is concerned, there are two types of directories, home directories and virtual directories. These are explained in the next two sections.

Home Directories

Each Web site must have a home directory. In most cases, this is <drive>\InetPub\wwwroot, wherein <drive> is the drive letter on which you installed IIS. You can specify any directory you want to be your home directory.

In order to create a home directory for your Web site, you can use the Windows Explorer or My Computer to create a directory on the drive or in the folder where you want it to reside. For example, to create a directory under the wwwroot directory of the InetPub directory, navigate to wwwroot using Windows Explorer. Select the wwwroot directory entry and choose New, Folder from the File menu. Give the new directory a name.

Figure 2.2 shows the Home Directory tab of the Default Web Site Properties dialog box.

FIGURE 2.2

The Home Directory tab is where you specify the location for the home directory of your Web site.

As you can see from Figure 2.2, there are three choices for a home directory:

- **A directory located on this computer**—Use this option if the home directory is on the same computer as IIS.

- **A share located on another computer**— This option is available if you have your home directory set up and shared on another computer on the network.

- **A redirection to a URL**—You would use this option if your home directory is located on a server on the Internet.

Virtual Directories

A virtual directory is used when you have a Web site that spans multiple directories, drives, or computers. An example of this might be a database accessed by an ASP page, in which the database resides on another server in your network, or if you have a common drive shared on the network that stores all your images' clip art. In order to access these files, you need to create a virtual directory.

To create a virtual directory, open the IIS snap-in in MMC. After you select the Web site in which you want to create the virtual directory, choose the Action menu, and then select New and Virtual Directory. The Virtual Directory Creation Wizard will walk you through the creation of the directory.

Alternatively, if you are using NTFS on your hard drive (as most self-respecting NT Administrators are), you can create a virtual directory in another way:

1. In Windows Explorer, right-click the directory you want to use.
2. From the context-sensitive menu, select Sharing.
3. Select the Web Sharing tab.

Figure 2.3 shows what this tab looks like.

The Share on drop-down combo box lists the available Web sites where you can share this directory.

By choosing the Share this folder radio button, you can give your virtual directory an alias.

You can delete a virtual directory by selecting it in the MMC console and then choosing Delete from the Action menu.

2

WEB SITE MANAGEMENT

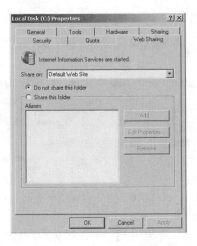

FIGURE 2.3
The Web Sharing tab is where you set properties for the virtual directory you want to create.

Redirecting Requests

Why should you have to redirect requests on your Web site? After all, your URLs are all up-to-date, aren't they?

For the most part, Web administrators do keep their URLs up-to-date and fix broken links on a regular basis. The main reason for redirection would be to accommodate clients when your site is under construction or renovation.

IIS 5.0 offers you the ability to redirect requests to other URLs or to programs on the server. We'll look at both in turn in the following sections.

Redirecting to a Directory

If you want to redirect requests to a file in a different directory, or perhaps to another URL, you can do so by using the IIS snap-in in MMC.

Figure 2.4 shows the Default Web Site Properties dialog box with the Home Directory tab selected.

In Figure 2.4, I have specified that any requests for my home directory will be sent to the URL entered in the text box.

Notice that there are three options you can select here:

1. **The exact URL entered above**—This setting will send the requesting client to the URL specified.

2. **A directory below this one**—This option is used to redirect a parent directory to a child directory. If your child directory is `newfolder`, then you would enter `/newfolder` in the text box and select this option.

3. **A permanent redirection for this resource**—If the browser supports the `301 Permanent Redirect` message, this option, with the correct new URL entered, will tell the browser to automatically update bookmarks that refer to the old URL.

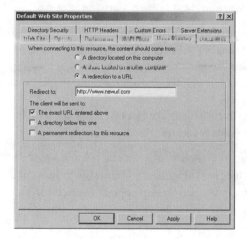

FIGURE 2.4
The Home Directory tab shows you how to redirect requests for the home directory to a different URL.

Redirecting to a Program

You can redirect requests to a program that you might use for logging purposes. In this case, you would make use of the redirect to pass the necessary parameters to the application.

Redirects can use wildcards and variables as well. The redirect variables are used to pass portions of the original URL with the new URL.

An example would be if you needed to pass parameters to the new URL, as in text strings in feedback:

```
http://www.myserver.com/feedback/newform.asp?age=35
```

The redirect variable that you would use to pass the parameters that are included with the URL, such as the `?age=35` parameter above, is the `$P` variable. By using the `$P` variable, you can cause the parameter portion to be added to the redirect URL.

The redirected URL is

`http://www.newserver.com/feedbacknew/newform.aspPARAMS=$P`

and the `parameter ?age=35` has been passed along with it.

Redirecting to a program is the same as redirecting to a URL or file with the exception that the program name is entered in the text box at the end of the URL:

`http://www.newserver.com/applications/createlog.exe`

You must select the option The exact URL entered above to prevent IIS from appending the filename to the URL and breaking your redirection request.

Content

We look at the content of your Web site here in two contexts. The first is the expiration of your content, and the second is content ratings.

The ability to manage these two aspects of your site content helps make browsing more efficient and pleasurable for the client. These two abilities help prevent clients from getting out-of-date information and enable parents to set up content restrictions on their browsers so that their children cannot view adult material on a site.

Content Expiration

In order to set expiration dates for content on your site, you can make use of HTTP headers. Browsers compare the date on the local computer to the expiration date in the header to determine if they should use a cached page, or download the updated content.

As with other management tasks, you use the IIS snap-in in MMC to gain access to the Properties dialog box. Selecting the Enable Content Expiration check box enables you to specify three different expiration options.

Figure 2.5 shows that I have chosen to expire the content in the `/scripts` directory of my Web site.

> **NOTE**
>
> You can expire content on files, directories, or the entire Web site by choosing the appropriate component in the MMC explorer panel.

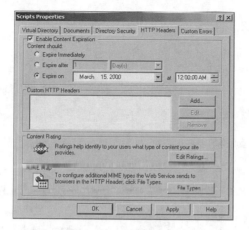

FIGURE 2.5
The HTTP Headers tab, in which you can enter the content expiration parameters.

In Figure 2.5, I have chosen to expire the content in my /scripts directory on a specific date, at a specific time,12:00 AM on March 15, 2000.

The other two options available are to have the content expire immediately or after *x* number of days. For the most part, you would expire content immediately if the page is generated on-the-fly, as in forms that a client would fill out. This content should not be cached. Also, you can have pages that display sale prices on stock items that are applicable only for a couple of days.

Content Ratings

Setting ratings on your Web content is only required if you have questionable information on your Web site. You can set the ratings based on violence, nudity, and language. This is available in the MMC by selecting the appropriate Web site and opening the properties dialog box for it.

You choose to enable ratings by clicking the Edit Ratings button under the Content Rating section of the properties dialog box (refer to Figure 2.5).

I recommend that you familiarize yourself with content ratings by selecting the More Info button on the initial page of the Content Ratings dialog box.

Figure 2.6 shows the Rating Service tab of the Content Ratings dialog box. Clicking the buttons on this tab takes you to sites on the Internet that explain the ratings in detail.

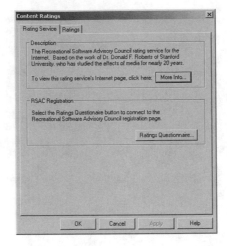

FIGURE 2.6
The Ratings Service Tab for setting ratings on the site.

You can also have the Recreational Software Advisory Council (RSAC) help you determine your ratings by clicking the Ratings Questionnaire button. This takes you to the RSAC Web site, where you can register your site and view sample questionnaires.

Select the Ratings tab to set ratings that reflect the content contained in the site or within a file or directory. Figure 2.7 gives you an example of a rating for violence. Moving the slider to the right will increase the rating level.

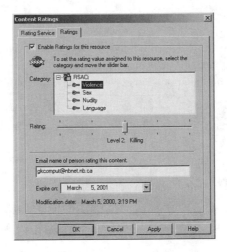

FIGURE 2.7
The Ratings tab enables you to specify a rating category, as well as the level of the rating.

I might have set the violence rating to Fighting (Level 1), which is less violent than Killing (Level 2), the rating shown in Figure 2.7.

Web Page Footers

Web page footers are used much like a footer in a word processing document. You place information in a footer file that you want displayed at the bottom of each Web page in your site.

You can use footers to place information at the bottom of the page such as contact information, page author information, or even a company logo.

First, create an HTML file with necessary HTML tags to define the content. Don't create a complete HTML document with the <HTML>, <HEAD>, <BODY>, and other tags; create just enough to display the contents in HTML form. Listing 2.5 shows a quick and simple concept of this.

LISTING 2.5 Web Page Footer

```
<I>Gerry O'Brien</I><p>
<a href=mailto:gkcomput@nbnet.nb.ca><I>gkcomput@nbnet.nb.ca</I>
```

In order to have your footer attached to each Web page, you need to set it up in the appropriate Web site or directory properties dialog box.

Fire up Internet Service Manager if it's not already running and choose the Default Web Site, or one of your own choosing. Bring up the properties dialog box as usual and select the Documents tab. You will see a screen similar to Figure 2.8.

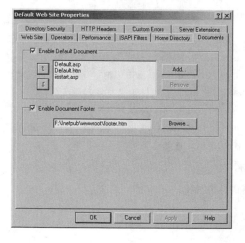

FIGURE 2.8
The Documents tab is where you specify the footer page location.

Select the Enable Document Footer check box and type in the location and name of the page you created as the footer. Or, you can choose the Browse button to locate the file on networked or local drives.

> **CAUTION**
>
> Using a Web footer can cause performance issues with IIS if the pages are accessed quite frequently.

> **NOTE**
>
> Web footers do not work with .asp pages. They only function in .html and .htm pages. You don't need a Web footer in .asp pages anyway because you can use #include files for the same purpose.

Server-Side Includes

As you saw in the section "Using ASP to Manage Sites," server-side includes are a great way to add common pieces of information to a Web page without the need to re-create that content for each page.

If you are familiar with the C and C++ programming languages, you will know that developers using these languages have enjoyed the use of #include files for some time now. They are pre-built, debugged, and tested procedures and functions already to be plugged into an application, and the developers didn't have to write a single line of code.

That is why we use #include files in IIS as well. You might have a copyright notice, a navigation bar, or an ad rotator already set up and working on a Web page now. Why rewrite that HTML code for each page you need it on. Using the #include directive, you can tell IIS to read the file into the location in your Web page where the directive is located. IIS places the code into the correct location before sending the HTML to the client and the included page's contents are displayed as if you had typed them in yourself.

You can also use #include directives to insert information about the file, such as its size, or to run shell commands or applications.

> **NOTE**
>
> `#include` files need to be named correctly in order for IIS to find them because of the special processing requirements for the directives. The default extensions for these are `.stm`, `.shtm`, and `.shtml`.

Enabling Includes

By default, IIS will process `#include` files. If you have the files named with the previously mentioned extensions, then IIS will process them.

One important consideration is to ensure that the files are placed into a directory that has scripts or execute permissions. These are determined by the NTFS permissions placed on the directories. You can check and set these permissions on the directory from its properties dialog box.

Figure 2.9 shows the properties dialog box for the `/inetpub/scripts` directory on my Web server. Note that the Execute Permissions option toward the bottom of the page is set to Scripts and Executables. It makes sense to have these permissions set on the directory that contains executable scripts.

FIGURE 2.9

The Properties dialog box for the `/inetpub/scripts` *directory.*

You can see that there are definite benefits to using server-side includes in your Web sites. However, careless use of includes can lead to pages not loading or displaying properly because the #include file cannot be found or IIS will not process it. In managing your site, you need to keep tight control over your #include files.

If, for some reason, you decide not to use #include files, or you want to disable processing of them, you can. Follow these steps to disable server-side includes:

1. In Internet Service Manager, select the Web site that you want to disable includes on and open its properties sheet.

2. Click the Home Directory (or Directory) tab.

3. In the Application Settings section, click the Configuration button.

4. You will see a dialog box similar to Figure 2.10. Ensure that the App Mappings tab is selected.

5. Select the .stm, .shtm, and/or .shtml listings, and click the Remove button.

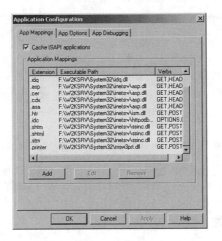

FIGURE 2.10
The list of available application mappings for my installation of IIS.

This procedure will remove the three extensions. (Remember that they are used to indicate #include files.) Now, whenever IIS sees a reference to a file with one of these extensions, IIS will ignore it and not process the file.

Using Server-Side #include Directives

As you have seen so far, you can use server-side #include directives to #include files in HTML pages before they are sent to the client's browser. There are other directives available as well that enable more capabilities.

You can use directives to format dates sent to the client, or to insert some output from an application. The section "Server-Side Includes Reference" will show you what directives are available and what they do.

Server-Side Includes Reference

#config

This directive is used to format dates, file sizes, or error messages sent to the client. It cannot be used in .asp files and is only used in static HTML pages.

Syntax

```
<!-- #config output=string -->
```

The *output* parameter is what is to be formatted. There are three possible choices for this:

- **ERRMSG**—This helps you control the error message that is sent to the client. When an error occurs processing a directive, the error message contains debugging information in regards to the error. You can send a custom message to the client instead by specifying the message as the *string* parameter.

  An example is

  ```
  <!-- #config ERRMSG="We apologize but a processing error has occurred" -->
  ```

- **TIMEFMT**—This enables you to specify the date/time format sent to the client browser. For example, by using the %A option in the *string* parameter, you will use the full day name, such as Wednesday. For a complete list of the available time-formatting options, see the online help file for IIS.

  ```
  <!-- #config TIMEFMT="%m/%d/%y" -->
  ```

  The preceding code will display the date as MM/DD/YY.

- **SIZEFMT**—Replace the *string* parameter with one of the two following options:

  ABBREV to display the size in KB

  BYTE to display the size in bytes

  ```
  <!-- #config SIZEFMT="bytes" -->
  ```

  The preceding code will display the file size in bytes instead of kilobytes.

#echo

You can use this directive to insert variables into the HTML file. Like the #config directive, this can only be used in HTML files and not .asp files.

> **NOTE**
>
> If you have variables that you want to insert into an `.asp` page, you can use the `Response.ServerVariables` methods. For more information on this method, see the ASP documentation.

Syntax

```
<!-- #echo var=variable -->
```

variable is used to specify the variable that you want to insert. Valid values for *variable* are

- **ALL_HTTP**—All HTTP headers that have not been parsed already into other variables. They consist of null-terminated strings. Individual headers are separated by linefeeds.
- **AUTH_PASSWORD**—Available only for basic authentication, this variable includes the value that the client entered in the Authentication dialog box.
- **AUTH_TYPE**—This indicates the type of authentication that is used, such as basic or integrated. If this value is empty, then no authentication was used.
- **AUTH_USER**—The user value entered in the Client Authentication dialog box.
- **CONTENT_LENGTH**—The number of bytes that the script is expecting from the client.
- **CONTENT_TYPE**—The type of information that is supplied in the POST request.
- **DOCUMENT_NAME**—This variable contains the current filename.
- **DOCUMENT_URI**—The virtual path, if any, of the current file.
- **DATE_GMT**—Used to pass the current date Greenwich Mean Time (GMT).
- **DATE_LOCAL**—Same as DATE_GMT, only in local time.
- **GATEWAY_INTERFACE**—The revision of the CGI specification used by the server.
- **HTTP_ACCEPT**—A special case HTTP header. If you have more than one accept case, they will be concatenated by commas.
- **LAST_MODIFIED**—This returns the date that the document was last modified.
- **PATH_INFO**—Any additional path information passed by the client.
- **PATH_TRANSLATED**—Takes the value of PATH_INFO and expands the virtual path, if any, into the directory specification.
- **QUERY_STRING**—This contains the information that follows the ? in the returned URL, such as form field information passed to .asp scripts.
- **QUERY_STRING_UNESCAPED**—A version of the query string that is not URL encoded.
- **REMOTE_ADDR**—IP address of the client that sent the request.

- **REMOTE_HOST**—Hostname of the client that sent the request.
- **REMOTE_USER**—The username that the client supplied and that was authenticated by the server. If an anonymous user was authenticated, this value will be blank.
- **REQUEST_METHOD**—The HTTP request method.
- **SCRIPT_NAME**—Name of the script being executed.
- **SERVER_NAME**—The server's hostname of IP address.
- **SERVER_PORT**—The port that the request was received on.
- **SERVER_PORT_SECURE**—Returns 1 if the request is on secure port, or 0 if it is not
- **SERVER_PROTOCOL**—The name and version of the retrieval protocol. Normally HTTP/1.0.
- **SERVER_SOFTWARE**—The name and version of the Web server that is answering the request.
- **URL**—The base portion of the URL without any parameters.

2

WEB SITE
MANAGEMENT

#exec

You use this directive to have the Web server run an application or shell command. This directive is not enabled in .asp files either but within HTML pages similar to #config.

Syntax

```
<!-- #exec commandtype=commanddesc -->
```

commandtype is the type of command and can be one of the following:

- **CGI**—This type will run a CGI script, ASP script, or ISAPI application. You must enter the path and filename of the application, followed by ? and any parameters in the *commanddesc* parameter.
- **CMD**—This will run a shell command. You specify the full path to the command and any parameters separated by spaces in the *commanddesc* parameter.

CAUTION

This feature is disabled by default, and you should use it with great care. A shell command such as *format* could be issued, resulting in the formatting of a drive.

#flastmod

This directive tells the Web server to insert the time that a specified file was modified. This cannot be used in .asp pages either, only in HTML pages.

Syntax

```
<!-- #flastmod PathType=FileName -->
```

PathType specifies whether this is a virtual path or a real path. The values used are

- `File`—A path relative to the directory containing the document
- `Virtual`—Path name of a virtual directory on the server

The *FileName* parameter lists the name of the file for which you want the last modified time.

#fsize

This will cause the server to insert the size of the file into the HTML page. You cannot use this directive in an `.asp` page, only in HTML pages.

Syntax

```
<!-- #fsize PathType=FileName -->
```

These two parameters are identical to the ones used for the #flastmod directive.

#include

We have already seen this directive used previously. It tells the server to read in the contents of the file specified at the location where the directive is placed. You can use this directive in `.asp` pages as well as HTML pages.

Syntax

```
<!-- #include PathType=FileName -->
```

PathType indicates if we are dealing with a virtual or real path.

FileName specifies the name of the file to include.

> **NOTE**
>
> Once again, we must stress that the filename extension needs to be `.stm`, `.shtm`, or `.shtml`. The only exception is if you have mapped another extension in the App Mappings section.

Summary

Managing a Web site involves more than just creating and updating the HTML pages that exist on the server. By using ASP code in the form of VBScript or JScript, you can perform repetitive tasks with ease.

Other concerns are dealing with redirection of client requests for relocated or deleted pages on the server. By using the ratings capabilities of IIS 5.0, you can offer your visitors the ability to screen your pages based on the content contained within them.

You also saw how you can use server-side includes to obtain and return information specific to files and documents that your server works with.

Administration

PART
II

IN THIS PART

Web and FTP Site Administration

IN THIS CHAPTER

Introduction to Administering Your Web and FTP Site

In this chapter, we will be discussing the tasks and issues involved in administering your IIS server for Web and FTP purposes. When you have an FTP or Web site set up and running, it will take a certain amount of resources to administer. It would be nice if IIS could run itself, and we wouldn't have to worry about babysitting it. In the real world, this is not the case.

Administering your Web and FTP sites thoroughly goes a long way to ensuring trouble-free operation. Although you cannot possibly predict and prevent all breakdowns or potential issues, you can help ensure that your server and sites operate at peak efficiency by performing the administrative tasks explained in this chapter.

Administration also becomes more critical with IIS 4.0 and 5.0 because of the capability of these Web platforms to host multiple, virtual Web and FTP sites. It is relatively easy to monitor and operate a server that is hosting one Web site with one IP address and one domain name. This task becomes more time-consuming and complicated when you start adding virtual Web sites to the server.

You can host multiple sites on IIS 5.0 using three possible scenarios. The first is to use multiple ports. Using Internet Services Manager, you can assign a port other than the standard port 80 to a different site, enabling you to run the second as a different Web site. Take note that this will require any clients to know and use the port of the alternative site as all browsers come with a standard configuration for the default port 80.

The second way to host multiple sites is to assign multiple IP addresses to multiple network interface cards (NICs). This method runs out of steam real fast because of the resources required to set this up.

The third method is new to IIS 5.0 and is by far the best choice available. You can now assign multiple IP addresses and domain names to one NIC by using host header names. This method relies on IIS to perform the necessary selection from the available Web sites based on the information passed to it from the header indicating the desired host.

> **NOTE**
>
> If you are going to use this last method to host multiple sites on the Internet instead of an intranet, be sure to register the names with the InterNIC.

Now you might ask, "How is hosting multiple Web sites on a single server going to make my administration any easier?" The answer lies in that wonderful concept of *delegation*. If you are hosting multiple Web sites on an intranet for each department in the company, you can assign the Web site maintenance duties to a member of its respective department.

Each Web site set up in this way acts as if it were on a server all its own.

> **CAUTION**
>
> Two words of caution here. First, you cannot use the host header method for multiple sites that will be using SSL because of the information being encrypted. Second, you must keep in mind that older browsers do not support host header names in this manner. Clients must be using Internet Explorer 3.0 or Netscape 2.0 or later.

As we have discussed thus far, you work with IIS and its components mostly with the Internet Services Manager. Figure 3.1 shows a screen shot of this component running within the MMC.

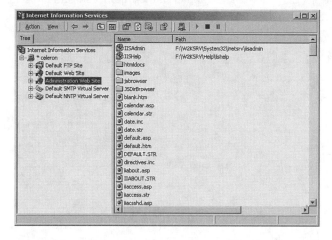

FIGURE 3.1
Internet Services Manager now runs as a snap-in to the MMC and is the focal point for IIS administration.

Starting and Stopping Sites

One of the first things that we will look at is how to start and stop the services of IIS. If you have performed a standard installation of IIS, you will find that the Web and FTP services will start automatically when Windows 2000 boots up. This is the default configuration, and we will see in a bit how to change that.

If you stop the Web Publishing Service, you effectively stop IIS from serving Web pages on the Internet of intranet. It will also unload those services from memory, which will free up resources for other applications.

You can pause the services as well. Pausing the Internet services will prevent IIS from accepting any new connections. This will not affect any connections that were already in progress. Pausing will not free up any memory resources either, so you cannot use this as a performance enhancer.

There are actually three different means of stopping the Internet services:

- Internet Service Manager
- The Services list (using the Services applet)
- The command line

The first method, using Internet Service Manager, is the easiest to use. If it is not already running, open the Internet Service Manager applet in the Internet Information Services MMC. Figure 3.2 shows the Internet Services Manager snap-in running on my server.

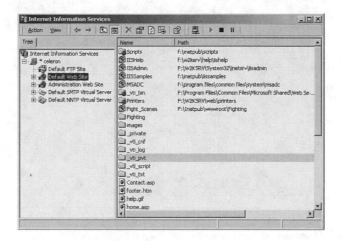

FIGURE 3.2

You use the VCR style buttons on the toolbar in the Internet Information Services console to start, stop, and pause the services.

To stop any of the currently running sites, click the site's name in the navigation pane (left pane) to highlight it, and then click the Stop button in the toolbar of MMC (indicated by the solid black square).

You might not notice any difference right off because of the refresh rate of the display for MMC. You can either choose the Action menu and select the Refresh option to refresh the

MMC display, or you can press the F5 key on your keyboard. When the display is refreshed, you should see the word (stopped) next to the site or service that you stopped.

For any site that is stopped, you can highlight that site and click the solid black arrow button (the Start button) to start the site or service. Clicking Start will also enable the site to publish its service to the Internet or an intranet.

By clicking the Pause button (indicated by two vertical lines), you can pause a site that is running. This will cause IIS to reject any new connections to the service while maintaining existing connections.

The second way to start, stop, or pause the sites is to use the Services applet. This applet is found under the Control Panel in Administrative Tools, as indicated by Figure 3.3.

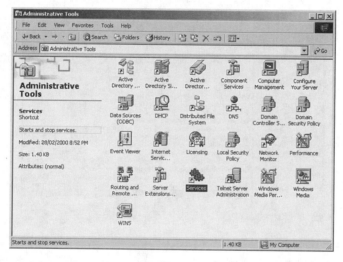

FIGURE 3.3

You access the Services applet under Administrative Tools to control the services installed on your server.

After you start the Services applet, you are given a window similar to that shown in Figure 3.4.

In Figure 3.4, I have the World Wide Web Publishing Service selected. The right pane displays the status of the service and the startup type.

The Status column tells you whether a service is running (Started), stopped, or paused. The Startup Type column tells you how the service is treated when the OS starts up. There are three possible values for this column: Automatic, Manual, and Disabled.

- *Automatic* means that the service will start up every time the OS boots up. This setting is ideal if you have your server set up to automatically reboot on memory dump errors, aka Blue Screens of Death (BSOD). Should an error occur that causes your server to reboot itself, a WWW service that is set to Automatic will restart as well allow your Web pages to be served without administrator intervention.

- *Manual* means that the service is available to be started by some other means, such as a script or an administrator, using any of the methods mentioned here.

- *Disabled* means that the service cannot be started by anyone or any script or application. Well, this is sort of misleading; it tends to indicate that if you were to disable the service, you can never restart it. All you need to do is change the startup type to Manual or Automatic.

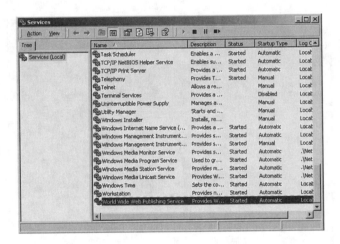

FIGURE 3.4
The Services applet runs in the MMC-like Internet Services Manager. This applet gives you more control over the running of the your computer's services.

You will also notice in Figure 3.4, that there is an extra button on the MMC toolbar that was not in the Internet Service Manager view. The furthest button to the right of the Pause button is the Restart button. By clicking this button, you essentially perform a service stop and start in one move. This is ideal for situations in which you have made a change to one of the services that requires a restart. An example of this would be an addition or deletion of authorized site operators.

The third method of running services, the Services list, is to use the command line. IIS provides nine commands for dealing with this:

- **stopsrv**—Stops the server or a list of servers specified
- **stopftp**—Stops the FTP server

- **stopweb**—Stops the Web server
- **startsrv**—Starts the server
- **startftp**—Starts the FTP server
- **startweb**—Starts the Web server
- **pausesrv**—Pauses the server or a list of servers specified
- **pauseftp**—Pauses the FTP server
- **pauseweb**—Pauses the Web server

Each of these commands can be executed remotely as well over the network using the NET command. I merely introduce the commands here because their syntax and use are explained more fully in Chapter 13, "Administration Scripts."

> **NOTE**
>
> If you are running a Web site that is using clustering, you must use the Cluster Administrator to start and stop your clustered sites. You can get more information on clustering in Chapter 12, "Replication and Clustering."

Adding Sites

Internet Information Server comes preconfigured for one Web site, one FTP site, one SMTP site, and one NNTP site. This doesn't mean that you have to stick with the same site in each format. As I mentioned before, you can create virtual sites on the same computer. This is a fantastic feature that allows you to host sites within your organization's intranet based on departments.

That means that Marketing can have its own Web and FTP sites, Legal can have its own sites, and Management can be off into a world all its own as well.

The first step involved in creating multiple sites on your server is to set up the default home directories. These directories can be anywhere on your local disk drive or on the network. You need to create them first because the wizard we are going to use asks us for this directory.

Let's assume that we are going to create a Web site for the Marketing department. Using Windows Explorer or My Computer, create the directory and name it Marketing. Make note of where you created the directory. I placed mine under the InetPub\wwwroot directory for ease of location.

If the marketing department or other department already has a Web site created and requires a server to place it on, you can publish it to the server using the publishing capabilities of the

Web development tool that that department used. Alternatively, you can copy the entire Web site directory structure to the server using Windows Explorer.

Now, start Internet Service Manager if it is not already running and select the server icon in the left pane, as shown in Figure 3.5.

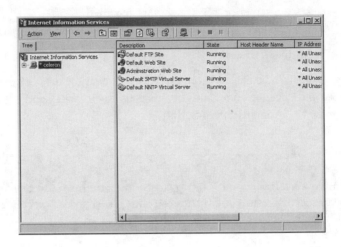

FIGURE 3.5

The server icon selected in Internet Service Manager on my computer called Celeron. *You will add a new site from this starting point.*

From the Action menu, choose New, Web Site. This starts the Web Site Creation Wizard. Click Next to advance past the introduction screen.

The first dialog box asks you to enter a description for the site. Figure 3.6 shows the dialog box.

The description you enter identifies the Web site to yourself or other administrators and is displayed in the left pane of MMC. Enter something here that pertains to the site's purpose of content and click the Next button.

You are then presented with the IP Address and Port Settings dialog box, as shown in Figure 3.7.

In Figure 3.7, I have entered the IP address of my server, 192.168.5.1, left the port at port 80, and defined a host header name of Marketing.

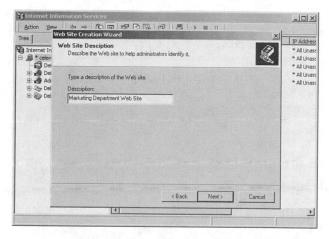

FIGURE 3.6

The Web Site Description dialog box enables you to enter a description for the new site.

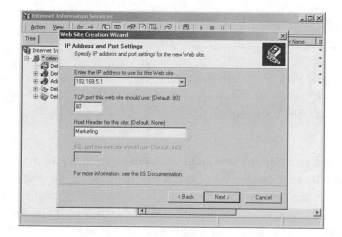

FIGURE 3.7

The IP Address and Port Settings dialog box is where you enter the IP and port information for the Web site that you are creating, along with the host header names for virtual sites.

In Figure 3.8, I only had to enter `http://Marketing` in the address bar of my Web browser, and IIS knew where to direct my request. This is because of the host header name defined in Figure 3.7.

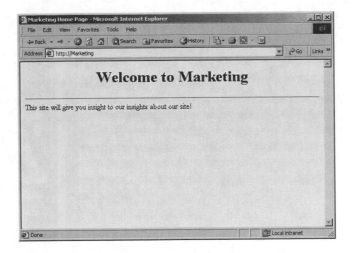

FIGURE 3.8

Using the host header name feature, you can locate virtual Web sites on IIS 5 with only the site's defined header name instead of a long URL.

NOTE

In order for this to work, you must define the host header information in your DNS server settings or in your hosts file. For example, the entry I added to my hosts file to make this work was 192.168.5.1 Marketing.

Click the Next button on the IP Address and Port Settings dialog box to advance the wizard to the Web Site Home Directory dialog box. Enter the path, or use the Browse button to locate the path, where you want the Web site to be located. This is the directory that you created earlier. Leave the Allow anonymous access to this Web site option checked if you want to allow anonymous access, or clear it if you will specify users later. Click the Next button.

The Web Site Access Permissions dialog box is displayed, as shown in Figure 3.9.

You will assign the appropriate permissions for the clients that will access this Web site:

- **Read**—Enables clients to view pages on this site.
- **Run scripts (such as ASP)**—Enables clients to request pages that contain ASP code and have that code execute.
- **Execute (such as ISAPI and CGI apps)**—This option enables CGI or ISAPI applications to execute on this site.

- **Write**—Selecting this option will enable the clients to upload, delete, or transfer files to this directory.
- **Browse**—Enables the clients to browse directories and collections.

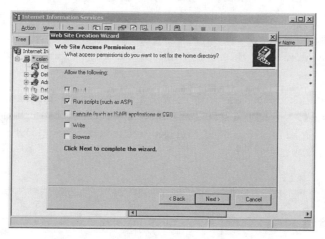

FIGURE 3.9

The Web Site Access Permissions dialog is used to indicate the permissions you want to assign to the Web directory.

After you have made your selections, click the Next button to advance to the last screen of the Wizard and choose Finish.

You have just added a Web site to your server. Now all you need to do is create the necessary content.

FTP sites can be created in a similar way. There are, of course, differences in the two types of sites. You still need to create a directory structure for the FTP site, and this can be done using Windows Explorer.

When you choose to add a new FTP site using the FTP Site Creation Wizard, you are asked to provide a descriptive name for the FTP site, and to select the IP address, the port number, and the directory location for the home directory. The wizard will also ask you to provide the access permissions for the home directory. These are Read and Write.

Once you have provided the necessary information to the wizard, the FTP site will be created and displayed in the MMC Console. You can now configure the site.

FTP Directories, Messages, and Output Styles

In order to maintain structure in your FTP site, you need to create a directory structure. The default FTP site contains one directory, *ftproot*. This directory does not show up in the MMC under the FTP site; only subdirectories under it do.

You can set up a directory structure in any way that you want, but you might want to take a look at a few sites on the Internet to see what they have in common and set up your structure in a similar manner. For example, most sites offer a *public* directory for general and anonymous use and an *incoming,* or *upload,* directory into which clients upload files. You can, of course, set up any other directories that you feel are necessary.

Almost every FTP server that you visit on the Internet greets visitors with a welcome message and acceptable use information. IIS 5.0 is no different; it enables specifying these types of messages as well.

It is usually a good idea to greet your visitors with a welcome to let them know that they are, in fact, using your FTP server. You should also place any pertinent instructions here as to where clients can upload files if enabled. You can even include a brief legal notice regarding liability relating to usage.

CAUTION

Keep in mind that some older browsers cannot display messages longer than one line.

IIS 5.0 also lets you set a message to be displayed when the user logs out of your FTP site and a message to indicate that the maximum number of connections has been reached.

Right-click the FTP site in MMC for which you want to configure messages and choose Properties. Select the Messages tab, as shown in Figure 3.10.

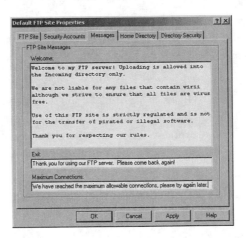

FIGURE 3.10

The Messages tab of the FTP Site Properties dialog box lets you enter messages to users of your FTP server.

In Figure 3.10, I have entered text that will be displayed when a user connects to my FTP server. Figure 3.11 shows how the welcome message is displayed to the user.

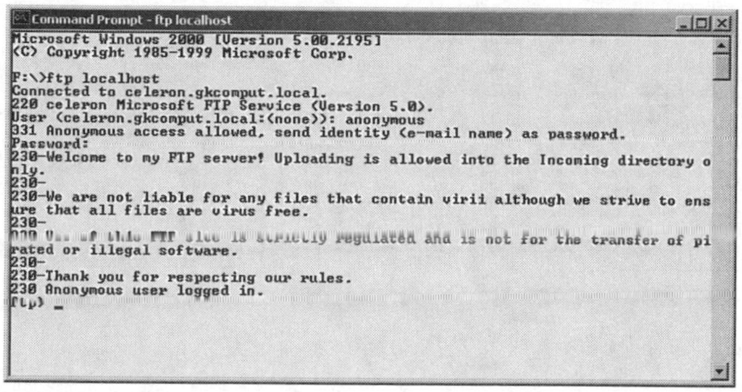

FIGURE 3.11

The welcome message is displayed when a user has been authenticated and granted access to the FTP site.

You can format the output that is displayed when a client requests a directory listing. The client computer sends a LIST command to the server, and the server responds by displaying a listing of the current working directory. IIS lets you specify that this directory listing be displayed in either an MS-DOS–style format or a UNIX style.

Figure 3.12 shows how the MS-DOS–style output looks, and Figure 3.13 shows the UNIX style.

FIGURE 3.12

The default setting for IIS is to display the working directory's contents in MS-DOS style.

With the almost constant attack on Microsoft's Web-based technologies, you should use any and all means available to thwart hackers attempting to access your sites.

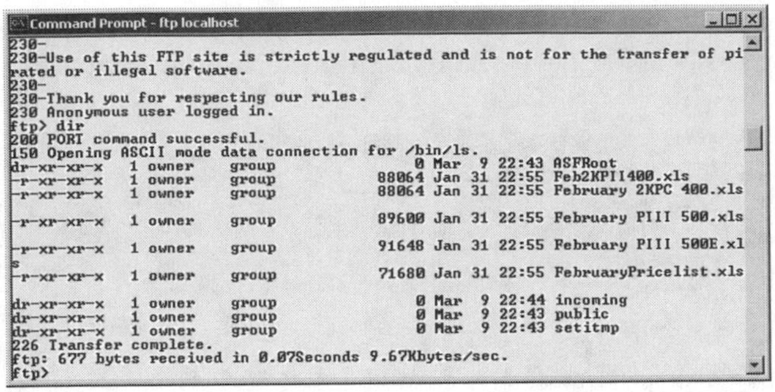

FIGURE 3.13
IIS 5.0 can also display the working directory in UNIX-style output.

> **NOTE**
>
> Although there are very sophisticated hackers who will attempt to break into your FTP sites through some very sophisticated means, you shouldn't make life any easier for them. Using the UNIX-style output can actually fend off some hackers because they cannot see the Microsoft FTP Service header at log on and see only the UNIX-style directory listing. This could make them believe they are using a UNIX/Linux server.
>
> You may also experience instances when some users will not be able to see any directory listing if you do not choose the UNIX style. Therefore, the recommended style for a server that will be used as a public Internet FTP server is the UNIX style.

There are a couple of final points to note before we end this section. Using the MS-DOS–style listing will result in the dates being formatted with a two-digit year; the UNIX style displays them with a four-digit year. You can change the default DOS style by enabling the `FtpDirBrowseShowLongDate` metabase property.

See Appendix B, "Administration Object Reference," for information on how to set this property using the `IISFtpServer` object.

Name Your Web Sites

When it comes to naming your Web site, you need to consider two names, a descriptive name and a host header name.

The *descriptive name* is the one given to the Web site that is visible in the Internet Services Manager under MMC. You set this name by opening the properties sheet of the Web site and entering the text into the Description box found on the Web Site tab. (If you gave the Web site a description when you created it, you won't need to do this here as it will already be named for you.) An example of this is shown in Figure 3.14.

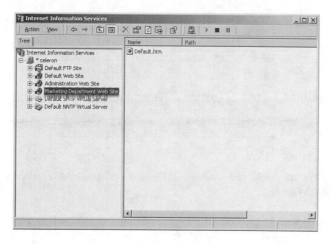

FIGURE 3.14
The highlighted entry shows the descriptive name of Marketing Department Web site.

As we mentioned before, the *host header name* can be used to enable a user to connect to a virtual Web site by typing the header name in the address bar of his browser.

We demonstrated this earlier when we gave the Marketing Web site a host header of Marketing and entered the IP/name combination into the hosts file. (You can also enter the information into a DNS server.)

In order to assign a host header name to a Web site, you need to open the Web site's property sheet. Locate the Advanced button under the Web Site Identification section. This will display the Advanced Multiple Web Site Configuration dialog box, shown in Figure 3.15.

There are two sections in this dialog box. The top section deals with standard sites, whereas the bottom portion deals with SSL site identities.

In Figure 3.15, I have my Marketing Web site set up with an IP address of 192.168.5.1, port 80, and a host header name of Marketing. The IP address of 192.168.5.1 is actually only used for internal TCP/IP networks as it is not a valid IP address on the Internet. The entire 192.168 range of IP addresses is reserved for internal use as is the 10 range of addresses. To create another identity, you click the Add button. This brings up the Advanced Web Site Identification dialog box, in which you can specify the IP, port number, and header name for the new identity.

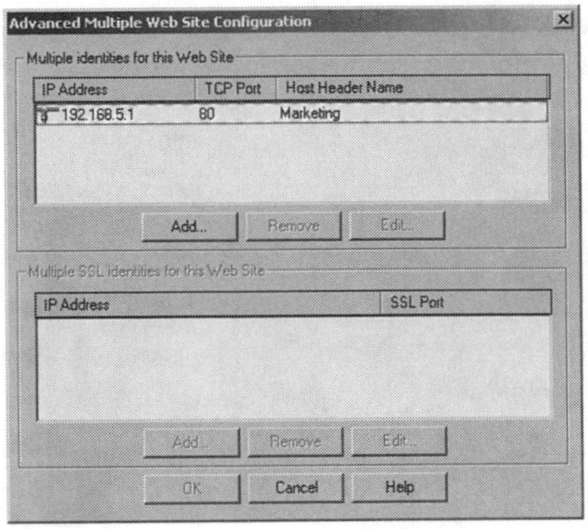

FIGURE 3.15
The Advanced Multiple Web Site Configuration dialog box is used to enter any multiple identities assigned to a Web site, including multiple SSL identities.

If the site were based on SSL, you could perform the same procedure to assign an IP and a port number to your SSL site.

NOTE

Remember that older browsers do not support host header names. IIS will send these browsers to the default Web site if one is set up. Because of this, it is a good idea to have a default site that will be served to these clients with information stating why they have been directed to the default site.

CAUTION

Because the domain name is specified in the certificate for SSL, you can assign only one host header name to an IP address. One way around this is to have multiple certificates, IP addresses, and ports for each Web site.

Restarting IIS

There are several reasons for restarting IIS. Most of them we hope we never encounter because they consist of server problems or application crashes. The application crashes that I refer to do not involve applications such as Microsoft Word but rather IIS applications.

You might also restart IIS because of changes in the site or the addition or deletion of operators.

The recommended and best way to restart IIS is to use the IIS snap-in in MMC. In the left pane of IIS, select the Web, FTP, SMTP, or NNTP service that you want to stop and click the Stop button in the MMC toolbar. Click the Start button to restart the service.

Alternatively, you can restart the entire IIS service by selecting the computer icon in the left pane and then choose Restart IIS from the Action menu. This will display the Stop/Start/Reboot dialog box, shown in Figure 3.16.

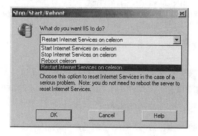

FIGURE 3.16

The Stop/Start/Reboot dialog box contains a drop-down list of available options for restarting IIS.

As you can see from the list displayed in Figure 3.16, you can start, stop, or restart the Internet Services on the computer, or you can actually reboot the server itself. Choose the appropriate option and click the OK button.

> **NOTE**
>
> When you stop IIS, you also stop some other services as well. All `Drwtsn32.exe`, `Mtx.exe`, and `Dllhost.exe` processes will be stopped. They will restart with IIS.

> **NOTE**
>
> You cannot restart IIS by using the Internet Service Manager (HTML). This service is the Web-based administration tool that you will see used in Chapter 15, "Remote Administration."

If you need to schedule the restarting of IIS or to integrate the restarting process into a custom or third-party software application, you can use the command line version of IIS restart. The syntax and use is described in the following section.

Syntax

```
iisreset [computername]
```

wherein *computername* is the name of the server running IIS.

This command also has optional parameters listed here:

- **/RESTART**—Stops and then starts all Internet services.
- **/START**—Starts all Internet services.
- **/STOP**—Stops all Internet services.
- **/REBOOT**—Reboots the computer.
- **/REBOOTONERROR**—Reboots the server if there are any errors encountered during a start, stop, or restart of the Internet services.
- **/NOFORCE**—Does not force a termination of services if a normal stop fails.
- **/TIMEOUT:val**—A timeout value, in seconds, to wait for a successful stop. If this timeout occurs and the /REBOOTONERROR option was used also, the computer will be rebooted. There are default settings such as 20 seconds for restart, 60 seconds for stop, and 0 seconds for reboot.
- **/STATUS**—Displays the status of the Internet services.
- **/ENABLE**—Enables restarting of IIS on the local computer.
- **/DISABLE**—Disables restarting of IIS on the local computer.

Figure 3.17 shows an example of using the iisreset command line with the /STATUS option.

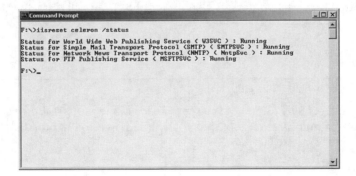

FIGURE 3.17

The Command Prompt window showing the use of the /STATUS option with iisreset *on my computer* celeron. *Note that only services are listed and not individual sites.*

Host Header Names Support

Internet Explorer browsers earlier than version 3.0 and pre–version 2.0 Netscape browsers do not support host header names. In an ideal world, every user would upgrade to the latest and greatest software packages when the packages were released. As you are well aware, we do not live in an ideal world. Therefore, we must take into consideration the fact that we will have visitors to our sites who are still using older browser technologies. IIS 5.0 can help.

Although you might not run into this situation very often, you will need to address it if you receive complaints from users that they cannot reach a particular site.

The procedure is fairly involved and is specific to the particular computer and Web site that you are running. It also involves editing the registry. If you need to support the header names in older browsers, I recommend that you read the section in the online help for the correct keys and values that need to be entered.

Changing Inherited Defaults

When you install IIS 5.0, it contains certain defaults that can be modified to suit your purposes. There are two possible ways to modify these defaults.

You can perform a modification on the server properties itself. This will cause a set of properties to be used for each Web or FTP site that does not have the specific property set. For example, if you right-click the server icon in the IIS snap-in and choose properties, the <computername> Properties dialog box appears, as in Figure 3.18.

FIGURE 3.18

The properties dialog box for the IIS server computer enables you to set defaults for Web and FTP sites that do not specify values for the various settings.

By selecting either the WWW Service or FTP Service from the drop-down list under Master Properties, you will display the services Master Properties dialog box. I show the WWW Services Master Properties dialog for my server named `celeron` in Figure 3.19.

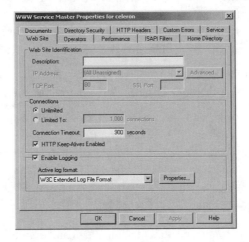

FIGURE 3.19
The WWW Services Master Properties for celeron *dialog box looks very much like the properties dialog box for any of the Web sites that I have on this computer.*

As you can see, you have the ability to set various default properties that will pertain to all the Web sites or all the FTP sites that you have on your server.

You can also perform the same procedure on each individual Web or FTP site on your server and set properties specific to that site.

> **NOTE**
>
> Any changes that you make to individual sites through this method will override any default master settings that you set earlier, for that site only.

Backing Up and Restoring Your IIS Configuration

As with anything related to a production server, you must consider a backup-and-restore scenario. This applies to IIS as well. What would happen if you were to make extensive changes to IIS configuration and a co-worker, or worse, a hacker, made extensive changes to that configuration? You could spend a considerable amount of time just trying to figure out what you had set in the first place, not to mention the amount of time required to rebuild that configuration.

Follow these steps to back up your current configuration:

1. Using the IIS snap-in, select the computer icon to highlight it in the left pane.
2. From the Action menu, choose the Backup/Restore Configuration option.
3. Click the Create Backup button, which displays a Configuration Backup dialog box enabling you to name your backup file. Enter a name for the backup file and click the OK button.

You have just created a backup of your current IIS configuration. You can test this by making some small changes to your existing configuration and noting them. Next, you can restore your backed-up configuration and verify that it does indeed replace the changes you just made with the original configuration that you backed up.

By default, the backup file is stored in the directory

```
<systemroot>\System32\inetsrv\Metaback
```

wherein *systemroot* is the directory into which you installed Windows 2000 Server.

Follow these steps to restore your configuration:

1. In the IIS snap-in, highlight the computer icon.
2. From the Action menu, select the Backup/Restore Configuration option.
3. From the Backup/Restore Configuration dialog box, locate the backup file you created in the Previous Backups section and select it.
4. Click the Restore button. Internet Services Manager informs you that the restore procedure can be a lengthy process and will wipe out all your current settings. Click Yes to restore the configuration or No to cancel the operation.

When the restore operation is complete, the services will be restarted, and your last configuration will be in place.

There is one other procedure that must be introduced here. That is restoring your IIS configuration after you have moved or reinstalled IIS. Follow these steps to perform this task:

1. Once again, select the computer icon in IIS and choose the Backup/Restore Configuration option from the Action menu.
2. Select the name of the backup file and choose Restore. You will receive an error message stating that the restore operation failed. A portion of the configuration will be restored regardless of this.

3. Go to a command prompt window and enter this command:

   `cscript.exe x:\InetPub\AdminScripts\Adsutil.vbs enum w3svc`.

   Replace the *x* with the drive letter where IIS is installed.

4. In this extensive and long list, locate the WAMUserName and WAMUserPass entries.

5. Open Computer Management under Administrative Tools in Control Panel.

6. Choose the Local User Managers and select the Users option. Double-click the IWAM_computername entry and change the password to the value that was displayed in the script listing in the command prompt.

7. Select the backup file again in the Backup/Restore Configuration dialog to fully back up the configuration.

CAUTION

If you are running the server as a Domain Controller, which you shouldn't be in a production environment for security reasons, you will not be able to read the password value returned by the script as it will be in the form of asterisks (********).

NOTE

To use step 3 in the preceding procedure, you must have the Windows Scripting host installed.

NOTE

You can back up your configuration using the Internet Services Manager (HTML), but you cannot restore it using this tool.

Dealing with Web Site Operator Accounts

Let's face it, you can't be everywhere at once. Although some management requires that as a part of your duties, I know of no one who has accomplished it yet. This is why it is important to be able to assign Web site operators on the server. These individuals can help administer the server in your absence.

You assign operators using the Web site properties dialog box, so open it now.

Selecting the Operators tab and clicking the Add button will open the Select User or Groups window, as displayed in Figure 3.20.

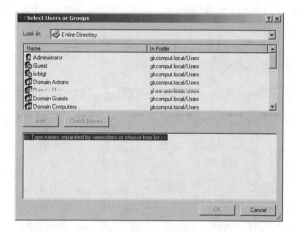

FIGURE 3.20

The Select Users or Groups dialog window enables you to specify users or groups as Web site operators.

Choose the user(s) or group(s) that you want, click the Add button, and then the OK button. This will add the selected user or group accounts to the Web Site Operators list.

> **TIP**
>
> As with all Windows NT/2000 privileges, it makes good sense to first create a group for the purpose you want and then add the individual accounts to that group. It makes administration so much easier.

You can also remove an operator account or group by using the Operators tab in the Properties dialog box. Select the user or group and click the Remove button.

Downlevel Site Administration

Downlevel site administration refers to the ability to administer IIS 5.0 from the IIS 4.0 and IIS 3.0 interfaces. You can perform this administration over an intranet because the preferred method—to administer your Web site over the Internet—happens through the HTML browser-based administration components.

If you want to use IIS 3.0 for administrative purposes, you will need to designate one Web site to be administered programmatically by an IIS 3.0–based application.

In order to enable IIS 3.0 administration, you need to perform the following steps:

1. Open the properties sheet for the IIS computer by clicking on the computer icon in the IIS snap-in.

2. Select either the WWW or FTP service and click the Edit button.

3. Select the Service tab, as shown in Figure 3.21.

4. Under the IIS 3.0 Administration section, select the Web site that you will administer.

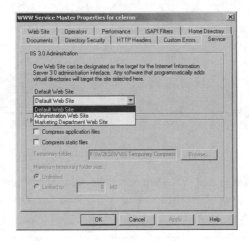

FIGURE 3.21

The Administration section of the Service tab is used to specify the Web or FTP site that you want to administer from IIS 3.0.

Summary

This chapter has taken you on a tour of the possibilities and procedures involved with administering your Web and FTP sites. There are a number of methods for dealing with the administrative issues that come up on a daily basis with IIS, and you are left to choose the methods you prefer or find the most convenient ones.

Remember to take advantage of ability to assign Web site operators administrative privileges to help you in your day-to-day administration of the server. Although you need to be careful what permissions you assign to them, site operators can be a big help to you.

IIS 5.0 also includes some features that help prevent the need to upgrade remote computers with newer administration software, by enabling downlevel administration and remote HTML-based administration, which we will look at later in the book.

Administering the SMTP and NNTP Services

IN THIS CHAPTER

IIS 5.0 includes the SMTP and NNTP services that enable you to send and receive SMTP mail to and from your IIS server. It also has the capability to set up internal discussion groups using the NNTP service.

Working with the SMTP Virtual Server

The SMTP Server that comes with IIS 5.0 is not a full-fledged mail server application like Microsoft Exchange. It does not offer the capability to create and maintain user email accounts for sending and receiving Internet or corporate email. Instead, the purpose of the SMTP server in IIS 5.0 is to provide the capability to send and receive email related to the operation of the IIS server.

You can use it to deliver messages over the Internet or your intranet. It includes support for basic SMTP functions. You can customize the configuration of the service for your specific security needs as well.

The SMTP service is composed of several components, which can be seen in the MMC console. In the left pane of the console, you can see the default components of the SMTP service by expanding the SMTP Virtual Server entry (click on the + sign). You should see a screen similar to the one shown in Figure 4.1.

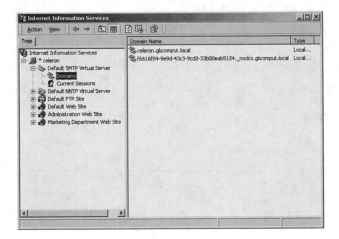

FIGURE 4.1

The Default SMTP Virtual Server installed on my computer lists the Domains and Current Sessions presently configured and running.

The Domains list shown in the details pane lets you configure those options by right-clicking the one you want and choosing Properties from the pop-up menu. The Current Sessions option will display status information for any active connection.

SMTP Features

Here is a list of features that are provided as a part of the SMTP service:

- **Full SMTP Protocol Support**—The SMTP server fully supports the Internet SMTP protocol and is compatible with SMTP clients.
- **Easy Administration**—The SMTP service can be administered with the familiar Microsoft Management Console.
- **Windows 2000 Server Integration**—You can use Windows 2000 Server's administration tools to work with the SMTP server as well. You can use Simple Network Management Protocol (SNMP) to administer the service. You can also use the event logs and transaction logs to monitor and report on the status of SMTP.
- **Scalable**—One server can support hundreds of clients by using multiple domains.
- **Mail Drop and Pickup**—You can configure the service to place all incoming mail into a single Drop directory enabling the service to be used as a receiver for other applications. You can also have other applications format the mail as a text file and place it into a Pickup directory. SMTP can then deliver the message.
- **Security**—The SMTP service supports Transport Layer Security (TLS) for encrypting your transmissions.

SMTP Directories

The SMTP service stores its mail in directories. No big secret. It does, however, follow a simple structure. By default, the directories are created under the `<systemroot>\InetPub\Mailroot` directory. This directory location is changeable when you set up IIS.

SMTP deals with five directories:

SortTemp	SMTP uses this directory to store temporary files.
BadMail	This directory serves as a place to store messages that, for some reason, cannot be delivered or returned to the sender.
Drop	All incoming messages are stored in this directory.
Pickup	Messages, formatted as text files, are copied to the Pickup directory for SMTP to deliver them.
Queue	Queue is a holding place for messages waiting for delivery. If a message cannot be delivered because a server is down, it will be placed in Queue and resent at a later interval.

4

ADMINISTERING THE SMTP AND NNTP SERVICES

Message Processing

The SMTP service delivers messages in accordance with RFCs 821 and 822. The delivery is between remote mailservers and the Drop directory.

When SMTP receives a message—either through the default TCP port 25 or by the message being copied into the Pickup directory—it will place that message into the Queue directory and check the destination address. If the destination is local, the message is delivered. If it is not local, SMTP will process it for remote delivery.

If SMTP has determined that the message is destined for a local client, it will remove the message from the Queue directory and place it in the Drop directory. This is considered a complete cycle.

SMTP uses a slightly different process for delivering remote messages. The messages that are destined for remote delivery are left in the Queue directory and sorted according to domain. That way, when SMTP delivers the messages, it can do so in a batch. Batching enables SMTP to optimize the connection by delivering these messages in one session.

Before SMTP delivers the messages to a remote server, it will check to see if the server is online and ready to receive the messages. If the server is not online, SMTP will store the messages in the Queue directory and will retry at specified intervals. I will discuss setting this interval later in the chapter when we look at setting the SMTP properties.

After a connection has been established, SMTP sends the messages and waits for acknowledgment from the receiving server before considering the service delivery complete. If you have TLS enabled for remote delivery, SMTP will encrypt the outgoing messages.

Administering the SMTP Service

You can perform the administrative tasks by using the procedures outlined in the following sections. Numerous options are available for configuring and administering the service.

Starting and Stopping the Service

The SMTP service runs as a service under Windows 2000. Although there can be only one SMTP service, you can have multiple SMTP virtual servers. I will show you how to create additional servers later in this section.

If you stop the SMTP service, you effectively stop all SMTP virtual servers. You can restart a virtual server without first restarting the SMTP service. In doing so, IIS will start the SMTP service first, and then the virtual server that you selected.

To stop a virtual server, select it in the left pane and then do one of three actions:

- Choose Stop from the Action menu
- Click the Stop button on the MMC toolbar
- Right-click the server and choose Stop from the pop-up menu

The choice is yours to make.

Using the same procedure, you can pause or start the virtual server of your choice as well. If you need to start, stop, or pause the SMTP service, you must use the Services tool. This tool can be accessed in one of two ways.

Select Start, Program, Administrative Tools, Component Services. Select the Services component in the left pane and scroll down the list until you find the Simple Mail Transport Protocol (SMTP) listing. This is shown in Figure 4.2 You can now start, stop, pause, or restart the service by using any of the previously mentioned methods.

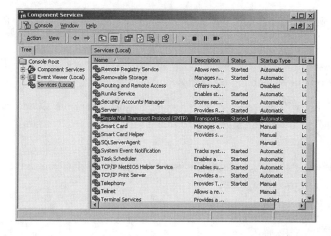

FIGURE 4.2
The Component Services applet enables you to start, stop, pause, or restart the SMTP service.

Another way to reach the services is to open the Administrative Tools folder under Control Panel and double-click the Services icon. I create a shortcut to the Services applet on my desktop for ease of use.

You can also use the Services applet or Component Services to change the default startup behavior of the SMTP service. Right-click the SMTP service entry and choose Properties to bring up the SMTP Properties dialog box, as shown in Figure 4.3.

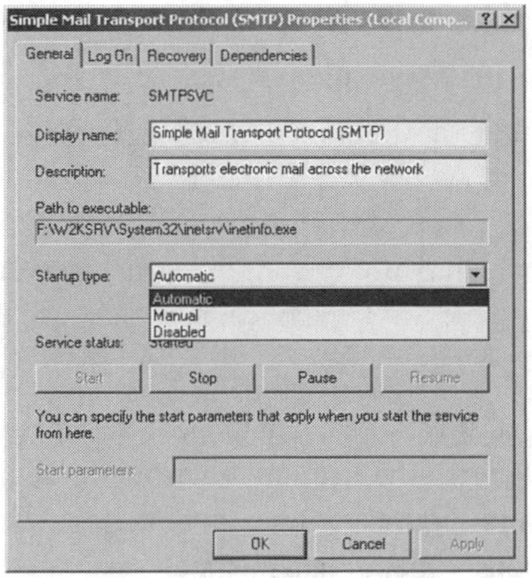

FIGURE 4.3

The Simple Mail Transport Protocol (SMTP) Properties dialog box is where you can change the default startup behavior of the SMTP service.

In the center of the dialog box, you will see the Startup type drop-down box. There are three choices listed: Automatic, Manual, and Disabled.

The Automatic setting will cause the SMTP service to start when the Windows 2000 operating system boots up. Manual will not start the service until you explicitly start it using one of the previously mentioned methods.

If you select Disabled, the service cannot be started until you select either the Manual or Automatic selection in this dialog box.

TIP

If you attempt to start the SMTP Virtual Server from MMC and you see the error message displayed in Figure 4.4, you know that the SMTP service has been disabled.

FIGURE 4.4

Here you can see the error message that is returned when you attempt to start the Virtual Server from MMC when the SMTP service has been disabled.

Creating Additional Virtual Servers

As I mentioned previously, you can have only one SMTP service, but many virtual servers. You only need one SMTP server per domain so, unless you are hosting multiple domains, you will not need to create more servers.

> **TIP**
>
> When you create a new virtual server, you will be asked for its home directory. Create the directory before starting this process.

After you have created a directory to hold the new virtual server, you can begin to create the new server as outlined here:

1. If you will be using a new IP address for the new virtual server, configure it first in Network and Dial-up Connections. See your Windows 2000 documentation for procedures to do this.
2. Open Internet Services Manager if it is not already open.
3. From the Action menu, choose New, Virtual Server.
4. The New SMTP Virtual Server Wizard starts up and asks you to provide a description for the new server. Enter the necessary information into the text box on the initial screen.
5. Click the Next button to advance to the Select IP Address window. Select the appropriate IP to use for this virtual server and click the Next button.
6. Select the directory that will host this virtual server. Browse to the directory that you created earlier and choose the Next button.
7. Enter the default domain in the Select Default Domain window of the wizard. This entry should reflect the name of the domain that will host the server.
8. Click the Finish button, and IIS will create the new virtual server for you.

Figure 4.5 shows the new virtual server that I created during this procedure.

After you have created the new server, you can right-click it, choose Properties, and begin to configure it.

Working with Connections

When an SMTP virtual server sends a message, or when one is received, a new connection is initiated. You can perform configuration options on incoming or outgoing connections.

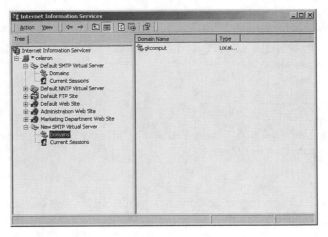

The new SMTP virtual server is displayed in the MMC with the appropriate domain name assigned to it.

To configure the connections, use the Properties sheet for the SMTP virtual server that you want to configure. Open the Internet Services Manager in the MMC and select the SMTP virtual server in the left pane. Choose Properties from the Action menu to bring up the Default SMTP Virtual Server Properties dialog box, as displayed in Figure 4.6.

The Default SMTP Virtual Server Properties dialog box is where you configure the incoming and outgoing properties for the connections.

Under the General tab, you will see a section called Connection. Click the Connection button to display the Connections dialog box, as shown in Figure 4.7.

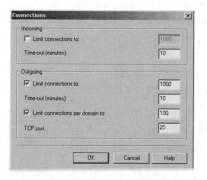

FIGURE 4.7
The Connections dialog box is used to limit the incoming and outgoing connections.

On this dialog box, you can specify a limit to incoming connections, or leave the check box unchecked to enable unlimited connections. The incoming connections are not limited by default. If you check the Limit connections to option, you can specify a minimum of 1 or as many connections as you would like. The default is 1000.

You can also set a timeout value in the Time-out (minutes) text box to specify how long SMTP waits before closing inactive connections. The default is 10 minutes.

From this same dialog box, you can configure the outgoing connections as well.

You set limits, if any, on the outgoing connections by checking the Limit connections to option under the Outgoing section. The default is 1000, which indicates that you can have 1000 simultaneous outgoing connections. You can change this value to a minimum of 1 or whatever you desire for an upper limit. Uncheck the option if you want unlimited outgoing connections.

> **TIP**
>
> You can help increase performance on the server by also limiting the number of outgoing messages using the Message tab of the Properties sheet.

4

ADMINISTERING THE SMTP AND NNTP SERVICES

The Time-out value is used for incoming connections, to indicate a time period in minutes to wait before closing an inactive connection. The default is 10 minutes.

You can also choose to limit the number of outgoing connections per domain. This option will work for any single remote domain. As you can see in Figure 4.7, the default is 100 connections. You should note that this number must be less than the Outgoing Limit connections to value to avoid connection refusal.

The TCP port setting enables you to specify the outgoing port that SMTP uses. The default is the same as for the incoming port, that is, 25. You can, of course, change this port number to another of your choosing, keeping in mind the other commonly used ports on your server such as 80, 119, and so on. The recommended approach is to choose port numbers higher than 1000. Doing so will lessen the chances of port conflicts or of a client making a request on a port that leads to the wrong application.

How do you determine the best settings for these limits? One way that I have found helpful is to do a baseline measurement of the server's performance before accepting or initiating connections. Set the limits to the defaults of 1000 and create a mail script or macro to send your server multiple messages. Watch the performance while the server works with these connections and see what the performance penalties are.

Increase the settings until you reach a point where the server performance is no longer acceptable.

Protocol Logging

Protocol logging enables you to track the commands that are sent to your SMTP server from the clients that connect to it. You can save these logs in one of four formats:

- **W3C Extended Log File**—This is a customizable ASCII text format that is the default format selected.
- **Microsoft IIS Log File**—This format is a fixed ASCII format log.
- **NCSA Common Log File**—This format is also an ASCII text format in line with the National Centre for Supercomputing Applications (NCSA) format.
- **ODBC Logging**—This logging option is also a fixed format, but it is logged to an ODBC-compliant database such as SQL Server.

Of the previously mentioned log formats, the W3C Extended format allows for the most configuration options and lets you track various items, as you will see in a moment. It is also important to note here that the ASCII format is the fastest format of the available options. This is an important concern when it comes to server performance. You will however, trade a friendly log format for this performance because the ASCII format is the easiest to work with.

CAUTION

When setting up your log file, you need to keep this in mind. If you use the default names that IIS sets up, all logged information for each service is kept in the same log file. For this reason, it is best to create a separate log file for each service that you want to log separately.

To enable logging for your SMTP virtual server, open the Internet Services Manger, highlight the virtual server you want to enable logging on and choose Properties from the Action menu.

This will display the SMTP Virtual Server Properties window, as seen in Figure 4.8.

FIGURE 4.8
The SMTP Virtual Server Properties dialog box shows the General tab and the list of available log file formats.

In Figure 4.8, I have expanded the drop-down list showing you the available formats. The default choice is the W3C Extended Log File Format. Before you can select from the list, however, you must select the Enable logging option box.

If you choose to use the default W3C log file format, you can customize the items that will be tracked and logged. Click the Properties button to display the dialog box shown in Figure 4.9.

On the General tab, you need to specify the time frame for the logging activity. The available options are

- **Hourly**—The log files will be created on an hourly basis.
- **Daily**—The log files are created daily. They are started on the first entry after midnight.
- **Weekly**—This option creates weekly log files. Like the Daily option, the log file is created, starting with the first entry after midnight but on a Saturday.
- **Monthly**—Creates log files monthly, starting with the first entry after midnight on the last day of the month.
- **Unlimited file size**—The log file will have new information appended to the end of the same file. In order to access a log file set up in this manner, you need to stop the server.
- **When the file size reaches**—When you select this option, you specify a file size that will be the maximum size created before a new log file is created.

Figure 4.9

The General Properties tab of the Extended Logging Properties dialog box allows you to set the interval for logging, as well as the directory in which to store the log file.

You can also check the Use local time for file naming and rollover option, if you want to use your local time instead of Greenwich Mean Time (GMT).

You can also change the default location for log file storage if you desire by entering the directory name into the Log file directory text box or by using the Browse button to locate a suitable directory. The log file name is displayed at the bottom of the page.

Selecting the Extended Properties tab will display the dialog box, as shown in Figure 4.10.

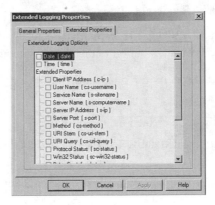

Figure 4.10

The Extended Properties tab is available only in the W3C Extended format and allows you to set a wealth of options to track regarding connections to the server.

As you can see, you can track quite a few different variables in regard to the clients that are connected to the server. Some variables, such as Client IP, Date, and Time, can be a great help in troubleshooting complaints of connection problems.

One other bit of information is necessary to add before I close my discussion of protocol logging. If you choose to create your log files using the ODBC format, you will find a slightly different Properties dialog box for this, shown in Figure 4.11.

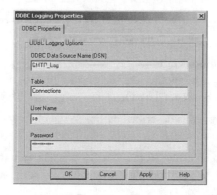

FIGURE 4.11

The ODBC Logging Properties dialog box is different from the other formats because you are saving the log information to an ODBC-compliant database.

As you can see from Figure 4.11, I have set the various options to enable the SMTP virtual server to connect to an ODBC data source. In this case, it is an SQL 7.0 database.

The ODBC Data Source Name (DSN) is a string value that tells the server what the data source name is. You will need to create a database for this feature to work first, and then set up the necessary DSN in the ODBC applet.

The Table variable is the table name within the database where the records will be stored.

If you are using a database that requires a username and password, such as SQL server, you enter those values in the corresponding boxes.

This book does not cover database concepts, so if you are unsure of how to accomplish these tasks, see your database administrator.

SMTP Virtual Servers and Clustering

Clustering is a feature of Windows 2000 Advanced Server and is not available on a Windows 2000 Server installation. Using SMTP clustering offers you fault tolerance and performance enhancements over those possible when using a single SMTP virtual server. If you have an SMTP server cluster, the workload is distributed over the available SMTP servers in the cluster.

If one server in the cluster fails, the remaining servers can take over the processing for the downed server.

I will not be covering clustering in this section or this book. If you need more information on clustering, see your Windows 2000 Advanced Server documentation.

In order to set up your SMTP server to be a part of a cluster, perform the following procedure:

1. Ensure that the startup behavior of SMTP is set to Manual.
2. Open the properties sheet for your default SMTP virtual server.
3. Click the Advanced button on the General tab and double-click the (All Unassigned) entry in the list box.
4. Change the assigned port to another unused port number to avoid conflicts with the new server that we will be creating. Click OK.
5. Create a new virtual server as described earlier in the chapter and set its default port at 25.
6. When you are asked to enter the Home Directory, make sure that you enter the path to the shared directory to be used for clustering and not a path on your local hard drive.
7. Open a command prompt window on your computer and change to the directory `<systemroot>\System32\inetsrv`, wherein `systemroot` is the directory into which you installed Windows 2000.
8. Enter the command *iissync servername*. (*servername* is the name of another node on the cluster.)
9. Use the Cluster Administrator to associate a resource type with the new virtual server.

For more information on clustering, see your Windows 2000 Advanced Server documentation.

Security

You set the security on your virtual server by using two tabs on the properties sheet, Access and Security. The available options on the Access tab enable working with access control, relay restrictions, connection control, and the security of the communications. The Security tab lets you specify operators. All its options are discussed here.

We will look at the Security tab first, which you can see in Figure 4.12.

Clicking the Add button will open a window to the available user and group accounts on the local computer or domain, from which you can select operators. Users entered here will have the right to start, stop, and pause the service, as well as configure it.

If you want to remove a user from the list, select that user or group name and click the Remove button.

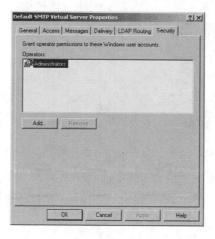

FIGURE 4.12
The Security tab on the SMTP Virtual Server Properties dialog box is where you add and remove authorized operators for the SMTP server.

TIP

It is recommended that you create a group on the domain controller that will be assigned in this step and add users to the group. This will make administration much easier.

The Access tab has four sections dealing with different aspects of securing the server communications and connections. You can see the Access tab and its sections in Figure 4.13.

The first section deals with Access control and authentication. To configure this, click the Authentication button. This will display the Authentication dialog box. The available options are

- **Anonymous Access**—Select this option if you do not want to use authentication on the server.
- **Basic Authentication**—Requires a username and password but sends them using clear text. You can append a domain name to the account name for authentication. You can also select the TLS option to use Transport Layer Security.
- **Windows Security Package**—The client and server negotiate this connection and use a Windows account name and password for authentication.

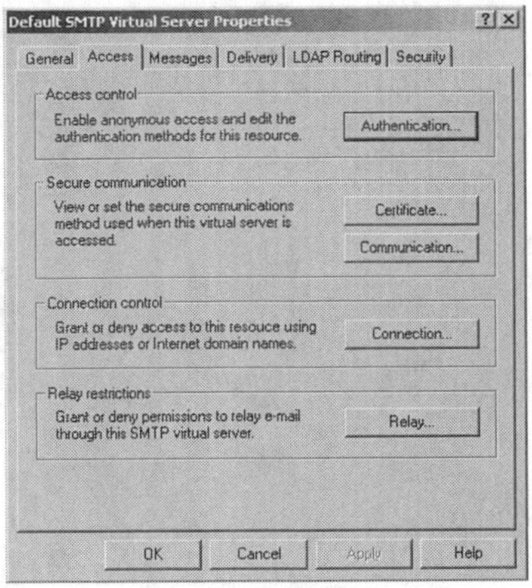

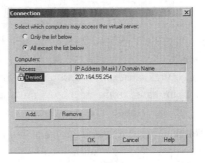

FIGURE 4.13
The Access tab contains sections for setting various security options relating to connections.

The Access tab's section on Secure communication deals with certificates and keys for secure communication. Certificates and Public Key Infrastructure (PKI) are beyond the scope of this book, so it is recommended that you learn about these security options before implementing them. By clicking on the Certificate button, you will invoke the Web Server Certificate Wizard, which will walk you through the process of creating a certificate request. You'll need such a certificate to send to an authorized Certificate Authority.

Clicking the Communication button will let you specify that secure communications should take place. This is only valid if you have a certificate installed.

Clicking the Connection button in the Connection control section will display the Connection dialog box, as shown in Figure 4.14.

FIGURE 4.14
The Connection dialog box will allow you to grant or deny access to the server by IP address or even by domain.

As you can see, I have granted access to all computers except the one with the IP address shown. This is only for display purposes, and the IP was just picked at random from my head, so please don't fret if the IP is yours. I hold nothing against you. You can also select a group of computers by specifying a network IP or using a subnet mask.

The final section of the Access tab concerns the use of your server as a relay agent for mail. You can grant or deny relay permissions for computers based on IP address, subnet address, and mask or domain name. These options allow you to select a single computer or a group of computers using the subnet mask or the domain name.

CAUTION

If you are unsure what to do with these Relay restrictions options, deny all relaying. If your server is discovered by Internet users as capable of relaying email, you can find yourself on the end of some very nasty emails and potential lawsuits as a result of someone else relaying spam mail through your server.

The security options I have been discussing are related to incoming messages. You can also set security on outbound messages as well. You need to access the security options for outbound messages by clicking the Outbound Security button at the bottom of the Delivery tab, as shown in Figure 4.15.

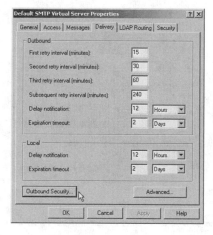

FIGURE 4.15

Clicking the Outbound Security button on this tab displays the Outbound Security dialog box, where you select the security options on outbound messages.

The options available for outbound message security are the same as for incoming messages, so I will not cover them in detail again. It is important to note, however, that these options pertain to messages that originate inside your organization or from outside users who might be relaying through your server, if you set up the relay feature as described earlier.

Managing Messages

You will need to deal with message issues on your server that relate to the number of messages to be delivered in a session or connection, message-size limits, recipients, and undeliverable messages. The following section explains procedures to help you work with these issues.

The options can be set on the Messages tab of the SMTP Virtual Server Properties dialog box.

As is the case with most production servers, performance is an issue that is important to the administrator. If your SMTP server is sending out a large number of messages in one connection, your server performance can slow down, and messages can take a long time to be delivered.

One way to avoid this problem is to limit the number of messages per connection. If you limit the number of messages per connection to, let's say, 30, and your server tries to send 120 messages, they won't all go in one session. The server will send the first 30, start a new connection for the next 30, and so on, until all messages are delivered.

If you want a good yardstick to measure the limit by, use the Performance Monitor and set a counter for the Messages Sent/sec object from the SMTP service objects, as shown in Figure 4.16.

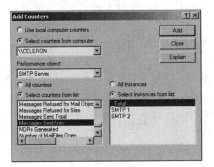

FIGURE 4.16

The Messages Sent/sec is a performance monitor counter object that can be used to determine a value to limit the messages per connection.

The limit value should be less than the number shown on the performance monitor.

To set the value, open the SMTP Virtual Server Properties dialog box and select the Messages tab. Select the Limit number of messages per connection to option and specify the value. The default is 20; you can enter a maximum value of 2,000,000,000. That's a lot of messages for one connection and if you are sending that many, I hope you are using a cluster.

You can also set a message size limit. You enter this value, in kilobytes, in the Limit message size to text box. If any clients attempt to send a message larger than this limit, they will receive an error message. The exception to this is if their server supports EHLO, in which case, the limit value will be detected, and the remote server will not attempt to deliver a message larger that this limit.

You can also set a limit on the amount of data sent during one session. Check the option Limit session size to and enter a value in the text box. This value will be the sum of all messages sent during a connection. Note that this applies only to the message body.

The final limit that can be set is the number of recipients per message. Select the Limit number of recipients per message to option and enter a value. The default is 100. If the SMTP server encounters a message with more than 100 recipients, it will open a new connection and process the remaining recipients.

SMTP also allows you to store non-deliverable mail on the server as well. A non-delivery report (NDR) will be placed in the directory that you specify in the properties dialog box. This is a copy of the NDR that is sent to the sender of the original message.

The SMTP server will try to resend the NDR up to the specified number of attempts before it will place it in the badmail directory that you specify. This directory is specified in the Badmail directory: text box. The default location is *x:\InetPub\mailroot\Badmail*, in which *x* is the drive letter where you installed IIS.

You can also deal with the delivery of messages on the Delivery tab of the properties dialog box. This tab is shown in Figure 4.17.

Under the Outbound section, the first four options allow you to set the First, Second, Third, and Subsequent retry intervals. These values, in minutes, are used to set the intervals at which the SMTP server will attempt to resend undeliverable messages.

The Delay notification option is used to set a delay timeout value before a delivery notice is set. This is useful to compensate for delays in network delivery. You can set the minimum to 1 minute, or the maximum to 9999 days. The default value is 12 hours.

The last option in the Outbound section is the Expiration timeout option. You set this value to have SMTP move the message(s) to the Badmail directory after it has exhausted all retry and delay intervals. As with the Delay notification, the minimum allowed value is 1 minute, and the maximum is 9999 days. SMTP starts with a default of 2 days.

4

ADMINISTERING THE SMTP AND NNTP SERVICES

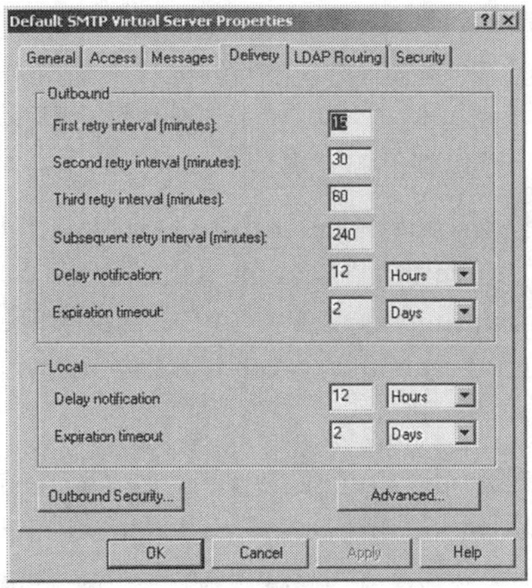

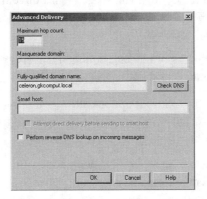

FIGURE 4.17

The Delivery tab of the SMTP Virtual Server Properties dialog box is used to enter retry intervals and timeout expiration periods for outbound messages

The lower section of this tab is the Local section. The two options available here function exactly as those in the Outbound section, but they deal with local connections only.

I will not cover the Outbound Security button, because I discussed it earlier in the "Security" section. There is however, an Advanced button that needs to be mentioned here. Clicking this button will display the Advanced Delivery dialog box, as shown in Figure 4.18.

FIGURE 4.18

The Advanced Delivery dialog box deals with routing issues in relation to your messages.

The first option that you see is the Maximum hop count. The default value of 15, indicates that the SMTP server will look at the number of routers that a message has crossed en route to its destination. If the message passes, or hops, more than 15 routers, the sender is issued an NDR. Of course, the message will be resent at the intervals specified earlier.

The next option is the Masquerade domain. The value that you enter here is displayed in the From field of the message. This is used to replace the local domain name.

Why would you want to do this? Well, if you are running a local domain that is not a Fully Qualified Domain Name (FQDN), some ISPs will reject the messages because of the From or MailFrom lines in the message header. By entering an FQDN in the Masquerade box, you can alleviate this problem.

> **CAUTION**
>
> Do not attempt to use this feature as a method of IP address or domain name spoofing.

The Fully-qualified domain name box contains the name of the server that you assigned when you installed Windows 2000. As you can see in Figure 4.18, I do not have an Internet domain available for this server, so I specified gkcomput.local during install. The server name is `celeron`, therefore, the FQDN of my server is `celeron.gkcomput.local`. If you have an FQDN for use on the Internet, it is recommended that you use it here. You can change this value to a new FQDN if you want.

If you click the Check DNS button, the SMTP server will attempt to validate the FQDN that you have entered. If you are using `local` as I am, the server will return the result almost immediately. It might take longer for Internet-connected computers to respond, based on the DNS server's response times.

You can also indicate a smart host on the Delivery tab. *Smart hosts* are computers on the network that are able to deliver messages over a connection that is less costly in terms of hops. If you have a smart host on your network, you can enter its IP address or hostname in this text box, and the SMTP server will redirect all outgoing messages to the smart host.

> **TIP**
>
> If you enter the smart host's IP address and surround it with brackets ([ ]), you can increase server performance by not requiring the server to do a DNS lookup on a hostname.

4

ADMINISTERING THE SMTP AND NNTP SERVICES

You will also notice that, as you enter a smart hostname or IP, the Attempt direct delivery before sending to smart host option becomes available. This option will cause SMTP to attempt to send the messages directly first. The default is not checked, and, in my opinion, you should leave it unchecked because it can defeat the purpose of a smart host.

The last option available on the Delivery tab is Perform reverse DNS lookup on incoming messages. If you select this option, SMTP will attempt to verify that the originating domain name and IP match. If they don't, the receive header will indicate "unverified" after the IP address.

This is actually a neat little feature, in that it can help to reduce mail coming from outside with forged headers.

NOTE

You need to be aware that, although it is useful, enabling this option can decrease server performance because the server must perform DNS lookups on each message that comes in the door.

Working with Domains

Sometimes I thank the powers that be for not allowing Microsoft to create a computer dictionary. Now, don't get me wrong. I am a Microsoft shop, and I use its software on a regular basis. But, Microsoft developers have a tendency to use their own terminology when it comes to their products.

You are already familiar with an Internet domain as well as a Microsoft Windows NT Server 4.0 domain and a Windows 2000 domain. Did you know that Microsoft has created a new domain for you to work with? Well, you now have an SMTP service domain. These domains are used to organize messages for delivery.

SMTP further divides its domains into local and remote domains. The local domain is serviced by a local SMTP server, whereas a remote domain is not within the local domain or network.

If you have a message that has a local domain address, it will be processed by the local SMTP server and placed into the Drop directory. Local domains are also sometimes referred to as service domains.

If you have a remote domain set up and you receive messages with remote addresses, the SMTP server will process the message and send it on to the remote domain. If you have multiple remote domains set up, you can specify different settings for each.

Creating a domain is an easy task. Remember when I said that there were two types of domains? Well, I sort of fibbed a bit. You can create a domain known as an *alias domain*. This type of domain is a secondary domain that points to the default domain. You can have messages sent to the alias, and they will be processed in the default domain.

Follow these procedures to create a domain:

1. Open Internet Services Manager and expand the SMTP Virtual Server entry.
2. Select the Domains entry in the Tree pane.
3. From the Action menu, select New and Domain. The New SMTP Domain Wizard starts up with the opening screen, as seen in Figure 4.19.

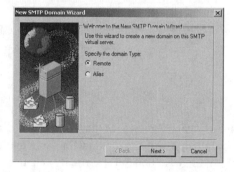

FIGURE 4.19
The New SMTP Domain Wizard lets you specify whether you are creating a remote or an alias domain.

4. Select either the Remote or Alias domain type, based on the type of domain you want to create.
5. When the Select Domain Name dialog box appears, enter the name of the domain such as microsoft.com for a remote domain or a name of your choosing for an alias domain and click the Finish button. The new domain and type will be displayed in the Internet Services Manager, as seen in Figure 4.20.

To delete an existing domain is even easier. Select the domain name in the Details pane and choose Delete from the Action menu, confirming the delete by choosing Yes on the SMTP Configuration message box.

NOTE

You cannot delete the default domain. If you have an existing domain that you want to delete but it is the default domain, create a new alias domain and make it the default. Then you can delete the previous domain.

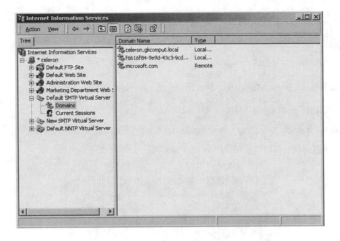

FIGURE 4.20

The Internet Services Manager shows the addition of the microsoft.com *SMTP domain and lists the type as Remote.*

SMTP uses a default domain to "stamp" messages that do not have a domain name attached to them. When SMTP is first installed, it will use the domain name that is specified in the Network Identification of the Windows 2000 Server. You can change the name of this domain within the Network identification area. For more information on how to do this, see the Windows 2000 help file on networking. If this name is changed, the SMTP default server name will be changed automatically when the service is restarted.

In order to change the default domain, you need to have more than one domain specified in the SMTP server. Although it doesn't indicate it, the top domain name is the default domain. In the details pane, right-click the domain name that you want to be the default and choose Set as default from the pop-up menu. Note that it now moves to the top of the list.

Remote domains have a few extra configuration options as compared to local or alias domains. To configure these options, right-click the remote domain name in the details pane and choose Properties from the pop-up menu. You will see a dialog box like that in Figure 4.21.

As you can see in Figure 4.21, I have the mcp.com remote domain's Properties window open with the General tab selected. The options on this tab are

- **Allow incoming mail to be relayed to this domain**—The default is to not allow the server to be used as a mail relay. Selecting this option overrides that.

- **Send HELO instead of EHLO**—If you have SMTP clients contacting your server that support ESMTP (an extension of SMTP), they will start the session by issuing the EHLO command. This command causes the server (if it supports ESMTP) to list the extensions that it supports. Select this option if your SMTP client is receiving error messages from a remote server that does not support EHLO.

- **Outbound Security button**—This button displays an Outbound Security dialog box that enables you to set authentication and TLS security options.

- **Route domain section**—This section contains two possible options. The default option is to Use DNS to route to this domain. With this option selected, the SMTP server will deliver the messages to the remote domain normally. If you select the Forward all mail to a smart host option, you must provide the name of the smart host to use. (See the section earlier in this chapter on smart hosts, for more information on their use).

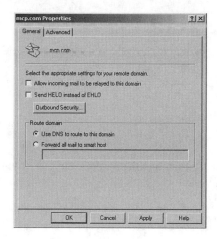

FIGURE 4.21
The mcp.com Properties dialog box contains two tabs with options for setting routing and security options for the remote domain.

The Advanced tab of this dialog box deals with Remote domains that dial in or connect periodically to acquire messages. You need to specify the option Queue messages for remote triggered delivery, to tell SMTP to hold the message sent to this remote domain until a valid login is initiated to retrieve the messages.

For security purposes, you need to click the Add button to add users or groups to the list of authorized users.

LDAP Server Connections

The Lightweight Directory Access Protocol (LDAP) was designed as an Internet protocol used to access directories and information regarding those directories from a server that supports LDAP. Windows 2000's Active Directory is LDAP compliant. SMTP can use LDAP to request a listing of mail users from an LDAP server. Figure 4.22 shows the LDAP Routing tab of the SMTP Virtual Server Properties dialog box.

4

ADMINISTERING
THE SMTP AND
NNTP SERVICES

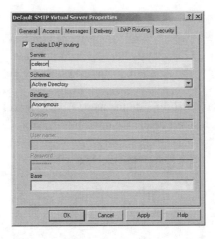

FIGURE 4.22

The LDAP tab of the SMTP Virtual Server Properties dialog box enables you to configure SMTP as a client to an LDAP server.

After you have entered the server name in the appropriate box, you need to determine the schema type. There are three schema types available from the drop-down list:

- **Active Directory**—Select this option if you will be contacting a Windows 2000 Active Directory server. You can use the Active Directory Users and Computers administrative tool on the server to manage mailboxes.

- **Site Server Membership Directory**—If you have the LDAP service installed as a part of the Microsoft Commercial Internet System 2.0 Mail, you would use this option.

- **Exchange LDAP**—This option should be selected if you are using Site Server 3.0 or later to manage the mailboxes.

Next, you need to concern yourself with setting the authentication level, through the Binding option. You have four choices:

- **Anonymous**—Requires no authenticaion.

- **Plain Text**—Account information is required but is transferred as clear text.

- **Windows SSPI**—Using this option will cause the client and server to negotiate security settings. The strongest method available to both will be used.

- **Service Accounts**—This option will use the information from the account that the SMTP service is being run under.

If you select the Plain Text or Windows SSPI options, you will be required to enter the domain name, as well as the username and password to be used.

In the Base field, enter the name of the container in the directory service you are contacting, where you want to start searching within the directory service. If there are sub-containers, entering the parent container's name will cause them to be searched as well.

Monitoring and Troubleshooting SMTP

Windows 2000 provides some tools to help you monitor your SMTP server for performance and troubleshooting requirements. These tools include the Performance Monitor, the Protocol Log, and the Windows 2000 System event log.

You use the System Monitor, found under Start, Programs, Administrative Tools, Performance. This tool is not specific to SMTP or IIS, but it is the performance tool used for monitoring system performance on many levels for the OS.

In order to use Performance Monitor for SMTP, you must add counters from the SMTP counter collection to the graph. Figure 4.23 shows some of the available counters for SMTP that can be added to the graph. You reach this dialog box by clicking the + button in the Performance Monitor toolbar.

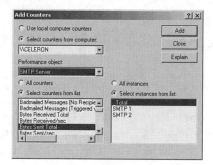

FIGURE 4.23

The SMTP service provides many counters to be used in Performance Monitor.

If you need to know more about using Performance Monitor, see the online help files or *Peter Norton's Complete Guide to Microsoft Windows 2000 Server* by Sams Publishing.

The Windows 2000 Server event log is a great way to review any error messages that were generated by the SMTP service. Figure 4.24 shows the Event Viewer window with some error messages generated by SMTP. You can access the Event Viewer by clicking Start, Programs, Administrative Tool, Event Viewer.

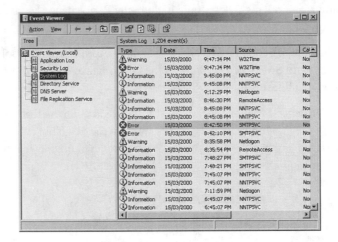

FIGURE 4.24
The Event Viewer window displays many different log types, but the System Log shows the SMTP error messages.

The other tool used to monitor SMTP is the Protocol Log. Protocol logging is used to track the commands that are received from SMTP clients. The log files can take on one of four formats: W3C Extended, Microsoft IIS Log, NCSA Common Log, and ODBC logging.

I won't delve into these log formats here as they were explained earlier in the chapter in the section "Protocol Logging."

The NNTP Service

The NNTP service provided with IIS 5.0 gives you the ability to host newsgroups and discussion forums on your server for internal purposes or customer-support forums.

The NNTP Service is not installed by default when you install IIS. In order to add the NNTP service to the IIS server, open the Internet Services Manager and select the computer icon in the Tree pane on the left. From the Action menu, choose New, NNTP Virtual Server.

This will open the New NNTP Virtual Server Wizard. You will be asked first to provide a server description. The next screen will ask for the NNTP server IP address and port number. If this is the first NNTP server, choose the typical port 119 for NNTP.

Select the Next button to advance to the Select Internal Files Path window where you can enter a path to store the files generated by the server. Choose the appropriate storage medium such as File System for the local computer or Remote Share if it will reside on a remote computer.

Next, select the path to the news content and click Finish to complete the NNTP Virtual Server creation.

The NNTP server that ships with IIS 5.0 fully supports the NNTP protocol and can be used to provide client-to-server and server-to-server communications. In addition, it also provides support for Multipurpose Internet Mail Extension (MIME), HTML, Graphics Interchange Format (GIF), and Joint Photographic Experts Group (JPEG).

Like the SMTP service, NNTP is integrated into the Microsoft Management Console for ease of administration. This also provides you the ability to manage multiple NNTP servers from one location over the network.

NNTP is also integrated into the Windows 2000 Server administration tools such as Performance Monitor and Event Viewer allowing for ease of troubleshooting and event logging. You can also make use of the Windows 2000 Access Control Lists (ACLs) for the security of your NNTP directories. By placing NTFS permission restrictions on the directories, you can prevent unauthorized access to certain newsgroups. You can also use the Content Replication System to perform updates on the ACLs across multiple servers helping to reduce administration.

If you have Microsoft's Index Server installed and configured on your server, you can also make use of the search capabilities provided by Index Server and perform searches on your newsgroups for specific groups or messages.

The NNTP service offers three possible authorization scenarios as well. These are

- **Anonymous Access**—Identical to anonymous access in the Web and FTP services, this allows all users access to the newsgroups on the server.
- **Standard NNTP Security Extension (AUTHINFO USER/PASS)**—This authentication requires a username and password that are passed as clear text.
- **Window Security Package (AUTHINFO GENERIC)**—If your users are working with Microsoft Mail and News clients, you can use this security option to enable passing usernames and passwords over the network in encrypted format.

Figure 4.25 shows the NNTP service in the MMC with some newsgroups installed and configured.

4

ADMINISTERING THE SMTP AND NNTP SERVICES

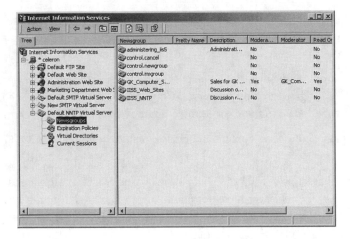

FIGURE 4.25

The NNTP service in MMC allows you to view and administer the service as well the newsgroups that are contained on the server.

NNTP Configuration

Before you can effectively configure the service, you need to understand the structure that NNTP uses for its groups and messages. Each newsgroup that is created in NNTP is actually a directory under the root directory. Each message in a newsgroup is a file under that particular group's directory. Figure 4.26 shows the directory structure for the NNTP service on my computer.

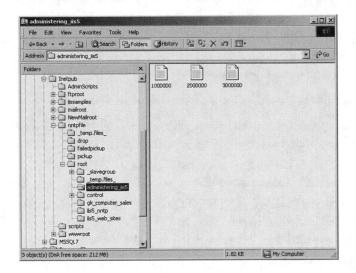

FIGURE 4.26

The NNTP service stores newsgroups as directories and the messages as files under the appropriate directory.

As you can see in Figure 4.26, the default root directory for NNTP is *x:\InetPub*
nntpfile\root, wherein *x* is the drive letter on which the NNTP service is installed. You can
change this directory by following the procedure outlined here:

1. Open Internet Services Manager, if it is not already open, and expand the server icon to
   display your NNTP virtual server.
2. Expand the NNTP server and select the Virtual Directories entry in the Tree pane.
3. Right-click the Default entry in the details pane and choose Properties from the pop-up
   menu, which will display the Default Properties dialog box, as shown in Figure 4.27.
4. Click the Contents button and enter the local path or network share where you want to
   place your default directory.

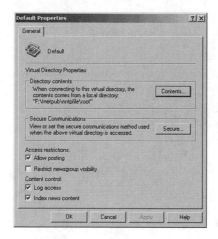

FIGURE 4.27
The Contents button gives you the option to specify the location and name of the default virtual directory for your
NNTP server.

One thing you might have noticed about the directories contained in the NNTP service is that
some directories and files are in the nntpfile directory. Do not delete or modify these files, as
they are internal data structures for NNTP's own use.

There are four entries under the NNTP Virtual Server in the Tree pane:

- **Newsgroups**—Selecting this option will display the available newsgroups that have been
  set up on the server.

- **Expiration Policies**—Select this entry and right-click it. Choose the New and Expiration
  Policies selections. This will start the NNTP Expiration Policy Wizard. Enter the appropriate information to set expiry lengths for articles on the server. This determines how
  long articles are kept on the server before they are deleted.

- **Virtual Directories**—This entry lets you set up virtual directories on your server. Right-click the entry and choose New and Virtual Directory to invoke the New NNTP Virtual Directory Wizard.
- **Current Sessions**—This lets you view the current connections to the server. Right-click the entry and choose Terminate All if you want to close all connections with the clients.

Right-clicking the NNTP Virtual Server in the MMC Tree pane and choosing Properties will display the Default NNTP Virtual Server Properties dialog box, shown in Figure 4.28. This is where you configure the service for your site.

FIGURE 4.28

The Default NNTP Virtual Server Properties dialog box controls the configuration options for the NNTP service.

Under the General tab, you can configure a name for the server as well the IP address in the same way you can for Web, FTP, and SMTP services. Clicking the Connection button displays a small dialog box that lets you set the connection limit and timeout values. When you select the Limit Connections to option, the default connection limit is 5000. You can specify your own limit here or clear the check box to enable unlimited connections. This value should be based on server performance monitoring for different levels of connections if you have a busy server.

You can also set a timeout limit for how long the server will maintain a connection on an idle client. The default is 10 minutes.

Below the Connection section of the General tab, you will see the now familiar Enable logging section. I won't go into the specifics here because the logging options are identical to those of the other services.

The last section on the General tab is the Path header option. You can specify a string value here that will be displayed in the Path line in your news postings.

Selecting the Access tab displays the dialog box shown in Figure 4.29.

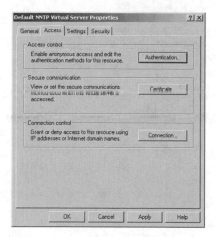

FIGURE 4.29

The Access tab allows you to set the various security and access control options available for the NNTP service.

Click the Authentication button to set up the access authentication as Anonymous, Basic, or Windows Security Package. These security options have already been explained, so I will not bore you with the details again.

You might note, however, that you can also enable SSL client authentication. This option will require clients to authenticate with a client certificate that can also be mapped to a user account on the server.

The Certificate button under the Secure Communication section will run the Web Server Certificate Wizard, enabling you to create a new certificate, assign existing certificates, or import a certificate from a key manager.

The last section, Connection control, lets you specify the computer that will be granted or denied access based on IP address, subnet mask, or domain name. These options are suited for external connections, and you would not normally use them in an intranet scenario.

The Settings tab controls setting relating to message sizes and moderators for the server. Figure 4.30 shows this tab.

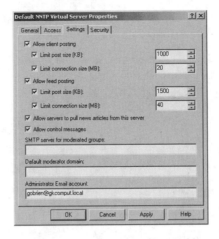

FIGURE 4.30
The Settings tab controls the message sizes, moderator information, and news feed settings.

I will start at the top of the tab sheet with the Allow client posting option. If this box is cleared, the server will not accept posts from clients, and the server is used only as a publication medium. Figure 4.31 shows the error message displayed in Outlook Express when I have disabled client posting.

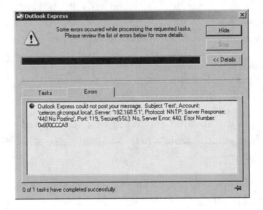

FIGURE 4.31
When the Allow client posting option is not checked, NNTP will not allow clients to post articles to the server.

When you do allow client posting to the news server, you can limit the size of each news article (message), as well as the maximum size of posts allowed in a single connection. The default setting for the maximum size of an article is set using the Limit post size (KB) option and specifying a value, in kilobytes. The default is 1000KB.

To limit the maximum size of all articles, a client can post in one connection session, select the Limit connection size (MB) option, and specify a value in megabytes. The default is 20MB. Some users will read and post offline; they can upload a considerable amount of data in the form of messages when they next connect to your server. This setting will help to reduce congestion on your connection by limiting the amount of data.

You can clear the check box of either option to impose no limits on these settings. Use your performance monitor and hard drive space as guides to the best values to use here.

The next option on the Settings tab determines if your server will accept articles from newsfeeds (refer to Figure 4.30). By selecting the check box, which is the default, you are allowing these newsfeeds to upload articles to your server.

Once again, you can limit the size of an article and the size of the data allowed in one connection in the same way as allowed in the client posting section.

Below this section is an option to enable news servers to pull feeds from your server. This means that another news server on the Internet, an intranet, or your WAN can download the newsgroups and messages that are posted on your server for use on that server. If you are running a WAN, you might benefit from this feature as it can provide an automated way to replicate newsgroups and messages to multiple servers or domains. You will want to monitor the connection status of your server if you have it publicly available on the Internet. Some outside users or companies might attempt to use your server as a source for newsgroups. Obviously you will set access restrictions on the directories that contain private company information.

The last option check box is Allow control messages. This option provides a way for you to allow or not allow the use of control messages on the server. *Control messages* are messages that the server processes as commands to delete messages or groups from the server. It is wise to restrict the use of control messages on the server if it is publicly available on the Internet.

There are three text boxes at the bottom of the Settings tab. The first one, SMTP server for moderated groups, is where you specify the mail server to send the posts for a moderated newsgroup. In a moderated newsgroup, a moderator receives the messages before they are placed on the server for access. In this way, the moderator can determine if the message or content is relevant.

The second text box is labeled Default moderator domain and is used to forward messages to the default moderator if those messages are sent to a moderated group without a specified moderator.

The last text box should contain the email address of an administrator who will receive NDR reports for messages that could be delivered to the newsgroup moderator.

4

ADMINISTERING
THE SMTP AND
NNTP SERVICES

Figure 4.32 shows the last tab on the properties dialog box, the Security tab. You use the Add button to open the accounts list for the computer or domain and specify the authorized users for the server. If you select a user in the list box and choose the Remove button, you will remove the user or group from the list of authorized users.

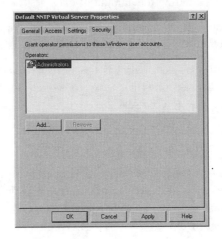

FIGURE 4.32
The Security tab sheet lists the available authorized operators of the NNTP server.

Maintaining and Monitoring NNTP

This is perhaps one of the most important areas that an administrator should be concerned with. Through proper monitoring and maintenance of your NNTP server, you can help avoid major outages and interruptions to the users of your news server. As with other services under Windows 2000, you can make use of the Performance Monitor and Event Viewer to monitor the performance of the news server and review any error messages.

You can use scripts to work with certain aspects of the NNTP service for maintenance purposes. These scripts are written in VBScript and can be run from a local or remote server. There are four scripts available:

- **Rexpire.vbs**—Use this script to modify, add, or delete expiration policies.
- **Rgroup.vbs**—This script can be used to modify, add, or delete groups to the server.
- **Rserver.vbs**—Use this script to modify, add, or delete virtual servers.
- **Rsess.vbs**—This is a session management script.

For each of these commands, there are command line options and return codes. There are too many to list them all here, so it is recommended that you review the script commands in the online help file for more information.

In order to monitor the performance of the NNTP service, Microsoft has provided various counters that can be added to the Performance Monitor graph. Figure 4.33 shows Performance Monitor's Add Counters dialog box that shows the NNTP Server selected and a few of the available counters. There are too many counters to mention them all here. It is recommended that you investigate them within Performance Monitor to see what each one measures.

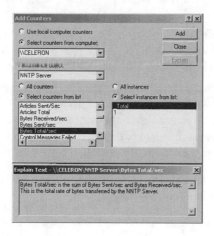

FIGURE 4.33

The Add Counters dialog box of Performance Monitor lists the available counters for the NNTP server. The Explain Text window displays the purpose of the counter.

If you need more information on what an individual counter measures, click the Explain button on the right side of the dialog box to have Performance Monitor display the Explain Text window.

There are two performance objects available for the NNTP service, NNTP Server and NNTP Commands. The Server object is used to measure the performance on articles and bytes sent and received and other counters related to the operation of the server. The Commands object deals with the possible commands that the server will process from clients.

In choosing counters to monitor, start with these:

- **Bytes Total/Sec**—This counter measures the total number of bytes per second that pass through the NNTP server. This can indicate bottlenecks existing in your server.

- **Maximum Connections**—Use this counter to monitor the connections made to the server. This value should always be less than the maximum value that you set earlier in the General tab.

- **Logon Attempts and Failures**—If you are running a secure server, monitoring this counter can show you that a break-in attempt has been made or is being attempted.

Although this is not an exhaustive list of the counters that you should have set up on the server, it is a good start toward giving you a picture of how your server is performing in relation to the NNTP service.

> **CAUTION**
>
> Although these counters are a great way to keep track of your server and monitor its performance, remember one thing—to track and monitor these counters also exacts a performance penalty on the server. Choose your counters wisely.

I have already showed you how to set up the logging features of NNTP. You can use these logs to determine if there are any discrepancies in the way the service is functioning. These log files have an entry for each and every time a user connects to the server, reads or posts an article, or logs on.

You can view these logs as a text file, or you can import them into other applications, such as in a spreadsheet or database, to monitor trends.

Another way to monitor the service is to use the Event Viewer. Click the Start button, select Administrative Tools, and then select Event Viewer. By selecting the System Log entry in the Tree pane, you can view the system logs that are created during the operation of the Windows 2000 Server.

Obviously, you are more interested at this point in the NNTP entries. With the System Log entry highlighted, select Filter from the View menu. This will display the System Log Properties dialog box, as shown in Figure 4.34.

By choosing the NNTPSVC entry from the drop-down list of available filters, you will filter the information presented in the Event Viewer window to be sent to only those concerned with the NNTP service.

During the scanning of the log files or the Event Viewer, you might come across some error messages that recommend you rebuild the NNTP server. This is an option that is available to you to help get the server back into operation quickly after a hard disk failure, accidental deletion of files, or trouble accessing the articles.

There are two rebuild levels that you can choose from. The Standard level is the fastest of the two, but it does not rebuild all the files. If you want to rebuild all the files, choose the Thorough rebuild.

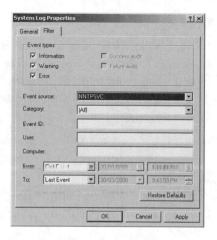

FIGURE 4.34
The System Log Properties dialog box with the Filter tab selected shows the Event Source as the NNTPSVC.

CAUTION

Before performing a rebuild of the server, be sure to stop the NNTP service.

After you have stopped the service, ensure that the NNTP Virtual Server is selected in the Tree pane and then click the Action menu. Choose All Tasks, Rebuild Server to display the Rebuild NNTP Virtual Server dialog box, as shown in Figure 4.35.

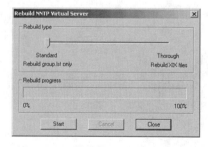

FIGURE 4.35
The Rebuild NNTP Virtual Server dialog box lets you choose the type of rebuild to perform, Standard or Thorough.

You use the slider shown on the screen to choose between the two levels of rebuild. After you have chosen the level, click the Start button to begin the rebuild process. The status indicator keeps you informed of the progress of the rebuild.

4

ADMINISTERING
THE SMTP AND
NNTP SERVICES

Troubleshooting NNTP

If you are having trouble with your NNTP server, there are a number of things that you can do to determine the problem and to rectify it. First, use the monitoring utilities mentioned earlier. The users of your server are a good resource for information pertaining to potential trouble. After all, they are the ones who use the server on a regular basis and would be the first to notice any discrepancies in the way it is working.

Using Event Viewer, you can determine if there are any issues related to service failures to start or stop. A server that has not started will not serve newsgroups to clients.

You can use the old standby PING program to verify connectivity of the server to the rest of the network. If you have the server set up to provide internal and external access to the newsgroups, it is wise to use a computer not connected to the internal network to determine connectivity to the outside world.

Last but not least, you can also use the Telnet program to help you determine where the problem lies, with the client or server.

Summary

In this chapter, we have looked at the SMTP and NNTP services that are provided as a part of IIS 5.0. I have shown you the various methods to manage and monitor the services to help you achieve optimum performance and usability of these two services.

By using the tools provided with Windows 2000 Server, you can monitor the performance of the services and tune them to work best on your server hardware and connections.

You have seen how an NNTP virtual server can be used to provide discussion forums for your company's employees or customers.

WebDAV Publishing

IN THIS CHAPTER

What Is WebDAV Publishing?

WebDAV stands for Web Distributed Authoring and Versioning. As an extension to the HTTP 1.1 protocol, it allows clients the ability to publish and manage resources on the server as well as give them the ability to place locks on the resources.

WebDAV also offers versioning control. The versioning capability is actually an extension to the WebDAV protocol. This versioning control is based on a two-level approach. The first level is classed as basic versioning, and the second level is advanced versioning.

Basic versioning allows authors to simultaneously create and access distinct resources such as files. It also provides automatic version control for clients that do not support a version or that are not "version-aware."

Advanced versioning provides capabilities such as tracking changes and managing any configuration issues. It also supports versioning of the URL namespace.

If you are familiar with Visual Source Safe, a code checking and storage component that is included with Microsoft Visual Studio Enterprise Edition, you will understand the concepts of version control. Basically, a file or any resource that can be controlled by versioning is "checked out" when it is first requested for editing. Instead of working with the actual resource, you are working with a copy of that resource. Once you have made the necessary revisions, you "check in" the resource, and updates are applied.

This is just a generic explanation of versioning, and you can read the entire 52-page document at http://www.webdav.org. Make sure that you are ready for some heavy reading because the document is a draft, and some of the wording seems to go around in circles based on the terminology used. This Web site is also a good place to keep track of any changes to the WebDAV protocol.

You must be running Windows 2000 Professional Server or Advanced Server before you can set up a WebDAV directory. Any client that supports a Windows 2000 Server can access this WebDAV directory. The most common clients that you will come into contact with are Windows 2000 itself, Internet Explorer 5, and Microsoft Office 2000.

Due to the fact that WebDAV is an industry-standard protocol, any client software that supports publishing to WebDAV directories can publish to your WebDAV directory if the appropriate user access permissions are set up. In this way, you can have a field office that perhaps does not use the previously mentioned Microsoft products, yet you will still be able to publish or read content within the WebDAV directory.

For an updated list of client software that supports WebDAV, visit http://www.webdav.org/.

You can add a WebDAV directory to your network places in Windows 2000 and then access it as if it were a local or networked drive. You can perform the same file operations on the WebDAV directory with IE5 that you can with Windows 2000.

If you are using Office 2000 on your network, users can publish files created with it to a WebDAV directory on an intranet.

Because WebDAV offers the ability for clients to manipulate the files by copying and moving them, modifying the properties, searching and locking, and so on, you need a good security model to help you deal with authentication issues. WebDAV integrates the security features of IE5 as well as Windows 2000.

WebDAV supports the Kerberos v5 authentication, Integrated Windows authentication, and the new-to-Windows-2000 Digest authentication. These authentication methods have already been mentioned in Chapter 1, "Internet Information Server 5.0 Features," and we will not delve into them here for the sake of brevity. There are many resources available to you in the online help and the Internet that can fully explain each of these authentication methods. If you would like to delve deeper into Kerberos, MIT—the creator of the Kerberos protocol—has a Web site that contains some fairly in-depth information relating to what Kerberos is, where it came from, plus known bugs and issues. The site even offers the source code and some binaries for it.

For more information on what MIT has to offer in regards to Kerberos, check out its Web page at `http://web.mit.edu/kerberos/www/index.html`.

Microsoft provides a technical document on its Windows 2000 Web site that explains the Kerberos protocol and how it is implemented in Windows 2000. The information can be found at `http://www.microsoft.com/windows2000/library/planning/security/kerbsteps.asp`.

Create a Directory for WebDAV Publishing

One of the first things you need to do after ensuring that you have one of the Windows 2000 operating systems installed is to set up a WebDAV publishing directory. Follow these steps:

1. Create a directory in the `InetPub` directory to use for WebDAV publishing. (Note: Do not create it under `wwwroot` because of the relatively lax security inherent in this directory.) The most common location for this directory is `\InetPub\WebDAV`, although you are free to choose a directory of your own.

2. Create a virtual directory in Internet Services Manager and call it `WebDAV`. Point the virtual directory to the one you just created.

3. Grant Read, Write, and Directory browsing permissions to the directory. This enables clients to publish to the directory and read the contents of the directory.

4. Click the Finish button of the Virtual Directory Wizard, and you have just created a WebDAV directory.

You now need to enable clients to publish to this directory. We will go into this a little later in the section "Publishing and Managing Files."

Managing WebDAV Security

Managing the security of WebDAV mostly involves client authentication, and controlling who has access and who is not allowed to use the service. We will look at each in turn.

As mentioned before, you have various levels of authentication for clients wanting to use the service. Anonymous access is available, but, because of the lack of security related to anonymous access, it is recommended that you do not use it for WebDAV.

Basic authentication is the lowest level of security that will require a username and password. This will authenticate users before they are allowed to publish to the directory but keep in mind that if you are not using SSL, your usernames and passwords are transmitted over the network in clear text and can be intercepted. If a hacker or other malicious user could intercept this information and use it to gain access to the published information, this would defeat the purpose of attempting to secure the directory.

You can use Integrated Windows authentication as well. Integrated authentication does not actually send a password across the network but instead, requires the client browser to prove that it knows what the password is through the use of a hashing algorithm.

You can also use Digest authentication, which, as we mentioned before, is a new feature available in Windows 2000. Digest authentication is the best method to use if you are providing publishing over the Internet or working through a firewall.

These authentication methods are described in more detail in Chapter 8, "Security."

Another important aspect of managing security for your WebDAV directories is access control. By using a combination of IIS 5.0 and Windows 2000 permissions, you can control who has access to these directories and what rights they have when connected to them.

Essentially you have three possible permissions that can be set on a WebDAV directory:

- **Read**—This permission allows clients to see the contents of the directory files and their properties. Clients cannot delete or otherwise modify the files.
- **Write**—This permission allows clients to publish or copy files into the directory. Clients can also delete and modify the files.
- **Directory Browsing**—With browsing enabled, clients can view listings of the files that reside in the directory. They cannot view file contents, nor can they modify them.

By using a combination of these permissions, you can customize the access on the directory or directories that you have set for WebDAV. A few examples follow.

If you enable Read, Write, and Directory Browsing, you are giving clients the ability to publish files to the directory, view and modify the contents and properties of the files, and view a directory listing.

Suppose you have a situation in which you want to allow clients to publish content to the directory but, for reasons of security, you do not want them to see what the directory is (for example, as with a poll or vote on a subject). To "hide" the directory from users, you can set the Write permission and clear the Read and Directory Browsing permissions.

You can set other possible combinations using the three access permissions, based on your own requirements.

To set these permissions, open Internet Services Manager and select the WebDAV directory that we created earlier. Right-click the directory entry and choose Properties from the pop-up menu. This displays the WebDAV Properties dialog box, as shown in Figure 5.1.

FIGURE 5.1
The WebDAV Properties dialog box showing the Virtual Directory tab where you select access permissions.

As you can see in Figure 5.1, you can specify the Read, Write, and Directory Browsing permissions along with some others.

The first permission option is *Script source access*. Although we are dealing with a WebDAV directory and not a Web directory that is serving Web pages to the public, you can use the directory for the latter purpose if you want. This permission allows clients to see the contents of your script files. This can be an issue if your developers do not want their ASP code being accessed.

The other two permissions that we haven't mentioned yet are Log visits and the Index this resource. You can choose to log access to this directory by selecting the Log visits option box. A log file will be recorded only if logging has been enabled for the site.

The other option, Index this resource, is not really a permission in one sense of the word. By selecting this option, you tell Index Server to index this directory. This will allow clients to perform searching on the contents of the directory.

> **CAUTION**
>
> One thing that you need to keep in mind when dealing with access control on an NTFS volume is that Windows 2000 assigns Full Control NTFS permissions to all directories by default. Remember this when creating new directories.

Searching WebDAV Directories

As we mentioned in the section on security, there is an option to have Index Server index your WebDAV directory. By doing so, users can search the directory on file or resource contents, as well as the properties of the files. An example of this would be a client searching for all files created by Gerry O'Brien in 1999.

There are a couple of items that need to be attended to so that the directory will be indexed and searchable. Obviously, the indexing service must be running. You can start the indexing service by opening the Services applet and locating Indexing Service and click the start button on the toolbar. Figure 5.2 shows the Services applet window.

In Figure 5.2, I have the Indexing Service highlighted, and it has been started.

> **TIP**
>
> If you want to provide the indexing service to the WebDAV directory on a continuous basis, you should set the startup option to Automatic in the Services applet. Indexing Service will start every time you reboot Windows 2000.

You can also start the Indexing Service from the command line or from Run on the Start menu. Choose Start, Run, and type in *net start cisvc*.

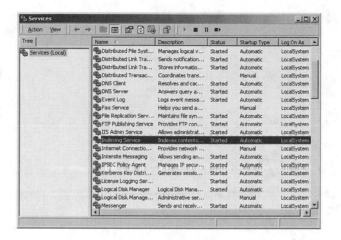

FIGURE 5.2

The Services applet window displays a list of all installed services and enables you to start, stop, and pause each service.

NOTE

If you didn't have the service running prior to now, it will take some time for it to index everything that you have chosen to be indexed. Therefore, if you do a search on your WebDAV directory only to find nothing listed, give the Indexing Service a little time to complete the index database. For more information on Indexing Service, see the online help file or *Peter Norton's Complete Guide to Microsoft Windows 2000 Server*.

CAUTION

If you have your drive formatted as NTFS, your clients will be able to perform full searches on the directory. If you have it formatted as FAT or FAT32, then the searches are limited to the resource contents and the properties will not be searched, as neither one of these provide support for this.

There different ways to search the WebDAV directory. Perhaps the easiest way is to use the Search option on the Start menu. This enables you to search for files by name in the directory or drives that you specify. This method offers various options for searching, as indicated in Figure 5.3.

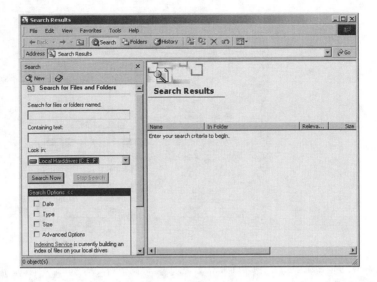

FIGURE 5.3

The Search Results dialog box enables you to choose search options and drives on which to perform searches.

Another easy way for your clients to perform searches is to create a Web page that allows searching. In Listing 5.1, I have provided HTML code that you can use to create a search page on your Web site. This code was generated by Microsoft FrontPage 2000.

LISTING 5.1   An Example of a Search Page

```
    <html>

<head>
    <meta http-equiv="Content-Type" content="text/html; charset=windows-1252">
    <meta http-equiv="Content-Language" content="en-us">
    <title>Customer Support -- Search</title>
    <meta name="GENERATOR" content="Microsoft FrontPage 4.0">
    <meta name="ProgId" content="FrontPage.Editor.Document">
    <meta name="Microsoft Theme" content="expeditn 001, default">
    <meta name="Microsoft Border" content="tlb, default">
    </head>

    <body>
    <p><a name="top">U</a>se the form below to search for documents in this
➥web containing specific words or combinations of words.
➥The text search engine will display a weighted list of matching
➥documents, with better matches shown first. Each list item is a link
➥to a matching document; if the document has a title it will
➥be shown, otherwise only the document's file name is displayed.
```

➥A brief <a href="#querylang">explanation</a> of the query language is
➥available, along with examples.</p>
```
    <!--WEBBOT
    bot=Search
    S-LINK
    S-FIELDS="TimeStamp,DocumentK,Weight"
    S-INDEX="All"
    S-DSN="default"
    TAG="BODY"
    S-Text="Search for:"
    I-Size="20"
    S-Submit="Start Search"
    S-Clear="Reset" b-useindexserver="1"
      -->
    <hr align="center">
    <h2><a name="querylang">Query Language</a></h2>
    <p>The text search engine allows queries to be formed from arbitrary
```
➥Boolean expressions containing the keywords AND, OR, and NOT,
➥and grouped with parentheses. For example:</p>
```
    <blockquote>
     <dl>
    <dt><strong><tt>information retrieval</tt></strong></dt>
    <dd>finds documents containing 'information' or 'retrieval'<br>
      <br>
    </dd>
    <dt><strong><tt>information or retrieval</tt></strong></dt>
    <dd>same as above<br>
      <br>
    </dd>
    <dt><strong><tt>information and retrieval</tt></strong></dt>
    <dd>finds documents containing both 'information' and 'retrieval'<br>
      <br>
    </dd>
    <dt><strong><tt>information not retrieval</tt></strong></dt>
    <dd>finds documents containing 'information' but not 'retrieval'<br>
      <br>
    </dd>
    <dt><strong><tt>(information not retrieval) and WAIS</tt></strong></dt>
    <dd>finds documents containing 'WAIS', plus 'information' but not
```
➥'retrieval'

```
      <br>
    </dd>
    <dt><strong><tt>web*</tt></strong></dt>
    <dd>finds documents containing words starting with 'web'<br>
      <br>
```

LISTING 5.1 Continued

```
</dd>
  </dl>
</blockquote>
<h5><a href="#top">Back to Top</a></h5>
</body>

</html>
```

Notice the section that starts with `<!--WEBBOT`. This is actually a FrontPage component that provides the searching capability.

The last line in the `WEBBOT` code, `S-Clear="Reset" b-useindexserver="1"`, indicates that the search will make use of Index Server by specifying the value of `"1"`.

The last method that will be mentioned here for searching is to make use of XML. This book does not intend to teach you XML because that would take another book in itself.

Another resource for building search tools using XML is the Windows 2000 Software Development Kit (SDK), which is available for download or online viewing on Microsoft's Web Site at `http://msdn.microsoft.com/windows2000/`.

Publishing and Managing Files

In this section, we will discuss the procedures users can perform to publish content to, and manipulate files in, a WebDAV directory. We will cover three scenarios, publishing with Windows 2000, publishing with Internet Explorer 5.0, and publishing with Office 2000.

Publishing with Windows 2000

If you remember from earlier in this chapter, we created a WebDAV directory under our default Web site. We will use this directory to demonstrate the capability to access it and publish to it using Windows 2000.

In order to make the directory available to work with in Windows 2000, you add the `WebDAV` directory to My Network Places. Follow this procedure:

1. Open My Network Places.

2. Double-click the Add Network Place icon to start the Add Network Place Wizard.

3. On the Welcome screen, you are asked to enter a URL, filename, and a Web folder or FTP site address. Use the Browse button to locate the network place, in our case, the `WebDAV` directory.

4. Enter the correct URL where you have placed the WebDAV directory. For example, if you placed it on your local IIS server, enter http://localhost/WebDAV. (Do this providing you used the WebDAV name for the directory; if not, enter the name you gave your WebDAV directory instead.)

5. Click the Next button. If your connection is successful, you will see the dialog box displayed in Figure 5.4. Click Finish. (If you do not get this or receive an error message, be sure that you are using the correct server and directory name.)

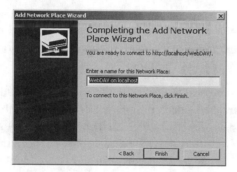

FIGURE 5.4
The Completing the Add Network Place Wizard screen indicates that the directory was found, and that you can now connect to it.

The WebDAV directory will now show up in the Network Places windows where you can begin to copy, move, delete, or modify files in much the same as you would files in any other directory.

Publishing with Internet Explorer 5.0

You can access the WebDAV directory for publishing use with IE 5.0 or higher. Instead of opening the directory with a URL, such as http://localhost/WebDAV, you need to open it as a file.

To do this, start IE 5.0 and select Open from the File menu. This will display the Open dialog box shown in Figure 5.5.

In Figure 5.5, I have specified the URL that we used earlier to connect to the WebDAV directory in My Network Places.

Be sure to select the Open as Web Folder check box to ensure that you open the folder correctly for publishing. Failing to check this option will result in the folder being opened in an identical fashion, as if you were connecting to an FTP directory through Internet Explorer. You will not be able to publish to the directory in this way.

FIGURE 5.5
The Open dialog box of IE 5.0 is where you specify the directory or filename to open in IE.

When the directory is opened, you can use the File menu to create new folders to which you can publish.

Publishing with Office 2000

If your organization uses Microsoft Office 2000, you can publish content to the WebDAV directory as well. This is an ideal situation for larger companies, in that it allows them to publish documents online such as human resources and corporate policy manuals for employees to access and read online. It also offers the capability to provide a central depository for policies, where they can be updated in one location only instead of on multiple computers.

Publishing to a WebDAV directory is no harder than saving a file normally under any Office application.

In order to publish the file to the WebDAV directory, you need to select the *My Network Places* icon in the left panel. This will display a list of available network places including the WebDAV directory that we created earlier.

Double-click the WebDAV on Localhost entry to open the folder and then click the Save button to save the file to the WebDAV directory.

That's all there is to it.

Summary

WebDAV is becoming an increasingly important protocol for Internet communication and is an extension to the HTTP 1.1 protocol. If you are interested in obtaining more information on the WebDAV specification, see RCF 2518 from the Internet Engineering Task Force (IETF).

You have seen that WebDAV can be used to provide a method for collaboration of documents and other files on a Web server running IIS 5.0 by creating a Web-publishing directory.

We have also discussed some security issues related to WebDAV directories. Providing security for your files in these directories is extremely important if you are publishing the directory on the Internet.

You saw some examples of searching WebDAV directories using the Windows 2000 search tools and Index Server. Further searching based on file properties and attributes can be achieved using XML.

Finally, you saw different methods of publishing content to the WebDAV directory using Windows 2000 itself, Internet Explorer 5.0, and Microsoft Office 2000.

Name Resolution

IN THIS CHAPTER

If you are familiar with Internet usage and the TCP/IP protocols, you know that all computers on a TCP/IP network require a unique IP address. Computers work best with numbers; humans do not. We prefer to identify things with a name. A Web site is no different.

In order to provide a somewhat friendly name for ease of remembering, TCP/IP networks use name resolution. Name resolution involves using a computer to provide mappings of friendly names to IP addresses. The friendly names are referred as *domain names* and *hostnames*.

There are various methods used for name resolution, and we will cover them here as they concern IIS 5.0.

Dealing with Name Resolution and IIS 5.0

There are two methods available for IP addressing in Windows 2000: static assignment and Dynamic Host Configuration Protocol (DHCP). You can use one or both methods as you see fit.

The static method of assigning IP addresses to your hosts can be time consuming if you have a large number of hosts. This method requires a little more administrative work because each computer must be configured manually for its IP address. Also, you must keep track of which addresses are assigned and which ones are available to be used on your network. If the network does not change very often, then this shouldn't be a major problem once you have it set up. I like to keep a network map on the wall that displays the IP addresses and where those hosts are located.

For ease of administration and to make life a bit easier for the user, you can set up and maintain the DHCP service on the Windows 2000 Server, or another Windows NT/2000 server to automatically provide IP addresses from a pool.

Normally you would set up a range of IP addresses that would be considered your network. For example, I use 192.168.5 for the network portion of the IP addresses that clients on my own network use. That leaves me with 254 possible hosts to assign IP addresses to— 192.168.5.1 through 192.168.5.254.

NOTE

The range of IP addresses actually spans from 0 to 255 but we can't use 0 or 255 because they are reserved. For more information on TCP/IP addressing, you should refer to a good text that describes it in depth.

My IIS server is set to use 192.168.5.1. That never changes on my network, hence it is known as a *static* IP address.

We won't go into TCP/IP in depth here because that is not the purpose of this book. However, it is important to know about the different classes of IP addresses as they relate to host and network addressing.

For the purposes of TCP/IP addressing, there are actually five classes of IP addresses, A, B, C, D, and E. Each class spans a range of addresses that provides a fixed number of hosts and networks. When I refer to a *host*, I am referring to the actual individual computer that receives an IP address. The network reference deals with what might be considered a zone for the purposes of separating groups of computers.

Class A addresses start at 0.0.0.1 and work up to 126.255.255.254. Class B spans the range of 128.0.0.1 to 191.255.255.254, and Class C uses 192.0.0.1 to 254.255.255.254. Class D and Class E are special classes and are not used in normal networking setups, so they will not be discussed here.

It is important to note a few things about IP addresses on a TCP/IP network. The first thing is the 127. addresses. These addresses are used for loopback testing to verify network operation internally on the local computer. If you issued the PING 127.0.0.1 command on your computer, you would receive PING responses from localhost, which is your own computer. This PING is internal and does not travel out onto the network.

Another issue to be aware of is that the Internet does not make use of certain ranges of IP addresses, in order to provide private TCP/IP networks with a range of addresses to use for internal networks. These addresses are in the 10.0.0 and 192.168. ranges. You may find that some ISPs are using the 10. range of IP addresses for certain types of network setups, such as xDSL or cable modem providers. These ISPs actually set up small internal networks using the 10. ranges to assign addresses dynamically to the clients and then assign an external, valid Internet IP when the client connects to the outside world.

One ISP in my home city uses this scenario for its ADSL implementation. This provides users with the ability to connect to each other internally, creating a small neighborhood of users within their own little network. Only when the client is issued a valid Internet IP can the outside world see the host computer.

Keeping this in mind, I recommend that for internal networks and intranets, you use the 192.168 range of IP addresses. Using this range, you can manipulate the addresses to create varying number of hosts and networks using subnet masking.

Within each class of IP address, there are two host addresses that you cannot use as well. These are the .0 and the .255. The .0 is meant as "this network," and the .255 is a broadcast address. TCP/IP makes special use of these two host addresses.

Let's take a look at the address 192.168.0. Using this range, you can have a total of 254 host computers on the network. Each would be contained in the IP addresses of 192.168.0.1 through to 192.168.0.254. This provides you with 254 hosts on one network segment.

If you need more hosts than this, you have a couple options. The first option is to create another network and use the next network range of 192. addresses. You could use 192.168.1.1 through 192.168.1.254 for another 254 hosts. You will need to use a subnet mask on your computers so that they can determine which host is on which network.

In the two examples given above, the network addresses are 192.168.0 and 192.168.1. Each network has the same numbered hosts, therefore you need a way to determine which host you want to talk to. This is where the subnet mask comes into play. On these addresses, you need to specify a subnet mask of 255.255.255.0. This ensures that when you send a message or data to a host computer, TCP/IP will first check the subnet mask to determine how to find the network and host address.

An example would be sending a data packet to the host computer with an IP address of 192.168.0.34. With 255.255.255.0 as the subnet mask, TCP/IP knows that it must first go to the network 192.168.0 before it starts to look for the host IP of .34. TCP/IP does this by using binary operations on the IP address.

As you may know, IP addresses are 32-bit numbers that are divided into four octets. We consider these numbers as decimal, but the computer sees them as binary. For example, the binary equivalent of the IP address 192.168.0.34 is 11000000 10101000 00000000 00100010. In order to determine the network address based on the netmask, TCP/IP does a binary AND operation. A binary AND uses what is known as a *truth table*. That table is displayed here:

	1	0
1	1	0
0	0	0

How this table works is that you take the left binary digit and the top binary digit. Where the two intersect in the middle indicates the ANDed value. For example, if you take the binary digit 0 in the left column, and then take the binary digit 0 in the top column, they will intersect on the 0 in the lower section.

Basically, ANDing states that if you have 1 AND 1, you have 1; if you have 1 AND 0, you have 0; if you have 0 AND 1, you have 0; and if you have 0 AND 0, you have 0. Confused yet?

So, let's apply the subnet mask to the above IP address for the purposes of ANDing. 255.255.255.0 gives us a binary number of 11111111 11111111 11111111 00000000.

IP Address	192.168.0.34	11000000 10101000 0000000000100010
Netmask	255.255.255.0	11111111 11111111 1111111100000000
Network Address		11000000 10101000 0000000000000000

So, if we take the binary number that we achieved as a result of the AND operation, remove the last octet, and convert it back to decimal, we see that the network address is 192.168.0.

An easier way to look at this without needing the binary arithmetic is that, when you see a 255 in the netmask, you will know that the portion of the address it refers to must match exactly. Therefore, with a netmask of 255.255.0.0 applied to the previous IP address, the network portion would then be 192.168, and the hosts would be .0.1 through 255.254.

This last example deals with *subnetting*, or splitting the network portion of the IP address to achieve more host addresses. This is the second option available to achieve more hosts and doesn't require you to use another range of IP addresses.

How subnetting works is an extension of the netmask example shown previously. By using the correct subnet mask, you can tell your TCP/IP network that you are using only the first two octets of the IP for the network portion and the last octet for the host portion. This will effectively give you 65,532 possible hosts on your network, instead of 254.

You can also use a dynamic assignment of IP addresses for your computers on the network. This involves setting up a Dynamic Host Configuration Protocol (DHCP) server. A DHCP server has the responsibility of assigning IP addresses to clients as they request them.

This method has been used on the Internet to help alleviate some of the shortage of IP addresses using the current 32-bit addressing scheme. The shortage will be resolved when the Internet starts to make use of the Ipv6 addressing scheme, which was designed to overcome the shortage.

DHCP helps right now by leasing IP addresses for a specified period of time. It is up to the client to initiate a periodic request to maintain that IP address. If the client fails to do so, the DHCP will enter the IP address back into the pool of available addresses to be assigned again if requested by another client.

Windows 2000 enables you to use DHCP as well on your own network. Most private networks don't run into an IP address shortage, but DHCP makes for easier administration. The DHCP service that comes with Windows 2000 provides automatic IP address assignment to clients requesting one when they log on. DCHP can also work in conjunction with the Windows Internet Name System (WINS) to automatically map NetBIOS computer names to IP addresses on the local network.

Your network might already have a DHCP server installed and functioning. If this is the case, you need not worry about assigning IP addresses. The DHCP server dynamically assigns these addresses when clients request them.

> **CAUTION**
>
> You should not configure your IIS server to acquire an IP address from a DHCP server. This will prevent you from being able to assign the server a friendly name and access it from the network. Configure your IIS server with a static IP.

After you have assigned an IP address to your IIS server, the server can then begin to serve requests to clients based on the IP address. Navigating to computers over the Internet using IP addresses is not exactly the easiest way to work, so assigning a static IP and a domain name makes it much easier for your clients to locate your server using fully qualified domain names (FQDN).

An FQDN consists of the server's hostname along with its domain name. An example is the Web server at Macmillan Publishing. You would type www.mcp.com in the address bar if you wanted to visit the Web site. The com portion is the top level domain, and the mcp portion is the next level down, or the corporate domain. The www portion is the Web service on that domain.

In order to allow your clients to use domain names, you need to have a method for resolving an IP address to a particular domain name. This is where the Domain Name System (DNS) server or HOSTS files come into play.

We will look at using a HOSTS file first because that is the simplest of the two methods. Simply put, a *HOSTS file* is a text file that resides on the local computer and provides a mapping of Internet hostnames to IP addresses. You can use the sample HOSTS file that comes with Windows 2000 if you want and simply modify it to suit your network. Listing 6.1 shows the HOSTS file that comes with Windows 2000.

LISTING 6.1 A Sample HOSTS File, Showing IP Addresses to Hostname Mappings

```
# This is a sample HOSTS file used by Microsoft TCP/IP for Windows.
#
# This file contains the mappings of IP addresses to host names. Each
# entry should be kept on an individual line. The IP address should
# be placed in the first column followed by the corresponding host name.
# The IP address and the host name should be separated by at least one
# space.
#
# Additionally, comments (such as these) may be inserted on individual
```

```
# lines or following the machine name denoted by a '#' symbol.
#
# For example:
#
#      102.54.94.97        rhino.acme.com          # source server
#       38.25.63.10        x.acme.com              # x client host

127.0.0.1               localhost
192.168.5.1      Marketing
```

As you can see in this listing, I have added two entries of my own at the end of the file. The 127.0.0.1 IP address is mapped to the hostname of localhost and is sometimes inserted automatically by Windows, whereas 192.168.5.1 maps to Marketing. The hash marks (#) are used to indicate a comment that is ignored by the client when processing the file.

The HOSTS file really is as simple as it looks. You simply enter the IP address of the host to which you want to connect and enter the hostname. The entries are separated by what is known as *whitespace*, a space or tab. This is so that the client can distinguish where the IP address ends and the hostname begins.

This file must reside in *systemroot*\system32\drivers\etc where *systemroot* is the directory where you have installed Windows 2000. If you are going to use this method of resolving hostnames to IP addresses, every computer on the network must have this file, and they must all be configured identically. For Windows 9x clients, you will modify and use the Hosts.sam file located in the Windows directory.

You can add descriptive comments to the each entry as well after the hostname as can be seen in the previous example. Any line that is a comment has the # hash symbol placed at the beginning of the line. The entry that contains the IP address 38.25.63.10, x.acme.com, has a hash mark and then x client host has a description of the host that uses that IP address.

This method is quick and simple for small networks, as you can see. You don't need to enter any DNS server IP address in your TCP/IP configuration if you are using the systems on an intranet only and only need to resolve hostnames on that intranet. If you are using the Internet, however, a HOSTS file is just not practical anymore. It is an administrative nightmare to try keeping up with new hosts being added and changed on a daily basis.

This is where you need a Domain Name System (DNS) server. Windows 2000 comes with DNS as a service that you can install and configure to perform the hostname–IP address resolution. One added benefit that the Windows 2000 DNS service has is that it can also work in conjunction with WINS to dynamically map the IP addresses to the computer names on your local network. WINS does not work on the Internet.

A DNS server can talk to other DNS servers as well. If it doesn't have an entry for a requested hostname, it can be configured to poll another DNS server to see if that server has the requested information. Figure 6.1 shows the DNS window on my Windows 2000 server with the default zones displayed.

Unfortunately, minutely examining the Domain Name System is beyond the scope of this book, and we do not have the space to instruct you on setting up such a server on your network. If you have installed the Microsoft Active Directory services on your server, DNS will be installed and configured in the process. Active Directory requires DNS to operate because of the fact that Active Directory does not use the previous concept of a Windows NT domain. Instead you are using a namespace that reflects the FQDNs used on the Internet.

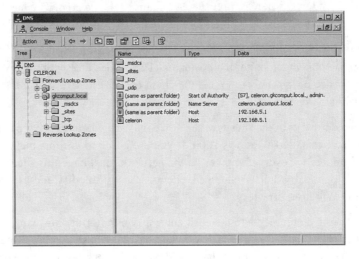

FIGURE 6.1
The DNS service is also an MMC snap-in that you use to configure DNS settings and zones on the network.

Registering an Internet Domain Name

In order to provide your Web pages to users on the Internet, a few things need to be set. Obviously, you are going to need a connection to the Internet. When sourcing a connection, take into consideration the fastest possible connection that you can afford. This will prevent connection or bottleneck problems down the road should your site become really busy. The last thing you want your visitors to see is a message stating, "The server is too busy. Please try again later." Approximately 95% of the time, the visitors won't come back.

After you have decided on a connection speed, make sure that you are getting a static IP address. You cannot use DNS with dynamic addressing.

Now that you have a connection and a static IP address, it's time to make a visit to the registration authority for the Internet. Point your browser to http://www.internic.net. You will find a directory or accredited registration companies with which you can register your domain name. When I registered my company's domain name, I used Network Solutions Inc., http://www.networksolutions.com. They are based in the United States of America. You should choose a registration company in your Web site's country of origin, if at all possible.

Each registration service charges for their services. The typical fee is $35 US per year for a domain name registration. In most cases, you must pay for two years' registration when you first register and set up a domain name.

Before you get all set to use that www.*yourname*.com domain name, you need to perform a search to verify that the name has not been used. It seems unlikely that you will encounter any problems, but keep in mind that there are quite a few companies and individuals who are registering domain names with the sole intent of being able to sell the name at a later time for a considerable amount of money.

One such case was an individual who registered www.mcdonalds.com before a certain fast food giant did so. McDonald's Corporation © already had www.mcd.com registered, but it couldn't use mcdonalds.com because it belonged to someone else.

McDonald's has since acquired that domain name for its own use from that individual under certain conditions. McDonald's must maintain and pay for a T1 connection to a high school in the Bronx. Not a bad trade-off. This is just to show you what you might be facing when it comes time to register a domain name on the Internet.

There are other issues to be aware of as well concerning domain names. For instance, if you are a commercial organization, you will be assigned to the .com hierarchy. Unless you are an educational institution, you will not be able to register as an .edu domain.

The other domain suffixes that are available to everyone for registration are .net, normally used for ISPs, and .org, which could indicate an organization of some sort, such as www.webdav.org or www.ashrae.org.

Another issue is the use of a country designator. These are the two letter designation for countries that serve as the top-level domain, such as the .ca in nbnet.nb.ca. The .ca domain is only available to organizations in Canada that are incorporated in more than one Canadian province.

Choose your domain name wisely to prevent having to change it later. Changes will make it quite difficult for your clients to find your site.

Verifying a Computer's Network Identity

I will break this section down into three areas: verifying a computer's identity on a local network, using a NetBIOS name, and verifying an identity on the Internet.

After you have all the necessary software installed and configured and IIS is up and running, it is a good idea to verify that other users can actually connect to your server and see its Web pages and FTP directories. As you might find out, being able to browse your local Web sites from the same computer that IIS is installed on does not mean that other clients with other computers can see the same results you do.

First, verify that you have connectivity by opening a browser on the local machine and entering http://localhost into the address bar. This should bring up the default page on your default Web site. If it does not, try using http://127.0.0.1. This will verify TCP/IP connectivity to the server. If this works, you have a name resolution problem on your local network.

Check your HOSTS file to ensure that you have the correct entry, as discussed earlier in the chapter.

After you have verified that the local computer can connect to the server and view Web pages, it is time to try another host on the network. Open a browser window on another client computer and enter the http://www.servername.com address, replacing servername with the one you used to name the server. If you cannot connect to the server, try using the IP address of the server.

If neither of these methods work, use PING to verify connectivity first or verify the server's IP address by using ipconfig or ipconfig/all from a command prompt. ipconfig /all will return information for all network adapters including PPP dial-up adapters. For ease of use, the ipconfig command will display only the information you really need.

Depending on the method you have chosen for name resolution, HOSTS file or DNS, you can also check the entries to ensure that they are accurate and entered into the appropriate file or zone.

You can check for connectivity over the Internet in much the same way as mentioned previously. PING is a good troubleshooting tool to verify connectivity, and it works with both IP addresses and domain names. I even use it sometimes to find out the IP address of a domain name, instead of using Finger or Whois. When you type in the PING command with a domain name, PING will always return the IP address as well. You can see this in Figure 6.2.

If the domain name is valid, PING will display the resolved IP address in square brackets immediately following the domain name that is entered. As you can see in Figure 6.2, I entered a domain name of celeron.gkcomput.local, which is the domain name for my Windows 2000 server. PING resolved the name to the 192.168.5.1 IP address and displayed it during the PING operation.

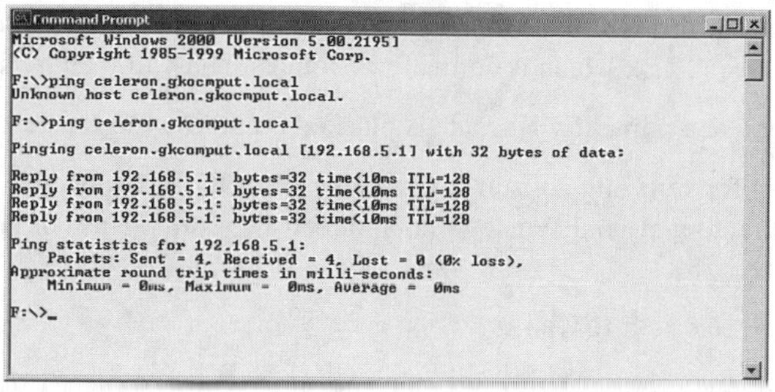

FIGURE 6.2

The Command Prompt window shows the IP address, in square brackets, immediately after the domain name.

TIP

If you have registered a domain name and have parked it on a DNS server somewhere on the Internet, you will not be able to resolve the domain name right away. It can take 48 hours or more for the information to propagate over the Internet. This is usually an area of frustration for first time users of the InterNIC registration services. Wait at least that long before launching any inquiries.

There are other tools available in your TCP/IP toolbox. For instance, sometimes you can verify that a host or server is running by making a phone call to the appropriate party, but you can still not reach it over the wire. Tracert is a utility that will display the routers that your request crosses on the way to the destination computer.

These are known as *route traces* and they can show you where there is a *lag*, or router stoppage, that is preventing you from getting where you need to go. Routers on the Internet talk to each other and discover routes to networks on an ongoing basis. In this way, a router can use information from other routers to build its own routing table. Based on this concept, the information is only as good as the most recent updates available in the other routers.

If you have one router that has failed, a router downstream may not know for a few minutes that the other router has failed. In this case, the routing information doesn't yet reflect the downed router and is not entirely accurate. If your router gets its routing information from any other router that does not know about the failure, you will have out-of-date routing information.

Now, based on this information, you could send a data packet to a host that was known by the failed router or needs to go through that failed router to reach its destination. If there are no other routes to your destination in the routing tables along your path, your data packet will exceed its time to live (TTL), which is normally 15 routers, and will then be discarded.

Tracert can help you determine if your route is blocked on the way to the destination.

Another useful tool for verifying domain names is the NSLOOKUP tool. This tool is located in the System32 directory of your Windows 2000 directory. A simple use of NSLOOKUP follows:

```
nslookup www.mcp.com 198.164.30.2
```

This command will contact the DNS server 198.164.30.2 and will query it for an entry of www.mcp.com. When I ran this command, I was returned an IP address of 63.69.110.193.

You can use this to verify that your domain name and IP address are correct in your lmhosts file or just to ensure that the domain name is actually assigned to the IP address.

Windows 2000 also includes another TCP/IP utility called route. This command is used to manipulate and display the contents of the routing table. The routing table is present on your system when you install TCP/IP.

The available options for the command are

- print—Causes the routing table to be printed to the screen
- add—Adds a route to the routing table
- delete—Deletes a route from the table
- change—Modifies an existing entry

The route command also accepts two parameters: -f will clear the routing table of all gateway entries, and –p is used with the add command to cause a route to persist across reboots of the server. By default, when the server is rebooted, the routing table is cleared.

Some example commands are

```
route -p add 197.168.0.20 255.255.255.0 156.34.25.0 1
```

This command will add a route in your routing table with a destination of 197.168.0.20, a netmask of 255.255.255.0 using the gateway of 156.34.25.0 and a metric of 1. The route will be persistent. These IP addresses are all arbitrary and hold no special significance to any hosts:

```
route delete 197.168.0.20 255.255.255.0 156.34.25.0 1
```

This command will remove the previously added route from the routing table.

6

Summary

We took a look at the various methods for name resolution on a local network and on the Internet in this chapter. Small networks that are used internally only as intranets can make use of HOSTS files to perform the necessary host-to-IP address resolutions for you. When you enter the realm of the Internet, you need the help of DNS.

We discussed IP addressing and pointed out that you can assign IP addresses dynamically and statically. Your IIS server should be configured to use a static IP address to make name resolution possible.

There are various ways to check for correct identity on a TCP/IP network including using IP addresses and domain names. PING is a fantastic little tool for ensuring connectivity and can even tell you the IP address of a domain name if it can resolve it correctly.

The tools and information presented in this chapter can help you verify that your IIS server is indeed connected and functioning before making it publicly available.

Configuring Applications

IN THIS CHAPTER

Application Configuration in IIS

What do we mean when we talk about IIS applications? Well, Microsoft defines it like this:

> "An IIS application is any file that is executed within a defined set of directories in your Web site."

Essentially, what Microsoft is saying is that an IIS application is a script or executable program that is executed on the Web server as a result of a request by a client or by IIS itself. These applications can be any of the following:

- ASP
- CGI
- ISAPI
- IDC
- SSI

Every application must have a starting point directory. This is considered the root of the application. You use the Internet Services Manager in MMC to specify the applications starting point. This, in combination with the directory boundaries you specify, sets the application's scope.

When you have created a starting point for the application, it will use a package icon displayed in the Tree pane of MMC. This can be seen in Figure 7.1.

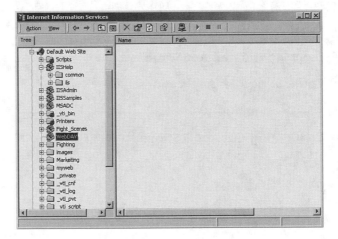

FIGURE 7.1

The package icon is used to indicate the starting point for an application.

In the Figure 7.1, you can see that there are many directories using the package icon here. IISHelp, IISAdmin, and WebDAV are just a few examples. It is also important to note that any subdirectories under the application root are considered part of the application.

In IIS 4.0, you had the option of running your applications in the same process space as IIS, which is known as `Inetinfo.exe`, (isolated) or in a separate process, known as `DLLhost.exe` (process). IIS 5.0 supports these two methods and adds a third, pooled.

By running a pooled process, you are taking two or more applications and running them in a process that is separate from `Inetinfo.exe` and combined into one `DLLhost.exe` session.

Why would you want to do this? For one very important reason, performance. It would be great if you could run each application in its own process. That way, if one app misbehaves, it doesn't take down other apps. However, for every `DLLhost.exe` instance that you run, you are consuming resources on the server. It is recommended by Microsoft that you run no more than 10 concurrent `DLLHost.exe` sessions.

In order to configure the application to use the appropriate model, select the application root folder in the Tree pane, right-click it, and choose properties from the pop-up menu. This will display the Properties window of that application directory, as shown in Figure 7.2.

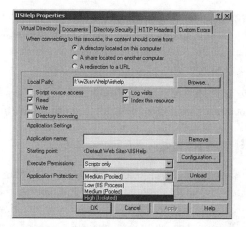

FIGURE 7.2

The Properties window of the application's root directory enables you to specify the protection options at the bottom.

As you can see, there are three choices here as we discussed earlier, Low (IIS Process), Medium (Pooled) and High (Isolated).

The recommended approach to assigning application protection while maintaining some performance is to run IIS in its own process, run any mission-critical applications in their own

7

CONFIGURING
APPLICATIONS

process, and then run all other applications in a pooled process. Obviously you can have more than 10 mission critical apps running on one server as well. You can use your best judgment as to the configuration or else look at adding a second IIS server and splitting up the application processing among them.

When thinking about which scripting language to use for your application, you should consider ease of use and of course server performance. Although we mentioned that IIS can make use of CGI, ISAPI, ASP and some other scripting technologies earlier, you need to weigh the pros and cons of each. You may of course already be well versed in CGI applications which is alright but why would you want to learn ASP or use ISAPI instead?

The answer to the first question is simplicity. ASP is a much easier language to learn than PERL. PERL stands for Practical Extraction and Reporting Language and is not the easiest language to learn. PERL is an interpreted language and is optimized for searching and reporting on text files.

By using ISAPI, you can create multithreaded dlls that can outperform CGI applications written in other languages. ISAPI applications can be run in-process or out-of-process and they make us of the Win32 API calls that offer a faster performance than CGI applications can achieve because of this.

ASP makes use of VBScript or Jscript languages by default with IIS. Both of these scripting languages are easy to learn but are extremely powerful. VBScript is the language responsible for the Melissa virus and all of the VBScript variants that followed it. This should give you a indication of the power of the language.

Jscript is almost as simple and equally as powerful. Jscript also offers the advantage of being able to convert Java applets or applications to Jscript with minimal effort.

Creating Applications

Creating an application is a relatively straightforward process. The first thing you need to do is to create the directory that will contain the application. You can use the default Web site directory if you want, especially if that is where you want to run applications. I recommend that you keep your applications in their own separate directories for ease of administration and also for reasons of security. This can prevent malicious users from running applications unauthorized in other directories on the server.

Under the Internet Services Manager snap-in, right-click the directory name in the Tree pane and choose Properties. This brings up the directory's Properties dialog box with the Directory or Virtual Directory tab selected, as shown in Figure 7.3.

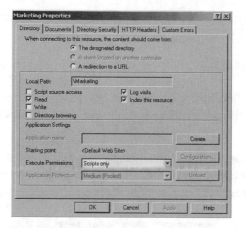

FIGURE 7.3

The Marketing Properties dialog box uses the Directory tab to create an application.

To create an application in this directory, click the Create button in the Application Settings section. This places the name Marketing in the Application Name: text box. You can rename this if you want.

After you have the application created, you can then begin to set up the permissions, application protection, and mapping configuration.

The first thing you need to decide is whether the application directory will allow scripts, executables, a combination of both, or none at all. This is done with the Execute Permissions drop-down combo box. The three possible permissions are

- **None**—This setting prevents any applications from running in the specified directory. This is a good setting for high security because it will not enable applications or scripts to execute.

- **Scripts only**—By choosing this option, you are enabling scripts to run, such as ASP scripts, Java script, IDC scripts, and so on. Applications cannot run with this option. This is still a secure way to configure the server while allowing some execution functionality.

- **Scripts and Executables**—This option enables any script or application to run in the directory. This can be a security issue as it will also enable applications to run that are mapped to Windows binary files such as .dll and .exe files. Potentially, a malicious client could run virus or Trojan horse applications on your server in this way. Enable this option carefully and make sure that you are up-to-date on all security issues relating to IIS 5.0.

After you set the necessary Execution Permissions, you should determine the process in which you want the application to run. We discussed the application protection processes earlier in the chapter. Select the process of your choice from the drop-down combo box called Application Protection.

Setting Mappings

Mappings for applications on IIS 5.0 act in the same manner as filename associations in Windows. The filename extension is used to determine which application is used to execute or view the file.

IIS 5.0 uses the Application Configuration dialog's App Mappings tab to configure and work with these mappings (see Figure 7.4). This dialog can be invoked by clicking the Configuration button in the Application Settings section of the Directory tab.

FIGURE 7.4
The Application Configuration dialog box is where you configure the application mappings and settings for your IIS server.

As you can see, there are quite a few extensions and filenames/paths listed here. Notice the fourth entry from the top. This tells you that there is a DLL file called `asp.dll` that contains the functionality or application used to process any requests for active server pages on your server.

CAUTION

Unless you are well informed as to the applications and DLL files used here for each application, it is recommended that you not change any of the default mappings. Add your own to handle custom applications, but for the most part, the defaults should serve you well enough.

The App Options tab on this dialog box is shown in Figure 7.5.

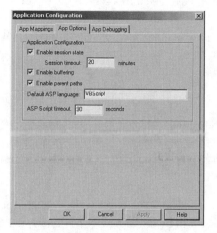

FIGURE 7.5

The App Options tab is used for configuring ASP application settings on the server.

This dialog box has some very important options in regards to ASP applications. The first of these, Enable session state, is used to create and maintain a session across pages for each user who accesses an ASP page. This helps the ASP programmer keep track of where the user has been, what pages she visited, any orders that she might have placed, and so on. Many ASP developers use this as a tool for presenting users with advertisements based on their interests as determined by the pages they have visited.

You can also customize the session state's timeout value, based on feedback from your ASP developers and your users' browsing habits. The default is 20 minutes. This will cause the session to end if the user has not refreshed the page or made any new requests within the specified time limit.

The next option is Enable buffering. Buffering is used on the Web server to hold the contents of the ASP page in memory on the server until all output is collected and ready to be sent. The server will then send the information to the client's browser. If this option is disabled, the output is sent to the browser as it is processed.

The Enable parent paths option enables ASP pages to use the relative path of a file or directory or parent directory. There is a security issue involved with this option. If you have execute permission set on the parent directory, a malicious script could run an unauthorized application in that directory.

The Default ASP Language text box holds the name of the scripting language that you intend to use as a default on your server. ASP can use VBScript or JScript, and the choice is that of your Web developers. The scripts on a Web page are embedded within <% %> script tags so that they do not display on the Web page when it is sent to the client. If your developers do not specify the script language explicitly in the HTML code like this, <%@ LANGUAGE="VBSCript" %> or <% @LANGUAGE="Vscript" %>, then the server will look to this option flag to see what language is being used when an ASP page is executed.

> **NOTE**
>
> If you have the default language to set VBScript, this does not mean that you or your developers cannot use JScript on the server or the page. VBScript and JScript can co-exist on the same HTML document.

The final option available on the App Options tab is the ASP Script timeout. The default value is 90 seconds, and you can set it to be in the range of 1–2,147,483,647 seconds. Personally I feel that if you have a script that takes that long to execute, you need to look at rewriting it.

This value will cause the script to end processing if it hasn't done so before the end of the timeout period, and it will write an event to the event log that you can view with Event Viewer. If you have scripts that are being cut short or not completing their execution, increase this value.

The Application Configuration dialog box also has an App Debugging tab. You can use the options on this tab sheet to enable debugging of the code on your ASP pages.

The first option available to you is the Enable Server-Side Script Debugging. This option will turn on debugging for scripts that run on the server using the Microsoft Script Debugger. This causes ASP to run in single-threaded mode and should be used only for testing. Never use it on a server that is in production and serving pages on the Internet or intranet because of the performance issues involved in single-threaded processing.

The Enable ASP Client-Side Script Debugging option is not implemented yet in IIS 5.0. Checking this box will not enable client-side debugging at this time.

The bottom section of the App Debugging tab sheet deals with script error messages. These are the messages that will be sent to the clients that have requested an ASP page that has encountered an error of some sort. There are two options available here.

Send Detailed ASP Error Messages to Client will send debugging specific error information to the client. This information will include the ASP filename, the error message, and the line number that the error occurred on. Figure 7.6 shows an example of such a message.

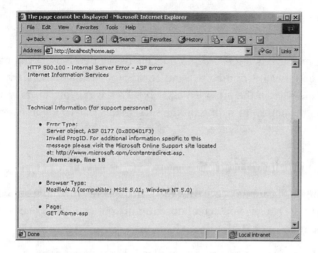

FIGURE 7.6
Internet Explorer shows a portion of the error message that was returned to the client using detailed messages.

LISTING 7.1   ASP File That Generates an Error

```
<%@ LANGUAGE=VBScript %>
<html>

<head>
<meta http-equiv="Content-Language" content="en-ca">
<meta http-equiv="Content-Type" content="text/html; charset=windows-1252">
<meta name="GENERATOR" content="Microsoft FrontPage 4.0">
<meta name="ProgId" content="FrontPage.Editor.Document">
<title>Home Page</title>
</head>

<body>
<!— #include file="navbar.stm" —>
<h1 align="center"><b>This is the Home Page</b></h1>
<hr>
<%
Dim dbGK
Set dbGK = Server.CreateObject("Database")
%>
```

Listing 7.1 shows a portion of the HTML code that I wrote to cause the error. As specified in the error message in Figure 7.6, if you count down to line 18, you see the code `Set dbGK = Server.CreateObject ("Database")`. This line causes the ASP script to attempt to create an object on the server to represent a database. Unfortunately, there doesn't exist a valid data source name on the server, so the error is generated.

The returned error message is a little cryptic for the average Web user. You can opt to send a generic text message instead. Choose the Send Text Error Message to Client option and enter the necessary text message in the provided text box. That way, your users will see a message telling them that something went wrong on the server side, but you won't bore them or confuse them with detailed ASP error messages.

Isolating Applications

The task of isolating applications deals with the processes in which the applications run. As discussed earlier in the chapter, you can choose to run applications in one of three different processes: Low, Medium, and High.

Running your application in a Low protection runs it in the same process space as Inetinfo.exe, which is the same as IIS itself. If the application crashes, it will take down IIS as well.

The Medium setting will run your application in a pooled, or shared, process with other applications set at Medium as well. This provides a little more protection for IIS because a malfunctioning application set to Medium will only take down other applications in the same process and not IIS. Your application can be affected by another misbehaving application running in the same process.

The High setting will cause your application to run in a process all by itself and protects it from any other application that can malfunction. If your application malfunctions, it will not take down IIS or any other pooled application.

CAUTION

Running all applications in a separate memory space, protection set to High, sounds like a good idea and it would be for a server that only runs a maximum of 10 applications. Any more than this will have a serious impact on the server's performance.

NOTE

If you are running server-side includes (SSI) or Internet Database Connector (IDC) applications, they must be run in the same process as IIS. That is, they must be set to Low (IIS Process).

Caching Applications

This area of configuration deals with tuning performance on your server. To properly tune your server's performance, you need to use the Performance Monitor and event viewer to see where any bottlenecks exist. They will also indicate where errors are occurring because of pages not being found, or scripts timing out.

Caching settings involves three areas or concern: CGI Script timeout, caching ISAPI extensions, and caching ASP script files. We will look at each in turn.

CGI Script Timeout

CGI scripts inherit the timeout settings that apply to the server as a whole. This means that you set the timeout value for the whole server using the Master WWW properties.

To set the timeout value, select the computer icon in the Tree pane of Internet Services Manager and open the Properties dialog box. Select the Home Directory tab to display the Application Configuration dialog box, as shown in Figure 7.7.

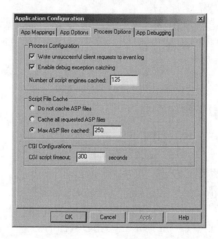

FIGURE 7.7

The Application Configuration dialog box contains a tab called Process Options, where you set the CGI timeout values.

As you can see from Figure 7.7, this configuration dialog box contains an extra tab that was not present on the same dialog box for the home directory of a specific Web site on the server. The Process Options tab enables us to set the CGI timeouts. As mentioned, this will affect the entire server and all Web sites on it.

The default value for the timeout is 300 seconds. There are no limits expressed anywhere so theoretically, you can have a script never time out. This, of course, is not a good idea.

Caching ISAPI Extensions

ISAPI DLL files that are accessed often can be cached to increase performance. By providing caching for these DLLs, you can reduce the amount of time that a client has to wait for the application to load and process because the DLL is already resident in the cache and can be accessed much quicker.

In order to enable caching, open the properties sheet for the application's directory that you want to cache. Select the Home Directory, Virtual Directory, or Directory tab, and click the Configuration button found in the Application Settings section. This will bring up an Application Configuration dialog box similar to what was shown in Figure 7.5.

The first option check box on the App Mappings tab sheet is the Cache ISAPI Applications option. Make sure that this check box is checked; your IIS server will cache ISAPI applications for each application directory that you have checked off. This feature must be selected for each Web site or application directory for which you want to enable caching.

> **TIP**
>
> It is best to leave this option checked for performance reasons. You might, however, want to turn it off if you are testing applications and a Web server in a debugging mode.

Caching ASP Script Files

ASP script files can also be cached to provide for better performance. In order to work with ASP caching, you must open the Home Directory tab sheet on the computer's properties dialog box as we did for CGI caching.

After you have the dialog box open, you will see the Script File Cache section in the middle of the dialog box. You have three options available to you. You can choose not to cache ASP script files; this will result in no caching of any ASO scripts.

You can choose to cache all ASP script files. This will cache all ASP scripts that are running.

You can also choose to limit the number of files cached by selecting the last option and entering the maximum number of files to cache. This is a good selection to use if your server is low on memory. The default is 250 files.

Stopping Isolated Applications

When your applications on the server need to be debugged or perhaps you just want to stop an application for a determined period or time, IIS enables you to do so by stopping only the required application and not the whole IIS service.

In order to stop an application you need to unload it. In order to do this, open the properties dialog box for the directory or site that contains the application that you want to stop. Choose the Home Directory, Virtual Directory, or Directory tab to display the Application Settings section. Figure 7.8 shows the IISHelp Properties dialog box.

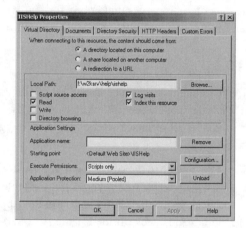

FIGURE 7.8
The IISHelp Properties dialog box with the Virtual Directory tab selected to unload the IISHelp application.

At the bottom-right corner of the Application Settings section, you can see the Unload button. Click this button to stop the application.

> **TIP**
>
> If this button is grayed out, it is an indication that you are not in the starting point of the application. Select the directory that was indicated as the starting point for the application.

7

CONFIGURING
APPLICATIONS

Configuring ASP Applications

As we mentioned earlier in the chapter, you can specify ASP options that will determine whether you will use buffering, session states, or ASP timeouts.

ASP applications are configured in two places. You can set defaults for all Web sites, and you can set specific settings for each Web site. These settings are specified in the Application Configuration dialog box under the App Options tab (refer to Figure 7.5).

If you were to set the ASP options on the Master Properties sheet, they would apply to all Web sites that did not have specific settings applied. If you want to specify settings specific for a Web site, you can do so by using the properties dialog box for that Web site instead of the master properties for the server. In this way, any settings made here will override defaults.

ASP Debugging

As any developer will tell you, debugging is a very important but dreaded aspect of developing software applications. ASP Web developers feel the same way. As a result of this, and even as an aside to it, bugs end up in your ASP scripts. You can turn on debugging to help find bugs before you put a script into production.

ASP uses the Microsoft Script Debugger to locate errors in your ASP code. Open the properties dialog box for the Web site or server for which you want to enable debugging. Choose the Home Directory tab and then click the Configuration button in the Application Settings section. Select the App Debugging tab and check off the Enable ASP Server-Side Debugging option box.

For more information on Microsoft Scripting technologies, visit their Scripting Web site at http://msdn.microsoft.com/scripting/.

Configuring CGI Applications

We won't delve into the intricacies of CGI applications because this can quickly become a complicated topic depending on which scripting language you are using. We will, however, show you how to set up your server to run CGI applications in the event that you have existing apps you don't want to port to ASP or cannot port to ASP.

The first issue that you need to deal with is directories. I recommend that you place all your CGI applications into a common directory. Most UNIX- or Linux-based Web servers place all CGI apps into a CGI-bin directory. You can do this on the IIS server as well.

Next, you must set the appropriate permissions on the directory. If your CGI apps are only scripts, you should only set the scripting permission on the directory; otherwise, set them to Scripts and Execute.

You also must download or purchase a script interpreter that is Windows 2000 compatible for your scripts. Microsoft does not provide any of these for you.

After you have the script interpreter installed, the directory set up, and the applications installed, you need to set the application mappings as described earlier in the chapter. This will ensure that any requests for pages that contain the CGI applications will get passed to the correct interpreter.

> **CAUTION**
>
> For security purposes, the server will not pass certain special characters to your application. These special characters are |, (, ,, ;, %, and <>.

ISAPI Filters

ISAPI filters are applications that reside on the server and are invoked by, or respond to, events generated by HTTP requests. You associate a filter with an event. When that event occurs, the application is called, and the filter is processed.

A common use for one type of filter would be to provide data encryption and decryption before sending and receiving data, respectively.

You can apply two types of filters. Although they are not named as such, I refer to them as *global filters* and *local filters*. These filters can behave in the same fashion as global and local permissions for NTFS drives.

The filters are applied as global first, and then local. The filters are merged this way and apply to the Web site that is processing the request.

To use an ISAPI filter, you must first add it to the Web server or Web site on which you want it to function. Open the Internet Services Manager if it is not already open. Select the Web site to which you will add the ISAPI filter and open its properties dialog box. Selecting the ISAPI Filters tab will display the tab sheet, as shown in Figure 7.9.

Clicking the Add button will let you specify the name and executable file of your ISAPI filters. If you have more than one installed, you can set the priority by selecting the filter from the list and using the up and down arrows on the left of the list box to move the selection up or down in the list.

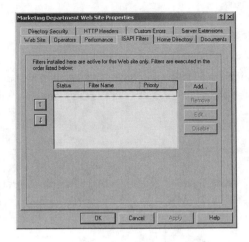

FIGURE 7.9
The ISAPI Filters tab sheet enables you to add and remove ISAPI filters, as well as to change the priority in which they are processed.

NOTE

ISAPI filters are always run in same process as IIS.

Summary

IIS 5.0 enables you to use a wide range of applications on your server. It makes transitioning from a UNIX-based Web environment to IIS a little easier by enabling the use of CGI applications written in languages like Perl.

Microsoft has taken great strides in making application development easier by incorporating ASP support into IIS. ASP is a much easier technology to deal with than CGI because ASP enables the developer to use VBScript or JScript to develop the application.

By using the information given in this chapter, you can configure your applications to operate securely and efficiently on your IIS server.

Security

IN THIS CHAPTER

One of the greatest issues facing any Web administrator today is the issue of security. Due to the impact that Microsoft has had on the computing industry and now on the Internet, there are a plethora of "hackers," who are continuously trying to discredit Microsoft and its products by breaking into Internet Information Server and its applications. This makes this chapter perhaps one of the most important in the book.

Securing Your IIS Server

Although we have mentioned the fact that hackers are just waiting for opportunities to break into Web servers and wreak havoc on your services and data, the issue of security for IIS involves more than just that aspect.

Security issues also relate to authorization of clients for restricted areas, encryption and certificates. Each of these areas plays a key role in the security of your IIS server. IIS 5.0 provides what are known as *task wizards* to help you deal with the security of your server.

The task wizards that you will work with in IIS 5.0 include the Certificates Wizard for obtaining and managing server certificates, the Certificate Trust List (CTL) Wizard for the creation and management of certificate trust lists, and the Permissions Wizard for setting permissions on the directories that make up the site.

You can use these wizards to make security easier on the server but they do not cover all possible aspects of security. There are still procedures that need to be performed outside of wizards, and they will be discussed in this chapter.

In order to set up security on your IIS server, you first need to examine the security requirements for your organization. If you are going to make sensitive information available on a server that will be connected to the Internet, you need to take extra precautions compared to the same scenario on an intranet that has no outside network connection.

Due to the fact that you are running your services on a Windows 2000 computer, much of your access control will be based on the Windows 2000 Access Control Lists (ACLs). In order to take maximum advantage of the security offered by Windows 2000, you need to ensure that your disk drives are formatted with the NTFS file system. Much of the security mechanisms discussed here will only work on NTFS volumes.

You will need to work side-by-side with the network administrator, if that person is someone other than yourself, to set up the necessary user and group accounts with the correct access permissions. You also want to make sure that you keep publicly available and restricted information in separate folders.

For the most part, your clients will be accessing the server using the IUSR_Computername account which maps its access permissions and password to the Guest account on the Windows

2000 server. This account is disabled by default when IIS is installed and should remain that way. Any account that needs to access restricted folders should be set up as a local group on the server and the appropriate permissions set. That way, if you have a group of user accounts that need access to the restricted resources, they can be made members of the group and administration is made easier.

Security Checklist

This section will give you, in table format, a checklist that you can use while configuring the security of your IIS server.

TABLE 8.1 IIS Server Security Checklist

Server Setting	How to Configure
File System	Use NTFS for all volumes.
Directory Permissions	Verify your directory permissions to ensure that only those containing scripts and applications have Script and Execute applied.
Verify IUSR_Computername Permissions	Assign access permissions correctly.
Verify Executable and Script file directories	Place your applications and scripts into directories separated from other files.
Review user accounts	Have the network administrator verify all ACLs for users and groups.
Passwords	Verify that all users who require authentication use long and hard to guess passwords.
Account Policies	Verify account and group policies.
Services on IIS computer	Review all services that will be running on the IIS server. Enable on those that are absolutely needed.
Domain Controllers	DO NOT run your IIS server on the domain controllers.
Auditing	Enable the appropriate auditing features to monitor security access violations.
Encryption	Use file encryption where possible and set up VPNs or other secure methods for remote administration.
Backup Configuration	Set up backup strategies for all important and sensitive data and store the backups in a secure area.
Virus Checks	Schedule automatic virus scans and virus updates.

8

SECURITY

TABLE 8.1   Continued

Server Setting	How to Configure
Service Bindings	Review the services that are bound to your NICs. Ensure that File and Printer sharing is not enabled over the Internet.
IIS Authentication	Verify that your clients and server are using the highest possible authentication methods available to both.
Certificate Mapping	Choose one-to-one or many-to-one mapping on your certificates.
Web and NTFS permission synchronization	Have your Web permissions coincide with the NTFS permissions. The most restrictive will apply.
IP Address restriction	Verify that only valid IP addresses are enabled for remote administration or remote access.
Physical Security	Verify that the server itself is physically secure and use password-protected screen savers.
Administrator Account	Rename the Administrator account to prevent hackers from utilizing it.

This checklist is a good starting point when setting up your security. You might come up with more checkpoints, and some of Table 8.1 might not apply depending on your environment.

Authentication

Authentication deals with clients or users proving to the server that they are whom they say. This is done through the use of a username and password combination. There might be other methods used in the future such as voice recognition or, for on site usage, biometrics. Only when authenticated can they be given access to the server.

With IIS, you can set authentication at the Web site, directory of file level. In this way, you can enable to the public section of the Web site and require authentication for specific directories of files that might contain sensitive information.

IIS uses five types of authentication:

- **Anonymous**—This is the basic authentication used for most Web sites and certain directories on FTP servers. Users are not required to enter a username/password combination except for when using FTP, where they can enter anonymous for the username and use their email address for a password.

- **Basic Authentication**—This method uses the username/password combination to authenticate users. There is one downfall to this method, however. The password is sent across the network as clear text. Any eavesdroppers can intercept the password and then later use it to gain access to the resources allotted to that username/password.

- **Digest Authentication**—This is new to IIS 5.0 and offers a different means of authentication. Digest authentication causes the user's credentials to go through a one-way hashing process. This is not reversible and never turns out the same.

- **Integrated Windows Authentication**—This method was formerly known as NTLM, or Windows Challenge/Response. This method does not send the username/password over the network. Instead, the client must prove that it knows the password through a cryptographic procedure. This method can also use the new Kerberos v5 protocol.

- **Certificate Authentication**—This method uses Secure Sockets Layer (SSL) to authenticate using either client or server certificates. Client certificates are used to process requests from client browsers, whereas the server certificates can be used to provide a secure way to transmit information over the network via encryption.

The FTP server is capable of using the Anonymous and the Basic authentication methods discussed previously. There is one thing to note concerning the FTP server: If you have both Anonymous access and Basic authentication enabled, the server will attempt to use the Anonymous method first. Take this into account when you set up security for the your FTP server.

Enabling and Configuring Authentication

Although the list above discussed the various authentication methods available, it is not an exhaustive explanation of each, and you should read more information in the online help files if you are still uncertain as to the method to use.

We will look at the procedures necessary to implement these methods next. You can enable only one method, or a combination of methods, if you so desire.

The first step is to ensure that you have a valid user or group account to which you can assign permissions. Using a group is the recommended approach because groups are easier to administer than multiple user accounts. Assigning all users to one group causes them to automatically inherit the group's access permissions.

After you have created the necessary accounts, it is time to set up the NTFS permissions on the directories. Select the folder or file in the Windows Explorer or My Computer and right-click it. From the pop-up menu, choose Properties. Select the Security tab, as shown in Figure 8.1.

The top list box displays the name of the users or accounts that have access to the folder. By clicking the Add button, you will invoke the Select Users, Computer, or Groups dialog box, as shown in Figure 8.2.

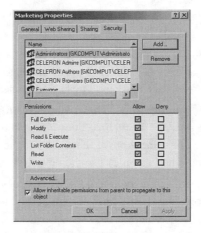

FIGURE 8.1
The Security Tab of the Marketing folder's Properties dialog box enables the setting of access permissions for users or groups.

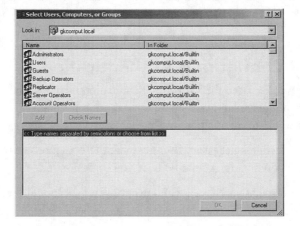

FIGURE 8.2
The Select Users, Computers, or Groups dialog box lists all available accounts on the network for use with access permissions.

Select a user or group account and click the Add button to place the account in the lower portion of the dialog box. When you have finished adding accounts, click the OK button to return to the Security tab of the folder's Properties dialog box. The new account should be added to the list.

After you have the new account added, you can begin to assign permissions to that account in the Permissions section. The available permissions and their meanings are

- **Full Control**—Gives the account complete control over the folder. This means that the user can add, delete, and modify the folder, as well as modify its attributes and take ownership of it. For obvious reasons, you only want to assign this permission to administrators.
- **Modify**—Enables users to view the folder contents and to modify the folder. They cannot modify the attributes, however.
- **Read & Execute**—Enables users to view the contents of the folder and execute any applications that reside in the folder. They cannot delete or modify the folder or its contents.
- **List Folder Contents**—Enables users to list the contents of the folder in Explorer or a dir command from a command prompt. They cannot execute any applications or modify the folder or its contents.
- **Read**—Permits users to view the folder and its contents as well as open the files in the folder with an associated application such as Microsoft Word for Word or RTF documents.
- **Write**—Enables users to copy files into the folder or delete existing files.

Click the Advanced button on the Marketing Properties Security tab sheet to display Figure 8.3.

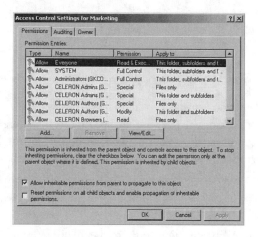

FIGURE 8.3
The Access Control Settings for the Marketing dialog box provides extra permissions and auditing settings for the resource.

The first tab of this dialog box deals with the account specific permissions. The columns display the Type of access, (Allow or Deny), the account Name, the Permission, and whether it applies to the folder, subfolders or files.

Using the buttons under the list box, you can add, remove, or edit the accounts and their permissions. The two bottom options enable you to set the inheritance of permissions from parent objects (if the selected account is a child of a parent object) and to reset the permissions on the child objects.

The Auditing tab enables you to add accounts to a list that will be audited. This can be useful for keeping track of specific accounts and their actions on the resource.

The Owner tab, displayed in Figure 8.4, enables you to view the owner of the object or resource and—if you have the appropriate rights on the system—to change the ownership.

FIGURE 8.4
The Owner tab of the Access Control Settings dialog box is where you view and change ownership of the resource.

All of the previously mentioned settings pertain to the Windows 2000 access permissions for the resources that you are looking at. They are not specific to IIS, therefore, we will not delve too deeply into this topic but refer it to your network administrator for configuration. From the IIS point of view, the main security features that we need to deal with are on the Security tab of the folder's Properties dialog box.

The Default Logon Domain

When a user logs on to the Web site using Basic Authentication, he must provide a username and password. For the most part, users will be on the same domain if you are using IIS for an intranet. However, any user coming from another domain, must have the domain name specified in his username as well. An example would be if I were to log on to my server from a domain other than gkcomput. My username is gobrien. If I were on a domain called SalesDom, then my username that would be passed for authentication would be SalesDom\gobrien.

If your users do not provide a domain name for authentication, the server will not know which domain they are originating from. In this case, you can configure IIS to use a default domain.

To set up a default domain, open the Properties dialog box for the Web site or folder that you want to enable the default domain on. Select the Directory Security tab to display the screen shown in Figure 8.5.

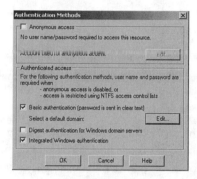

FIGURE 8.5

The Authentication Methods dialog box is where you set authentication methods for the Web site.

As you can see, I have the Basic authentication option box checked. After you have the option checked, click the Edit button to display the screen in Figure 8.6.

FIGURE 8.6

The Basic Authentication Domain dialog box is where you can set the default logon domain when none is given with a username.

You can enter the domain name that will be used as the authentication domain for the Web server. Normally, this is the domain that the Web server resides on, but it doesn't have to be. You can use the Browse button to locate another domain to use.

Using Fortezza

IIS 5.0 supports the U.S. Government's Fortezza security standard. Fortezza uses a cryptographic mechanism to provide the following:

- Message integrity
- Message confidentiality
- Authentication
- Access control to messages and components

We will show you how to use Fortezza on your IIS server, but we will not go into detail on the protocol. If you need more information, visit the National Security Agency's Web site at `http://www.armadillo.huntsville.al.us/`.

Fortezza uses a hardware device for authentication. It is actually a card similar to a PCMCIA card and requires a card reader connected to the server. Along with the hardware, you will also need the necessary software. This can be obtained from Microsoft at `http://www.microsoft.com/security`. The software that you will be using is not for export.

Next you will need to install the drivers and software that came with your card reader. Refer to the manufacturers' instructions for this procedure. At the same time, you will need to install the Cryptographic Service Provider (CSP) that should be supplied by the card reader manufacturer.

After you have all the necessary software installed, you need to run the Fortutil.exe command line utility, which is used to add, delete, or confirm card certificates. The command has four command line options:

- **fortutil.exe /a**—Causes a certificate to be added. It requires a Web site name, PIN, card serial number, and card personality as parameters.
- **fortutil.exe /q**—Use this option to confirm a certificate giving the Web server name as a parameter.
- **fortutil.exe /r**—Deletes a certificate and also takes a Web server name as a parameter.
- **fortutil.exe /?**—Invokes the help file for the `fortutil.exe` command.

> **CAUTION**
>
> If a card has been removed from the reader while IIS is running and then is reinserted, you will likely experience an SSL connection error. When this happens, you will need to place the card into the reader and restart the IIS service.

Access Control

For the most part, if you are running IIS on Windows 2000 for use as a Web server on the Internet, access control is not a concern. You want to enable Anonymous access to the Web and

FTP sites to make the experience as pleasurable as possible for your visitors to keep them coming back, especially if you are running an e-commerce site.

Some companies provide Web servers on the Internet to enable their employees or business partners to access sensitive data or their Web sites. For the most part, this is not a good idea without the correct security measures in place. But that is the reason we have this chapter on security—to help you implement these measures. After all, the main reason for using the Internet for this style of communication is because it is somewhat cheaper than using leased lines.

We have discussed authentication methods, and this section on access control works hand-in-hand with authentication. Essentially, access control is all about controlling who has access to your site.

One of the control methods that is most popular for Web and FTP sites is the Anonymous access. Users logging in to your Web or FTP sites through Anonymous access are allowed to view only those areas that you designate as available to them.

During installation, IIS creates a user account called *IUSR_computername* wherein *computername* is the name of your server. This account takes its lead from the Guest account that resides on your Windows 2000 SAM database. In this way, the users cannot gain access to every file or resource on your server. FTP directories can be seen by anonymous users, but, if you have access control set on specific directories, they will not be permitted to view the directories' contents.

As we mentioned earlier in the book, IIS 5.0 includes WebDAV, which enables remote access to drives, folders, and files on the server over the Internet. Obviously this can be a very dangerous access control area if it is not configured correctly. See Chapter 5, "WebDAV Publishing," for more information on how to configure WebDAV for your server.

8

CAUTION

WebDAV can be used on FAT as well as NTFS-formatted volumes. You need to pay special attention to any drives with FAT formats because of the lack of security features available at the individual file level.

Using the standard flowcharting symbols, Figure 8.7 shows how access control takes place.

The four permissions you see in Figure 8.7 determine access control. When a request is made, IIS first checks to see whether you have allowed or denied the particular IP address. If it is not specifically denied, the check will continue; otherwise, the request is refused. IIS then checks to see whether the user is allowed access based on the username. If this is allowed, IIS moves on to checking any Web permissions that you might have set for the resource. Once again, if this is allowed, IIS will then perform a last check based on the NTFS permissions assigned to the resource.

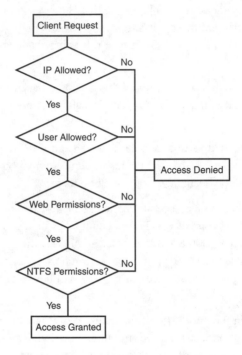

FIGURE 8.7
This flowchart gives you a view of the access control process.

The user will see a couple of possible error messages based on the point of access control failure. If the IP address, username, or Web permissions test fails, the user will be given a `403 Access Forbidden` error message. For a failure of an NTFS access test, the `401 Access Denied` message is sent. This is where you can get creative with your custom error messages and inform users of the exact problem with their access attempts.

In the sections that follow, we will look at how you set these access control restrictions.

Securing Files with NTFS

Of the available file systems that Windows 2000 can use, NTFS offers the highest level of security. If your drive is not formatted as NTFS, it is recommended that you convert it to NTFS. Some of the security and access items we will be discussing apply only to NTFS and cannot be used on FAT- or FAT32-based file systems.

You can perform a one-way conversion of your FAT/FAT32 drive to NTFS with a command line utility. Note that I said one-way. This procedure is not reversible except by reformatting and reinstalling Windows 2000 OS.

From the command prompt window (or after clicking Start,Run), type in `convert.exe [drive:] /fs:ntfs /v. [drive:]` refers to the drive you want to convert such as C:. The `/fs:ntfs` switch simply tells convert.exe to perform an NTFS conversion. You can leave off the `/v` option; it is used for verbose mode and will display messages as the conversion takes place.

You will then be asked to reboot the server so that the conversion can take place. You might as well use this time to go for a quick coffee. The conversion actually takes place on the reboot. When the conversion is completed, you will have much more control over the security of your files and folders.

To work with NTFS security on your folders and files, you will need to open Windows Explorer or gain access to them through My Computer. Select the folder or file on which you want to set the NTFS permissions. Right-click the folder or file and choose Properties from the menu. Figure 8.8 shows the Security tab selected on the Marketing Properties dialog box.

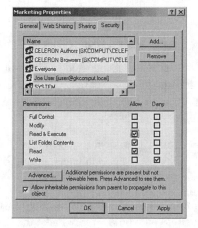

FIGURE 8.8
The Security tab lets you set the necessary NTFS permissions on folders or files.

This dialog box looks familiar because you saw it earlier in the section "Enabling and Configuring Authentication" (refer to Figure 8.1). The Name list box at the top displays the accounts that are assigned permissions of some kind to the resource, in this case, the Marketing folder. You can add or remove accounts by using the appropriate button.

8

SECURITY

To set the NTFS permissions for the Marketing folder for a specific account, ensure that the account has been added to the list box. You can see in Figure 8.8 that I have added an account called juser@gkcomput.local and set some permissions for him. Specifically, he is allowed Read & Execute, Read, and List Folder Contents; he is denied Write.

Simply put, he cannot delete or add files to the Marketing folder but he can perform a directory listing on the folder and view file contents. Also, with the Read & Execute permission, he is able to run applications or scripts that might reside in the folder.

For more information on the NTFS permissions, see the following section "NTFS File and Directory Permissions."

CAUTION

You need to take an important point into consideration when assigning Read & Execute permission for users or group accounts. As I mentioned, this enables the user to run applications that reside in that directory. However, if that application relies on a .dll file in another directory to which the user or account has been denied specific access, the application will not execute for the user.

NTFS File and Directory Permissions

AS we have seen thus far, NTFS permissions are used to allow or deny access to the folders and files on your Web server. This is the main reason why it is recommended that you use NTFS for your drive format. FAT and FAT32 partitions do not have the necessary file attributes to enable the added security available in NTFS.

NTFS enables you to set permissions right down to the file level. In order to effectively use these permissions, you should really have a good understanding of what they are and how they are implemented and applied.

For the most part, if you are not the network administrator, you would not need to be concerned with this aspect of security. You would simply make the request to the administrator and have her make the necessary changes for you. It is my belief that a good basic understanding of NTFS permissions is useful to the Web administrator and is an aid in resolving access issues. As they say, if you don't know what's broken, you can't fix it.

NTFS uses additional file attributes to assign and maintain access permissions. When dealing with access to resources on a Windows 2000 server active directory or domain, you work with what are known as Access Control Lists (ACLs). Some people pronounce this as *ackel*. Whatever the pronunciation, these ACLs are used to determine permission levels for resources.

As you saw in the previous section, when we assigned the Allow and Deny permissions on the Security tab of the Marketing folder, we were assigning ACLs to the resource. When a user attempts to access this folder, the user's name and group are compared to the ACL for the folder. If the username or group name is not listed, the user is denied access.

If the account does exist, Windows 2000 compares the access permissions against what the user is trying to do. This is where the specific Allow and Deny permissions take effect.

> **CAUTION**
>
> When you first create a folder or file on Windows 2000, the Full Control permission is assigned to everyone. This means that, unless you configure the access permissions for the resource, all users will be able to read, view, delete, modify and take ownership of the resource. These permissions will be explained later in the chapter.

Table 8.2 lists the capabilities of each of the permissions that you can assign to the resources on the server. Use it to determine what permissions to set on your Web and FTP sites.

TABLE 8.2 Resource Permissions

Permissions	Full Control	Modify	Read & Execute	Read	Write
Navigate Folder/ Execute File	Yes	Yes	Yes	No	No
List Folder and Read Data	Yes	Yes	Yes	Yes	No
Read Attributes	Yes	Yes	Yes	Yes	No
Read Extended Attributes	Yes	Yes	Yes	Yes	No
Create Files/Folders	Yes	Yes	No	No	Yes
Write Attributes	Yes	Yes	No	No	Yes
Write Extended Attributes	Yes	Yes	No	No	Yes
Delete Files and Subfolders	Yes	No	No	No	No
Delete	Yes	Yes	No	No	No
Read Permissions	Yes	Yes	Yes	Yes	Yes
Change Permissions	Yes	No	No	No	No
Take Ownership	Yes	No	No	No	No
Synchronize	Yes	Yes	Yes	Yes	Yes

Grant and Deny Access

Along with access permissions that you can assign based on users, IIS 5.0 also enables you to restrict access to your server based on computer identification. You have the option of denying all but the computer that you specify, or allowing all except those that are specified. In order to set this up, you need to select the Directory Security tab on the Web site's Properties dialog box. Figure 8.9 shows the Directory Security tab for the Marketing Web site on my server.

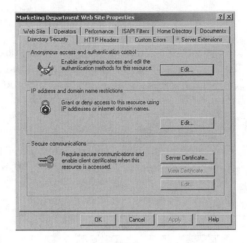

FIGURE 8.9
The Directory Security tab offers security features related to access control on your server.

Click the Edit button in the section titled IP address and domain name restrictions. This will display the dialog box shown in Figure 8.10.

FIGURE 8.10
The IP Address and Domain Name Restrictions dialog box is used to grant or deny computers by IP address or domain name.

In Figure 8.10, three entries are denied access to my server. The first entry denies any computer or user coming from the `netmail.com` domain. Any users with the `netmail.com` domain within their credentials are denied access to my server.

> **NOTE**
>
> I must confess, that I did not do a search on the domain name of netmail.com, and I have nothing against netmail.com if it does exist. This is just for illustrative purposes.

The second entry lists a single IP address, 142.166.17.25. The third entry in the table is a range of IP addresses. No computers within the 192.168.2.0 network are allowed access. This is determined by the netmask of 255.255.255.0. For more information on network subnet masks and network addresses in TCP/IP, see Chapter 6, "Name Resolution."

Notice that there are two options available for access control. I can specifically deny or allow access. By having no entries in the list box, you are stating that there are no access restrictions for this Web or FTP site based on computer identification.

To add an entry to the list, click the Add button. This will display the dialog box shown in Figure 8.11.

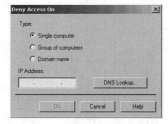

FIGURE 8.11
The Deny Access On dialog box has three choices to use for access restriction.

The first option is to restrict by a single computer IP address. You can enter the IP address of the computer that you want to restrict in the supplied box or perform a DNS lookup. Clicking the DNS Lookup button will cause Windows 2000 to look for a DNS server to poll for an IP address.

The second option, Group of computers, changes the dialog box a bit, as can be seen in Figure 8.12.

Using this option, you can restrict access based on network ID and subnet mask. This is a good choice if you want to block out an entire group of IP addresses.

The third option lets you enter a restriction based on a fully qualified domain name.

FIGURE 8.12
The Group of Computers option enables you to specify a network ID and subnet mask.

Any one of the three methods you choose offers you the ability to control access to the server itself.

> **NOTE**
>
> If you do not have any security settings placed on the folders or files within your Web site and you apply the access restrictions mentioned previously, those folders and files will inherit the security settings of the Web or FTP site.

Web Server Permissions

Up to this point, we have talked a lot about NTFS permissions. This section discusses Web Server permissions. There is a difference between the two, and you need to be aware of that.

NTFS permissions apply to valid Windows 2000 user accounts. If you have a user accessing the server using an existing account that is on the server, then the NTFS permissions will apply to that user's access.

For the most part, users accessing your Web server are doing so with an Anonymous login. In other words, to access your publicly available Web pages, the user does not need to enter a username/password combination. This is known as Anonymous access, and it makes use of a special account on the server called *IUSR_computername*. On my server, it is IUSR_celeron.

> **NOTE**
>
> If you have both Web Server permissions and NTFS permissions assigned to the same resource, the more restrictive permissions will be the one used.

In order to set the Web Server permissions, you need to have the Properties dialog box opened for the Web site. If it is not open, do so now.

Select the Home Directory, Directory, or Virtual Directory tab to display a window similar to Figure 8.13.

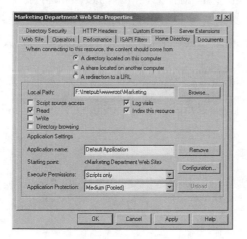

FIGURE 8.13

The Home Directory tab sheet offers the options for setting Web Server permissions.

The available permissions appear as option check boxes in the middle section of the tab sheet under the Local Path text box. They are

- **Script source access**—If users have Read or Write permission and you select this check box, they can access your source code used in ASP applications.

- **Read**—Enables users to read your Web pages and to download files.

- **Write**—Enables users to upload files to a directory on the server and to change the contents of a file if it is Write-enabled.

- **Directory browsing**—User can see a listing of the folders and subfolders in a hypertext format. Virtual directories do not appear in the listings, but, if a user knows the name of the virtual directory, the user can reach it.

- **Log visits**—This option is not really an access permission but enables you to use the logging features on a site or directory.

- **Index this resource**—Also not an access permission but sets up indexing of the contents of the directory in Index Server.

In the Application Settings section, there is another option that you need to be concerned with in regards to the Web Server permissions. The Execute Permissions drop-down box configures the permissions for applications running on the server. There are three options:

- **None** does not allow any scripts or applications to be run on the server. This is the safest of all permissions but limits your server to static Web pages.
- **Scripts only** will enable your server to run scripts such as ASP scripts.
- **Scripts and Executables** will permit ASP scripts, CGI scripts, or applications to run on the server.

These options should be investigated carefully to ensure server security.

After you have made the necessary selections, click the OK button to apply the settings.

> **CAUTION**
>
> Sometimes ASP scripts use passwords in them that are displayed as plain text. Be aware of this fact when enabling the Script Source Access permission because passwords can be viewed in the script files this way.

Controlling Database Access

A good portion of Web sites makes use of some form of data storage and retrieval. Your site might use a database to store inventory items displayed on an e-commerce site in a consumer catalog. You might use a database to store the account information for customers or clients that connect to your site so that you can provide authentication.

Whatever the reason for using a data store based on a database, you need to be aware that the data can be accessed outside of the methods that you have provided in your Web pages' interfaces.

Picture a large computer OEM that offers complete computer systems, custom-built systems, and components for sale on the Internet using a Web site. In order to provide for ease of administration, the company would likely use a database on the server that stores all the components and their related prices.

Now, it can be much easier to store the cost price in the database and have the Web page use ASP to pull the information from the database to display. In this way, you can display the same data on more than one page in the site and only have to update the information in one location.

For the site that I am currently building, we use a table in the database to store the product or component name and the cost that is paid to the wholesaler. I use a query to pull the component name and cost price from the table, perform a percentage markup on the cost, and enter that value into a price column that displays the client's cost instead of the company's cost.

What I have done here is reduce the amount of work that I have to do when updating prices or profit margins. The customer never sees any of my processing responsible for the pricing calculations; it goes on behind the scenes.

By using this scenario, I am actually putting my data at risk of being viewed in a way that I never intended. If a user knows or thinks that a database might be on the back end somewhere, he could hack into my server and view the data that is private, such as the wholesale cost or the markup percentages. This is one of the reasons why you need to secure the database and data files.

There are various methods available to you that enable you to secure your database and its data. They are described in the following sections.

Make sure that you use the security and authorization features of your database software. SQL, for instance, can require a user to enter a valid username and password to access the data. If you want to secure the data but still not require the users to enter this information when browsing the site using a Web browser client, you can place the username and password into an ASP script file. Be aware, though, that this can be compromised because ASP scripts store this information in plain text.

As we mentioned earlier in the chapter, you can use NTFS permissions to secure your files.

Database access on a Web server requires the use of a Data Source Name (DSN). Make sure that the file containing the DSN is properly protected from unauthorized access; it contains the database access username and password.

We have mentioned that ASP scripts contain the username and password as plain text. You can ensure that these files are secure as well. If you have highly sensitive information, I recommend that you convert the ASP script files to a COM component and use that to access the database. For more information on COM components, see the Internet Information Services SDK.

Using these methods will help ensure that your data can safely reside on the server without fear of the data being compromised.

Encryption

When talking about encryption for IIS, we are not talking about the capability to encrypt the data or files on the server. Instead, in this context, *encryption* deals with the use of Secure Sockets Layer (SSL), to encrypt the data before it gets transmitted over the network, whether it be an intranet or the Internet.

Obviously you do not want to encrypt transmissions on publicly available Web sites because of the overhead involved and the fact that not all clients will support it. If your sales force is contacting a sales Web site on your server over the Internet, you would almost definitely want to encrypt the transmissions to ensure that nobody eavesdrops on the connections.

To better explain encryption, we will present a brief background here.

In its basic form, encryption is the scrambling of information to make it unintelligible to anyone but the intended recipient. The first attempts at encryption occurred during the various wars. The sender and receiver would agree on a method to code messages that didn't make sense unless the reader knew the code. These early codes were sometimes mathematically based. When the sender coded a message, he applied a mathematical formula to change the ordering of the letters. This made the message unreadable. The receiver used a similar mathematical formula that reversed the work of the encoder, to return the message to its original state.

This method worked for a while, but it had one major flaw. The formula could be figured out by applying what is known as a *brute force attack*. This involved using many people trying every possible combination available to decode the message. These simple codes could be broken today in a matter of seconds or minutes with a desktop PC.

The encryption that is used today is still based on mathematical formulas, but they are much more sophisticated and not usually vulnerable to brute force attacks.

One of the reasons for this is because of what is known as the *encryption strength*. This is expressed in bits and refers to the length of the key used to encrypt and decrypt the data. At present, the strongest available in IIS 5.0 is 128-bit encryption. A user must have the key in order to decrypt the data at the other end. It is not impossible to crack 128-bit encryption, but the time required with today's available computer technology would exceed the value of the data by the time it was extracted.

IIS uses what is known as *Public Key Encryption*. Public Key Encryption uses two keys, one public key and one private key. The private key resides on the server and is used to encrypt and decrypt data sent to and from a client.

During a communication session using SSL, the Web browser will issue a request for a secure connection to the server by using the `https://` protocol heading, instead of the normal `http://`. The server and client will negotiate the encryption strength.

When this negotiation is complete, the server will send the browser a public key. The browser will use this public key to encrypt the data sent from it to the server, and the server can use its private key to decrypt the data. Both server and client will use what is known as a *session key* during the session. When the session ends, the session key is no longer valid.

CAUTION
The private key held by your server is the weak link in the security aspects of Public Key Encryption. It is extremely important that you protect the private key from discovery by using the strongest encryption strength available.

Enabling Encryption

Encryption is activated on the server when a client makes a request using `https://` in the header of the browser's URL. If you do not have encryption enabled on your server, the session will not use it.

You will need to have a server certificate installed on the server in order to make use of encryption. The procedure to acquire a certificate can be found in the later section "Certificates."

To enable encryption, follow this procedure:

1. Acquire and install a server certificate.
2. Open the Properties sheet for the Web site, directory, or file that you want to protect with encryption.
3. Select the Directory Security tab sheet, which is shown in Figure 8.14, and click the Edit button in the Secure Communications section. If this button is grayed out, you do not have a certificate installed on the server.
4. In the Secure Communications dialog box, select the Require secure channel (SSL) check box (see Figure 8.15).
5. Instruct all users that connect to this Web site to use `https://`, instead of `http://`.

Encryption Strength

The encryption strength used for secure communications deals with the bit-key length. By default, IIS uses 40-bit encryption strength. You can increase this to 128-bit by selecting the Require 128-bit encryption check box on the Secure Communications dialog box (refer to Figure 8.15).

The stronger your encryption strength, the more secure your communications are.

FIGURE 8.14

The Marketing Department Web Site Properties dialog box with the Directory Security tab selected enables you to work with server certificates for encryption.

FIGURE 8.15

Use the Secure Communications dialog box to enable SSL security for the Web site.

> **NOTE**
>
> Because of export restrictions, 128-bit encryption is only available in Canada and the United States. Be aware that if you require 128-bit encryption, each browser that needs access to the encryption-enabled Web site will require 128-bit encryption as well. This can leave out clients from other parts of the world.

Financial institutions can make use of an extension to SSL known as *Server-Gated Cryptography* (SGC). This method uses 128-bit encryption and can fall back to 40-bit encryption. In order to use SGC, you will need to contact your certificate authority and request an SGC certificate.

Certificates

We touched a bit on certificates in the previous section on encryption. The use of certificates is a means for a browser and a server to prove their identification by a digital signature. Essentially there are two types of certificates, server certificates and client certificates.

Server certificates reside on the server and perform three functions. They authenticate users on the server, they can validate Web content, and they are used to establish secure communications using SSL or SGC.

Client certificates reside on the client computer and are used to identify the user to your server. The client certificates are also issued by a certificate authority. The client certificate and the public key provided by a server act as a *key pair* for secure communications.

The client certificate contains information that identifies the user, the issuing authority, a public key, serial number, and expiration date.

Setting Up SSL

Secure Sockets Layer (SSL) 3.0 is used with IIS 5.0 to verify your Web Server's content, to authenticate users, and to encrypt the data that is transmitted over the wire. In order to use SSL on IIS 5.0, you need to do some installation and configuration tasks.

In order to use SSL, you need a server certificate installed on your IIS server. You obtain these certificates from a certificate authority such as Verisign. If you visit Microsoft's Web site at `http://backoffice.microsoft.com/securitypartners/`, you can search for a list of certificates providers by name or product.

Verisign offers a 14-day trial certificate if you would like to test certificates first and make sure that is what you want. You can get the free trial at `http://www.verisign.com`. Select the link Free Trial under Web Server Certificates.

If you already have a certificate installed on the server, you can go ahead and configure it. Open the properties sheet for the Web site on which you will use the certificate. You can only have one certificate per Web site.

Select the Directory Security tab sheet and click the Edit button in the Secure Communications section. When the Secure Communication dialog box opens, check off the Require secure channel (SSL) option box to enable SSL and the certificate. You can also choose Require

128-bit encryption here as well. We mentioned earlier about cautions to bear in mind when using 128-bit encryption strength.

You now have SSL set up on the computer. But wait—what if you don't have a certificate? How do you go about obtaining one? The later section "Obtaining Server Certificates" describes the process of obtaining certificates from third-party authorities. First though, let's look at the new security wizards that come with IIS 5.0.

Using the Security Wizards

IIS 5.0 has three new wizards that make working with security on your IIS server a little easier.

You can use the Web Server Certificate Wizard, to obtain a certificate from a third-party provider and install it on your server. The Web Server Certificate Wizard will walk you through the process of creating a certificate request that you will send to a certificate authority for issuance of a server certificate.

If you are not connected to the Internet at the time that you generate the request, you can save the request in a text file for later submission to the authority. You will see this procedure later when we send a request to Verisign for a certificate.

IIS also includes the Certificate Trust Lists (CTL) Wizard that enables you to manage a list of trusted certification authorities for each Web site. In this way, you can maintain a separate list of trusted and non-trusted Certificate Authorities (CAs) for different Web sites.

The last wizard, the Permissions Wizard, can be used to maintain the permissions for access on your IIS server.

The Permissions Wizard offers with a scenario-based approach to applying permissions to a Web site. There are two scenarios that the wizard will set up.

The first scenario is that of a public site wherein the public will have access to the content on the server.

Scenario two deals with tighter security; it is based on the idea of running an extranet over the Internet for sensitive data access.

Each of these wizards provide the necessary step-by-step instructions and simple question/answer screens during the configurations that make it really easy to perform the security chores they cover.

Obtaining Server Certificates

As I mentioned previously, you can obtain a certificate for your IIS server from a third-party certificate authority for use on your server. There are quite a few CAs available now, and you are free to choose the one that feels comfortable. For the purposes of this book, I requested a trial certificate from Verisign.

The first item to take care of is to generate the certificate request file using the Web Server Certificate Wizard. To access the wizard, open the Web site's Properties sheet and select the Directory Security tab. Click the Server Certificate button in the Secure Communications section.

Click Next on the Welcome screen to display the IIS Certificate Wizard screen, as shown in Figure 8.16.

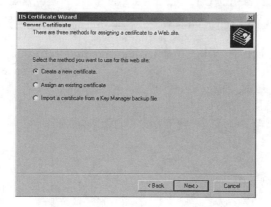

FIGURE 8.16

The IIS Certificate Wizard enables you to create a new certificate, assign an already existing one, or import a certificate.

For our purposes, we want to create a new certificate, so leave the default option, Create a new certificate, checked. Click the Next button to advance the wizard to the Delayed or Immediate Request screen. This is where you decide either to make the request now, or to create a request file to be used later. If you are not directly connected to the Internet, you will need to select the default of Prepare the request now, but send it later. Click the Next button.

The Name and Security Settings screen enables you to set a name for the new certificate; it will take the default name of the Web site. On the bottom section of the screen, you can select the bit length. The default is 512, but I recommend that you choose the 1024 bit length for added security. If you are going to be using export versions of the certificate you can select the Server Gated Cryptography option at the bottom. Click the Next button.

The next screen asks for the company name and the organizational unit for inclusion in the certificate. Enter the appropriate information for your company and click Next.

The next screen is titled Your Site's Common Name. If you will be using the server on the Internet, enter the FQDN here. If you are on an intranet, you can use the NetBIOS name. Click the Next button to advance the wizard.

The Geographical Information screen asks you to enter your country, state/province, and city. When you have entered this information and clicked Next, you are asked to provide a path and filename for the request certificate request. This is the text file that will be sent to the CA for certificate issuance. You can just accept the default here, if you would like, but remember the directory that the text file is stored in. You will need it later.

When you have finished creating the request file, you are ready to request a certificate. Connect to the Verisign Web site, http://www.verisign.com, to request your certificate. Verisign will ask you to provide the request file that was created on your server. You are asked to open the file in an ASCII text editor—Notepad works fine—and to copy and paste the encrypted information to the provided text box on the Verisign Web page. Figure 8.17 shows Notepad with my request file open.

FIGURE 8.17
The certificate request file is an encrypted text file that contains all the information you entered using the wizard.

As you can see in Figure 8.17, the file is encrypted. This prevents your information from being intercepted during transmission.

Verisign will take all the credentials that you supply and verify them before sending you a certificate for your server. If you are using the trial certificate as I did, you should receive it in about an hour via email. The certificate information will be in encrypted form at the bottom of the email message. You will use this to install the certificate on your server. Copy and paste the encrypted portion into Notepad and save it as a text file in a directory where you can gain access to it. I chose to name mine certresponse.txt for the ease of finding it.

Go back to the Directory Security tab sheet on the Web site's Properties sheet and click the Server Certificate button again. After clicking past the Welcome screen, you are presented with a new screen, as shown in Figure 8.18.

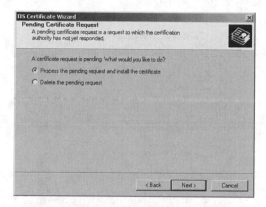

FIGURE 8.18

The Pending Certificate Request screen enables you to process a pending request or delete it.

Leave the default option, Process the pending request and install the certificate, checked and click Next. You are asked to locate the filename of the response file. This is the file that we created from the email response from Verisign. Select the file and click the Next button to complete installation of the certificate. You should see a Certificate Summary screen, as shown in Figure 8.19.

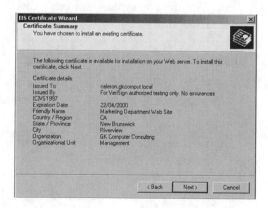

FIGURE 8.19

The Certificate Summary dialog box shows the details of the certificate that you have just installed.

After the certificate is installed, you can view the certificate's information by clicking the View Certificate button in the Secure Communications section on the Properties sheet for the Web site. You can also enable the SSL encryption by clicking the Edit button. Figure 8.20 shows the server certificate that I received from Verisign.

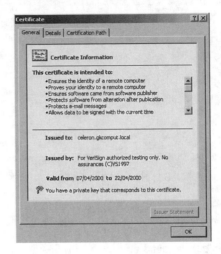

Figure 8.20

The certificate displays some general information such as the issuer, to whom the certificate was issued, and the expiration date.

As you can see, this certificate is only good for 14 days as it is only a trial certificate. You can select the Details tab to view detailed information about the certificate, such as its serial number, public key information, and thumbprint.

Certificate Trust Lists

Certificate Trust Lists (CTLs) offer you a way to maintain a list of trusted authorities for issuing certificates to your servers. You can specify a list of CAs for individual Web sites if you so choose.

This feature enables you to have the server automatically verify client certificates based on the CTL. To create and edit your CTLs, use the CTL Wizard.

Note

CTLs can be applied to Web sites only and not to virtual directories or directories.

To create a CTL on your Web server, click the Edit button on the Secure Communications section of the Directory Security dialog box that we have been working with all along.

At the bottom of the Secure Communications dialog box is an option, Enable certificate trust list. Check this option box to enable CTLs on your server. Click the New button to start the CTL Wizard. Click Next to bypass the Welcome screen, and you are shown the Certificates in the CTL screen as shown in Figure 8.21.

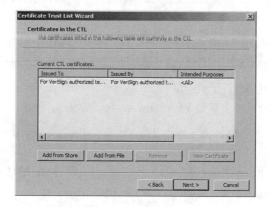

FIGURE 8.21
The Certificates in the CTL screen lists the currently available CTL certificates.

I already have the certificate from Verisign added to the list. To add certificates to your list, click the Add from Store button to display the dialog box shown in Figure 8.22.

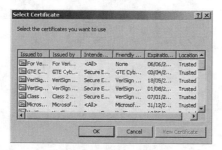

FIGURE 8.22
The Select Certificate dialog box shows a list of available certificates that are preinstalled with IIS 5.0.

Select the appropriate certificate from the list and click OK. Click Next on the Certificates in the CTL screen to advance to the Name and Description screen of the wizard. Enter a friendly name and description here if you wish and click Next.

The wizard displays the Completing the Certificate Trust List Wizard screen, which gives you a summary of the settings you made. Click Finish. If all went well, you will receive a confirmation message.

Client Certificates

In the same way as you acquire a server certificate from a trusted authority, you can obtain a client certificate as well. Some authorities will ask that you provide some credentials to verify your identity.

The procedure that is used here is for Internet Explorer. If you are using Netscape or another browser, refer to the online files for information on how to obtain a client certificate.

Obtaining Client Certificates

To obtain a client certificate for your Web browser, follow these steps:

1. Locate a trusted certificate authority with which to deal and verify the information that they will require from you.

2. Read the specific instructions or information that pertains to that CA's procedures.

3. Fill out the necessary information and order the certificate.

4. When you receive the certificate, install it in your browser. For IE 5.0, select the Tools menu and then choose Internet Options and select the Content tab, as shown in Figure 8.23.

FIGURE 8.23

The Content tab of the Internet Options dialog box in IE 5.0 enables you to install client certificates.

As we have mentioned, each Certificate Authority and each browser software have their own methods for dealing with client certificates, and we can't cover them all here. Familiarize yourself with the procedures of your chosen CA and browser.

Enabling Client Certificates

Enabling client certificates on your server is a way to prevent any users from connecting to the server without a client certificate. Keep one thing in mind—the requirement of a client certificate does not guarantee that your data is safe from unauthorized view. You will need to use an authentication method such as Basic, Digest or Integrated authentication.

Another way to track users is account mapping to client certificates. In this way, you can ensure that the client is who he says and that he has a valid Windows account with NTFS permissions set. If you do not already have the Properties sheet open for the Web site for which you want to enable client certificates, open it now and select the Directory Security tab.

Under the Secure Communications section, click the Edit button to open the Secure Communications dialog box, as shown in Figure 8.24.

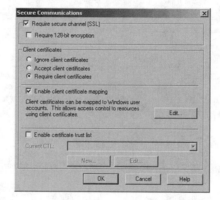

FIGURE 8.24

The Secure Communication dialog box is where you determine the use of client certificates for your Web site.

Make sure that the Require secure channel (SSL) option is selected. This will ensure that any client connecting to this Web site must do so using the https:// protocol.

The Client Certificates section in the middle of the dialog box enables you to choose between three different options for client certificates. These options are

- **Ignore client certificates** —Grants access to clients whether or not they have a client certificate.

- **Accept client certificates** —Enables the server to accept connections from clients that have certificates as well as those that do not have certificates.
- **Require client certificates** —Requires the client to have a certificate to connect to the server. If the client does not have a certificate, access will be denied.

NOTE

In order for your server to use client certificate requirements, you must have a server certificate installed on the server.

Mapping Certificates to User Accounts

As was mentioned in the previous section, "Enabling Client Certificates," a certificate alone does not protect resources from unauthorized access. A user with a valid client certificate still might not have any valid reason for connecting to your server other than to steal information. He might have a valid certificate but no user account on the server. To maintain security for your sensitive data, it is recommended that you use the client certificate mapping features of IIS 5.0 to map the certificate to a valid user account.

NOTE

In order for the procedures in this section to take effect on the server, you must stop and restart the Web site.

There are three types of mapping available: One-to-One mapping, Many-to-One mapping, and Directory Services mapping.

One-to-One mapping uses a single client certificate mapped to a user account. When a request comes from a browser, the browser must send the certificate for verification. The server will check the certificate against the one that it holds for the user account. The certificates must match exactly; otherwise, access is denied.

TIP

If a user renews a client certificate, you must perform the mapping again to ensure matching certificates.

Many-to-One mapping is not as strict as the One-to-One mapping. The server will check to verify that a certificate contains specific information such as an issuer.

The server will accept certificates that meet the criteria. In this way, a client can renew a certificate and still gain access to the resources if information such as the user information remains the same as on the older certificate.

Directory Services mapping is useful in a distributed environment where your organization is using the Windows 2000 Active Directory services. This can enable client certificates to be authenticated and shared among the various servers on the network.

CAUTION

If you use this style of mapping, be aware that it is applied at the Master level and will disable the One-to-One and Many-to-One mapping on the server. Your computer must also be a member of a Windows 2000 domain.

To enable One-to-One mapping, open our now familiar Directory Security tab on the Web site properties sheet and click the Edit button under Secure Communications. This opens the Secure Communications dialog box.

Select the Enable client certificate mapping option and click the Edit button in that section. This will display the Account Mappings dialog box, as shown in Figure 8.25.

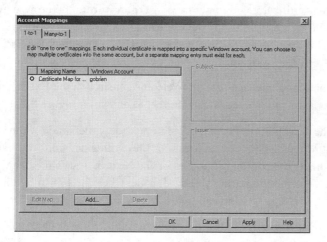

FIGURE 8.25

The Account Mappings dialog box is used to add, delete, and edit certificates to account mappings.

8

From this dialog box, you can see that I have already added a mapping in the 1-to-1 tab sheet. Click the Add button to start the process of adding a client certificate to an account mapping. A file open dialog box will appear, enabling you to locate the certificate that you want to add to the mappings box.

When you have located the certificate that you want to map, the Map to Account dialog box shown in Figure 8.26 appears.

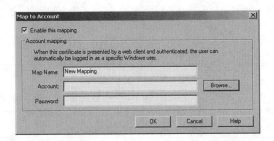

FIGURE 8.26

The Map to Account dialog box is where you specify the user account and password to map the certificate.

You can enter the user account and password if you know it or use the Browse button to open a dialog box that will display user accounts for you to choose from. Enter the account and password and click the OK button. The wizard will ask for a password confirmation and then add the certificate to the list.

If you cannot find a certificate, you might have to export it from the browser. For IE 5.0, select the Tool menu and Internet options. On the Content tab, select the Certificates button to open the certificates dialog box. Select the appropriate certificate and click the Export button. This starts the Export Certificate Wizard.

Choose the Next button to advance past the Welcome screen. On the Export File Format screen, choose the Base-64 encoded X-509, format as shown in Figure 8.27.

When you click the Next button, you are asked to provide a filename for the exported certificate. The Account Mappings dialog box looks for files with extensions of .cer, .crt, .spc, or .key, so name the file accordingly and choose the Next button. The wizard will then display a summary screen showing the setting you have made. Click the Finish button and if all goes well, you will see a message box indicating that the export was successful.

To add a Many-to-One mapping, follow the procedure for a One-to-One mapping to open the Account Mappings dialog box, but select the Many-to-1 tab. Click the Add button to display the General dialog box, as shown in Figure 8.28.

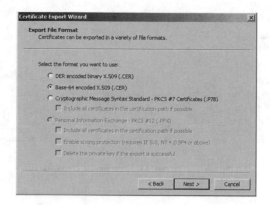

FIGURE 8.27

The Export File Format screen of the Export Certificate Wizard lets you choose the export format.

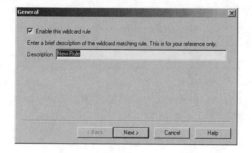

FIGURE 8.28

The General dialog box of the Many-to-1 tab requires a description for the mapping.

Select the Enable this wildcard rule option, enter a description that will be used for your reference, and click the Next button.

You will see the Rules dialog box. It enables you to add the rules that will form the wildcard matches for the mapping. Click the New button to add a rule, and you will see the screen shown in Figure 8.29.

Based on the information provided in this dialog box, select the appropriate criteria that will be used to perform the Many-to-One mapping and click the OK button. This will return you to the Rules dialog box, where you can click New to add another rule or Next to continue with the mapping.

When you click Next, you are given the opportunity to enter the user account to which this rule will map. Enter the user account name. Browse to locate the account and enter the appropriate password.

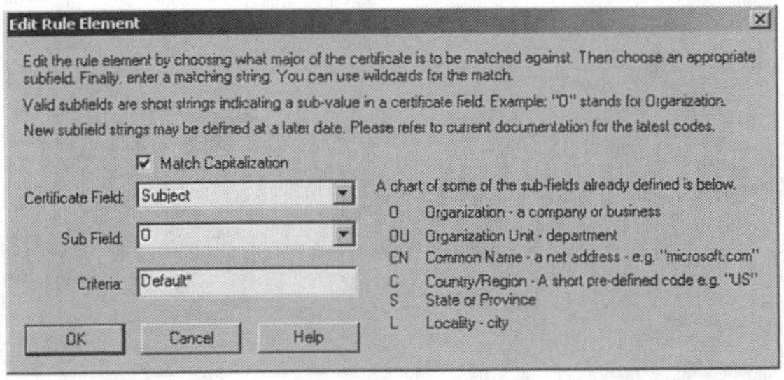

FIGURE 8.29
The Edit Rule Element dialog box enables you to set the criteria for matching when performing the mapping.

Click Finish and confirm the password to add the rule to the Many-to-One mapping list of rules.

Click OK on the Account Mappings dialog box (refer to Figure 8.25) to close it and apply the changes. Click OK on the Secure Communications dialog box to close it , and then stop and restart the Web site that you made the changes to in order to apply the mappings.

> **NOTE**
>
> If you have both One-to-One mappings and Many-to-One mappings, the specific One-to-One mappings will take priority over the Many-to-One mapping if they conflict.

Auditing

Auditing is a great feature that can offer information on successful and unsuccessful logon attempts, users attempting to access restricted resources that they do not have access to, and users attempting to use restricted commands.

Although auditing does not prevent break-ins, it can help you monitor patterns that could indicate break-in attempts or to notice any improper use or access of your Web server.

Configure and Monitor Auditing

Although Windows 2000 offers some features of its own regarding auditing, we will concentrate on auditing as it relates to IIS 5.0. In order to use the auditing that we will discuss here, you need to install the Group Policy snap-in.

The Group Policy snap-in needs to be run in its own MMC console apart from the Computer Management MMC. Click Start and choose Run. Type in MMC to start a new MMC console. From the Console Menu, select Add/Remove Snap-In and then choose the Add button from the

Add/Remove Snap-in dialog box to display the Add Standalone Snap-in dialog box, as shown in Figure 8.30.

FIGURE 8.30

The Add Standalone Snap-in dialog box shows the Group Policy snap-in selected.

Scroll the list until you find the Group Policy entry, select it, and click the Add button. The Select Group Policy Object dialog box displayed lets you enter the computer that you will audit. Leave the default selection if you are going to audit the local computer and click Finish.

Click Close on the Add/Remove Standalone Snap-in dialog box and then OK on the Add/Remove Snap-in dialog box to return to the MMC console with the newly added snap-in. Your screen should look similar to Figure 8.31, which verifies that the Group Policy snap-in was, indeed, added.

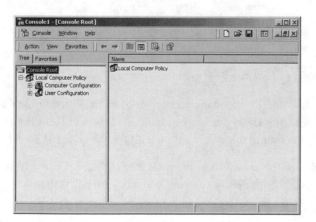

FIGURE 8.31

The Console1 MMC shows the newly added Group Policy snap-in.

8

SECURITY

> **NOTE**
>
> The auditing features require the NTFS file system. This is why, earlier on in the book, we recommended that you use NTFS or convert your FAT volumes over to NTFS.

In order to audit directory and file access events, you need to use Windows Explorer to navigate to the directory or file. When you have a directory selected, right-click it and choose Properties from the pop-up menu.

Select the Security tab on the Property dialog box and then click the Advanced button at the bottom of the tab sheet. This will open the Access Control Settings dialog box for the directory or file that you chose to audit. Select the Auditing tab, as shown in Figure 8.32.

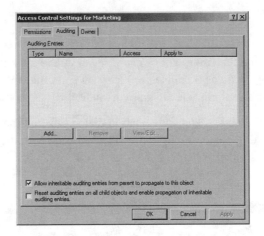

FIGURE 8.32

The Access Control Settings for Marketing directory has the Auditing tab selected for adding user or group accounts.

Click the Add button to add an account or computer to audit. When you click the OK button, you are shown the Auditing Entry for Marketing dialog box, shown in Figure 8.33. Select the check boxes next to the events that you want to audit for the selected account.

When you have selected the events to audit, click the OK button. You will be returned to the Access Control Settings dialog box, where you can verify that the entries were added to the list.

At the bottom of the dialog box are two options for inheritance settings. The first option will cause the resource that you have selected to inherit any auditing entries from a parent object.

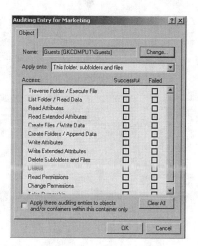

FIGURE 8.33

The Auditing Entry for Marketing dialog box lists the events you can audit for the selected resource.

This is useful if you want a file or subfolder to use the audit events of a parent folder as well as the specific entries you just added.

The second option will cause all child objects of this resource, such as subfolders or files, to inherit the auditing settings that you have specified here. Click OK to apply the settings.

If you receive the error message that auditing is not turned on for the server, you will have to use the Group Policy snap-in that we created earlier.

From the Tree pane in the Group Policy MMC, expand the tree as shown in Figure 8.34 to gain access to the Audit Policy for the local computer.

To enable auditing for the events listed in the Details pane, right-click the event and choose Security from the pop-up menu. Choose the Success or Failure option to audit the resource.

CAUTION

Auditing can be a wonderful tool to use on the server for monitoring the successes and failures of resource access attempts, but it can also be a huge resource hog. Use auditing sparingly to achieve the results you want without placing too much strain on the server resources.

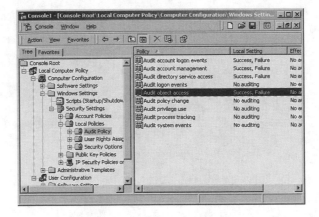

FIGURE 8.34
The Group Policy snap-in in MMC shows the Audit Policy for the local computer.

Detecting Unauthorized Access

If you suspect that your Web site is experiencing unauthorized access, you can use the logs
generated by IIS and Windows 2000 to view the security events that have taken place on the
server. In order to view the security logs for the server, you can use the Event Viewer application that comes with Windows 2000.

NOTE

You must have administrative rights on the server to view the Security logs in Event
Viewer.

You can start the Event Viewer application from the Start menu by navigating to
Administrative Tools and then Event Viewer or you can open it from within Control Panel and
Administrative tools. Either method will bring up the Event Viewer, as shown in Figure 8.35.

Although the Security Log is empty on my server, which is what you would want to see ideally, it can provide you with information that can point to potential break-ins by repeated
unsuccessful logons, unsuccessful resource access, or unsuccessful attempts to upload files to
the server. Any entry in the Security Log should be taken seriously and should be investigated
to determine its cause.

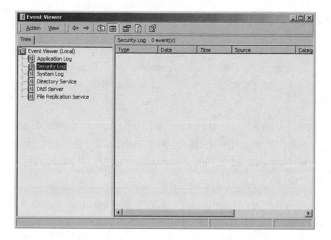

FIGURE 8.35

The Event Viewer window is where you can monitor any security events that pertain to your Web server.

IPSec

Internet Protocol Security (IPSec) is a security mechanism that was designed by the Internet Engineering Task Force (IETF). It is used to provide IP data packet formatting which can provide for a strong end-to-end authentication mechanism for your Internet traffic. It also offers data integrity, anti-replay and confidentiality.

Microsoft has taken the IPSec architecture and built on it by integrating the Windows 2000 domains and Active Directory directory services. Because of this, you can use the standard authentication methods such as Kerberos v5, Public/Private key scenarios or password based authentication, for establishing trusts between computers.

When these computers have established their trust, they can then begin to transmit encrypted information. This works similarly to a virtual private network (VPN) in that the data transferred between computers might still be intercepted, but the interceptor does not have the decryption mechanisms. This renders the data unusable.

There are two scenarios involved in setting up IPSec on your server. You can use a built-in IPSec policy or you can create your own. Both procedures are somewhat involved and I will not explain them here due to space considerations. However, you can download an excellent white paper on IPSec which includes setting it up on your server and monitoring it. You can locate this white paper at
`http://www.microsoft.com/WINDOWS2000/library/planning/security/ipsecsteps.asp`.

8

SECURITY

Summary

This is perhaps the largest chapter in the entire book and for good reason. The Internet is open to the world for access to anyone with a computer and an ISP. If you have a server or computer connected to the Internet, that same computer is also available to be connected to by those same people.

Microsoft has had its fair share of security breaches over the past couple of years. Some have been discovered by reputable organizations trying to verify the security and safety of their own networks. Others have been discovered by companies as a result of a malicious activity by an outsider.

One such instance just came out recently, regarding a vulnerability in IIS 4.0 that was a part of Windows NT 4.0 Option pack. Its back door enables a Web developer with authoring privileges on the server to execute malicious code, gain access to other Web sites hosted on the server, and view the contents of certain files on the server.

The vulnerability was found in a file called `Dvwssr.dll` and was present on IIS servers that had FrontPage Server Extensions installed. The recommended fix is to delete the `Dvwssr.dll` file from the computer. Microsoft has also stated that the vulnerability does not exist in IIS 5.0 on Windows 2000. If you have upgraded from NT 4.0 and IIS 4.0, the upgrade will remove the vulnerability.

Just for safety's sake, I searched my hard drive and found it still present. Why? Because I am running a dual-boot scenario with NT 4.0 and Windows 2000 Server. Microsoft has not mentioned that this is a cause for concern, and most IIS 5.0 installation will not be a dual-boot scenario anyway. However, the general consensus from Microsoft is that the file is not needed, so it can be safely deleted. For more information, check out their security bulletin at `http://www.microsoft.com/technet/security/bulletin/ms00-025.asp`.

You can use the information presented here to help you set up and maintain security for your Web server and to help you monitor it for signs of any break-in attempts.

One of the best decisions that a company can make when placing a Web server on the Internet is to use a standalone server that is not connected to the company's internal network in any way. This will result in the complete isolation of the internal network from any outside attack through the Internet.

There is of course a simple way to provide some security for the web site that you don't want viewed publicly. You may simply assign it a different port number. This is the scenario with the Administration web site that is a part of IIS. If you have installed more than one IIS installation, you will notice that the port number is randomly selected for each installation. This means that not every IIS remote administration web site is available on the same port number.

This adds another layer of complexity that an intruder must overcome.

IPSec can offer you varying options for security on your IIS server as well. Microsoft makes a white paper available that shows how to set up IPSec policies and monitor them.

If you need to place sensitive information on a Web server, consider the issues and procedures presented here as a means to protect that data.

One other method that wasn't discussed here was the use of Virtual Private Networking for security in communications. This topic is somewhat new, about a year or two old. Microsoft has a protocol for Virtual Private Networking that you can use with Windows 2000, or you can look into third-party software and hardware implementations as well.

Custom Error Messages

IN THIS CHAPTER

The HTTP 1.1 protocol defines a set of generic error messages that are sent to a client when a problem occurs with the connection or connection attempt. These error messages do not go into specific detail as to what the problem is. There are some rather familiar messages such as the 404 File Not Found message, which appears when the requested Web page does not exist on the server.

As far as your clients are concerned, there should not be any error messages on a well-maintained site. Well, this is next to impossible to achieve on large Web sites with more than one Web site developer working on it. Error messages are inevitable. You can, however, relieve some of your clients' grief by providing custom error messages that can better explain what the problem is, rather than showing the standard HTTP 1.1 error message codes. Table 9.1 lists the standard HTTP 1.1 error codes and messages.

TABLE 9.1 Error Messages and Associated Codes

Error Code	Error Message
400	Bad request
401.1	Logon failed
401.2	Logon failed due to server configuration
401.3	Unauthorized due to ACL on resource
401.4	Authorization failed by filter
401.5	Authorization failed by ISAPI/CGI application
403.1	Execute access forbidden
403.2	Read access forbidden
403.3	Write access forbidden
403.4	SSL required
403.5	SSL 128 required
403.6	IP address rejected
403.7	Client certificate required
403.8	Site access denied
403.9	Too many users
403.10	Invalid configuration
403.11	Password change
403.12	Mapper denied access
403.13	Client certificate revoked
403.14	Directory listing denied
403.15	Client Access Licenses exceeded

403.16	Client certificate untrusted or invalid
403.17	Client certificate has expired or is not yet valid
404	File not found
404.1	Site not found
405	Method not allowed
406	Not acceptable
407	Proxy authentication required
412	Precondition Failed
414	Request-URI too long
500	Internal server error
500.12	Application restarting
500.13	Server too busy
500.15	Requests for Global.asa not allowed
500-100.asp	ASP error
501	Not implemented
502	Bad gateway

As you can see, most of these messages are cryptic and would mean nothing to the average Web site visitor. Luckily, IIS 5.0 enables us to configure custom messages to replace these.

Customizing and Working with Error Messages

If you take a look at Figure 9.1, you will see that the error messages provided with IIS 5.0 are nothing more than HTML pages located in a directory.

> **CAUTION**
>
> Each of these files can be modified or customized to the way you want with a simple text editor or with an HTML editor. It is recommended that you leave these message files as is and create new ones for customization instead.

Open any text editor or HTML editor and create the HTML file that you want to use for a custom error message. Listing 9.1 shows some HTML code for a quick and simple customized error page that you can use instead of the standard 404 File Not Found.

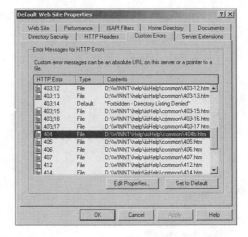

FIGURE 9.1
The Custom Errors tab sheet of the Default Web Site Properties dialog box lists the custom error messages on your server.

LISTING 9.1   Sample Custom Error Message

```
<HTML>
<HEAD>
<TITLE>Page Not Found</TITLE>
<BODY>
<CENTER><H2>We apologize that the page you were looking for cannot be displayed
at this
time.</H2></CENTER>
<p>
<br>
<CENTER>Please send an e-mail to <a
href="mailto:webmaster@gkcomput.com">webmaster@gkcomput.com</a>
describing what file or page you were attempting to access.
<p>We apologize for any inconvenience!
</BODY>
</HTML>
```

This code generates an HTML page that simply replaces the generic 404 File Not Found error message. You can include whatever text you would like or other email addresses.

In order to test this code, copy this new file into the same directory that holds the error messages. In the Custom Error message dialog box, change the File Not Found error message to the new file. Attempt to access a nonexistent file in the Web site to verify that your new custom message is returned.

Not only can you generate static HTML pages, but you can also use ASP or ISAPI applications to perform more complex responses to the client, including references to the requested page, in case he made a typo. Listing 9.2 shows an Active Server Page that provides this type of information.

LISTING 9.2 Custom Error Message That Generates an Email

```
<%@ LANGUAGE=VBScript %>
<html>

<head>
<title>Page Not found!</title>
</head>

<body>
<%
' 404custom.asp
' This asp file serves to handle 404 File Not Found error messages.
' It maps to a URL so you need to indicate a URL instead of a file
' in the Custom Error Properties for the 404 message.

Dim strQueryString
Dim strRequestedURL
Dim errMail

' Get the requested URL string including the error number
strQueryString = Request.ServerVariables("Query_String")

' We need to parse the string to remove the error number
strRequestedURL = Replace(strQueryString, "404;", "")

'Create a mail object
Set errMail = Server.CreateObject("CDONTS.NewMail")

'Set up the mail header information
errMail.From = "webclients@gkcomput.com"
errMail.To = "gkcomput@fundy.net"
errMail.Subject = "ERROR - 404 Page Not Found"
errMail.Body = "The client requested " & strRequestedURL
errMail.Importance = 2
errMail.Send


Set errMail = Nothing     ' destroy the object to free resources
```

LISTING 9.2   Continued

```
%>

<p>We apologize but, the page you were looking for, <% =strQueryString %> was
➥not found on the server.<br>
Please check the URL above and ensure that there are no spelling errors.<br>
We have sent an e-mail alert to our webmaster in regards to this matter.<br>
If you would prefer, you can visit our <a href="http://www.hompage.com">Home
➥Page</a> </p>
</body>
</html>
```

This page is a little more complex than the static HTML page in that it adds some ASP functionality. We first declare some variables to hold the data that we want returned from the Not Found error. We need to know the URL that was requested so we can figure out if it is indeed missing or was never meant to be there.

We then create a new CDONTS mail object and set up the necessary To, From, and Subject headers. We place some text and the returned URL into the body of the message, set the message importance, and send the email.

At the end of the page, we also display some informative text for the user, explaining what happened and informing him that the error has been reported to the Webmaster for review.

Once again, copy this error message into the error message folder and configure the properties for the Web site to point to this URL for the File Not Found error message. Attempt to access a nonexistent file in the Web site to verify that the error message is displayed and that it does indeed send an email to the Webmaster.

> **NOTE**
>
> This example uses the CDONTS object. You must make sure that it is installed and configured on the server for the email portion of the code to work.
>
> For more information on CDONTS, visit
> http://support.microsoft.com/support/kb/articles/Q186/2/04.asp.

As you can see, using ASP has many advantages over using static error message pages. This small example provides the user some good feedback as to what went wrong and also sends an email notification to the Webmaster so that the client doesn't have to worry about doing it. Not only that—some users wouldn't let you know anyway. They would just go away with a bad feeling toward your Web site and likely never visit it again.

If you are creating .asp files or ISAPI applications as custom error messages, select the URL type instead of the File type in the Error Mapping Properties dialog box. This way, the necessary parameters are passed to the script.

Enabling Detailed Messages

As mentioned earlier in the chapter, the HTTP 1.1 protocol defines generic error messages that are sometimes rather cryptic. You can create your own custom error messages as well. If you don't want to create these error messages yourself and don't want to use the generic ones provided by the HTTP 1.1 protocol, you need not worry. IIS 5.0 provides, by default, more user-friendly error messages to take the place of the generic ones.

These error messages are installed by default into the `%systemroot%\help\iishelp\common` directory, wherein `%systemroot%` refers to the directory in which Windows 2000 is installed.

NOTE

If you have upgraded your IIS 4.0 server to IIS 5.0, your custom error message will have been copied over to the new directory automatically.

To enable these detailed error messages for your Web sites, open the Properties sheet for your Web or virtual Web and choose the Custom Errors tab on the Properties dialog box. Figure 9.1 showed the custom error messages that are available. By default, these are applied to the default Web site.

Simply selecting the error message you want to work with and clicking the Edit Properties button, you can browse for the custom error message to use for that particular error. Once again, by default, IIS 5.0 stores these files in the `%systemroot%\help\iishelp\common` directory.

ASP Error Processing

If you are using ASP files on your Web site, any errors generated by these files are handled somewhat differently depending on the location of the file. For example, by default, IIS 5.0 will pass any .asp file errors to the `500-100.asp` file for processing only if the .asp file with the error is on the default Web site.

If you have created another Web site on the server alongside the default Web site, you are going to have to create your own `.asp` error-processing file or, map your 500-100 errors to the `500-100.asp` file for processing.

You can map these using the information provided in the section on customizing and working with custom error messages.

This book is not about teaching you ASP, so it is recommended that you refer the task to your Web developers to create any custom `.asp` error-handling files.

> **NOTE**
>
> If you do not create or map a custom file to handle your `.asp` errors, IIS will act as if no custom error file exists. This behavior will be the same if your custom `.asp` error file has errors. Check and verify the script code before assigning the `.asp` processing file to your `.asp` errors.

Summary

The HTTP 1.1 protocol sets a standard for error messages returned to client's browsers in the event of errors. These messages are short and sometimes cryptic, which makes them hard for the average user to decipher.

IIS 5.0 comes with a set of custom error messages built in and applies them to the default Web site. These error messages are a little more user-friendly than the generic HTTP 1.1 messages are.

If you are still not satisfied with the available custom messages provided by IIS, you could create your own custom error messages and map them to the appropriate errors.

You can also set up custom `.asp` files that will process `.asp` error messages when they occur on your server. These files provide a means to give feedback to the user as to what the error was and can also write that information to an email message and send it to the Webmaster for action.

We know that most Web developers work hard to maintain a Web site and ensure that their visitors see the pages they expect to see and enjoy the content as it was intended. In the same way that a software developer cannot develop an entire software application without inadvertently creating bugs, a Web developer is likely to run into some problems because of unforeseen circumstances.

The error message capabilities of IIS 5.0 can help to ensure clients that the Web site is being looked after and that errors will get reported and fixed.

Site Activity Logging

IN THIS CHAPTER

One of the nicest features of IIS 5.0 from a troubleshooting and monitoring point of view is the capability to log the activity for the site. The information gathered can be a great resource for Webmasters, Web developers, and even a Web site sponsor's marketing department.

Reviewing the log files, which are ASCII text files, can uncover such information as who visited the site, how many hits various pages are experiencing, and even error messages for troubleshooting.

Logging Activity on Your IIS Server

The logging features of IIS are quite extensive and operate independently of other operating system logging events. You have the option of choosing the logging file formats as well as the site, folder, and file logging options. You can choose whether or not to log right to an individual file.

IIS gives you four different formats for logging. These formats are listed and explained in the following sections.

Microsoft IIS Log File Format

This is an ASCII fixed-format log file that you cannot customize. This log file will record the following information:

- Client IP address
- Username
- Request time
- Request date
- HTTP status codes
- Bytes received

Listing 10.1 shows a sample of the Microsoft IIS log file format on my local server.

LISTING 10.1   Log File Entry

```
192.168.1.20, -, 04/04/2000, 9:26:32, W3SVC1, PENTHOUSE, 192.168.1.23, 230,
➥278, 1109, 200, 0, GET,
/Default.htm, -,
```

You can see the IP that made the request, which is 192.168.1.20. Next you see the date and time as well as the service that recorded the log (W3SVC1) and then the server's NetBIOS name of PENTHOUSE.

The second line displays the IP address of the server, 192.168.1.23. The next set of numbers is interesting. The first, 230, indicates the length of time in seconds that the request took to complete. We then see 278. This is the number of bytes received, followed by the bytes sent, 1109.

The number 200 in the second line indicates the HTTP status code. It is followed by a Windows 2000 status code of 0. We then see the GET statement, which is merely the type of request that was made, and finally, the file that was requested.

As you can see from this example, the Microsoft IIS log file format is fairly easy to read.

National Computer Security Association (NCSA) Common Log File Format

This format is also an ASCII text file that is not customizable. This file is used only for Web sites though and is not available for FTP site logging.

Listing 10.2 shows a sample of this log format.

LISTING 10.2   Log File Format

```
192.168.1.20 - - [04/Apr/2000:09:37:47 -0400] "GET /Default.htm HTTP/1.0" 304
➥212
```

The first entry is the IP address of the requesting client. Next, in square brackets, you see the date and time, along with the Greenwich Mean Time (GMT) offset.

In double quotation marks, you can see the command that was issued, GET, along with the filename and protocol version.

The last two entries are the IIS status code of 304 and the bytes sent, 212.

W3C Extended Log File Format

This is the only customizable format of those available on IIS. By customizing this file format, you can include only that information that is pertinent to you. Listing 10.3 shows a sample of a log file on my server in the W3C Extended log file format.

LISTING 10.3   W3C Extended Log File Format

```
#Software: Microsoft Internet Information Services 5.0
#Version: 1.0
#Date: 2000-04-04 12:47:04
#Fields: time c-ip cs-method cs-uri-stem sc-status
12:47:04 192.168.1.20 GET /Default.htm 304
```

This file definitely looks different from the last two. The first two lines of Listing 10.3 tell you that you are using IIS 5.0 in version 1.0.

You may have noticed a small discrepancy in the Date field as compared to the previous logs. All requests were made within 15 minutes of each other. The time shown in this log indicates 12:47:04. However, I accessed the page at 09:47:04 a.m. local time. This means that the time shown in Listing 10.3 is in GMT format. My time zone is –4:00 GMT, which means that my local time is four hours behind GMT.

The next line, #Fields, holds some more interesting information. Although they are not perfectly lined up, the last two lines are in a column/row format.

Field	Log Entry	Description
Time	12:47:04	Time of request
c-ip	192.168.1.20	Client location

You first see time, the first entry in the last line is the time of the request. Next is c-ip, in the second location of the last line, you see the client IP. We then have cs- method, which corresponds to the GET method. Cs-uri-stem refers to the URL or filename that was requested, and finally, we see sc-status and the status code of 304.

We will look at the process for customizing this format in the section "W3C Extended Logging Customization" later in the chapter. If you would like more information on this log file format, visit http://www.w3c.org.

ODBC Logging Format

This logging format is only available on a Windows 2000 Server and not on the Professional version of Windows 2000. The ODBC logging format is fixed and is logged to a database format.

Clicking the Properties button will enable you to specify the ODBC Data Source Name (DSN), which defaults to HTTPLOG.

TIP

If you have been using the different log file formats on your server and want to look at a log in a specific format, you can do so by using Notepad or any text editor to open the files. You can differentiate the formats by their names. W3C files start with ex and then the date, such as ex000404. Microsoft IIS formatted files start with in and then the date, such as in000404. The NCSA format uses nc, as in nc000404.

CAUTION

Because logging is enabled by default and every visit is logged, your log files can quickly become large and take up disk space. You should regularly review and compress or back up these files so you can delete them to free up space.

Enabling Logging

As mentioned previously in this chapter, you can enable logging on your Web site, on the FTP site, on directories, or even individual files. By default, when IIS is installed, it enables W3C Extended log file formats for the Default Web site.

The procedure for enabling logging on a Web site is straightforward. Open the Internet Services Manager and select the Web site in the Tree pane on which you want to enable logging. Right-click and choose Properties to open the Properties dialog box for that Web site. Figure 10.1 shows the Properties dialog box.

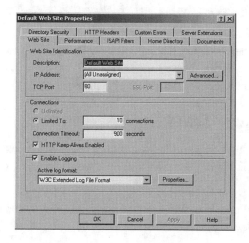

FIGURE 10.1

The Default Web Site Properties dialog box shows the Enable Logging option checked at the bottom of the Web Site tab sheet.

I have enabled logging for the Default Web Site and set the log file format to W3C Extended. That's all there is to enabling logging for a Web site.

As I mentioned before, you can selectively enable and disable logging for individual directories and files as well. In this way, you can choose to log only the information that you need, which will help to reduce the log file size.

10

SITE ACTIVITY LOGGING

To work with directory or file logging, open the Properties dialog box for that directory or file. Figure 10.2 shows the Properties dialog box for the gkcomput directory on my Web server.

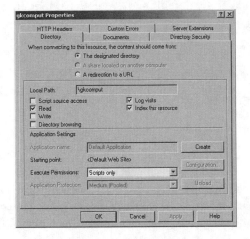

FIGURE 10.2

The Properties dialog box for the gkcomput *directory with the Directory tab sheet selected. You enable or disable logging here.*

In the middle section of the Directory tab sheet, you will see the various permissions for this directory such as Read and Write. There is an option here called Log visits. Check this option to enable logging of the directory, or clear it, to disable the logging feature.

Processor Usage Tracking

IIS 5.0 includes a new feature that enables you to monitor the CPU usage of the server that is a result of the Web site. This feature is only available if you have selected the W3C Extended logging format.

Processor usage is logged on a per–Web site basis and does not include any tracking based on the script or application level. The process tracking deals with the processor usage by the Web site as a whole.

To enable process tracking, open the Properties dialog box for the Web site on which you want to track processor usage. On the Web Site tab, make sure that the W3C Extended logging format is chosen and that logging has been enabled.

Click the Properties button in the logging section to display the Extended Logging Properties dialog box and select the Extended Properties tab. Scroll down to the Process Accounting entry, as shown in Figure 10.3.

FIGURE 10.3

The Extended Properties tab is where you select the Process Accounting information to log processor usage.

Select the check box next to Process Accounting to enable tracking of processor usage on the Web site. The various options are

- **Process Event**—This is the type of process that triggers an event, such as an application or script file.

- **Process Type**—The event that was triggered, such as Site-Stop, Site-Pause, and others that can be found in the online help files.

- **Total User Time**—Accumulated time for User Mode processor time used during the current interval. This is measured in seconds.

- **Total Kernel Time**—Total accumulated Kernel Mode time used during the current interval in seconds.

- **Total Page Faults**—The number of memory page faults that occurred.

- **Total Processes**—The number of CGI and other out-of-process applications that were created during the logging period.

- **Active Processes**—Total CGI and out-of-process applications that were running when the log file was recorded.

- **Total Terminated Processes**—Total number of CGI and out-of-process applications that were halted in execution because of Process Throttling.

Once you have made your selections, click the OK button to return to the Web Site Properties sheet. Click the OK button to apply the changes and close the Properties dialog box.

NOTE

Process Accounting is only available for Web sites and not for FTP sites.

10

W3C Extended Logging Customization

In the previous section on the log file formats, we mentioned that the W3C log files could be customized. This customization enables you to select the columns or pieces of information that you want logged. With the Web Site Properties dialog box opened, click the Properties button in the Logging section. This will display the screen shown in Figure 10.4.

FIGURE 10.4

The Extended Logging Properties dialog box with the Extended Properties tab sheet selected for customizing the W3C log file.

As you scroll the list, you can see that there is a considerable number of logging options available. We will explain each, to help you choose those that will best serve your purpose. Obviously choosing them all would generate rather large log files, so you need to be selective in the information you collect.

Date	This option records the date on which the event occurred.
Time	Similar to Date, it records the time on which the event occurred.
Client IP Address	IP address of the requesting client.
User Name	Username of the requesting client.
Service Name	Client of the Internet service making the request.
Server Name	The name of the server that generated the log entry.
Server IP	IP address of the server.
Server Port	The port used for the connection.
Method	Action performed by the client, such as a GET command.
URI Stem	What resource was accessed, such as an HTML page or ASP script.

URI Query	Search strings that the client was using.
HTTP Status	Status of the action in HTTP terms.
Win32 Status	Status of the action in Windows terms.
Bytes Sent	Number of bytes out of the server.
Bytes Received	Number of bytes into the server.
Time Taken	Length of transaction.
Protocol Version	HTTP or FTP version used by client.
User Agent	Browser used by client.
Cookie	Content of sent or received cookies.
Referer	Name of site that redirected the user to current site, if any.
Process Event	Type of process that triggered an event, such as an application or CGI script.
Process Type	The event that was triggered, such as a site stoppage or restart.
Total User Time	Total time the client used the connection.
Total Kernel Time	Processor Kernel Mode time used by connection.
Total Page Faults	Total of memory page faults generated, if any.
Total Processes	Total number of out-of-process applications created.
Active Processes	Total number of out-of-process applications running when the log was recorded.
Total Terminated Processes	Total number of out-of-process applications that were stopped because of Process Throttling during the session.

This is quite an extensive list of available options for the W3C Extended log format. You obviously don't need to include all options in every log, but there should be a few that will serve the purposes for most sites.

Saving Log Files

When dealing with log files, we have mentioned numerous times that you can easily fill a drive with log files if you do not manage them carefully. One of the best ways to do this is to provide a means of backing up the log files so you can delete older files to make room for newer files.

IIS offers the capability to save the log files to a directory that you specify. You can also set the frequency of when your log files are generated. The default names of these log files will also change based on the log file format that you choose. The available options are

- **Hourly**—This option creates log files hourly and is normally used for high traffic sites.

- **Daily**—Log files will be created daily. The first entry after midnight is the start of a new log file.

- **Weekly**—This creates a weekly log file that takes its start point as the first entry after midnight on Saturdays.

- **Monthly**—Monthly log files that start with the first entry after midnight of the last day of the previous month.

- **Unlimited File Size**—The log file continues to grow as new entries are appended to it. You must stop the IIS server to access this log file.

- **When The File Size Reaches**—You specify the size, in megabytes, to limit the log file too. When that limit is reached, a new log file is generated.

NOTE

In the options described here, midnight is measured in local time except for the W3C Extended format, which uses GMT. You can tell W3C to use local time instead if you prefer.

To configure the file saving and interval features of logging, open the Web or FTP Properties dialog box and select the Web Site or FTP site tab sheet. Click the Properties button in the Enable Logging section at the bottom of the tab sheet. This displays the screen shown in Figure 10.5.

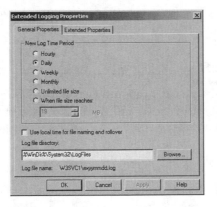

FIGURE 10.5

The General Properties tab where you determine the logging time intervals.

The General Properties tab sheet is selected by default. You set the intervals for the log files (the frequency of their generation) in the New Log Time Period section.

Below this section is an option, Use local time for file naming and rollover. This option is where you set the time zone style for the W3C log file format, as indicated in the preceding Note.

In the Log file directory text box at the bottom of the tab sheet, you can see that, by default, the log files are stored in the `%WinDir%\System32\LogFiles` directory. (`%WinDir%` is the directory in which Windows 2000 is installed.) You can type in your own preference here or use the Browse button to locate a directory or drive of your choice.

Note the Log file name label on the bottom of the tab sheet. This indicates the format of the name that will be used when saving the log files . As you can see on the dialog box, log files generated with the present settings on my computer will be named starting with an e (indicative of the W3C Extended format), followed by a two-digit year, two-digit month, and two-digit day with an extension of `.log`. This information can help you locate specific log files when you need to.

Converting Log Files to NCSA Format

You can perform a conversion of your W3C or Microsoft IIS log files to the NCSA format. This is done through the use of a command line utility. The syntax for the command is

```
convlog -i,n,e filename.log -t -l(0,1,2) -o -x -d
```

This command uses the following options:

-i	Input file type.
-n	NCSA log file input.
-e	W3C Extended file input.
filename.log	Input log filename.
-t(*ncsa:GMTOffset*)	Default output to NCSA log file format. GMTOffset indicates hours to offset from GMT.
-l(0,1,2)	Date format used in the Microsoft IIS log file format.
	0 (MM/DD/YY) default.
	1 (YY/MM/DD)Japanese.
	2 (DD.MM.YY) German format.
-o	Output directory to use.
-x	Saves transaction entries (non-HTTP) to a dump file with the `.dmp` extension.
-d	Can use a domain name instead of IP address during the conversion process.

To convert a W3C Extended log file on my server over to NCSA with a four-hour offset time from GMT (my time zone), the syntax would look like this:

```
convlog -ie ex000407.log -t ncsa:-0400
```

Summary

Logging the activity on your network has many advantages and benefits. It provides a good way to determine how your site is being used and by whom.

Your company's marketing department is likely to be very interested in collecting some of the information to help them determine areas of the Web site that need to be spruced up a bit or to aid them in seeing what products or services most interest the site's visitors, based on the areas or pages that they visit.

The log information is also very useful to administrators for troubleshooting connectivity issues, lost links, and busy versus slow areas of the site.

You can also use the logs for some security purposes because they can tell you the IP address and domain names of visitors. If you find that a restricted area of your site was broken into, you can utilize the logs to see the identity of the clients who were on your system at the time, and what resources they were using.

The various formats available to you help you work with ASCII text files for Microsoft IIS and NCSA formats or a customizable format using the W3C Extended format. If you are so inclined, you can import the text files into a spreadsheet or database application for analysis and trending.

All in all, the logging features of IIS 5.0 are a useful addition to the product and can provide you with useful information and feedback on the activities of your Web and FTP sites, making you a better Web administrator.

Performance Tuning

IN THIS CHAPTER

Performance tuning is a must for any Web server. The reasons are varied but all valid. Web servers place more demand on a server's resources than an FTP site does. This is because an FTP site merely serves up files, whereas a Web site serves up static HTML files along with server side applications. As was noted in previous chapters, you can run multiple applications inside of and outside of the IIS server's process space.

You want your visitors to have a good experience when they visit your Web site and not to have to deal with server delays or slow loading pages and applications. The information in this chapter will help you to tune your server to achieve the best performance you can get from it.

Factors that affect performance are related to hardware and software. We will look at performance monitoring from different perspectives—from testing and tuning, monitoring tools, and disk optimization.

It is important to establish a baseline for measuring performance. As a result, testing and tuning aspects are ongoing tasks that you need to perform on a regular basis. This will provide you with a good understanding of how the server's resources are being used and when it is time to upgrade or replace hardware.

Tweaking IIS Performance

In order to tweak the performance of your server, you need to look all the variables present and determine where bottlenecks are occurring. IIS 5.0 and Windows 2000 have a few tools to help you do this. By effectively using these tools, you can determine the best place to concentrate your efforts.

As we mentioned previously, performance monitoring is an ongoing process, and you will find yourself locating a bottleneck, fixing it, and then searching for another one. This process can continue for quite some time, and you could end up replacing all your server's components. This is certainly not the idea of the exercise.

The tools that are provided for you and their functions are described in the following sections.

System Monitor is a tool that you can use to monitor the server's performance at intervals selected by you. You can use the information in a variety of ways to determine the performance of the server.

System Monitor uses object counters to monitor server performance. Some of the more common counters are listed here, along with recommended limits:

- **Memory Pages/Sec**—Should be in the range of 0–20 pages per second.
- **Memory Available Bytes**—Needs to be at least 4MB.
- **Memory Committed Bytes**—Microsoft recommends committing no more than 75% of the physical memory on the server.

- **% Processor Time**—Should be less than 75%.
- **System Processor Queue Length**—Should not exceed a count of 2.
- **Disk Queue Length**—Should also be 2 or less.
- **Active Server Pages Requests Queued**—Should be 0, indicating that no ASP request should be queued.

This is not the entire list of available counters that you can use with IIS, but it presents a good starting point for looking at your server's performance. For more information and to see what other counters are available, see the documentation for Performance Monitor.

Event Viewer is another tool that can help you to monitor your Web server as well. Although Event Viewer is designed to log errors and events from the applications, the system, and the security aspects of the server, you can view the logs to see whether any trends are building on the application side. Error messages regarding applications not responding or running can show a reason other than a bottleneck for poor server performance.

Task Manager is a great tool that comes with Windows 2000. You can use Task Manager to check which resources each process running on the computer is using. Figure 11.1 shows the Task Manager window.

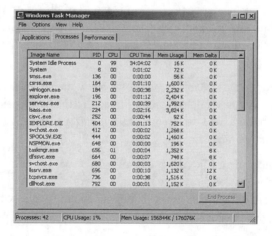

FIGURE 11.1

The Windows Task Manager is a great tool for monitoring system resources for each running process.

The Task Manager's Processes tab has six columns of information. The first five are displayed by default, but I have added one column, Memory Usage Delta, that is beneficial in determining whether you have misbehaving applications The columns are

- **Image Name**—This column lists the processes that are running on the computer at the time. The process name is usually the actual .exe filename such as IEXPLORE.EXE for Internet Explorer.
- **PID**—Windows NT and 2000 have a Process ID (PID) like that in UNIX and Linux. The PID is used internally by the OS to keep track of the application or process as it is running. This PID will not be the same if the application is stopped and restarted.
- **CPU**—This column tells you how much CPU time the process is utilizing. If you have a process that is using 85% or more, either you have a misbehaving application or the processor needs to be upgraded.
- **CPU Time**—This is the total CPU time that the process has taken since it was started. The System Idle Process normally has the highest count here.
- **Mem Usage**—This is the total number of pages currently in memory for the process.
- **Mem Delta**—This is actually the change in memory usage since the last update that the process is using. This figure can go up and down.

One of the reasons why I always add the Mem Delta column to my Task Manager is that it is a great way to determine if you have an application with a memory leak. A memory leak occurs when an application requests memory but doesn't release it back to the operating system when it is finished. This is more common in the world of object-oriented programming, wherein a programmer might forget to release an object after he is finished with it in code. The Mem Delta counter will continue to rise, and the application will continue to use memory until there is no more left.

To add extra columns to the Task Manager, select the View menu, then Select Columns. You will be given a dialog box with available columns to add to the processes view. Select the Memory Usage Delta option to add the Mem Delta column. Clearing a check box on the dialog will remove the selected columns.

Network Monitor monitors the traffic on the network. This tool can provide you with detailed information about the data packets traveling on your network. You can set up a capture filter to look for specific information, and you can configure a capture trigger with the capability to run an application when a specific event happens on the network.

Disk Optimization is not really a tool, but it can help minimize server bottlenecks on systems that are not appropriately equipped with the correct hardware and software for data storage and retrieval. A hard disk drive must deal with *latency*, that is, the time the drive takes to locate data before it can be retrieved. In newer hard drives with faster drive motors, this latency time period is shrinking.

There is one disk optimization you can perform that will serve as a double bonus. If you have at least three physical disks in the server, and they each have the same amount of space available, consider using a stripe set with parity. This disk configuration gives you a faster read performance and offers data redundancy. If one drive fails, you can rebuild the data from the parity information on the remaining two disks when a third disk is replaced. This option is not the most efficient in disk space because it requires one complete disk to deal with the parity information.

Stripe sets with parity are known as software RAID level 5. Microsoft implemented this RAID level in Windows NT and it has carried over to Windows 2000.

Essentially, striping with parity will make use of a minimum of three disks to provide its fault tolerance. This is accomplished by storing the data on two disks and performing a mathematical algorithm to determine parity information. This parity information is then stored on the third disk. The sole purpose of this parity information is for the purposes of reconstructing the data should one of the disks fail.

To set up RAID 5 on your server, ensure that you have four hard disks installed. The reason that you need four is because the system and boot partitions cannot be a part of the stripe set with parity.

Go into Control Panel and then choose Administrative Tools. Double click Computer Management. In the Tree pane, select the Disk Management option under the Storage heading.

Ensure that the three disks to be used are partitioned and formatted with the NTFS file system. Select the unpartitioned space on the first drive and click the right mouse button. Select the Create Volume menu option and choose Next in the Create Volume Wizard welcome screen. Choose Raid-5 Volume and follow the instructions provided with the wizard.

If you do not need the fault tolerance provided with striping with parity, you can implement a plain stripe set. This scenario divides the data up into the same size chunks on the disk as striping with parity does, but its performance is faster. A plain stripe set doesn't have the overhead of calculating the parity information.

TIP

If you want the fault tolerance and performance both, look at implementing a hardware fault tolerance solution such as hardware RAID devices. These hardware disk controllers perform the necessary parity calculations on board, leaving the CPU to its own tasks.

These are just some of the ways in which you can tweak a little better performance from your Web server to maybe gain a competitive edge over your competition. Well, these optimizations aren't exactly going to catapult your Web server into the Guinness Book of Records for the fastest Web server ever, but they can help you to eke that last little bit of performance from your hardware investment.

Memory Management

Aside from the CPU, memory in a computer is one of the biggest factors that can affect system performance. The old adage was that the more RAM you had, the faster the performance of the computer. On Windows NT 4.0 this was true until you reached the 128MB mark. Any more RAM added after that amount did not have the same effect on the performance increase, so there was no immediate return on investment. This issue has been addressed with Windows 2000, which uses all the memory available and will give you performance increases as RAM is increased.

When we deal with RAM usage on a server, there are several factors to take into consideration. First, if you do not have a large quantity of RAM installed on the server, Windows will use the swap space on the hard drive. This can cause a performance penalty on two sides: Excessive swapping reduces application performance and also interferes with disk reads and writes for data.

Another reason to have as much RAM as possible is that IIS and Windows 2000 will use it for caching. RAM is much faster than any hard disk, so it makes sense to store frequently requested files in cache rather than on the hard drive because it speeds up access. This cache is actually the RAM on the computer and not the cache Ram that sits between the CPU and memory. IIS will store a file handle in cache, and Windows 2000 will store the file itself in the cache.

One way to optimize the RAM you do have is to configure Windows 2000 as an application server, rather than as a file server. Although, theoretically, you are serving up files by using the application server setting, you are telling Windows 2000 to configure the RAM usage as if you were serving up applications to a local network. In effect, if you are using ASP or CGI scripts and applications, you are running an application server. To configure Windows 2000 as an application server, follow this procedure:

1. Click the Start button and choose Settings, Network and Dial-up Connections.

2. Right-click the Local Network icon and choose Properties to open the Properties sheet, as displayed in Figure 11.2.

3. Double-click the File and Printer Sharing icon to open the File and Printer Sharing for Microsoft Networks Properties dialog box.

4. Select the Maximize data throughput for network applications option and click the OK button to close the dialog box.

5. Click OK on the Local Area Network Properties dialog box to close it and apply the changes.

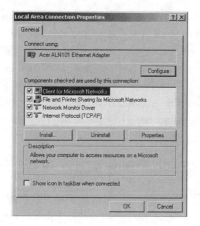

FIGURE 11.2

The Local Area Network Properties dialog box uses the File and Printer Sharing option to set the memory optimizations.

If you want to monitor your memory performance, you can do so by using the memory counters in Performance Monitor. There are counters available for the cache. You can implement these counters within Performance Monitor as well. The cache monitors are

- **File Cache Flushes**—This counter measures the number of file cache flushes that have taken place since the server was started.
- **File Cache Hits**—The total number of successful lookups in the cache.
- **File Cache Hits %**—This value indicates a ratio that measures the number of hits based on the number of requests.
- **File Cache Misses**—This is the total number of unsuccessful lookups in the cache.

This is not an exhaustive list of the available counters for the IIS memory objects. There are other counters that deal with Binary Large Object (BLOB) Cache counters as well as URI cache counters.

To access these counters, you need to have Performance Monitor up and running and choose the Add button on the button bar, indicated by a + sign. From the drop-down list of Performance Objects, select the Internet Information Services Global entry to expose the available counters.

NOTE

Don't confuse the cache counters available here with the cache counters that are available as a part of the memory object in Performance Monitor.

So how does this information help you to optimize the server's performance? Basically, you can determine whether you have enough RAM on the server by monitoring the successful and failed cache hits. If the number of failed hits is high, that is an indication that IIS has to go to the disk for the requested files instead of having them available in the cache. You can verify this by also including a % Disk Time counter in the same graph. If this counter shows a high value as well, that is a very good indicator that you need more RAM. If your server cannot accommodate more RAM, you might need to look at upgrading the server mainboard or perhaps getting into a clustering solution.

One other method to improve performance on the memory side is *traffic estimating*. In this procedure, you provide IIS with an estimate of the expected server traffic, and IIS adjusts its memory usage accordingly. If you set the number just slightly higher than the estimated or actual figure, you will find an increased performance. If you set this value too high, however, you will end up wasting memory resources that could be used elsewhere on the server. Even though you are running a Web site on the server, you might still be running other applications, and Windows 2000 itself needs quite a few services running in the background in order to perform its operating system functions.

So, how do we get this estimate? One of the best ways is to not really guess at the figure but to use Performance Monitor to track the Total Connection Requests and Current Connections counters. These counters can be found in the Web Service object in the Performance Monitor. Use the log file to collect approximately one full week's worth of data, including weekends. Use this number as your base.

In order to set the number of daily connections for the Web server, open the Properties sheet for the Web site and select the Performance tab sheet. In Figure 11.3, you will notice a slider bar in the Performance Tuning section. The bar has three indicator marks: Fewer than 10,000, Fewer than 100,000, and More than 100,000. Move the slider to indicate the number of connection attempts that you determined from the log files.

While trying to set this slider bar, you will notice that it doesn't really work like a normal slider; you cannot select any position in between two of the three indicator marks. You can only select one of the entered values. In a sense, this can throw my previous statement about setting the value "slightly higher" than your estimate. Just simply use the next highest setting.

Before we leave the section on memory I must reiterate—you should place as much RAM in your Web server as you can afford, especially if you are running scripts and applications on the server. The investment is worth it in the long run and can offer a short payback period.

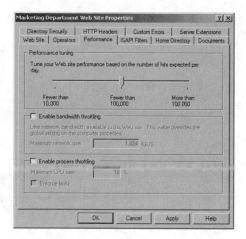

FIGURE 11.3
The Performance Tab indicating the performance tuning slider bar.

Processor Utilization

In discussing any performance issue related to the server, you have to take the CPU into consideration. After all, it is responsible for processing the instructions that serve up the Web pages and run the applications. Obviously, we do not want to have a bottleneck at the processor.

One of the ways that you can determine whether the CPU is the bottleneck is to add some CPU counters to the Performance Monitor chart and see where usage occurs. The main counter that you want to add is the % Processor Time. I also recommend the Interrupts/sec counter so that you can track excessive use on the CPU. Keep in mind, however, that high interrupts per second might not be a result of applications tying up the CPU cycles. You might have a bad Network Interface Card (NIC), or another I/O device in the computer that is misbehaving and causing frequent interrupt requests.

I mention this is because I had a NIC that was doing this, and it took awhile before I found out what it was. The original issue with the computer was that it was extremely slow. I used Performance Monitor to see where the high utilization was occurring. I actually added the Interrupts/sec counter by mistake, but it's a good thing that I did.

Figure 11.4 shows the Performance Monitor running on `Celeron` with the two counters added and graphed. Unfortunately, the screen shots are in gray scale, so you will have to trust me when I say that the highest peaks are the % Processor Time and the lower scale, barely visible, is the Interrupts/sec. As you can see from the figure, I have replaced the bad NIC.

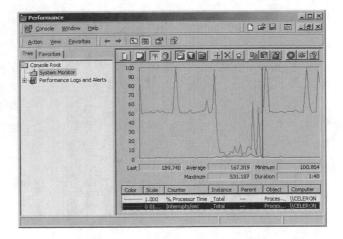

FIGURE 11.4
The Performance Monitor shows some high peaks of usage on the % Processor Time counter.

The peaks you see in Figure 11.4 do not indicate that my CPU is creating a bottleneck because they only last for a brief moment. The CPU should be replaced if this value remains at or above the 80% mark. If the Interrupts/sec counter value is also high, don't replace the CPU until you verify that all I/O cards are working okay.

What are some of your options if you find that CPU utilization is high? Well, you might not have to replace the CPU. This can be a good thing, especially if you just convinced Accounting's gurus to spend the money on the new Web server anyway. They won't be too impressed if you come looking for more money to replace the CPU in the new server, not to mention the fact that their confidence, and the boss's confidence, in your abilities might drop off.

If you have the option, you can split the Web site or sites over more than one server and use replication to decrease the load on one server.

If you have the option, you can add additional processors to the server. Windows 2000 Server will support 8 processors in the same box. Windows 2000 Data Center Server, not available at the time of this writing, will support 32 processors. You likely will not be running a Web site on Data Center anyway.

Another option that doesn't require a hardware upgrade is to move any processor-intensive applications to another server. You could apply this strategy if, for example, you are using a Web site that makes use of ASP and a database such as SQL Server. It would make more sense to move the database onto another server. This will place the processor demands on a server other than the Web server.

IIS 5.0 does offer one other advantage, and that is that you can make use of processor throttling. By implementing processor throttling, you can effectively limit the amount of time that the CPU will spend processing out-of-process applications. One scenario that could make use of this feature is a hosting service that is actually hosting multiple Web sites on the same server. You can use this feature to prevent a site that contains many out-of-process applications or CGI scripts from hogging the CPU resources and causing the other sites to suffer as a result.

This throttling can be applied to individual Web sites so you can set up what are known as *restriction levels*. Using this feature, you can have IIS log an event when a site goes over its restricted amount of CPU time during a specified interval. If this happens, consequences will occur based on the amount of overrun. The three levels of consequence are

Level 1—This level simply writes an event to the Windows 2000 event log.

Level 2—For this level to be reached, the CPU time must exceed 150% of the limit. An event is written to the Event Log, and all the out-of-process applications will have their CPU priority set to idle.

Level 3—When the CPU time exceeds the 200% limit, an event gets written as before, but, this time, all out-of-process applications are stopped on that Web site.

All process accounting is reset after 24 hours of operation. An administrator can override this by simply stopping and restarting the Web site. Web site operators do not have control over this setting.

> **TIP**
>
> If your site makes use of CGI applications and you are going to use processor throttling, you should look at lowering the timeout value on your CGI applications. In the event that a CGI application fails, the thread is not released until the timeout has expired. This will count towards the time restriction.

Let's show you how to set up processor throttling now. First, open the Properties dialog box for the Web site that you want to throttle processor use on. When you have the Properties dialog box open, select the Performance tab sheet. Figure 11.5 shows the Performance tab on the Properties for GK Computer Consulting's Web site on my server.

Select the Enable process throttling check box at the bottom of the tab sheet. Then enter a percentage value in the Maximum CPU Use box to limit the processor usage. Check Enforce Limits to tell IIS to enable the Level 2 and Level 3 enforcements.

So far we have discussed performance from a memory, disk, and CPU viewpoint. There is one other issue that plays a major role in the performance of your Web site, both real and perceived. That is the network, covered in the next section.

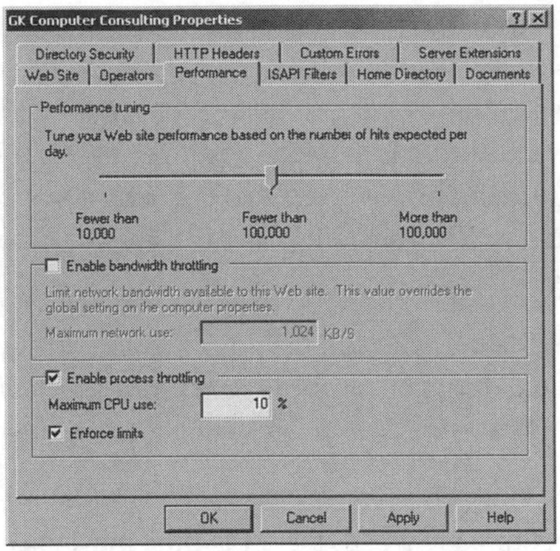

FIGURE 11.5

The Performance tab sheet enables you to set and enforce processor throttling on individual Web sites.

Network Capacity

As we all know, network capacity can have an adverse effect on a server's performance in relation to the transfer of data. A Web server basically just transfers data across the network media. This can be an intranet or the Internet. Either way, you can have the fastest CPU made and the most RAM ever configured in one server, and it still won't matter if your network bandwidth or NIC can't get that data out of the computer fast enough.

Sometimes, you might have all the bandwidth you need, or even the maximum available to you, and still run into problems with data choking up or not getting out. This can get to be a large problem for a Web server because it must run on the TCP/IP protocol.

TCP/IP is not the problem. The point I am trying to make is that by its nature, TCP/IP is a connection-oriented protocol and is designed for reliable delivery. This means that it has a lot of overhead in ensuring that the data that was transmitted actually made it to its destination and arrived without modification. If it doesn't, TCP/IP will resend the message. This can be a great bandwidth hog so you want to keep the retransmissions of data to a minimum.

If you have a Web site on the server that is using up most of the bandwidth, other sites cannot get their data out on the wire. You might need to look at bandwidth throttling.

Bandwidth throttling only throttles static HTML pages. You can set it on the computer level and on the individual Web site level. Web site level settings will override computer-wide settings.

To determine whether you have a network bandwidth problem, you need to use Performance Monitor. Figure 11.6 shows the Performance Monitor screen again with some network-specific counters added this time.

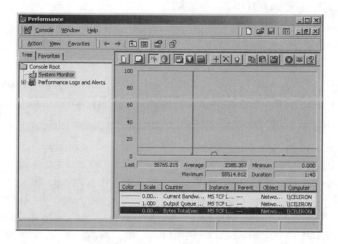

FIGURE 11.6

The Performance Monitor screen with network-specific counters added.

Once again, it is much easier to read in color. The top line indicates the current bandwidth. As you can see, the value is approximately 10, which indicates that my NIC is a 10Mbps network card. This is the total bandwidth that is available to my network connection.

The next highest counter that you can see with a few little peaks is the Bytes Total/sec. This value indicates the rate at which bytes are sent and received on the interface. Bearing in mind that there are 8 bits in one byte, you can do some math here to see how well your bandwidth is being used.

The last counter that I have added does not show a very high value. As a matter of fact, the counter hasn't moved, which is perfect. It is what you would like to see ideally. This counter measures the length of the output packet queue in packets. It should never exceed 2. If it does, it is an indication that your data is being held up on the server instead of being sent over the wire. This could be a slow NIC, that is to say, you might need to upgrade that 10Mbps NIC to a 100Mbps or even a Gigabit Ethernet. It could also mean that your connection downstream, at the ISP maybe, is causing a bottleneck.

One way to help reduce the use of the network connection is to restrict the amount of simultaneous connections allowed to a Web site. This can help to free up resources for other services that are using the same connection. A good example here is if your Web server is also your email server running Microsoft Exchange Server. If your Web site is using the bandwidth that is available on the NIC, Exchange will not be able to send email using the Internet Mail Connector or mail delivery will be delayed.

Choosing Connections

One of the questions facing you as a Web administrator is, what speed should you use for the Internet connection? Do you need a T1, a T3? Will a leased 56K do, or would you be better off with a fractional T1? The question of speed can be answered mathematically.

First, determine the average size of the files that are on your Web server and the amount of time it will take to send those files over the Internet or network. Then, determine the estimated number of users that will connect to the site.

To figure out the file's size, use this procedure. To determine the bits per page, multiply 66 by 80 and multiply that number by 8. These numbers represent 80 characters per column, 66 lines per page, and 8 bits per character. This will equal 42,240 bits per page. Next, you need to multiply the 42,240 by 1.5 to arrive at the figure of 63,360 bits per page. The 1.5 multiplier is used because it takes 4 bits of overhead to transmit every 8 bits of data. Note that these numbers are for text only pages and do not take into consideration any graphics. To determine the time it will take a graphic to download, I like to use Microsoft FrontPage. When you insert a graphic into a page, it will tell you the estimated download time in the status bar at the bottom of the FrontPage editor window. The time is based on a 28.8Kbps speed.

Now, you can divide the connection speed that you intend to use by the estimated file size. This would yield approximately 24 pages per second on a T1 line.

You can also use another calculation to determine the amount of hits or connections that your line speed will support.

We will use the T1 line speed as the factor here. T1 lines can transmit at 1.54Mbps, so take that number and divide it by the previously determined 12 bits per byte (8 bits/byte + 4 bits overhead). This value will equal 125KB per second.

Now, there are 86,400 seconds in a day. Multiply that by the 125KB/sec calculated previously and to come up with 10,800,000KB per day. Put that figure into Gigabytes by dividing it by 1,048,576. This will yield 10.3GB per day.

Now, if you take your average page size, say 20K for easy figuring, you can divide the 10,777,994KB/day value by 20 to come up with 538,899.7 hits per day.

Table 11.1 shows the simultaneous connections supported by the more popular connection types.

TABLE 11.1   Simultaneous Connections

Connection	Users Supported
56K Frame Relay	10–20
ISDN	10–50
T1	100–500
T3	5000 or more

Connection Performance Calculation

The online help file for IIS contains a great little tool that can help you to calculate the performance of your connections based on the connection type, the page size in KB, and the expected or accepted page load time.

You can find this tool by opening your Web browser and typing `http://localhost/iishelp` in the address bar of the browser.

Expand the Administration, Server Administration, Performance Tuning, and Network Capacity headings. Select the Calculating Connection Performance entry.

Bandwidth Throttling

Throttling bandwidth can be used to help other network services running on the same computer get a piece of the network bandwidth. A fair number of companies use the same Internet-connected server as a Web server, a mail server and sometimes as a news server. When you have all these services running on the same computer, they must use the same network connection to the Internet in order to transfer data.

If you have more than one Web site, you can also throttle bandwidth based on an individual Web site. In this way, as we mentioned previously, you can prevent a Web site from taking all of the available bandwidth at the expense of the other sites of services running on the server.

First, we will look at throttling the use of bandwidth by IIS itself. This will help to free up more bandwidth for other services, as mentioned at the start of this section.

Open the Internet Services Manager. Select the Computer icon in the Tree pane and then right-click it to open the Properties dialog box for IIS on that server. Figure 11.7 shows the Properties dialog box for my server.

You can set the maximum kilobits per second that IIS will use for all its Web and FTP sites. This value applies to IIS as a whole. The default value is 1,024Kbps.

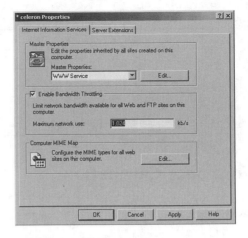

FIGURE 11.7
The celeron *Properties dialog box shows the Enable Bandwidth Throttling value set.*

You can also set up throttling based on individual Web sites by opening a Web site's Properties dialog box and selecting the Performance tab, as displayed in Figure 11.8.

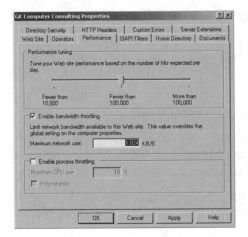

FIGURE 11.8
The Web Site Properties dialog box with the Performance tab selected for bandwidth throttling.

You can check the Enable Bandwidth Throttling option box and enter a value as you did in the previous procedure.

NOTE

Text in this dialog box, explains that when you set a value here, this setting will override the settings that were made in the IIS performance for the server.

Connection Limiting and Timeouts

We have talked about using bandwidth throttling as a way to limit a Web site or the IIS service itself from using all available network bandwidth. There is another limitation that you can apply to the Web sites to free up some more bandwidth for the other services.

IIS offers you the ability to limit connections to the Web site as well. By limiting connections, you are telling IIS to allow only so many simultaneous users to be connected to the Web or FTP site. This can reserve connection bandwidth by reducing the amount of traffic over the connection.

Most of you have likely run across a situation in which you tried to connect to an FTP server and were refused with the message that the server had reached its maximum allowable connections. This is the same idea.

The recommended approach to determine whether you need to enforce connection limits is to use the Performance Monitor program to monitor the current, maximum, and total connections' counters. If you log the counters on the Web and FTP services over several days, you should be able to see an average scope of operation on which you can base your decisions.

To limit connections on the server, open the Web or FTP site Properties dialog box. Choose the Web Site or FTP Site tab sheet and select the Limited to: option under the Connection section. You can then enter a value for the maximum simultaneous connections allowed. The default for the Web sites is 1000 connections, whereas the FTP site uses 100,000 connections.

You can also enter a connection timeout value here as well. This option is used to disconnect idle connections to free up the resources and bandwidth taken by those connections. This value can prove to be useful if you are limiting connections on the site because an idle or broken connection takes an available connection away from the rest of the users.

HTTP Keep-Alives

When a browser makes a request for a Web page from your server, it actually makes numerous requests each time it needs information. If your page contains graphics, a Web browser can make a request for the text portion of the page, followed by a request for the graphics. Obviously, this can slow down your connections and performance.

Browsers also like to keep the connection open across multiple requests. IIS enables HTTP Keep-Alives by default as a way for the server to maintain the same connection for the Web browser. This prevents the multiple connections for each request.

To enable the HTTP Keep-Alives on your server, open the Properties dialog box for the Web site on which you want to enable the Keep-Alives and choose the Web site tab sheet (see Figure 11.9).

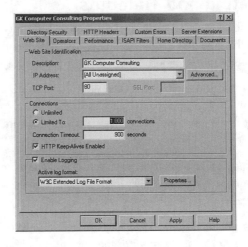

FIGURE 11.9
The HTTP Keep-Alives option is enabled by default with IIS 5.0.

In the Connections section, you can see that the HTTP Keep-Alives option is selected. You can clear this option, but it will have serious performance impacts on your server.

HTTP Compression

IIS 5.0 can support the compression of your HTTP traffic to reduce download time to browsers that support it. This feature can be a double-edged sword so you need to weigh your options in implementing it.

If you decide to use compression, you need to understand that in order to perform the compression, IIS will take up some CPU resources. This can affect the performance of the server as a whole and can eliminate any benefit that was gained from the compression.

A good idea is to monitor the CPU utilization before and after you implement compression. Of course, if your CPU is at or above the 80% mark already, then compression should not be considered.

HTTP compression is set on the IIS server as a whole. Therefore to enable it, we need to open the Properties dialog box for the IIS server itself.

Select the computer icon in the Tree pane of Internet Services Manager and choose Properties from the Action menu. This will display the Properties dialog box for your IIS server, as shown in Figure 11.10.

FIGURE 11.10

The celeron *Properties dialog box enables the setting of Properties that pertain to the entire IIS server.*

Select the WWW Service from Master Properties drop-down list. Click the Edit button to open the WWW Master Properties dialog box for the server, as shown in Figure 11.11. Select the Service tab.

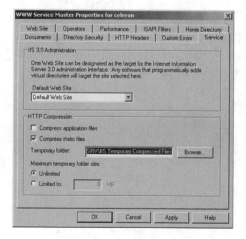

FIGURE 11.11

The WWW ServiceMaster Properties dialog box with the Service Tab selected to show the available HTTP Compression options.

You have the option of compressing static HTML files as well as applications running on the Web site. Select one or both of the options.

You can enter a location for the temporary folder that will hold the compressed files. You can enter a full pathname here or use the Browse button to locate a folder on your server's hard disk.

At the bottom of the Compression section, you can also limit the folder size. This is a good idea to help reduce the chance of filling the hard drive with the compressed files. It also reduces the amount of storage space needed for your HTTP files as well as other files required by the various services you have installed on the server.

> **NOTE**
>
> The temporary directory for the compressed files must reside on the local hard drive, and that hard drive must be formatted with the NTFS file system.

Summary

Performance tuning is an ongoing function for your IIS server. Usage changes, and hardware gets added to the server, which affects the performance.

By using the monitoring tools and procedures that IIS and Windows 2000 provide, you can determine the best routes to take to increase server performance not only in serving Web pages and FTP files, but also in the processing of the applications running on the server.

If performance is a critical issue for your Web server, make sure that you do not run any other services such as mail servers on the same computer. This will allow IIS to make the most efficient use of the resources available on the server.

Replication and Clustering

IN THIS CHAPTER

In this chapter, we will go over some of the more common ways to provide a highly scalable architecture that offers fault tolerance and a means to balance your workload across all your servers. This chapter will teach you how to install, configure, and maintain some of the software necessary for a High Availability Architecture.

This chapter will address

- The clustering of Internet Information Server 5.0
- Load balancing using Network Load Balancing
- The replication of content across the cluster
- Replication technologies, such as Distributed File System (DFS), Site Server's Content Replication Component, Robocopy.exe, and IISsync.exe

With the Windows 2000 Server feature, Network Load Balancing (NLB), you can create an architecture that lets you sleep at night. NLB makes your Web site, FTP site, or another application available when your clients need it. NLB also automatically removes a host from the cluster in the event of a failure. Network Load Balancing Service (NLBS) gives you the freedom to scale your cluster and allows you to expand your cluster up to 32 servers.

The most important piece of the Network Load Balancing utility is the Virtual Network Interface Card (VNIC). This is the cornerstone of the Network Load Balancing Service; it is what enables NLB to have up to 32 hosts in a cluster. The VNIC will be discussed in detail later on in the chapter.

Within a clustered system, you need to have synchronicity of content, which leads us to our next topic of discussion—replication among the hosts in the cluster. Clustering is an undisputed necessity, but, without identical content across all the members, the cluster is disparate. Microsoft offers several technologies that will automatically ensure the continuity of content across your cluster. Later in this chapter, I will go over general configuration and implementation of some of these products and the value that each of these utilities can add to your cluster.

Clustering of a Network Application

One of a network administrator's major concerns, when he deploys an application, is the question of availability. As an administrator, you want to ensure that the solution you are putting on the network is always there—your clients need it. This concern inspired the concept of clustering a group of similar computers to do the work of one.

Robert Metcalfe, the inventor of Ethernet, states in the much quoted Metcalfe's Law, "Connect any number, *n,* of machines—computers, phones, or even cars—and you get *n* squared potential value. Think of phones without networks or cars without roads. Conversely, imagine the benefits of linking up tens of millions of computers and sense the exponential power of the telecosm." This is clustering, bringing together multiple computers to increase their potential for reliability, performance, and scalability.

Clustering servers creates a "virtual" server—several servers seen as one *logical* server—to serve a load intensive application, enable fault tolerance, or perform a mission-critical task.

One example of a clustered network application would be four individual servers, each running an instance of Internet Information Server (IIS) and serving a hospital's intranet Web page. The page provides vital patient information, such as records of allergies and treatments. Obviously, this page would need to be available 24x7; there is no room for downtime in this scenario. If this Web site were run on just one machine, there would be no room for maintenance or failure. If you brought that machine down, the doctors would have no access to the patient information, and there could be serious ramifications. However, with a clustered solution, should one of the machines need to be taken offline to perform maintenance, then the other three instances of IIS are still running on the other servers and can provide the application to its clients. Microsoft's Network Load Balancing Service provides this kind of clustering functionality. It gives you the ability to bring multiple computers, or *hosts*, together to form a cluster of application servers. When brought together, the aggregate of the many is a powerful solution.

> **NOTE**
>
> Microsoft's Network Load Balancing Service can cluster up to 32 hosts. This makes NLBS a better solution for scenarios in which you want to have many hosts, such as for Web Servers or FTP servers. Other clustering solutions can't handle that many hosts. For example, the Microsoft Cluster Server (MSCS), designed for applications like Microsoft SQL Server, has a limitation of only two hosts in a cluster.

NLBS provides a method of load-balancing through the use of, Virtual Network Interface Cards (VNICs) and, Virtual IP addresses (VIPs). This chapter will go into depth on the topics of Virtual NIC's and Virtual IP addresses.

Why Should You Cluster Your Network Application?

Clustering a network application lets you provide a method of scalability. The ability to add more servers or hosts to the cluster, or *scale up*, is paramount in a clustered environment. If you are hosting an Internet Web site on one server and you get 2,000 hits per day, you might be safe. If you are hosting an Internet Web site that gets 2,000 hits on Monday, but on Tuesday you are expecting 20,000 hits, you might not be safe. Having implemented a cluster, you have the power to add more hosts to your cluster and give your Internet Web site the extra boost that it will need to handle 20,000 hits.

Another reason to cluster your application is to balance the workload among all your hosts. By balancing the load, you are regulating the number of requests that are directed to each host. Host A is not resting on its laurels while Host B is close to its breaking point from overload.

NLB load-balances requests received for individual TCP/IP services across the cluster and enables a proportional balancing of the TCP/IP requests that are serviced. This means that you can assign a certain percentage of traffic to each host in the cluster, depending on the amount of traffic that each host can handle. With Network Load Balancing, you can automatically redistribute the network load when the cluster set changes. If you add or remove a host, the cluster will automatically sense this and rebalance the load within 10 seconds.

When you cluster an application, one of the biggest tangible results that your clients can see is an increase in an application's speed. When you cluster, you have multiple computers all working together to handle a task. This means that the application's execution queue—the string of requests that are waiting to be handled—is much shorter. Client's requests are responded to faster. It's just like waiting in line at the supermarket—the more checkout personnel there are, the less time you spend waiting in line. And, the more servers you have performing a task, the faster it will get done.

NLB supports up to 32 servers in a single cluster. This means that you can multiply your computing power by 32. You can launch an application and go with the theory of many hosts making the workload light.

NLBS can provide high availability for your application. In the event of a disaster, whether it be hardware or software failure, if your network application is not clustered, you will no longer have a network application. Hopefully, it will never happen, but if one or more hosts in a cluster fail, your architecture will be able to continue serving that application. A *single point of failure* (SPOF) is any one malfunctioning point in your network, application, server, or architecture that will stop the servicing of client requests. Having only one server hosting an application is considered an SPOF. Clustering will help reduce the number of SPOFs in your architecture. NLBS automatically detects and recovers from a failed or offline computer, thus providing automatic fault tolerance. Servers in your cluster can be taken offline for preventive maintenance without disturbing cluster operations. Hence, the show goes on, even when you bring down three of your four servers for maintenance.

A cluster requires little to no human intervention after it is configured and operational. To the network administrator, this is a dream come true—the cluster can dynamically remove hosts from, and add hosts to, itself without the administrator performing complex tasks.

When you cluster clients, you only need to provide one host name or IP address to access the application, while retaining individual names for each computer. NLB clients use one IP address to access the entire cluster. For example, if www.xyz.com resolves to 10.1.1.2, when a client makes a request to www.xyz.com, it can be served from any one of the servers that are in the cluster serving www.xyz.com. Figure 12.1 illustrates this cluster.

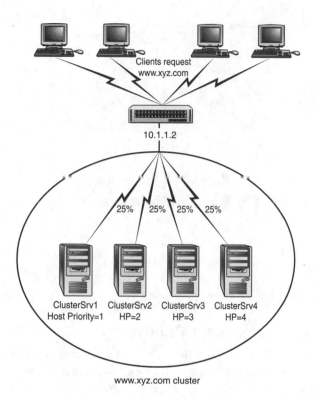

Clients request
www.xyz.com

10.1.1.2

25%   25%   25%   25%

ClusterSrv1   ClusterSrv2   ClusterSrv3   ClusterSrv4
Host Priority=1   HP=2   HP=3   HP=4

www.xyz.com cluster

FIGURE 12.1

Four cluster hosts serving up the Web site www.xyz.com.

www.xyz.com resolves to the VIP of 10.1.1.2, and each host in the cluster has its own unique Real IP address, such as 10.1.1.3, 10.1.1.4, and so on.

You might be wondering about application compatibility with clustering. Rest assured when setting up your cluster, server applications need not be modified to run in an NLB cluster. For example, if you are hosting an FTP site on one server, when you cluster, you won't need to make any changes to the application to accommodate clustering functionality.

Installing Network Load Balancing

Network Load Balancing comes preinstalled on all Windows 2000 Advanced Server installations. You must invoke NLBS to operate on your Windows 2000 Server. Here's how:

1. Click Start, point to Settings, and then click Network and Dial-up Connections.

2. Right-click the interface that should act as the virtual adapter, and then click Properties.

3. Click to select the Network Load Balancing check box, shown in Figure 12.2.

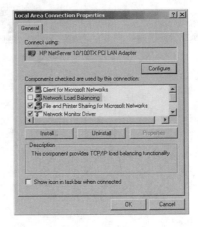

FIGURE 12.2
Installing NLB on your Windows 2000 Server.

Network Load Balancing is now instantiated on your server.

Configuring Network Load Balancing

To set up the base configurations, click the Network Load Balancing component, and then click Properties. Type your cluster-specific data on the Cluster Parameters tab (see Figure 12.3), the Host Parameters tab (see Figure 12.4), and the Port Rules tab (see Figure 12.5). For example, in the Primary IP Address box, type the IP address you want the cluster to load balance (also known as the *virtual IP address*, or VIP). To receive information about the data to be entered in any box, click the question mark button in the top-right corner of the window, and then click the appropriate field. When you are finished, click OK.

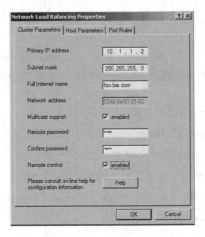

FIGURE 12.3
The Cluster Parameters tab for NLBS.

In the Cluster Parameters tab, you enter the Primary IP address, subnet mask of the cluster's VIP, and the remote password for cluster administration.

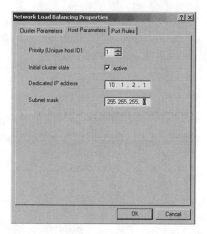

FIGURE 12.4
Host Parameters tab.

The Host Parameters tab is used for configuring the individual host's parameters, which define the host's unique IP address. The host uses the unique IP address for intracluster and LAN communications. The Priority ID is the priority number that the host holds in the cluster. If a host's Priority ID is 1, then that host holds the highest priority. If its Priority ID is 2, then it has the second highest priority, and so on.

Click Internet Protocol (TCP/IP), and then click Properties. Type the virtual IP address in the IP Address box by first clicking Use the following IP address. If the interface already has an IP address that differs from the virtual IP address, click Advanced. Then add the virtual IP address in the IP Addresses box on the IP Settings tab.

Setting Up the Port Rules

By default, all cluster network traffic is handled by the host with the highest host priority (lowest numeric value) among the current members of the cluster. This host handles all of the cluster network traffic. If the highest-priority host fails or goes offline, the host with the next highest priority will take over the traffic. This default behavior ensures that NLBS does not affect cluster network traffic for ports that you do not specifically manage with the WLBS load-balancing mechanisms. It also provides high availability in the handling of your cluster network traffic.

To maximize control of various types of TCP/IP traffic, you can configure how each port's cluster network traffic is handled. Figure 12.5 shows the three different types of filtering modes for which NLB can be configured: single host, multiple host, and disabled modes.

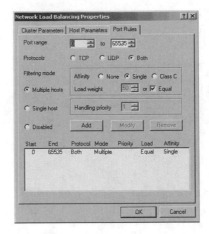

FIGURE 12.5

The Port Rules tab.

Use this tab for setting up port rules and the filtering mode that the host will operate in.

Single Host Filtering Mode

In the event that you have multiple servers in your cluster and you only want to provide a scenario for fault tolerance, you can implement single mode filtering. This mode directs all of the TCP/IP traffic to the host in the cluster with the highest priority. This will not load-balance your cluster because you are only directing traffic to the host with the highest priority. All others will remain idle, and no traffic will be directed to them. Single host mode will give you a method for fault tolerance only. In the event of a failure of the host with the highest priority, the host with the next highest priority will take over all the subsequent requests, as shown in Figure 12.6.

Note that there is no traffic being routed to the hosts with the lower host numbers. Only the host with the highest priority number will receive traffic in single host mode.

Multiple Host Filtering Mode

Multiple host mode is the mode that provides the most robustness; it enables load-balancing and fault tolerance within a cluster. This mode provides load-balancing by sending a TCP/IP request to a member of the cluster. If there is no response, then that member of the cluster is taken out of the cluster, and traffic is no longer directed to that server. By enabling you to set the load percentage among the servers in a cluster, you can direct traffic to the most appropriate member of the cluster. Refer to Figure 12.2 for an example of an even distribution of the load across an NLB cluster.

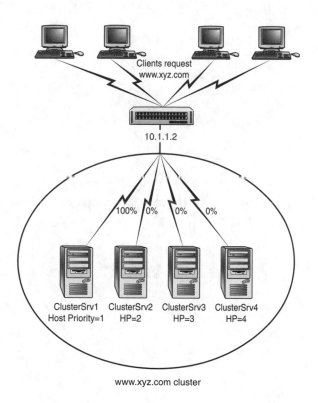

FIGURE 12.6

An example of a single host mode with multiple hosts and their corresponding Host Priorities.

For example, if your cluster was serving an application that was processor intensive and you were using the Multiple Host Mode of the NLB system, you could balance the load that the servers would experience, based upon the processor speed of the individual machine (50/50, 60/40, and so on). If one server was an 800Mhz Pentium III and a second server was a 133Mhz processor, you might want to implement a balance of 90/10 (refer to Figure 12.3). You can control the precise load-balancing behavior of this filtering mode by indicating that all hosts should maintain an equal load distribution or by setting the load percentage for each host. When you specify load percentages, NLB adds up the load percentages for all participating cluster hosts and directs the proportional amounts of work to each host. The total load percentage for the cluster need not add up to 100%. For example, if the cluster has Hosts A and B with load percentages of 30% and 60%, respectively, NLB will direct one-third (30/90) of the traffic to Host A and two-thirds (60/90) to Host B. Hosts with equal loads would service the same number of requests, as shown in Figure 12.7.

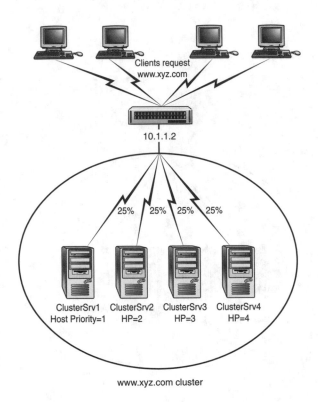

FIGURE 12.7

NLB hosts set with equal loads, so all servers are servicing the same number of requests.

The cluster load-balancing shown in Figure 12.8 will result in the hosts with the most processing power servicing the most requests.

The last configuration option for this mode is the affinity that you want the client to maintain with each host within the cluster. There are three options:

- **Single**—A client maintains affinity to the same host that it originally contacted.
- **None**—A client will have no affinity to any of the servers, therefore, it will be directed to the next available host in the cluster.
- **Class C**—In this mode, the same host in a cluster will service all requests that come from the same Class C IP range.

Using affinity will increase your ability to use client sessions for your session enabled applications.

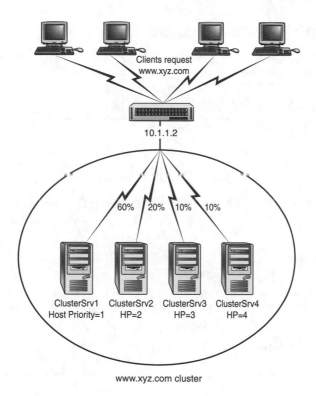

FIGURE 12.8

NLB hosts with the load set appropriately if you were to cluster a processing-intensive application on your network.

Disabled Filtering Mode

This mode blocks all traffic to a port to provide a firewall against unwanted network access to your cluster. You can specify that a filtering mode apply to a numerical range of ports, that is, 1–79 and 81–65,000, leaving only port 80 open for http traffic. You do this by defining a port rule with a set of configuration parameters that define the filtering mode. Each rule consists of the following configuration parameters:

- The TCP or UDP port range to which this rule should be applied
- The protocols to which this rule should apply, including TCP, UDP, or both
- The filtering mode that specifies how the cluster handles traffic described by the port range and protocols

Troubleshooting Network Load Balancing

Table 12.1 describes some of the problems that you might run into with Network Load Balancing and how to resolve them.

TABLE 12.1 Troubleshooting Network Load Balancing

Problem	Solution
Cannot ping virtual/dedicated IP address	Make sure that you have entered the IP address in the TCP/IP properties as well as the NLB configuration panel.
Cannot ping another host in the cluster	The problem can result from no intracluster communications. Make sure that the cluster is not configured for unicast mode.
Host cannot join cluster	Check the Virtual IP to make sure that it matches the cluster IP.
Host not responding to requests	Make sure that you have not set up a port rule to deny the port that the request runs on, that is, blocking http (port 80).
All traffic goes to one host	Check that all the hosts are configured multiple hosts. when you are configured for with the multiple host rule.

Summary

Clustering and load-balancing is a very large topic. This chapter has covered just a few of the technologies that Microsoft makes available. The most important point to remember from this lesson is that one server—no matter how much processing power you put into it, no matter how much RAM you install, no matter how much RAID you implement—is still just one server and will eventually fail. The presence of a single point of failure is never a good thing. Many hosts in a cluster allow for downtime from hardware or software failure, or for maintenance. Multiple hosts let you have the peace of mind to sleep at night. Load-balancing provides not only a way to prevent one server from being overworked, but also a means for increased performance. By spreading the workload across multiple hosts, your performance will increase because of the presence of many servers working together to achieve a common goal.

Replication

Replication is the process of copying data between one or more servers to achieve synchronicity of content. Whether it is on FTP servers, WWW servers, mail servers, or file servers, all the data that is being served needs to be the same in a cluster. If the data is disparate, the end users will get a different experience each time they visit your site. Additionally, the disparity could result in errors because of a service or action requiring the most up-to-date content available to that service.

In order to operate a Web Server farm that serves up the same set of data to each of its clients, you will need to introduce replication into the equation. This can be accomplished using a utility such as Microsoft Site Server 3.0's Content Replication component, IISsync.exe, Robocopy.exe, or Distributed File System. Each of these utilities has its own strengths and weaknesses. Your needs and special circumstances dictate the best utility for your network.

One of Windows 2000 Server's exciting new features is a utility called Distributed File System (DFS). Its dynamic replication and error-checking capabilities make it an attractive option to Win2k administrators. This portion of the chapter will expand more on DFS because it is a native utility of Windows 2000 Server.

Types of Replication Utilities

Everyone's network is different due to different requirements, topologies, geographic locations, and operating systems. This means that there is not just one correct tool for every network environment, each one requires a different kind of utility that can serve the individual needs of an administrator. Some administrators may prefer the Command Line Interface, some may prefer a very robust solution, some may even need to heavily script their replication. Microsoft offers up several solutions to the problem of replication within a cluster. The solutions include, but are not limited to, IISsync.exe, Site Server's Content Replication Component, Robocopy, and the Distributed File System. Let's take a look at some of the features and benefits of each of these solutions.

IISSync.exe

IISSync.exe, the Internet Information Server Synchronization utility, comes native with the installation of IIS. It can be found in the `%system root%\winnt\system32\inetsrv` directory. This tool works with IIS to provide a scriptable and scalable environment for serving up a scalable and fault-tolerant Web farm. IISsync.exe was not designed to replicate content, but its design does keep the replication of the metabase in mind. Replicating the metabase is an important feature within a cluster of servers in which the metabase changes often, and the changes need to be made across all servers.

The command for IISsync.exe is very simple. From the command line on the source server, or the server from which you want to replicate the metabase, type *iissync \\targetserver*, wherein *targetserver* is the NetBIOS name of the server to which you want to replicate the metabase.

Site Server's Content Replication Component

The second tool, the Content Replication Component of Site Server 3.0, does not come native with IIS. It is a part of the MS suite of services called Site Server. (The current version is available for evaluation download at `http://www.microsoft.com/siteserver/site/default.htm`.) The Content Replication Component is the most scriptable and robust tool that MS provides for replication throughout a server farm. This chapter will not delve too deeply into Site Server, because it is a broad subject range.

Robocopy.exe

Robocopy is a utility that comes with the Win2k Resource Kit. This command line utility is scheduled through the Task Scheduler feature of the Windows 2000 operating system. Robocopy.exe can recursively replicate all directories and files below it at scheduled intervals.

Distributed File System

Distributed File System (DFS) can be used in your cluster implementation to ensure that all the hosts in the cluster are serving identical data. DFS is automatically installed with Windows 2000 Server. It ensures that all data within a DFS root, a directory, or a share that contains data to be replicated with other DFS servers is synchronous. With DFS, an administrator can change one document or file within a DFS share and have it replicate to all other members of the DFS replication set.

Why Should You Replicate Data?

Continuity of content is paramount in a cluster and can be an administrative hassle. If you are administering a 32-host cluster wherein the content is changing daily, you need to ensure that there is no disparity between any of the servers. Handling a task like this can become an administrator's worst nightmare. You would have to hand-copy each changed file to the individual servers and check that you are copying the latest data. Performing a task like this lends itself to human error. If you copied the wrong file to a host that is in production, you could jeopardize the site's uptime and also jeopardize your company's name. With the use of an automated replication utility, the administrative tasks are reduced greatly, and content can be automatically deployed from a single point.

Setting Up a DFS Share for Replication

To use the Distributed File System, you need to use the DFS admin snap-in to the Microsoft Management Console. To get started with this user interface, do the following:

1. Click Start, point to Programs, point to Administrative Tools, and then click Distributed File System.

2. Right-click Distributed File System in the left pane, and click New Dfs Root. The Create New Dfs Root Wizard appears, and then click Next.

3. Make sure that Create a domain Dfs root is selected, and then click Next.

4. Select the host domain for the Dfs root and click Next.

5. Accept the name of the host server for the Dfs root. Click Next.

6. Choose the local share point to be used on the target to host the Dfs root, where you would have your replication content. If it is the first time that you are setting up a DFS share, you will need to create a share point. Click Create a new share and type the path to share as **d:\content** and the share name as an easily recognizable name. The snap-in lets you create both a new share point and a new directory, if they do not already exist.

7. Click Next. If the specified folder does not exist, you are asked if you want to create it. Click Yes to continue. Add a comment if you want to further describe this root. Click Next.

8. Click Finish to create the Dfs root. After the Create New Dfs Root wizard has finished, you are ready to administer your Dfs root.

You are now ready to start replication throughout your cluster. Using this tool will reduce your duties by making sure that all your content is spread across all the hosts in the cluster.

TIP

When you implement a replication scheme, be sure to replicate with caution. Use a test lab or a test directory that is filled with test content. I would not recommend testing with production content on production hosts. If the content replication is misconfigured, you run the risk of overwriting all your valuable production content. Create a directory such as **d:\test** and populate the directory with other directories that are similarly named, replicate the content of this directory to the identical directory on the target servers. When you feel confident using the replication utility on this test directory, you can implement your production replication.

Summary

When deploying identical servers to be hosts in a cluster, one of the most important considerations is the synchronicity of the content they are serving. In order to reduce the huge administrative task of ensuring that all data is the same across several hosts in a cluster, there are several products that automate this task. You choice of products depends on the nature of your cluster implementation. Setting up the replication in a test environment is very important to ensure that you do not replicate the wrong content into a production directory. Windows 2000 Server provides a very scalable and configurable utility, DFS, which will enable you to perform replication of content with multiple servers in a domain.

Administration Scripts

IN THIS CHAPTER

If you are coming from a UNIX/Linux environment or are a hard-core command-line guru, you will appreciate the administration scripts capabilities of IIS 5.0. You can use these scripts to automate some of your administrative tasks. You can make use of the scripts to create Web sites and the directories and applications within them.

Working with IIS Administration Scripts

You can run administration scripts by using `adsutil.vbs` or `adsutil.exe`. The two differ in the language that is used to work with them. `adsutil.vbs` uses VBScript files to run the scripts, whereas `adsutil.exe` offers you the ability to manipulate the metabase using the Active Directory Services Interface (ADSI) in the C/C++ programming language. It is also important to note that `adsutil.exe` is capable of accepting or reading commands from a file and `adsutil.vbs` is not.

If you are planning to use the VBScript Administration scripts, you should note that they are intended to be used with the `Cscript.exe` command-line scripting utility. Cscript will work best if it is registered. There are two methods for registering Cscript.

The first method is to issue the `adsutil.vbs` command all by itself at the command prompt. This will cause Windows 2000 to generate an error and state that `adsutil` will not work with Wscript. When you click OK, you are given another message box, as displayed in Figure 13.1, where you can choose to register `adsutil`.

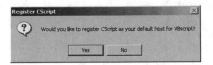

FIGURE 13.1

This dialog box asks if you want to register cscript *as your default host for VBScript applications.* adsutil *is a VBScript application.*

When you choose Yes, Windows 2000 will register `adsutil` and associate it as a vbs file with `cscript`. It will then inform you of the success or failure of the registration. You can now use it from the command line or in batch files.

The other method of registering `adsutil` is to use the Cscript.exe application through the command line. By issuing the command *cscript //H:cscript*, all on one line, you will register `cscript` as the default script host, as is indicated in Figure 13.2.

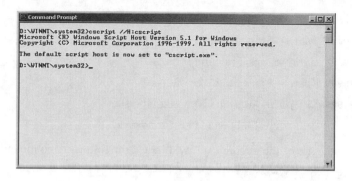

13

ADMINISTRATION SCRIPTS

FIGURE 13.2
The Command Prompt window shows the cscript *command issued and the response that* cscript *is now the default script host.*

Administration Script Utility (`adsutil`)

We have shown a small bit of the `adsutil` utility previously, but we will discuss it in a little more detail here. As we stated, it is an administration utility that makes use of VBScript and ADSI. It is recommended that you use `adsutil` with `cscript`.

`adsutil` has the following syntax:

`adsutil Command <path> [parameters]`

The commands are

- **GET_** *path*—Displays the chosen parameter.
- **SET_** *path value*—Assigns a new value.
- **ENUM_** *path[/P, /A]*—Enumerates all the parameters for the path with /P enumerating the paths without data and /A enumerating all the data that can be set on the node.
- **ENUM_ALL** *[/P, /A]*—Enumerates all parameters. The /P and /A options act in the same manner as for ENUM.
- **DELETE_** *path*—Deletes the path or parameter.
- **CREATE_** *path [keyType]*—Creates a new path and assigns to it the KeyType value.
- **APPCREATEINPROC_** *path*—Creates an in-process application.
- **APPCREATEOUTPROC_** *path*—Creates an out-of-process application.
- **APPDELETE_** *path*—Deletes an existing application.
- **APPUNLOAD_** *path*— Unloads the specified out-of-process application.
- **APPGETSTATUS_** *path*—Gets the status of the application.

- **FIND_** *path*—Finds out the path of where a parameter starts.
- **START_SERVER_** *path*—Starts the server if it is not running.
- **STOP_SERVER_** *path*—Stops a running server.
- **PAUSE_SERVER_** *path*—Pauses the Web site.
- **CONTINUE_SERVER_** *path*—Restarts a paused Web site.
- **HELP**—Displays a listing of all commands for *adsutil*.

As an example of the use of the *adsutil* utility, I issued the following command on my server:

Adsutil STOP_SERVER W3SVC/1

Figure 13.3 shows this in the command prompt window and a confirmation that indicates that the server was stopped.

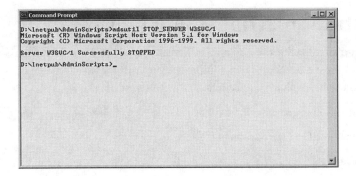

FIGURE 13.3
The Command Prompt window indicating the adsutil *command that was issued and the response from the server.*

> **NOTE**
>
> These commands do not stop the Windows 2000 server but merely the IIS portion of the server.

Display Administrative Node

This command is used to display the fields in an Administrative node in the tree. An example appears in Figure 13.4.

Syntax

dispnode -a ADSPath, -h

ADSPath is the full path to the node that you want to display.

-h displays help for the command.

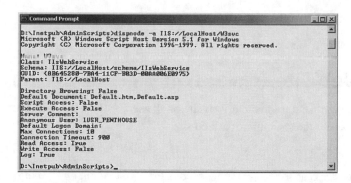

FIGURE 13.4

An example of the dispnode -a *command.*

Display Administrative Tree (`disptree`)

This command is used to display a tree of administration objects starting with the specified root. If you do not specify a root node, the default is IIS://Localhost.

Syntax

> *disptree -a ROOT, -n, -h*

-a ROOT is the full ADSI path to the root.

-n tells the command not to recurse into container objects.

-h displays help for the command.

Example

disptree -a IIS://Localhost/w3svc -n

Find Web Site (`findweb`)

This command finds the specified Web site on the specified computer.

Syntax

findweb [-c Computer] WEBSITE, -?

-c *Computer* indicates the computer to be searched. If none is specified, localhost will be used.

WEBSITE is the Web site to search. You can specify this value as the server number, server name, server domain name, or server IP address.

-? displays help.

Example

findweb -c celeron2 www.gkcomput.com

Create Web Site (mkw3site)

You can use this command to create a Web site on the server. This doesn't create any content for the site but merely the structure of a Web site.

Syntax

mkw3site -r *root directory*, -t *server comment*, -c *computer*, -o *port number*,
➥-i *IP address*, -a *Administrator*, -h *Host name*, -DontStart, -? *Help*

-r specifies the full path for the root directory.

-t enables you to enter a server comment that will appear in the Internet Services Manager.

-c is the name of the computer on which the site will be created. This is optional and if not specified, the default is localhost.

-o specifies the port number that you want the Web site to monitor for HTTP requests.

-i is the IP address of the server that the site will be assigned. This is also optional.

-a specifies an administrator that will be responsible for working with the site.

-h specifies the hostname to use for this site. Only use this option if you are using DNS for name resolution.

-DontStart tells IIS not to try to start the server after it has been created. You might need to make some changes before you actually bring the site online.

-? will display help for the command.

Example

mkw3site -r D:\InetPub\wwwroot\testweb -t TestSite -h www.newweb.com

Figure 13.5 shows the result of the command being run and how it has added the new Web site to MMC.

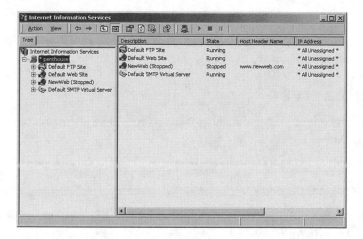

FIGURE 13.5
The MMC console now shows the new Web site that has been added as a result of the mkw3site *command.*

One of the best uses for this script is if you have a need to create more than one Web site structure on your server at a time. Perhaps you are the administrator of an ISP or Web hosting service that hosts multiple Web sites on one server. This script command can help you to create these site structures by using one batch file.

Create Virtual Web Directory (`mkwebdir`)

We have mentioned virtual directories before and that you can create them using the Internet Services Manager application in the MMC, but you can also create a virtual Web directory using the `mkwebdir` script command as well.

You will find this command useful for creating multiple virtual directories simultaneously when used in a batch file.

Syntax

```
mkwebdir -c computer name, -w website, -v name, path, -h help
```

-c specifies the computer name to create the virtual directory on. You can specify multiple computers by separating their names with commas. If no computer is specified, localhost is assumed.

-w specifies the Web site on which to create the virtual directory. Website can be the server number, server description, hostname, or IP address.

-v specifies the name and the path of the virtual directory to create. You can create multiple entries here as well by separating the entities with a comma.

-h is the now familiar option to receive help on the command.

13

ADMINISTRATION
SCRIPTS

Example

```
mkwebdir -c -w "Marketing Department Web Site" -v images, F:\Inetpub\
➥wwwroot\Marketing\images
```

Stop Web Server

This command can be used to stop a running Web server. It is an alternative to using the Internet Services Manager.

Syntax

```
stopweb -a server, -c computer, -v verbose, -? Help
```

-a indicates the number of the server to stop given as SERVERx. You can stop multiple servers by separating the entries with a comma.

-c indicates the computer. Multiple entries can be separated by commas.

-v (verbose mode) will cause the script engine to display comments as it completes the script.

-? accesses help for the command.

Example

```
stopweb -a 1
```

Figure 13.6 shows the Internet Services Manager window where you can see that the Default Web Site has been stopped as a result of the stopweb command being issued. The Default Web Site is classed as Web site 1 on my server.

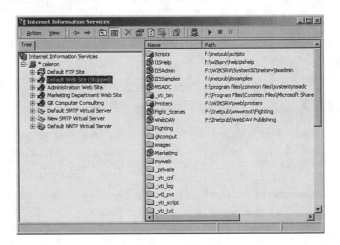

FIGURE 13.6

The Internet Services Manager showing the Default Web Site as stopped because of the stopweb *command.*

Stop Server (`stopsrv`)

You can use this command to stop a single server or a list of servers. You can separate the list of server names with commas.

Syntax

```
stopsrv -a SERVERx, -c computer, -v verbose, -h help45
```

-`a` specifies the server number that you want to stop.

-`c` specifies the computer name or names separated by commas. If no name is given, `localhost` is assumed.

-`v` causes the script engine to display comments as it processes the script.

-`h` displays help for the command.

Example

```
stopsrv -a w3svc/1
```

This command will stop the Web service on the `localhost` computer.

Stop FTP Server (`stopftp`)

You can use this command to stop the FTP server on a computer that is specified in the command.

Syntax

```
stopftp -a SERVERx, -c computer, -v verbose, -h help
```

-`a` lists the number of the server(s) to stop.

-`c` gives a list of computer(s) to stop.

-`v` (verbose mode) displays the script engine output as the commands are processed.

-`h` displays help for the command.

Example

```
stopftp -a 1
```

This command will stop the first FTP server that you have on your computer.

Start Web Server (`startweb`)

Stopping the Web server from the command line is not much good to the administrator if he cannot start it from the command line as well. IIS offers the `startweb` command for this purpose.

Syntax

```
startweb -a SERVERx, -c computer, -v verbose, -h help
```

-*a* indicates the number of the server that you want to start. A list of server numbers can be given separated by commas.

-*c* specifies the computer or list of computers on which to start the Web service.

-*v* causes the script to use verbose mode.

-*h* displays help on the command.

Example

```
startweb -a 1
```

This command will restart the Web server that we shut down earlier with the stopweb command.

Start Server (startsrv)

You use this command to start a server or a list of servers from the command line.

Syntax

```
startsrv -a SERVERx, -c computer, -v verbose, -h help
```

-*a* specifies the server number or numbers separated by commas.

-*c* gives the computer name or list of computer names to start.

-*v* (verbose mode) displays script output to the screen.

-*h* displays help for the command.

Example

```
startsrv -c celeron -a w3svc/1
```

This will start the Web service on the celeron computer.

Start FTP Server (startftp)

This command is used to start a previously stopped or newly created FTP site.

Syntax

```
startftp -a SERVERx, -c computer, -v verbose, -h help
```

-*a* lists the server number(s) to start.

-c is used to specifies the computer name(s) to start.

-v is for verbose mode.

-h displays help for the command.

Example

```
startftp -c celeron -a 1
```

This example will start the first FTP service on the computer named celeron.

Pause Web Server (pauseweb)

You can use this command to pause a Web server. You might want to pause a server in the event that you are making some quick changes that could affect the display of a page or cause out-of-date information to be displayed before you actually got the information updated.

Syntax

```
pauseweb -a SERVERx, -c computer, -v verbose, -h help
```

-a lists the server number(s) to pause.

-c gives a list of computer name(s) on which to pause the Web server.

-v is for verbose mode.

-h displays help for the command.

Example

```
pauseweb -c celeron -a 1
```

This command will pause the first Web server found on the computer named celeron. In my case, it is the Default Web server.

Pause Server (pausesrv)

This command is used to pause a server or list of servers. If you use more than one server in the command, separate the names with commas.

Syntax

```
pausesrv -a SERVERx, -c computer, -v verbose, -h help
```

-a lists the server number(s) to pause.

-c lists the computer name(s) on which to pause the server.

-v uses verbose mode.

-h displays help for the command.

Example

pausesrv -c celeron -a w3svc/1

This command will pause the Web server on the computer named celeron.

Pause FTP Server (pauseftp)

You can use this command to pause an FTP server on the network.

Syntax

pauseftp -a SERVERx, -c computer, -v verbose, -h help

-a lists the server number(s) to pause.

-c lists the computer name(s) on which to pause the service.

-v uses verbose mode.

-h displays help for the command.

Example

pauseftp -c celeron -a 1

This command will pause the first FTP server on the computer named celeron.

Continue Web Server (contweb)

Obviously, if you have a way to pause a Web server, you should have a way to restart it. With Internet Service Manager, you can use the restart button. From the command line, you use contweb.

Syntax

contweb -a SERVERx, -c computer, -v verbose, -h help

-a lists the server number(s) on which to restart the Web server.

-c lists the computer name(s) on which to restart the Web server.

-v uses verbose mode.

-h displays help on the command.

Example

```
contweb -c celeron -a 1
```

Using this command will restart the paused Web server running on the computer named `celeron`.

Continue Server (`contsrv`)

This command is used to restart paused servers.

Syntax

```
contsrv -a SERVERx, -c computer, -v verbose, -h help
```

`-a` lists the server number(s) to restart.

`-c` lists the computer name(s) to restart.

`-v` uses verbose mode.

`-h` display help for the command.

Example

```
contsrv -c celeron -a msftpsvc/1
```

This command will restart the previously paused FTP service on the `celeron` computer.

Continue FTP Server (`contftp`)

In the same way as the `contweb` and `contsrv` commands will restart their respectively paused services, `contftp` will restart a paused FTP service.

Syntax

```
contftp -a SERVERx, -c computer, -v verbose, -h
```

`-a` lists the server number(s) to restart.

`-c` lists the computer name(s) on which to restart the FTP service.

`-v` uses verbose mode.

`-h` displays help for the command.

Example

```
contftp -c celeron -a 1
```

This command will restart the paused FTP server number one on the computer named `celeron`.

13

ADMINISTRATION
SCRIPTS

Change Access Restrictions (chaccess)

You can change the access restrictions on a server by using the chaccess command in a batch file or at the command line. The available access restrictions are Read, Write, Script, Execute, and Browse. These restrictions coincide with those listed on the Home Directory tab sheet of the Web site properties dialog box, as shown in Figure 13.7.

FIGURE 13.7
The Home Directory lists access restriction options that can be set on this tab sheet or from the command line using chaccess.

Syntax

```
chaccess -a ADSPATH, -c computer,

        +/- read
        +/- write
        +/- script
        +/- browse
        +/- execute

        -v verbose, -h help
```

-a specifies the machine relative path.

-c is a list of computer name(s) to which to apply the changes.

+/- controls restrictions. Use the + to turn a restriction on or the - to turn it off followed by the restriction.

-*v* uses verbose mode.

-*h* displays help for the command.

Example

```
chaccess -a w3svc/1 -c celeron +read +write +browse
```

This command will set the read, write, and browse access restrictions for the first Web service on the computer named celeron.

Summary

Administration scripts are a great way to provide remote and automated administration relating to certain aspects of the Web and FTP services running on the computer.

By using these commands in batch files, you can automate the creation of Web sites and virtual directories on a server saving you countless hours of manual configuration of each site through Internet Services Manager.

Making changes to a Web or FTP site sometimes involves restarting or stopping the service while the changes are made. Using the script commands shown here, you can achieve these tasks without ever having to start the Internet Services Manager.

Another good use for these scripts is to create an automated way to shut down a service based on a time frame. For example, you might want to shut down the Web or FTP service after hours as an added measure of security. This should prevent unauthorized access because your sales staff or other workers are finished with work for the day and don't require access to the sites after hours.

There are many more uses and advantages relating to these administration scripts, and each office might have its own need for them. Whatever your reason, I am sure that you will find them advantageous.

13

ADMINISTRATION
SCRIPTS

Administering IIS Programmatically

IN THIS CHAPTER

IIS offers tools that enable you to administer services using scripts or applications. The information that you manipulate and work with is stored in what is known as the metabase.

The *metabase* is a memory resident data store that offers fast access to the stored information because the data doesn't have to come from a disk. As most of us are already aware, disk access has not quite made it to the speed of memory access yet.

Administering IIS Through Objects and ADSI

Information relating to the configuration of IIS is stored in the metabase as binary values. In order to manipulate these values, you use the IIS Admin Objects. There are IIS Admin Objects that correspond to specific key types in the metabase. By using ASP or scripts, you can create your own applications for remotely administering your IIS server. Chapter 15 discusses remote administration of IIS; the HTML-based interface that you will see in Chapter 15 was created using the IIS Admin Objects.

There are two ways to program IIS: You can use the IIS Admin Objects, which is what we will be covering in this chapter, or you can use the IIS Admin Base Object. The IIS Admin Base Object provides you with more advanced programming capabilities.

The IIS Admin Base Object is a low-level interface used with COM+–compliant languages such as C++. You use the IMSAdminBase interface to work with the IIS Admin Base Object. Using this interface and the C++ programming language, you can create applications to manipulate the IIS configuration by gaining access to the metabase keys and values.

In order to access this functionality, you work with what are known as *handles*. These handles refer to the keys in the metabase. You need to use the OpenKey method to gain access to a handle for a metabase key. You provide the full metabase path to the key. An example would be /LM/MSFTPSVC/1. This path points to the first FTP server on the local machine.

The IIS Admin Base Object has a master handle, called the METADATA_MASTER_ROOT_HANDLE. Although this is the master handle, it does not offer any protection in relation to multiple-thread access of the metabase. What this means is that you can have a multithreaded application accessing the metabase, and one thread may change a key's value without another thread being aware of this change. This may be an issue if one thread's execution depends on the value stored in another key. If that value is inadvertently changed, it may cause a malfunction in the application.

The IIS Base Admin Object makes use of inheritance as well. This means that you can assign a value to a root object or parent object and indicate that each subkey or subobject should inherit these settings. This feature will apply settings across an entire server or site. It can be overridden by specifying a new setting for individual objects.

When dealing with the IIS Admin Base Object, you will work with some user types. These user types allow you to assign a classification to your identifiers by application. IIS currently uses four user types. These are

- IIS_MD_UT_FILE—Used for directory and file properties
- IIS_MD_UT_SERVER[—Configures server parameters
- IIS_MD_UT_WAM[—Deals with Web application management
- ASP_MD_UT_APP[—Configures ASP applications

Appendix D lists a complete administrative reference that indicates the user types for each object. You can download the Windows 2000 Platform Software Development Kit (SDK) from the Microsoft Web site at `http://msdn.microsoft.com/downloads/sdks/platform/platform.asp`.

The bottom of the page breaks the SDK into components so that you can download only what you require. This platform SDK provides a wealth of information on using the IIS Admin Base Object to develop applications for IIS manipulation.

The IIS Admin Objects that I will be presenting are known as *automation-enabled*. This means that they expose their interfaces to languages such as Visual Basic, VBScript, C++, or JScript for manipulation. They are based on the Active Directory Service Interfaces (ADSI).

I will delve into these objects and the ADSI a little later in the chapter, but, first, I need to introduce you to the metabase. After all, this is where the configuration information for IIS 5.0 is stored, and it is what you will be manipulating with the IIS Admin Objects.

IIS Metabase

As mentioned previously, the metabase is the single repository or location for the storage of configuration information relating to IIS 5.0.

Structure

The metabase is organized similarly to the Registry, in that it uses a hierarchical structure of keys and values. The nodes in the metabase tree are called *keys*. These keys contain values that relate to IIS configuration values and are known as metabase properties.

If you are coming to IIS 5.0 from earlier versions, you are probably used to dealing with the IIS configuration keys in the Registry. These values are now stored in the metabase, which offers a unique capability to assign the same property differently for different nodes. You will also find that the metabase provides faster access times because it is stored in RAM when the server is running.

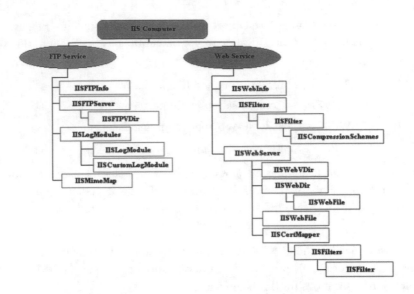

FIGURE 14.1
The IIS Administration Objects are displayed, showing their relationships.

The topmost key is the IIS Computer key. This key contains properties that will be set for the entire IIS service on the computer. The keys then break into separate services, one for the FTP services and one for the Web services running on the computer.

Each service contains keys that are specific to it. Under the FTP Service key, you will find keys relating to FTP servers. Notice that I said *servers* because you can have more than one. Likewise, the Web Service key can have more than one Web Server under it. If you make changes to the Web service or the FTP service, it will affect all servers running on the computer. As we discussed previously, you can make changes at an individual Web or FTP server, and have those changes override the global ones set at the service or computer level.

Keynames and Paths

When talking about keys in the sense of the metabase, you can compare them to a directory in a file structure. These keys can form a path by being placed in sequence and being separated by a forward slash (/).

You can have keys with the same name in the metabase, provided they are placed in unique paths in much the same way as you can have two files with the same name in different directories in the computer.

In order to access a specific key with the IIS Admin Objects, you need to specify the complete path to that key. This path is known as the ADSI path and is called AdsPath. This path always starts with IIS:// and then the IP address or hostname of the computer. An example would be *IIS://localhost/W3SVC/1*, which would access the first Web Server located on the local server.

Each Web or FTP server has a root directory or virtual root associated with it. In order to access the root directory in the previous example, you would specify it like this, *IIS://localhost/W3SVC/1/ROOT*. All other directories will be subdirectories of this.

Property Inheritance

Most of the properties that make up the metabase are inheritable. This means that you can get away with only a few settings and minimize the memory used by the metabase. Higher-level keys can assign their properties to lower-level keys; that is, the lower-level keys can *inherit* the settings of the upper-level keys. A good example of this is when you set file permissions such as Write or Execute at the service level, W3SVC. All identical keys under this root key inherit these settings, unless you set a specific key differently.

> **NOTE**
>
> If you are using the IIS snap-in and you set an inheritable property, you will see a dialog box asking on which subnodes you would like to set the property. If you set an inheritable property through script, the subnodes will inherit the settings automatically.

Appendix D, "Script Reference," lists the properties and indicates which are inheritable.

Security and Reliability

The metabase resides in memory. Obviously, it will not persist if the computer is rebooted or shut down. For this reason, the metabase is stored on disk and is loaded into memory when IIS starts. Periodically, IIS will save the metabase to disk to ensure that recent changes are preserved. When you shut down IIS, the metabase gets resaved to disk.

The metabase file is named Metabase.bin by default and is located in the Inetsrv directory. It is very important that this file be protected against unauthorized access and should be placed on an NTFS partition where the proper security access permissions can be set.

You can move this file to another directory or rename it. When you do this, however, you will need to make the necessary changes to the Registry so that IIS can find the file when it starts up. The Registry key that you need to configure is

HKEY_LOCAL_MACHINE

14

ADMINISTERING IIS
PROGRAMMATICALLY

```
\SOFTWARE
     \Microsoft
          \InetMgr
               \Parameters
```

You need to add a value to this key of type REG-SZ and name it `MetadataFile`. `MetadataFile` specifies the complete path to the metabase, which must include the drive letter and filename.

IIS Administration Objects

Microsoft provides the IIS Admin Objects to make the task of programmatic administration easier. These objects are automation enabled and are based on the ADSI. This means that any language which supports automation can access these objects and manipulate them. VBScript and JScript are both automation enabled, and because both are included with IIS, you already have all the tools you need.

Overview

Using the IIS Admin Objects, you can develop an ASP page or any custom application and manipulate the metabase properties by accessing the correct objects.

Keeping in mind the structure of the metabase as described earlier in this chapter, you can use the IIS Admin Objects to manipulate and set the properties on a server-wide basis or on individual files or services. All you need to do is to access the correct object by using the full path to that object starting with the root.

The IIS Admin Objects mirror the metabase object hierarchy, which you can review by looking at Figure 14.1. You will see how you can gain access to the required object by traversing the hierarchy.

ADSI

Active Directory Service Interfaces (ADSI) provide you a standard syntax for dealing with the IIS Admin Objects. Using this syntax, you can gain access to the necessary configuration data. As mentioned previously, the IIS HTML-based administration tool uses these objects to perform remote configuration.

Their metabase path references the IIS Admin Objects. If you wanted to reference the second Web Server on the computer named `websrvone`, you would use the full ADSI path, called the AdsPath, like this—`IIS://websrvone/W3SVC/2`.

ADSI Objects

The IIS Admin Objects implement the IADs interface, which is defined by the ADSI standard. As a result, the following functionality is implemented:

- A method of retrieving the namespace properties
- A path to the schema definition of an object
- Identification information such as name and type of object
- A caching system
- A method of setting and retrieving properties for a specific node of the metabase
- A way of retrieving the path for an object's parent
- Binding information for uniquely identifying object instances in a directory tree

ADSI Container Objects

ADSI Container Objects are the IIS Admin Objects that can contain other objects by implementing the IADsContainer interface.

The IIS Admin Objects classed as container objects are the IISComputer and IISWebVirtualDir objects. IISComputer contains IISWebService and IISFtpService as the two objects directly below IISComputer. IISWebVirtualDir can contain an IISWebDirectory object, an IISWebVirtualDir object, and an IISWebFile object.

The IADsContainer interface enables the following procedures to be performed in relation to containers and their objects:

- Create objects in a container
- Delete objects from a container
- Provide a count of the number of objects in a container
- Access the objects in the container
- Enumerate the objects

The `Create`, `Delete`, and `Count` methods and the `GetObject` and `_NewEnum` properties support these functions, respectively.

An example of how to use each method follows:

`Create`—Set newObj = *Object(KeyType, Name)*

`newObj` is used to access the new object in the container.

Object is the name of an IIS object that is normally returned by the `GetObject` method, as shown in the code example that follows.

14

ADMINISTERING IIS
PROGRAMMATICALLY

KeyType is the type of IIS Admin Object to create.

Name is the name for the new object.

Example

```
<%
Dim WebSrvObject, SrvObject
Set WebSrvObject = GetObject("IIS://celeron/W3SVC")
Set SrvObject = WebSrvObject.Create("IISWebServer", "5")
%>
```

This code snippet will first return the name of the W3SVC object located on the computer named celeron and assign it to the WebSrvObject variable. The next line of code sets the SrvObject variable to be the newly created IISWebServer object number 5.

Delete—*Object*.Delete *KeyType, Name*

Object is the IIS Admin Object returned by the GetObject method.

KeyType is the type of IIS Admin Object to delete.

Name is the name of the IIS Admin Object to delete.

Example

```
<%
Dim WebSrvObject
Set WebSrvObject = GetObject("IIS://celeron/W3SVC")
WebSrvObject.Delete "IISWebServer", "5"
%>
```

This code snippet will delete the object that was created with the Create method used earlier.

NOTE

If the object that you are deleting is a part of an application, the AppDelete method will be called first to remove the application definition before the object is removed. Be sure that is what you want to do before deleting the object.

Count—This is a property of the ADSI Container Object and returns the number of objects in the container.

_NewEnum—This property will return an enumerator object that can be used by VBScript or JScript to retrieve the objects in the container using a For Each loop.

Administrative Tasks

As mentioned before, the metabase stores the configuration properties for IIS. By making use of the IIS Admin Objects, you can manipulate these properties to configure IIS, create new Web and FTP sites, assign permissions, and perform other configuration tasks.

The HTML-based administrative tool is a good example of the use of the IIS Admin Objects. This tool uses Web browser interface for remotely administering IIS and is described in Chapter 15, "Remote Administration." You can use this tool to become familiar with the various tasks that can be accomplished with the IIS Admin Objects and the metabase properties.

You can create HTML-based applications that run in a Web browser to administer your IIS server in much the same way that IIS's HTML-based administration tool does.

Manipulating the Metabase

In order to gain access to the IIS Admin Objects in the metabase, you need to navigate a hierarchical structure using what is known as the AdsPath. The AdsPath uses a syntax that looks similar to a URL. The general syntax looks like IIS://[path] wherein *path* is used to indicate the directory path of the object you are trying to access.

An example of an AdsPath would be *IIS://celeron/MSFTPSVC*, which would provide access to the FTP service running on my server celeron. This can be considered the root object for the FTP service, and it contains all the other objects that are considered children or subobjects of this root object.

In order to work with the objects in code, you normally use the GetObject method to return the name of the object that you want to work with so that you can use this name in your code.

LISTING 14.1 Sample Code for Returning ADSI Object Properties

```
<%@ LANGUAGE=VBSCript %>
<HTML>
<HEAD><TITLE>       </TITLE></HEAD>
<BODY>
<%
Dim WebSrvObject
Set WebSrvObject = GetObject("IIS://celeron/W3SVC")
%>
<B>Web Service Name</B>....<%= WebSrvObject.Name %> <BR>
<B>ADsPath</B>....<%= WebSrvObject.ADsPath %> <BR>
<B>Class</B>....<%= WebSrvObject.Class %> <BR>
<B>GUID</B>....<%= WebSrvObject.GUID %> <BR>
<B>Parent</B>....<%= WebSrvObject.Parent %> <BR>
<B>Schema</B>....<%= WebSrvObject.Schema %> <BR>
</BODY>
</HTML>
```

14

ADMINISTERING IIS
PROGRAMMATICALLY

If you place this code into an `.asp` file and run it on your server, you will see a display similar to that shown in Figure 14.2.

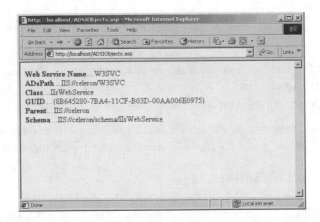

FIGURE 14.2
Internet Explorer showing the six properties of the W3SVC ADSI Object.

As you can see, using the `GetObject` method returned the object necessary for me to access the properties for the W3SVC. This is a simple `.asp` file that merely displays the properties that are associated with the W3SVC object that was returned.

The first line of code declares a variable, `WebSrvObject`, that will be used to hold the object returned by the `GetObject` method. In this way, we can use the variable name to refer to the object when we access its properties instead of needing to use the full AdsPath every time we need a property.

In order to use the `GetObject` method or any `.asp` script that accesses the metabase on your Web Server, you will need to access the `.asp` page using an administrative account. If you attempt to access the file without this, you will receive an error message stating that the server cannot open the page because permission has been denied for the `GetObject` method.

The easiest way around this is to assign the appropriate permissions to the `InetPub` directory. For example, I added the group Everyone to the users list in the Security settings for the `InetPub` directory and allowed Full Control of the directory. This does have one inherent security risk. If the server is a production server connected to the Internet, you can allow any user from the outside or inside to connect to the `InetPub` directory and run applications; modify or delete files; and even upload and run Trojan horse programs or viruses. If you decide to do this, try to set up on a test system first. When your scripts are working as you want them to, transfer them to a production server.

Alternatively, you can create a logon page that will require a user to provide a username and password to be authenticated on the server using the NTLM or Basic authentication methods. This way, you are protecting your production server from being easily compromised. This will, however, create an extra step that you must go through in order to test your pages using the `GetObject` method.

Summary

This chapter presented an overview of the possibilities of administering IIS through `.asp` script code. I recommended the HTML version of the Internet Service Manager as the tool for your remote administration of IIS.

You were shown the structure of the metabase, the configuration storage database for IIS, and how the keys and values pertain to the various IIS Admin Objects.

The chapter also covered the ADSI hierarchy discussing the ADSI objects and ADSI container objects.

If you would like to see how the HTML Administration tool handles setting the properties and manipulating the IIS services, the scripts are mostly all JScripts. The `.asp` files can be found in the `%winnt%\system32\inetsrv\iisadmin` directory. Do not change these files without ensuring that the originals are backed up. Should you modify these files incorrectly, you will render your IIS HTML-based administration tool inoperable.

14

ADMINISTERING IIS
PROGRAMMATICALLY

Remote Administration

IN THIS CHAPTER

For most administrators, the option of sitting in front of the server is not really an option at all. Most of the time you are at your own desk in front of your own workstation performing other administrative tasks. Not only that but you can't really use the server as your desktop workstation anyway. Most companies want the server locked in a climate- and access-controlled room. If the hum of power supply fans doesn't drive you crazy within the first couple of days, the 68° Fahrenheit temperature will ensure a steady shiver.

Let's face it, remotely administering the server is the preferred way to go and IIS offers you the ability to do just that. You can perform remote administration using two methods. The first method involves accessing the IIS server over an intranet or internal network. The second method provides a way to access IIS over the Internet.

We will look at each option in turn and explain some of the advantages and disadvantages of each method. There is no one best method for working remotely on the server and you must decide what your preference is. Of course, sometimes you will have no option based on what procedures your company might have in place.

Remote Administration over the Internet

You can reach your IIS server over the Internet for administrative purposes by using a Web browser such as Internet Explorer or Netscape Navigator. IIS offers an HTML-based administration facility for this purpose. Of course, the first thing that we must do is enable it.

Enabling the Remote Administration features of IIS involves a simple step. Open the Internet Services Manager and expand the server icon to display the available Web sites on the server, as shown in Figure 15.1.

If the Administration Web Site is not running, select its entry in the Tree pane and select the Run button on the toolbar, or select Start from the Action menu. This will enable remote administration of the IIS server. If you do not intend to allow remote administration of the server for security purposes, make sure that this Web site is not running.

When you have the Administration Web Site running, right-click it and open the Properties dialog box for it, as shown in Figure 15.2.

Take note of the TCP port number in the Web Site Identification section. This is the number that you will use to gain access to the administration portion of the Web site from your browser. You can change this port to one that you would like to use or to one that is made available on your network behind a firewall. Make sure that you do not use any ports that are common TCP/IP port numbers such as 21 for FTP or 119 for News servers.

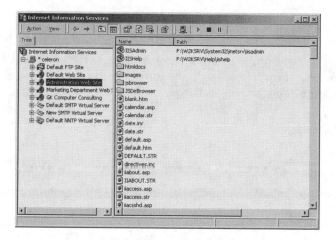

FIGURE 15.1

The Internet Services Manager MMC snap-in contains an Administration Web Site used for remote administration of IIS using a Web browser.

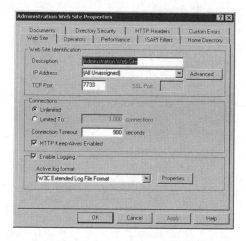

FIGURE 15.2

The Administration Web Site Properties dialog box gives you the opportunity to set configuration parameters for the Administration Web Site.

> **NOTE**
>
> Make sure that you talk to the network administrator or the individual who is responsible for your corporate firewall to ensure that the port is open on the firewall or a proxy server to allow you to gain access to the Administrative Web Site.

> **TIP**
>
> TCP/IP port numbers indicate an application on a TCP/IP server, rather than on a physical port.

When you have the port number configured, you need to set up the access rights for the administrative site. The first option to set is the operators that will be allowed to access the administrative Web site over an HTTP connection. Select the Operators tab on the properties sheet for the Administration Web Site. Figure 15.3 shows the Operators tab.

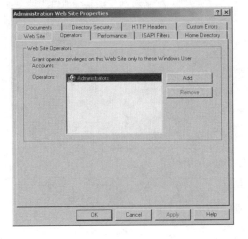

FIGURE 15.3

The Operators tab sheet on the Administration Web Site Properties sheet enables you to add Windows accounts or groups to the list of valid operators allowed to connect to and administer the Web Server of HTTP connections.

As you can see, Windows 2000 defaults to allowing only the administrators access to the administration site. You can add other Windows accounts or groups to this list by clicking the Add button. This will bring up the Select Users or Groups dialog box, as shown in Figure 15.4, allowing you to select the groups or user accounts that you want to add.

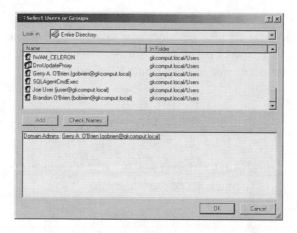

FIGURE 15.4

The Select Users or Groups dialog box gives you access to the Windows 2000 Active Directory Users and Groups that reside on the server so that you can choose operators for the administration of the Web site.

Select the users or groups and click the Add button to add them to the list of available users. When you have all the users and groups that you want, click the OK button to return to the Operators tab of the Properties dialog box.

One other security precaution that you can take is to restrict access to the Administration Web Site to only those computers that you specify. You can do this by clicking the Directory Security tab on the Properties sheet. This will display the screen shown in Figure 15.5.

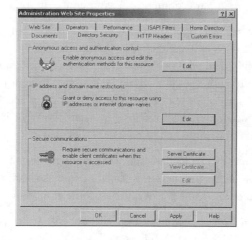

FIGURE 15.5

Use the Edit button in the IP Address and Domain Name restriction section to restrict the computers that can connect to the Administration Web Site.

We have seen this tab sheet before when we looked at security earlier in the book. Clicking the Edit button will enable you to set the restrictions based on a single computer IP address, on a group of computers as in a network range, or by domain name. You must select the Denied Access option on the IP Address and Domain Name Restrictions dialog box, as shown in Figure 15.6.

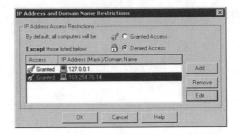

FIGURE 15.6

The IP Address and Domain Name Restrictions dialog box showing that the only computers allowed to connect to the Administration Web Site on my server are the computers that have the IP address of 169.254.76.14 and 127.0.0.1.

This option is a good one to use if you know the IP address ahead of time for the computer that you will use to connect to the server. If you have a typical account from an ISP that assigns IP addresses dynamically, this option will not work for you. Your IP will be different each time that you connect. Also, some ISPs work with a pool of IP addresses that are not only dynamically assigned at connection time but can be reassigned if your connection is idle. This makes it even harder as you cannot maintain an IP for the duration of a connection if there is not a steady stream of data being transmitted over your connection.

The other two options can offer a slightly better offset. For instance, if you choose the Group of Computer option, you can usually contact your ISP and determine what its range of IP addresses is. Most ISPs only deal with one class of IP, such as class A, B, or C. This way, you can cover all the possible IP addresses that would be assigned to your computer. The only downfall of this option is that someone else on your ISPs range of addresses could also administer your Web site. This would only be possible if he knew the Web site address, port number, and username/password combination. Not likely but still possible.

The last option of computer domain name could work similarly to the Group of Computer option except any computers that use the same domain name as specified would be able to administer the Web based on the same restrictions set forth in the Group of Computer option.

For the most part, you will likely be administering the web site from within your own company's network. This can be done over HTTP as well or with the use of the MMC on another computer. We will look at this option in the section "Remote Administration over an Intranet."

Now that you have the necessary access restrictions in place, click OK to apply the changes and close the Properties dialog box. Now, open your favorite browser and using the address bar, enter the name or IP address of your Web site followed by a colon and the port number as in this example:

```
http://207.169.52.31:6765
```

After a bit, you should see the administration screen displayed in your browser, as shown in Figure 15.7.

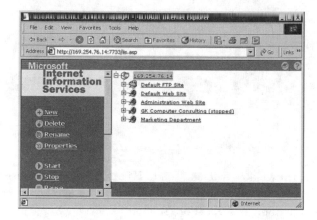

FIGURE 15.7
Internet Explorer shows the Internet Services Manager Web interface that you can use to administer the Web site.

As you can see from the screen, you have full access to the Web Server for purposes of administering the Web and FTP sites. You can select a site in the right window and stop start or pause the site by selecting one of the hyperlinks on the left window.

TIP

If you pay attention to the status bar when you move your mouse over one of the hyperlinks, you will notice that the functionality is implemented using JavaScript. Each hyperlink will cause a JavaScript function to be executed that will send the necessary commands to the server to perform the actions that you specify.

Scrolling down the list in the left window will display the available commands and functions that you can perform. You will see that the same functionality available in the MMC console is available to you in the Web interface. See Figure 15.8 for an example of some administration functions.

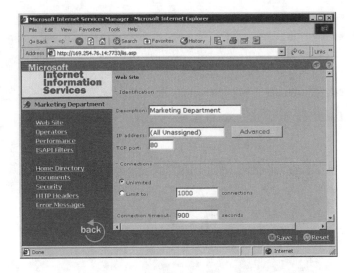

FIGURE 15.8
The Marketing Department Web Site properties are displayed as an HTML page.

The hyperlinks on the left window will take you to HTML pages that correspond to the same tab sheets in the properties for the Web or FTP sites. When you make changes using this interface, you do not have an Apply or OK button. You must select the Save button at the bottom of the page. This will make the changes necessary to the Web or FTP site. Using the Back button in the left pane will cause the browser to load the home page, as you saw in Figure 15.7.

The nice advantage of using the HTTP approach to administering your Web server is that you can do so from any operating system using any Web browser that supports JavaScript and graphics. This means that you can use Internet Explorer on the Intel platform or Netscape on the Linux platform.

You can also access the online help files and documentation for IIS by entering the URL `http://%servername%/iishelp/iis/misc/default.asp`. You can replace the `%servername%` variable with the name of the server or IP address.

> **NOTE**
>
> One little quirk that you will notice if you select the Permissions Wizard, or one of the Security options such as IP and Domain Name Restrictions, is that the computer will open a separate browser window giving you the HTML-based screens related to the function that you have chosen.

Create a New Web Site

For a little practice, let's create a new Web site using the HTML Administration Tool. First, make sure that there is a directory created on the server to hold the Web site that you will create. Open the Administration Web site from a remote computer using your Web browser as shown previously.

Make sure that the IP address of the server is selected and then click the New option in the left frame. A new browser window will open, welcoming you to the New Web Site Wizard. Click Next to continue. You are then given the opportunity to create a new Web or FTP site. Leave the default choice or Web site selected and click the Next button.

Enter a Web site description in the text box provided on the Web Site Description page. When you click the Next button, you are asked to enter the Web site bindings. This information includes the IP address to use, the port number, and the SSL port number for secure sites. Fill in the appropriate information and click the Next button.

When the Path page is displayed, you can enter the path to the directory that will hold the Web site content or use the Browse button to locate the directory on the server. You can also choose to allow Anonymous access to this site on this page as well by checking the Allow anonymous access to this site option. After you have entered the path name, click the Next button to advance to the Access Permissions screen.

Using the options presented on the Access Permissions screen, you can set up the necessary read, write, and script access permissions for this Web site. Any settings you make here will override the global settings that were set at the Web site, if any. These overrides apply to this Web site only and to no others on the server.

Click the Finish button; after a few seconds you will see the newly created site in the list of Web sites available on the server. You will notice that the site has not been started. This is a good time to practice some more administrative tasks by highlighting the new Web site and clicking the Start option in the left frame to start the Web site. You can now use a Web publishing tool, such as Microsoft FrontPage, to create the content for the newly created site.

NOTE

The speed at which you will see the new site added depends on the speed of your Internet connection.

Remote Administration over an Intranet

As we mentioned previously, you can use the HTML-based interface for remote administration of the Web Server over the Internet or an intranet. If you have Web site operators that are not familiar with the Internet Services Manager or MMC, you can offer those operators the ability to administer using the procedures outlined previously.

The method that I recommend for an intranet site is to use the remote capabilities built in to the MMC. Figure 15.9 shows a screen shot of Internet Services Manager with a connection to another server on my network called Pii350.

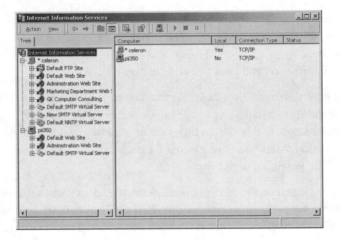

FIGURE 15.9

Internet Services Manager enables you to connect to other IIS servers for administration and configuration.

As you can see from Figure 15.9, I have an identical interface to what I am using on my local server, but instead, I am accessing a remote server. Notice the subtle differences in the console that indicate I am on a remote server. In the Tree pane, the icon for the remote server is similar to that of a network computer icon. In the Details pane on the right, the column labeled *Local* indicates that Pii350 is not local.

Aside from these simple cosmetic indications, the user would not really know that they were working with a remote server because the commands, menu choices, and dialog boxes are identical.

Figure 15.10 shows the Default Web Site Properties dialog box for the Default Web Site on the remote server. As you can see, there is no difference from that of a local server.

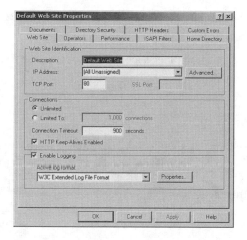

FIGURE 15.10

The Default Web Site Properties dialog box is identical for remote and local servers.

> **NOTE**
>
> Depending on the speed of your network, you might notice a delay in the displaying of dialog boxes or properties relating to remote sites. This is because of the lag in transferring the data over the network.

The one thing that we haven't covered yet is how to connect to a remote server to administer it using the Internet Services Manager. The procedure is simple.

Open the Internet Services Manager if it is not already open. Select the Internet Information Services entry in the Tree pane on the left. Choose Connect from the Action menu. This will bring up the Connect to Computer dialog box, as displayed in Figure 15.11.

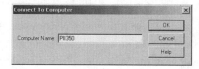

FIGURE 15.11

The Connect to Computer dialog box is where you enter the name of the server to which you want to connect.

In the text box provided, enter the name of the server that contains the IIS service that you want to administer from this MMC console and choose OK. There will be a delay as MMC searches the network for the computer and enumerates the entries in the IIS service on that computer.

That is all there is to it. The new computer's icon will appear in the Tree pane of your Internet Services Manager MMC console.

> **NOTE**
>
> You do not have to be running a Windows 2000 Server to remotely administer another Windows 2000 Server IIS installation. You can use Windows 2000 Professional as well because it uses the same MMC and IIS version as the Windows 2000 Server. You can also reverse the procedure.

Change Directory Security Remotely Using MMC

To provide a little practice in using the MMC to remotely administer another IIS server, we will walk through setting the Directory Security options on a remote server.

Open the Internet Services Manager console from the Administrative tools folder. Select the Internet Information Services entry in the Tree pane to highlight it.

From the Action menu, choose Connect. When the Connect To Computer dialog appears, enter the NetBios name or the IP address of the computer to which you want to connect for remote administration. Click OK.

When the connection is established, you will see the available sites and services on the remote computer listed under its own heading directly beneath the sites and services for the local computer. Select the Default Web Site entry or another Web site under the remote server, and click the right mouse button to open the pop-up menu. Choose Properties.

The dialogs are identical for remote computers as they are for local computers. Select the Directory Security tab on the Properties dialog box. Click the Edit button in the Anonymous access and authentication control section. This displays the Authentication Methods dialog box.

Make sure that the Anonymous access and Integrated Windows authentication options are selected. You can also choose the Edit button under the Anonymous access section to select the account used for anonymous access to the Web site. Click the OK button to close the Authentication Methods dialog box.

Click the Edit button in the IP address and domain name restrictions section to configure the access control based on IP address or domain name.

Once you have made the necessary changes to the security options, click the OK button to close the Web site's Properties dialog box.

NOTE

The only security procedure that you cannot perform remotely is the Server Certificate procedure. You need to perform that procedure at the server to apply for and configure a server certificate.

Summary

Remotely administering the IIS server is often a desirable approach because, most of the time, you will not be in front of the actual server that is hosting IIS. You can take advantage of the remote administration capabilities built in to IIS to perform the duties from another workstation, server, or computer.

If you are the sole administrator of all IIS servers in your company and you administer those servers on the local network, you might it find it beneficial to work with the Internet Services Manager in the MMC console for the sake of keeping the interface consistent.

If you have operators who are not familiar with the MMC and would prefer working with a more familiar interface, you can set up the HTML-based administrative services using the Administration Web Site. This way, these operators can administer the site remotely using an HTML-based interface on their favorite Web browser.

It is very important to remember to use the security features of IIS when you are allowing remote administration on the Web-based administration site. By using the available Windows 2000 accounts and the appropriate computer restrictions, you can provide a secure method of administering IIS over the Internet.

Application Development

PART

III

IN THIS PART

Active Server Pages

IN THIS CHAPTER

Introduction to Active Server Pages

Active Server Pages (ASP) is designed as a server-side scripting environment. You can use VBScript or JScript in ASP pages to create dynamic Web pages, provide database access on the server, call COM components, and run applications. The nicest thing about ASP is that it is browser neutral. When ASP scripts are run on the server, any Web-based browser that supports the HTML 4.0 tags will render the pages in the browser.

So what does this have to do with administering IIS? Well, aside from the fact that ASP can make life a lot easier for a Web developer, you can use ASP to work with IIS and not just to create dynamic content. In order to figure out how to do this, you need a basic understanding of ASP. I will not provide a complete tutorial on the subject here, but I will give you enough information to use it for simple tasks with an idea of where to go for more information.

You can use the information presented here and that found in Chapter 14, "Administering IIS Programmatically," to use ASP to administer your server. Using the IIS Admin Objects and any COM components that your internal development department might create, you can use ASP to your advantage with IIS.

One of the most compelling reasons that I have found to use ASP for site administration purposes is to provide personal customization for a visitor to your Web site by generating scripted cookies or ASP to maintain session state. Knowing ASP also means that you don't have to learn Perl or other CGI scripting languages.

ASP can also make it very easy for you to maintain a site that requires authorization. You can use scripting to access a database of usernames and passwords. You can allow a user to create his own username/password combination. This will be stored in the database where you can determine the access level the user has to the site. When you make this change and the user next logs in, she will gain the access provided by her assigned level.

If you are familiar with earlier versions of ASP, you will find that the version that comes with IIS 5.0 has added some new features and made some changes in others.

Two new methods, `Server.Transfer` and `Server.Execute`, have added flow control to this version of ASP. These two methods enable you to transfer requests to `.asp` files without using redirects that require round-trips to the client.

Although error handling existed in earlier versions, ASP 3.0 includes a new method, `Server.GetLastError`. This method can return a description of the error and the line number where the error occurred.

ASP 3.0 also has the capability to process files that contain the `.asp` extension, even if they do not contain any server-side scripting. This is a benefit to the administrator and developer in ensuring that neither have to worry about going through the Web site and manually renaming static HTML files as `.asp` files, should scripting be added later. You can now name all your files with an `.asp` extension.

XML integration makes it easier for you to host these types of documents on the server and have them read by XML parsers, such as Internet Explorer 4.0 or later. Keep in mind that there are still browsers being used on the Internet today that do not support XML. Due to the popularity of XML and the speed at which it is being adopted, you will see other non-Microsoft browsers implement XML in the next releases.

ASP includes new functionality in the Browser Capabilities component that can retrieve a browser's capabilities in cookies to help adjust your applications accordingly.

ASP is self-tuning, in that it can detect requests have been blocked, even by external sources. It will provide more threads automatically so that it can execute additional requests and continue processing. It can also reduce the number of threads if it detects that the CPU is overburdened.

One of the features that your developers will like is the use of script encoding. Previously, developers worried about the client being able to view the logic in their scripts. Although not all scripts are a concern, if you run any that contain company proprietary procedures, you do not necessarily want just anyone being able to view that source code. With this version of ASP, you can encode the script so that it appears as scrambled and unreadable ASCII text. Both scripting engines, VBScript and JScript 5.0, can decode this on-the-fly and execute the scripts normally.

If your company's developers have developed ASP pages in previous versions, the following paragraphs will be of particular interest to them. They contain information relating to some important changes that have been made in this version of ASP.

In IIS 4.0, ASP content buffering was not turned on by default. IIS 5.0 defaults to buffering on. This means that the results of an ASP script are not sent to the client until the processing has been completed. You can turn this feature off in the script, or you can have the content sent to the client at any time in the script with the `Response.Flush` method.

With the `IsClientConnected` method, IIS 5.0 can determine whether the browser is connected before sending any content to it. In IIS 4.0, the `Response.IsClientConnected` method would return the correct information from a client only after sending content to the browser.

ASP in IIS 5.0 also uses enhanced security when dealing with `#include` files. IIS 5.0 will apply the credentials of the physical path when it processes these `#include` files. IIS 4.0 did not use these credentials.

When a request is sent with a parameter, IIS 5.0 handles default files differently than the way IIS 4.0 did. Previous to IIS 5.0, if a URL were requested, such as `http://www.gkcomput.com/?newuser=true`, the request or URL would be passed to default.htm because the .asp file was not specified. IIS 5.0 passes any request, at any time to the default .asp file.

IIS 5.0 has moved the ProcessorThreadMax and ErrorsToNTLog entries from the registry in IIS 4.0 to the metabase.

Creating Active Server Pages

Before you create ASP pages you must select a scripting language. ASP can make use of both VBScript and JScript language files out of the box, but you can add scripting engines yourself for other languages, such as REXX, Perl, or Python. However, why use these scripting languages when IIS includes two easy and very powerful languages already?

IIS 5.0 defaults to VBScript, but you can change that default to another language, or you can use a mixture of both approaches in your ASP pages. To set the default scripting language, open the Internet Services Manager. Right-click the icon for the server and choose Properties from the pop-up menu, or you can select the server icon and choose Action and Properties. This will display the dialog box shown in Figure 16.1.

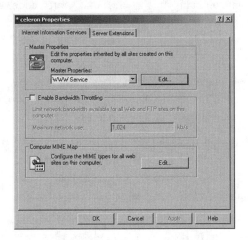

FIGURE 16.1

The *celeron* *Properties dialog box displays the master properties for the entire IIS server.*

Click the Edit button in the Master Properties section to open the WWW Service Master Properties dialog box and select the Home Directory tab on that dialog box.

In the Application Settings section, click the Configuration button to open the Application Configuration dialog box, as shown in Figure 16.2. Select the App Options tab.

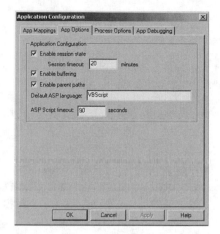

FIGURE 16.2

The App Options tab of the Application Configuration dialog box showing the default ASP language.

As you can see from Figure 16.2, the language on my server is VBScript. This is partly because it is the default language and partly because I am a Visual Basic developer, and I know VBScript better than JScript. You can choose the language of your choice or that of your in-house developers.

After you have made your choice, click the various OK buttons to close the dialog boxes and apply the changes. You are now ready to begin developing pages in your language of choice.

Believe it or not, by renaming a static HTML file with an extension of .htm or .html to have an extension of .asp, you have created an .asp file. Of course, it doesn't have any special functionality just because you have renamed it. You need to add scripting commands to the page to create any functionality. Listing 16.1 shows a really simple ASP page that uses the time on the client computer to display an appropriate message.

LISTING 16.1 time.asp

```
<%@ LANGUAGE = "VBScript" %>
<HTML>
<HEAD><TITLE>Server Time</TITLE></HEAD>
<BODY>
<CENTER><H1><FONT Color="Blue">GK Computer Consulting Order Entry Page
</FONT></H1></CENTER><HR>
<%
Dim timeframe
```

LISTING 16.1 Continued

```
If Time < #12:00PM# Then
    timeframe = "morning"
ElseIf Time >= #12:00PM# AND Time < #5:00PM# Then
    timeframe = "afternoon"
Else
    timeframe = "evening"
End If
%>

Welcome to our web site! At present, it is <% =timeframe %> here.<P>
Any transactions that you perform on our site today, will be stamped<BR>
with our local date and time which is <B><% =Now() %></B>
</BODY>
</HTML>
```

If you type this code into the notepad of your favorite HTML editor and save the file as
time.asp in a directory on your Web Server, you can access it from the server or another computer over the network. It will display the correct greeting based on the time set on the server
computer. You can play with the time settings to verify that each greeting works as intended.

One of the first things that you must do in order for your ASP page to work is to place the language tag at the top of the page before any HTML tags. The language tag follows this syntax:

```
<%@ LANGUAGE="VBScript" %>
```

You will also notice in the code snippet that the <% %> delimiters enclose all script commands,
so that the server will not send the script text to the client's browser. Figure 16.3 shows what
happens if I leave off the leading <% delimiter in the previous code.

The screen shot in Figure 16.4 indicates what the code should produce when the script delimiters are used.

This is not something that you want to happen for two reasons. First, the code didn't function,
and your clients didn't see the intended message. Second, your logic behind the code is displayed for all the connecting clients to see. If this were proprietary information, you wouldn't
want that getting out.

You have seen in the code example that I have used the script and the normal HTML text output in separate areas of the page. I can actually have the server output HTML text and tags
from within our script delimiters as well, if I want. Listing 16.2 shows an example of this.

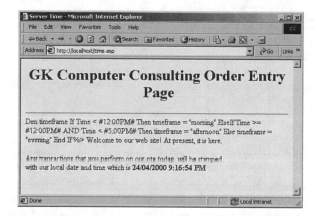

FIGURE 16.3
Internet Explorer showing the full text of my VBScript code in the browser window.

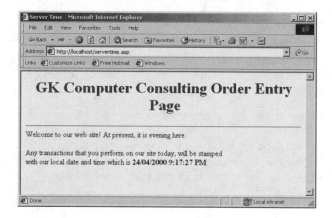

FIGURE 16.4
Internet Explorer showing what the ASP page is intended to produce with the code correctly executed.

LISTING 16.2   HTML_Output.asp

```
<%@ LANGUAGE = "VBScript" %>
<HTML>
<HEAD><TITLE>HTML Output Within Script</TITLE></HEAD>
<BODY>
<CENTER><H2><FONT Color="Blue">Output Text From Within Script</FONT></H2>
</CENTER><HR>
<%
```

LISTING 16.2 Continued

```
Response.Write "<FONT SIZE=14 FACE='Script'>"
Response.Write "<B>This text is Script, Bold and is 14 point.</B></FONT>
<BR>"Response.Write "It was sent to the client from within the script
delimiters<P>"Response.Write "The date on the server is " & Date()

%>
</BODY>
</HTML>
```

Now let's take a look at the differences between what you have written for code and what is displayed when a user chooses to view the source code of the page. First, bring up the page that you just created in your browser window. If you are using Internet Explorer, choose Source from the View menu. Contrast the code that you see in this window with that of the actual code written for the page. You will notice that none of the script code is displayed, only the HTML code and the output that resulted from the code.

This is how .asp files react when you use the <% %> delimiters. Any code that is within these tags is not displayed when the code is being run on the server. If you embed the code in a set of <SCRIPT> </SCRIPT> tags so that it will be executed on the client instead, then that code will be seen as a source when the user chooses the View Source option.

> **NOTE**
>
> Just because a user cannot see the code in your page does not mean that he cannot download the file from your server and view the code that way. The user cannot simply choose Save from the File menu and view the code. He must download the actual file.

Now that you have seen the basic structure of an ASP page, the next few sections will take you through a quick introduction to the rest of the information that you need to know in order to work effectively with ASP pages.

Scripting Languages

IIS 5.0 offers you the capability to use a scripting language of your choice providing that you have the scripting engine installed on the server. For the most part, scripting languages are unlike low-level programming languages such as C or C++ and a little more like Visual Basic and Java in that they are interpreted. An interpreter must read each line of script code and execute it. Scripts are never compiled into a binary executable though.

The two languages that come as part of IIS 5.0 are VBScript and JScript. VBScript is a subset of the Visual Basic programming language. If you have any Visual Basic developers in house, they already know the code constructs for VBScript. They can begin developing ASP pages for you almost immediately.

JScript is Microsoft's version of JavaScript. It closely models the syntax and structure of the Java programming language.

I will use VBScript for all the code examples in this book for three reasons. First, because it comes with IIS and is the default scripting language. Second, because I know VBScript better than I know JScript. Third, VBScript is much easier to master than JScript or other languages, such as Perl or REXX.

You have already seen how to set the default language for the server to use in the first part of this chapter. You can also determine a default language for an ASP page by placing the script language name into the script directive at the start of the page, as in this example:

```
<%@ LANGUAGE=ScriptingLanguage %>
```

Replace *ScriptingLanguage* with the language name of your choice, such as VBScript or JScript.

NOTE

There are certain peculiarities with VBScript when running within .asp files. Your developers should familiarize themselves with them. For example, you cannot use InputBox or MsgBox functions in .asp files because there is no user interface to an .asp file.

If you need to comment your code for clarity, you'll also need to know the different comment styles for the different languages. VBScript enables the use of apostrophe comments like Visual Basic.

```
<%

' Write a line to the screen and include the current date
Response.Write "Today's date is " & Date()

%>
```

This code uses the apostrophe ['] to create a comment before the line of code; the comment explains what the code does.

In JScript, you use of the // comment style, that is used by Java and C++ programmers.

```
<%

// Write a line to the screen and include the current date
var x
x = new Date()
Response.Write (x.ToString())

%>
```

When the server processes the code, it will strip out, and not process, the comments because of the comment delimiters.

Another important point to keep in mind when dealing with VBScript or JScript is that they are both *typeless* languages. This means that any variables you declare do not take any special data type. In Visual Basic, if you had to deal with a string of characters, you declared a variable of type String, as in this example:

```
Dim strNewString As String
```

This would ensure that you could only store character data in this variable. In the two scripting languages discussed here, all variables are of type variant. Variant will be discussed next in the following section.

Variables and Constants

If you're not familiar with *variables*, the term means a name for an area of memory that is set aside for storing data to which the variable name refers. In this way, you can gain access to the data from memory by name, which is easier to remember than a memory address. Because the name used to refer to the data is a variable, you can assign different values to the name at different times.

For example, suppose that you want to create a variable name that will hold an integer value used to perform a loop in your code. You would declare the name as

```
Dim intCounter
```

Then, in your loop code, you could specify something similar to this:

```
For intCounter = 1 to 10
        Do something with your code
Next
```

This is what is known as a For loop. You are going to change the value in the intCounter variable name, and also the data at the memory location reserved for intCounter, from 1 to 10 in single step increments.

A *constant* is another type of data store with one major difference from the variable—the data in a constant like the following cannot be changed:

```
Const pi = 3.14159265
```

This would indicate that the data name of `pi` is assigned the value of 3.14159265, and it cannot be changed by any code segment. If you declare a data store as a constant, you must also initialize it with a value at that time as you cannot modify or assign it later in code.

VBScript does not require that you declare a variable before using it. Explicitly declaring variables first is just good programming practice, and you can actually make use of a feature in VBScript that can help force you to learn this habit. If you place a statement such as Option Explicit at the start of your `.asp` files, VBScript will complain when you attempt to reference an undeclared variable. This tells the compiler that every variable must be declared explicitly before it is used. You must place Option Explicit after any `.asp` directives, such as `#include`, but before any HTML or script code.

Declaring Variables

To declare a variable in VBScript, use one of these four statements:

- `Dim`—Declares a variable normally and is the most common statement used. An example is *Dim intCounter*.

- `Public`—Makes a variable available in more than one function or procedure. An example is *Public strName*.

- `Private`—Makes a variable private to the procedure or function in which it is declared. An example is *Private m_lngPi*.

- `ReDim`—Use when working with arrays. If you had an array that was already declared and you used the `ReDim` statement, you would effectively clear the original data and formatting of the array and replace it with the new data. The example *ReDim arDice(9)* would reconfigure the `arDice` array with 9 elements.

In the list of statements I mentioned making variables public and private. These issues are known as the *scope* of a variable. Scope refers to where the variable can be accessed from and when it no longer exists.

A normal variable is visible only within the function in which it is declared. No other function can access it. You can have a variable with the same name exist in another function, and the two will not get mixed up. When the function or procedure ends, the variable is no longer valid and goes *out-of-scope*. This means that the variable name doesn't exist anymore. The data still resides in memory, but that memory location is now available to be used by another variable or even another application.

This information is important to know because, a good portion of the time, you want to maintain state within an application on your server. The only way to do this is to make your variables available and visible to the entire application. This is done by using global variables. These are declared with Session or Application scope. *Session scope* makes your variable available to all pages within the application that are requested by one user. *Application scope* makes the variables available to all pages in the application requested by any user.

To declare variables with these types of scope, you use the Session and Application objects, respectively. For example, to declare a variable with Session scope, such as the first name of a user, use the following code:

```
<% Session("Fname") = "Gerry" %>
```

You can now access and use this variable across all pages that are used within the session, by simply placing this line within your page where you want to use the first name:

```
<%= Session("Fname") %>
```

In the same way, you can use the Application scope object by replacing `Session` in the code snippet with `Application`.

I am not trying to provide you with a complete ASP tutorial here, just some good background information to help you understand how it works so you can use it in your IIS environment.

Client-Side Script Interaction

You can mix client-side scripting and server-side scripting within the same page if you want to. There is a caution in doing this—not all browsers support all scripting languages. Netscape does not support VBScript, so you would not be able to use VBScript for the client-side portion if you wanted to be compatible with all browsers.

The newest browsers provide varying degrees of support for Java applets and Java Script or JScript. This could be a fairly safe bet to use for client-side scripting. Listing 16.3 demonstrates the use of this technique.

LISTING 16.3 `mixscript.asp`

```
<%@ LANGUAGE = "VBScript" %>
<HTML>
<HEAD><TITLE>Mixing Script</TITLE></HEAD>
<BODY>
<%
  Dim tmTime, strServerName, strServerSoftware, intGreeting
  tmTime = Time()
  strServerName = Request.ServerVariables("SERVER_NAME")
```

```
    strServerSoftware = Request.ServerVariables("SERVER_SOFTWARE")
    'Generate a random number.
    Randomize
    intGreeting = int(rnd * 3)
%>
    <SCRIPT LANGUAGE="JScript">
    <!--
    //Call function to display greeting
    showIntroMsg()
    function showIntroMsg()
    {
      switch(<%= intGreeting %>)
      {
      case 0:
        msg =  "Welcome to <%= strServerName%> Web server running
            <%= strServerSoftware %> software."
        break
      case 1:
        msg = "This is my <%= strServerName%> Web server. The time on the
server is             <%= mTime %>."
        break
      case 2:
        msg = "I am running <%= strServerSoftware %> on this computer."
        break
      }

    document.write(msg)

    }
-->
</SCRIPT>
</BODY>
</HTML>
```

This code will create a page that requests the server time, name, and software version on the server side. It then passes these parameters to the JScript function, which runs on the client's computer.

One benefit of this technique is that you can take the burden of processing the JScript function away from the server and move it to the client. A lot of little scripts like this can mean a performance enhancement on your server. Now, don't get me wrong. I'm not saying that you need to load down the client's computer with scripting either, but the more processing you can offload from your server, the better it will perform the remaining processing.

Procedures

In the documentation for IIS 5.0, Microsoft states "a procedure is a group of script commands that performs a specific task and can return a value." In my experience with programming languages, a procedure (such as a subprocedure) is indeed a group of commands or statements that will perform a specific task. However, for returning a value, I prefer to stick to calling that a *function*. In this way, you can differentiate between a procedure that will only perform a function and one that will return a value to the calling procedure.

In keeping with typical scenarios of functions and procedures used by other development tools, you can write your procedure/function within the same page that will use it. Alternatively, you can write common procedures/functions into a common file and use the #include directive to bring the file and the functions into the page. This can help reduce having to write the procedure or function each time you want to use it in a page.

Procedures are written to be executed either on the server or on the client. Most of the script commands that I have written have been within <% %> delimiters. However, for functions or procedures, you normally enclose them within the <SCRIPT> </SCRIPT> tags. When you do this, the code will run on the client computer. If your code is VBScript, any non-Microsoft browser will have trouble processing it.

To cause your function and procedures to run on the server only, you can include an extra directive in the <SCRIPT> opening tag:

```
<SCRIPT LANGUAGE=VBScript RUNAT=SERVER>
```

This tells IIS that the script within this set of script tags must run on the server.

> **CAUTION**
>
> Make sure that all your functions or procedures are completely within the script tags. Also, do not use any script commands that do not form part of the procedure within the same script tags. This can result in code with unpredictable behavior.

When your page needs to make use of the functionality of a procedure or function, you need to call that procedure/function. There are various ways to do this based on what the procedure is and what scripting language you have used.

If you are calling a JScript routine, you must include parentheses at the end of the function name. The following code snippet shows the correct syntax for calling a JScript function called RunMe:

```
<HTML>
<HEAD><TITLE></TITLE></HEAD>
<BODY>
<% RunMe() %>
</BODY>
</HTML>
```

For VBScript, you can omit the parentheses unless the function or procedure you are calling requires parameters to be passed to it. The parameters must be placed within the parentheses, regardless of whether you are calling a VBScript or JScript procedure. The following snippet demonstrates this:

```
<HTML>
<HEAD><TITLE></TITLE></HEAD>
<BODY>
<% Sum(10, 25) %>
</BODY>
</HTML>
```

This procedure will send the two integers 10 and 25 to the procedure named Sum. By the name of the procedure, you can figure out that it will add the two numbers.

Collections

If you are used to working with arrays for storing related data, you might welcome the use of collections. Collections are like arrays in that they store a group of related items. You can store numbers, characters, strings, and objects in collections.

You can access the data in a collection by the index value similar to that of an array, or you can access the data by way of its unique string key. Of course, you can use a loop to iterate through a collection as well.

The advantage that a collection has over an array is that it can expand and collapse automatically as data is added or removed, and you don't have to re-dimension it.

A good example of a collection is the Contents collection of the Session object. You use this collection to store information for session state, so that you can retrieve any of the values as needed for a particular page or function. Consider the following code snippet:

```
<%
Session.Contents("Fname") = "Gerry"
Session.Contents("Lname") = "O'Brien"
Session.Contents("Phone") = "387-0000"
%>
```

If I need to access any of the data items within this collection, I can do so by using the key string or the index. The following lines of code show how to extract the last name from the collection:

```
<%= Session.Contents("Lname") %>
<%= Session.Contents(2) %>
```

Either line will return O'Brien as the value. The index value is 2 and not 1 because collection index numbers start with 1 (unlike an array that, by default, starts with 0).

Determining a Collection's Item Count

You might be asking yourself, "Well, okay, but how do I know how many items are in a collection?" With an array, you know up front because, for the most part, you create the array with the correct number of items. With a collection's capability to add and remove items automatically, the upper limit can change at any time.

The easiest way to determine how many items are in the collection is to iterate through the collection. You can use a loop to print the contents of a collection, as shown in Listing 16.4.

LISTING 16.4   Iterating Through a Collection

```
<%
Dim strItem

For Each strItem in Session.Contents
    Response.Write Session.Contents(strItem) & "<BR>"
Next
%>
```

This code uses the For...Each loop to iterate through the collection and print out the values "for each" item in the collection. It doesn't matter how big or small the collection is; the loop will stop after the last item is accessed.

Alternatively, you can use a For...Next loop. Its code sequence would look like this:

```
<%
Dim intCounter

For intCounter = 1 TO Session.Contents.Count
    Response.Write Session.Contents(intCounter) & "<BR>"
Next
%>
```

This code does the same thing as the previous For...Each loop. You are free to choose whichever one you like.

> **NOTE**
>
> If you are a VB programmer and used to dealing with collections in that language, there is one change that you need to be aware of in regard to collections in ASP. In ASP, collections support the Item, Count, Remove, and RemoveAll methods, but they do not support the Add method. You will have to build your collections at design time.

User Input Processing

User input processing is perhaps one of the greatest features of ASP from an administrative standpoint. You can use the forms processing capabilities of ASP to collect and validate user input. Forms have been the standard for some time now with HTML pages for collecting data from users. You can use ASP to validate data sent to an ASP page from a static .htm file or from another .asp file. You can also create a form using ASP and send the data on that form back to an ASP page again.

Listing 16.5 creates a sample page that contains a couple of input boxes for user information, such as first and last names. Listing 16.6 uses that data and passes it to an .asp file that will process the data and display it on the screen with a welcome message.

LISTING 16.5   inputuser.htm

```
<HTML>
<HEAD><TITLE>Form Data Collection</TITLE></HEAD>
<BODY>
<H2>Please enter your first and last names in the appropriate
boxes below and click the Enter button.</H2>

<FORM METHOD="GET" ACTION="userinfo.asp">
First Name <INPUT TYPE="Text" NAME="FirstName"> <P>
Last Name <INPUT TYPE="Text" NAME="LastName"> <P>
<INPUT TYPE="Hidden" NAME="UserStatus" VALUE="New">
<INPUT TYPE="Submit" VALUE="Enter">
</FORM>

</BODY>
</HTML>
```

LISTING 16.6 userinfo.asp

```
<%@ LANGUAGE="VBScript" %>
<HTML>
<HEAD><TITLE>userinfo.asp</TITLE></HEAD>
<BODY>
<CENTER><H1>UserInfo.asp</H1></CENTER>
<HR>
Welcome <% =Request.QueryString("FirstName") & " " %>
<% =Request.QueryString("LastName") %>
</BODY>
</HTML>
```

Listing 16.5 gathers the user's information. It is just a static HTML file that includes a form. In the form section, the method is GET, and the action is listed as the userinfo.asp file. This means that IIS will gather the information from the form fields and keep that information in the FirstName and LastName variables declared in the form's INPUT Name. The information is then passed to the userinfo.asp file in the URL and looks like this:

http://localhost/userinfo.asp?FirstName=Gerry&LastName=O%27Brien&UserStatus=New

The userinfo.asp page extracts the information using the Request.QueryString method and then displays it on the page. This information can be sent to a database or to a text file that you can later examine.

This example is not that elaborate, but it gives an idea of the possibilities with ASP for gaining access to user information. This information can be used by the marketing department for potential sales contacts or any other internal uses that you might have.

One of the main advantages in processing user input from a form is the ability to use validation functions to determine if the information is valid. You could use this functionality to have a user enter a username and password when connecting to an initial page. This username and password could be sent to another ASP page that will query a database and validate the user information. If the information is valid, the user can be given access to the Web pages. If not, the ASP script could generate a custom error message based on the validation. This is a great timesaving feature in that it can be used to generate pages dynamically and doesn't require you to store multiple pages on the server, taking up disk space and man hours to build.

Components and Objects

Almost all software development has turned to Object-Oriented Programming (OOP). The concept of OOP is that you create objects based on real world objects and try to mimic the real world objects as closely as possible in the code.

Creating objects requires that you create an interface for the object. This interface is not necessarily a graphical interface, like a Windows application has. It's more like a set of procedures, properties, and methods that are exposed to programmers, so that they can make use of the object in their own projects.

Microsoft uses this concept in their COM, COM+, and DCOM components. These COM components are reusable pieces of code that can be plugged into an application and used without having to re-create that functionality from scratch.

A good example would be the Microsoft Office Suite of applications. Microsoft includes Visual Basic for Applications (VBA) with Office, which enables you to customize the software product to add functionality that doesn't exist in it. When you use VBA, you are accessing COM components.

Other software developers can create an application entirely separate from the Office Suite but can make use of Microsoft Word's spell checking feature, if Word is installed on the system. Again, you are accessing and working with COM components.

The biggest advantage of components to Web developers is that developers can call a component's functionality from within their scripts. This means that you could create a COM component in whatever programming language that supports it and access that component from within your VBScript or JScript. This COM component could be written in C++, which would offer better optimization that an ASP script could.

You can encapsulate your business logic into COM components, which makes the logic portable. It also means that, if you need to change the logic, you can do so and maintain the access mechanisms without breaking your existing code that accesses the logic.

Using COM Objects in ASP

In order to use a COM component or object in your script, you must create an instance of it first. Do so with the following code:

```
<% Set adOne = Server.CreateObject("MSWC.AdRotator") %>
```

This line of code will create an instance of the Ad Rotator component, which comes with IIS 5.0 and will be covered in Chapter 17, "Installable ASP Components."

Of course, after you have created an object, you need a way to access its functionality. Each object exposes methods that you can call from within your code. These methods are responsible for setting or getting properties of the object or for performing specific actions.

A good example of this is in some of the code that you have used previously. IIS has a built-in object called the *Response Object*. You have used it in your ASP scripts to write something to the HTML page, like this:

```
<% Response.Write "<B>Write method of the Reponse Object</B>" %>
```

The Write method causes the HTML following it to be displayed on the page. Write is one of the methods of the Response Object that you do not have to create. You simply call the method and pass it the necessary parameters; it takes care of the processing necessary to display the text you entered.

You can set the available properties of an object from your script code as well. The Ad Rotator object that you instantiated earlier contains three properties, Width, Height, and Border. You can set any one or all of these properties with your code, as in the following example:

```
<% adOne.Width = 440 %>
```

I have set the width of the Ad Rotator control to be 440 pixels wide. Notice that I used adOne instead of MSWC.AdRotator. This is because I created a copy of the object and called it adOne. I can set the properties of adOne as an instance of the object, but I cannot set the properties on the MSWC.AdRotator itself.

As mentioned earlier, you can make use of COM components and objects to make administration easier by incorporating the logic you need into these components and making that code reusable across many Web applications without the need to re-create it.

Object Scope

When dealing with objects, you need to be aware of an object's *scope*, that is, its visibility to functions or scripts. If an object doesn't have the correct scope, scripts will not be able to access the functionality of the object.

Page Scope

Normally, an object has what is called *page scope*. This means that any script on the page where the object was created can see the object and can gain access to the functionality of that object. If you created an Ad Rotator object on default.asp, only scripts on default.asp can access the Ad Rotator object. Any script on another page, such as contact.asp, would not be able to access the Ad Rotator object on the default.asp page.

Any object created with the Server.CreateObject method has page scope. When the page has finished processing, the object is released. This is a good idea because it frees the resources used by that object.

Session Scope

You can also create an object and give it Session scope. *Session scope* means that the object is available to all scripts processing within the session. Use Session scope for components that deal with user info that must be manipulated over many pages during the course of the session.

Session scope requires a knowledge of threading, which is another topic altogether. Therefore, I will not cover it in any detail here.

Application Scope

The third type of scope available is *Application scope*, which means that an object is available over an entire application. This can have benefits in relation to performance issues. Assume that you want to use an Ad Rotator component to display your ads to the users of your Web site. If you were to create this object using Page scope, each time a user opened a page that contained the object, it would create an instance of that object. Each page opened would create another instance. Each instance would exact a toll on your server performance.

Now, if you were to take that same Ad Rotator object and give it Application scope, each page could then access that one object and make use of it, instead of creating a new one. This can save server resources.

For more information on object scope and how to implement threading, see the IIS help file in the Active Server Pages Guide, Active Server Pages, Building ASP Pages, Setting object Scope section or visit Microsoft Developer Network at http://msdn.microsoft.com/library/default.asp under the Platform SDK, Web Services, Internet Information Services SDK, Active Server Pages Guide, Active Server Pages, Building ASP Pages, Setting Object Scope.

Sending Content

Any text in an .asp file that is not an HTML tag, or is not enclosed within the <% %> delimiters or the <SCRIPT> </SCRIPT> tags, is sent to the browser for display. As shown in Listing 16.7, you sometimes need to send output to the browser from within the code by using the Write method of the Response object.

LISTING 16.7   newtime.asp

```
<%@ LANGUAGE = "VBScript" %>
<HTML>
<HEAD><TITLE>Server Time</TITLE></HEAD>
<BODY>
<CENTER><H1><FONT Color="Blue">GK Computer Consulting Order Entry Page
</FONT></H1></CENTER><HR>
<%
Dim timeframe
If Time < #12:00PM# Then
    Response.Write "<B>Good Morning</B>"
```

LISTING 16.7 Continued

```
ElseIf Time >= #12:00PM# AND Time < #5:00PM# Then
    Response.Write "<B>Good Afternoon</B>"
Else
    Response.Write "<B>Good Evening</B>"
End If
%>
Welcome to our web site!<P>
Any transactions that you perform on our site today, will be stamped<BR>
with our local date and time which is <B><% =Now() %></B>
</BODY>
</HTML>
```

In Listing 16.7, I have reproduced some of Listing 16.1 with some modifications to show the use of the `Response.Write` method. The code still checks to see what time it is on the server and greets the user accordingly, but, this time, I have used the `Response.Write` method to send the correct text to the browser. Because the text is inside the script delimiters, I had to use `Response.Write` because the browser will ignore anything between them and will not display the text.

You can also send other information to the client browser besides text. The Response object has a property known as `ContentType`, which is used to specify the type of content being sent to the browser. Browsers use this information to determine whether they can display the data themselves or whether they need to call a helper application.

Examples of this can be found at most computer hardware manufacturers' Web support Web sites, where they maintain a list of component manuals for downloading or viewing. Most are formatted using Adobe®'s PDF and require the Acrobat® Reader to view them. If you download the page, you would open the reader yourself and view the document. If you choose to view it from the Web site, the server must send the content type of `pdf` to your browser so that it can open the Acrobat Reader, if it is installed on your system, and configure it in the browser.

The browser recognizes these content types by using file extension mapping to MIME (Multipurpose Internet Mail Extensions).

Redirect Method

One method for sending content to the client that can prove a valuable tool for the IIS administrator is the `Redirect` method. Technically, you are not sending content to the client with this method; you are just causing the client's browser to be redirected to another page or location. If you change a page or content's location in a Web site, you can use the `Redirect` method to ensure that clients are taken to the correct location until you make the necessary changes to the appropriate links in the various pages. On extremely large sites, this can take quite some time, so the `Redirect` method is a welcome addition.

Another reason to use the `Redirect` method is to ensure that users who have actually logged in to a site that requires authorization have a valid userID. You can check to see that they have a valid user ID, and, if not, you can redirect them to the registration page with the following code snippet:

```
<% If Session("userID")="" then
    Response.Redirect "registration.asp"
 End If
%>
```

Using this code, check in a session variable called `userID` to see if it contains an entry. If it is blank, the user has not registered and needs to be sent to the registration page. The `Response.Redirect` method does this.

These are just some of the examples of how you can send content to the client. The online help files offer some more information and examples of usage.

Including Files

You can make your life and that of your Web developers a little easier with the use of `#include` files. C and C++ programmers have long enjoyed the benefit of being able to use pre-written code in their applications, code that was written by them or someone else and already debugged and tested. This is a fantastic timesaver in that you don't have to re-create something that already exists.

IIS 5.0 has the `#include` directive, which enables you to do the same thing that the C++ programmers do. Your Web developers might already have pre-coded `ASP` or `HTML` pages that are company standards and that need to be displayed on each Web page that the Web site uses.

Whenever I use FrontPage templates to design a site on IIS, I create a navigation frame or section in the page that contains the necessary links to the main pages in the Web site. I then use the `#include` directive to place these files into the correct frame or section of each page that needs them. This means that I create the code once and include it in each page that needs it.

The syntax for the `#include` directive is

```
<!-- #include virtual|file ="filename" -->
```

You will notice that the directive is placed inside the comment `<!-- -->` tags. You use either virtual or file to indicate if the `#include` file resides in a virtual or regular directory. The filename is the complete path and name of the file that you want to include.

When naming your #include files, it is recommended that you use the .inc or .stm extensions to distinguish these files from regular .html files in a directory listing.

#include files can contain #include directives to other files as well. This can be a confusing and potentially error-prone procedure, especially if you inadvertently create a loop such as include1.inc calling include2.inc, which in turn calls include1.inc.

CAUTION

#include files will execute before any scripting commands on the page, so you cannot use a script to dynamically create #include filenames.

TIP

It is always a good idea to review your #include files to ensure that they do not contain any unnecessary code that will include the pages. This can cause excessive processing.

Managing Sessions

As you are aware, HTTP is a stateless protocol. Each request that comes into the server is treated as a completely new request with no link to any previous request or user information. This makes it rather difficult to develop any applications that need to maintain user information and choices that they have made during their visit to your Web site. A good example of an application requiring this is a shopping basket application like that used by many online purchasing sites, such as Amazon.com or Barnes and Noble.

The Session Object

ASP offers a solution to this dilemma with the session object. With the session object, the server can create a unique user ID and maintain that ID across a session for a user.

NOTE

There is one downfall to this method that is very important to keep in mind. The session object makes use of cookies. If your user's browser is set to refuse cookies, this method will not work.

To give you a better understanding of how the session object works, it is important to point out how a session is started. This can happen in one of four ways:

- The server receives a request for a page or application that requires a sessionID cookie, but one does not exist.
- A requested URL contains a reference to the Global.asa file, and that file contains a Session_OnStart procedure.
- The user stores a value in the session object.
- An .asp file's Global.asa file contains an <OBJECT> that instantiates an object with Session scope.

Each of these scenarios triggers the Session_Onstart event, in which you can place the necessary code to perform the functions you want to take place at that time. This can include such things as setting the session timeout value.

This value is the amount of time in seconds that the session will last if a user has not made a request or refreshed a page. This value needs to be adjusted based on the expected time it will take a user to click other pages or refresh existing pages. If the timeout is too short, you will disconnect the user from his session and, if he was using a shopping cart application, he would lose all information that was placed in his cart. He would need to restart the procedure from scratch.

Making a timeout too long is not a good idea either because a user could disconnect from a session before completing the transaction. The objects that were created as a result would remain in memory until the timeout released them. This could cause an unnecessary load on the server's memory usage.

Using the session object, the server will create a unique ID for the user when he starts a session. The server will send this user ID to the client browser in a cookie and will request that cookie when new requests are made, in order to maintain a state for that user. You can also use the session object to store variables relating to the user, as in the following code snippet:

```
<%
Session("Fname") = "Joseph"
Session("Lname") = "Smith"
%>
```

This kind of flexibility enables you to customize the pages returned to the client by using these variables in the code:

```
Welcome to our online shopping center <% =Session("Fname") %>
```

As you can see here, it wouldn't make any difference what user was visiting the page. The correct name would be placed in the Fname variable. Although a small thing, being called by name can actually make a client's visit more pleasing. It adds a personal experience to the visit.

There are many more tasks that you can perform with the session object, but, instead of filling an administrative book with a slew of programming topics, I will just discuss some of the methods here and leave the remaining exploration of the topic to you or your developers. The online help files provide more information on the session object and uses for it.

Accessing Data Sources

Using ASP, you can access data sources from scripting on your Web pages. The data source can be a Microsoft Access database residing on the server, or it can be any Open DataBase Connectivity (ODBC)–compliant data source, such as SQL Server, DB/2, or Oracle. You can even access data that resides in a text file or a spreadsheet using the correct methods.

The most common approach with data sources is to use a back-end database that supports multiuser, high performance access mechanisms, such as Microsoft SQL Server.

You can store information that changes often in one database, allowing access to that data from many pages within the Web site. This is a major timesaver. You only need to change the database, and all pages that access the data will be updated the next time they access the source.

You can also use a database to store user information such as usernames and passwords that map to access levels or other information related to authentication. You can then use ASP's data access capabilities to poll the data from the database and apply it as needed.

The ActiveX Data Objects (ADO) provide this connectivity to the database in ASP. ADO is a high-level access interface to the underlying structure of an ODBC–compliant data source; that means you don't have to deal with the low-level APIs that actually make up the ODBC interface.

In order to access a data source from ASP, you need to create the necessary connection information. This consists of a connection string that the script will use to locate the data source; the string provides the data source type and any authentication that might be needed.

For the examples in this section, you will use a Microsoft Access database that contains four pieces of information, the users' first names, last names, passwords, and access levels. Using Microsoft Access, create a table that contains this information and name it Users. Name the database itself userinfo.mdb and place it in the wwwroot directory. I have added three users to the database for illustrative purposes.

Setting an ODBC Data Source

Before you create an object to be used as the database access mechanism, you must set up the ODBC data source on the server. Follow this procedure to add the necessary information to the server to access the data source:

1. Open the Control Panel applet on the server.

2. Double-click the Administrative Tools icon to open the Administrative Tools window and then double-click the Data Sources (ODBC) icon, as shown in Figure 16.5.

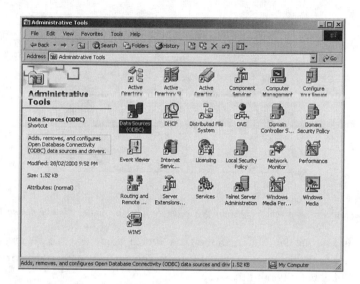

FIGURE 16.5

The Administrative Tools window is where you will find the Data Sources (ODBC) icon to configure data sources.

3. From the ODBC Data Source Administrator window, select the System DSN tab, as shown in Figure 16.6.

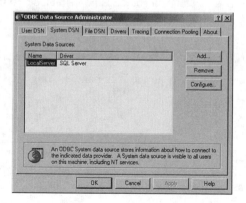

FIGURE 16.6

The ODBC Source Administrator window enables you to select the various options for data source names.

4. Click the Add button to open the Create New Data Source dialog box, select the Microsoft Access Driver (*.mdb) entry, and click Finish. The ODBC Microsoft Access Setup dialog box will appear, as shown in Figure 16.7.

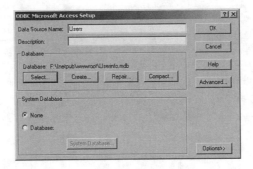

FIGURE 16.7

The ODBC Microsoft Access Setup window is where you locate the database and give it a name and description.

5. Enter a name for the data source in the Data Source Name text box. We will use this name to refer to the database in the ASP code. You can also enter a description here if you would like, but it is not necessary.

6. In the Database section in the middle of the dialog box, click the Select button to locate the database that you just created. Leave the remaining options at the defaults and click the OK button.

The new data source name will appear in the System Data Sources list on the ODBC Data Source Administrator dialog box. The data source is now created and installed on the server for access by ASP code.

Accessing the Database from a Web Page

Now you need to access the database from the Web page. Listing 16.8 will perform the necessary database connection.

LISTING 16.8   database.asp

```
<%@ LANGUAGE = "VBScript" %>
   <HTML>
   <HEAD><TITLE>Database Access Example</TITLE></HEAD>
   <BODY>
   <CENTER><H1><FONT Color="Blue">Accessing a Database</FONT></H1>
</CENTER><HR>
   <%
```

```
    Dim db
    Dim rs
    Dim strSQL
    Set db = Server.CreateObject("ADODB.Connection")
    db.Open "Users"
    strSQL = "SELECT * FROM Users"
    Set rs = db.Execute(strSQL)
    %>
    <table BORDER="1" WIDTH="100%">
    <tr>
        <td bgcolor="#C0C0C0"><font face="times new roman, times">
        <p align="center"><b><font color="#FF0000">First Name</font></b>
</font></td>
        <td bgcolor="#C0C0C0"><font face="times new roman, times">
        <p align="center"><b><font color="#FF0000">Last Name</font>
</b></font></td>
        <td bgcolor="#C0C0C0"><font face="times new roman, times">
        <p align="center"><b><font color="#FF0000">Access Level</font>
</b></font></td>
    </tr>
    <%
    Do While Not rs.EOF
    %>
    <tr>
    <td align="center"><font face="times new roman, times"><% =rs("FName")
    %>
    </font></td>
    <td align="center" ><font face="times new roman, times"><% =rs("LName")
    %>
    </font></td>
 <td align="center" ><font face="times new roman, times"><% =rs
("Access_Level")
 %>
 </font></td>
</tr>

    <%
    rs.MoveNext
    Loop
    db.Close
    %>
</BODY>
</HTML>
```

This code will contact the Userinfo database created earlier using the User data source name. The first thing to do with the code is to create an ADODB connection and open the database.

To extract the records from the database, use an SQL statement, SELECT * From Users. This statement tells ADO to select all the records that it finds in the Users table, located in the database just opened. You'll use this information to create a recordset, which is the data mechanism that manipulates the records returned from the database.

After populating the recordset, you'll dynamically create a table and fill it with the first name, last name, and access level fields from the database. Note the use of the line <% Do While Not rs.EOF %> in the code. By using this style of loop and comparing the counter to the rs.EOF, you will be able to fill the table with the data. You don't need to know how many records the table contains. This code will cause the loop to stop when the recordset reaches the end indicated by the EOF property. For more information on recordset properties, see the documentation on ADO at http://msdn.microsoft.com/library/psdk/dasdk/adot9elu.htm.

Figure 16.8 shows Internet Explorer displaying the results of opening the database.asp file. Note that it doesn't show the password field, as that can be considered a security risk.

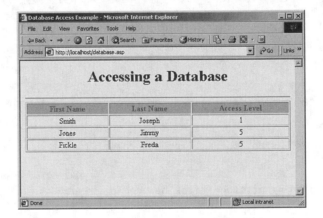

FIGURE 16.8

Internet Explorer shows the results of accessing the Userinfo database from ASP code.

The preceding example is only a simple use of ASP's data access. You can create a database such as this and access the same information to make decisions in your ASP code regarding how user access is granted on a Web site.

Transactions

If you have set up an electronic storefront on your Web Server so users can place orders online for your products, you want to provide a reliable means for them to place an order, have the dollar amount billed to an account, or charge purchases to a credit card and then see the order confirmed.

You need a way of ensuring that all the steps of the purchase take place, or, if one step fails, that the purchase doesn't take place at all. You accomplish this through *transactions*.

ASP uses the Component Services transactioning environment to enable transaction processing. This environment lets you create high performance, scalable, and reliable Internet applications. It is actually a programming model that also provides a runtime environment for developing and managing these types of applications.

In order for your ASP page to use a transaction, you initiate it with the following code:

```
<%@ TRANSACTION=Required %>
```

This section has provided just an introduction to the possibility of using transactions in your ASP scripts. Transactions and COM programming is another topic that could easily take up an entire book, and it will not covered here.

Debugging Scripts

I have been writing ASP scripts for more than a year now and developing in Visual Basic for three years, and I still cannot get a page or application completed without running into errors. Then again, I'm aiming for the impossible because no programmer before me has been able to do this either.

These errors can be as simple as spelling mistakes or as complex as incorrect syntax. Whatever the cause, there are debugging features in ASP that can help you find and fix these errors.

Believe it or not, the easiest "debugger" to use, and the tool I use most often, is the browser itself. If you attempt to open a page in IE that contains an error in the script, you will receive an error message in the browser window. Figure 16.9 shows an example of this.

As you can see from the Error Type information provided in Figure 16.9, the script attempted to access a table in the database that does not exist. It even tells you what line the error can be found on. The reason for this error is because I changed the name of the table in the code from Users to User. This example shows how a simple typographical error can render a script not functional. It is always best to test your scripts in a test environment before sending them to the production server.

If you would like to have more control over your script debugging, you can use the Microsoft Script Debugger tool. This tool enables you to step through your code one line at a time, view variables in a window, set pauses or stop points in your code, and trace procedures. One disadvantage of this tool is that you cannot edit your scripts from within the tool itself.

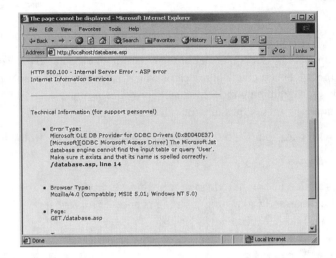

FIGURE 16.9
Internet Explorer shows an ASP script error.

Built-In ASP Objects

ASP contains built-in objects that allow you to access information from the server, respond to browser requests, and store information about users. Each of these objects is introduced in the following list. Refer to the online help files for more information on using these objects.

- **Application Object**—Provides a mechanism for sharing information among all the users of the application.
- **Request Object**—Collects information from the HTTP headers or information passed in from form fields using the GET or POST methods. Request Object can also gain access to information stored in cookies and binary data in files uploaded to the server.
- **Response Object**—Gives you control over information that you send to the user in HTML or cookies.
- **Server Object**—Gains access to the properties and objects of the server. You have already seen the use of this object in this chapter in the Server.CreateObject methods.
- **Session Object**—Stores information that pertains to a session, such as user information, in order to maintain the data across multiple page requests.
- **ObjectContext Object**—Used in transaction processing to cause the committal or abortion of a transaction.
- **ASPError Object**—Traps ASP errors that enable you to return more descriptive or more friendly error messages to the user.

16

All these methods are covered in detail in the sections on ASP in the IIS help files. Most administrators do not need to deal with creating or working with these components, so I will leave the details to the Web developers.

Summary

The information presented in this chapter was intended as an introduction to Active Server Pages and was in no way meant to be a tutorial on the subject.

I showed you some examples of using ASP to make your life a little easier when it comes to administering your Web Server. Making use of the built-in objects that ASP provides, you can automate some of the tasks of administering your server.

I presented some procedures that show you how to use ASP to reduce the load on the server by setting timeout values of script objects. This lets resources be released earlier.

You also saw how to use ASP script `#include` files to reduce Web site development time by reusing existing `.asp` and `.html` pages in other pages.

Although ASP is not entirely meant as an administrative tool, these examples showed you how to use ASP to your benefit. I highly recommend that you visit the MSDN Web site for further reading on ASP and the many uses for it.

Installable ASP Components

IN THIS CHAPTER

Active Server Pages includes some installable components that you can use on your Web sites to create interactivity and dynamic content. This chapter describes these components and provides an example of their usage.

Ad Rotator Component

The Ad Rotator component is used to create an Ad Rotator object within an `.asp` page that will automatically rotate advertisement images in much the same way as ad banners do.

Instead of changing the images on a timed basis, this component will display a new image whenever the user connects to the page or hits the refresh button.

Overview

The Ad Rotator makes use of a Rotator Schedule File, which is an ASCII text file, to determine the schedule and file information for the advertisements.

The Ad Rotator also uses a Redirection File. This optional file keeps track of how many times a particular ad has been clicked and provides the necessary redirection to the correct URL.

Listing 17.1 shows the code for our Web page that contains that Ad Rotator component. This code simply displays the Ad Rotator component at the top of the screen. Each time the page is accessed or refreshed, the ad will rotate.

LISTING 17.1   rotator.asp

```
<%@ LANGUAGE="VBScript" %>
<HTML>
<HEAD><TITLE>Ad Rotator Component</TITLE></HEAD>
<BODY>
<CENTER><%  Set ad = Server.CreateObject("MSWC.AdRotator") %>

<%= ad.GetAdvertisement("adrot.txt") %>

<HR>
<H1> Welcome to Our Ad Page!</H1></Center>
</BODY>
</HTML>
```

In order for this page to work correctly, you need to set up the `adrot.txt` file correctly. This file is displayed in Listing 17.2.

LISTING 17.2   adrot.txt

```
REDIRECT redirect.asp
WIDTH 440
HEIGHT 60
BORDER 1
*
http://localhost/gkad.gif
http://www.gkcomput.com/
Bringing You The World!
33
http://localhost/samsad.gif
http://www.mcp.com/sams
Sams Publishing
33
http://localhost/macad.gif
http://www.mcp.com/
Macmillan Computer Publishing
33
```

This file is an ASCII text file and follows a certain syntax. The first section indicates the REDIRECT file to use, if any, and then goes on to set the width, height, and border size of the images. This is important to note so that when you place images on your server for use with the Ad Rotator, you can size them correctly.

An asterisk separates the two sections (*). The second section details the image location and name, the URL that the redirect will take you to, and the replacement text for any browsers that do not support graphics or that have graphics turned off. These are each on a separate line. The last option for each entry in the file is an integer number indicating the percentage of time that the ad should be displayed.

The last file that was mentioned was the REDIRECT file. This file contains the ASP script code responsible for redirecting the users to the correct URL when they click on the ad image. For our little example, Listing 17.3 shows a really simple redirection file.

LISTING 17.3   redirect.asp

```
<%@ LANGUAGE="VBScript" %>
<HTML>
<HEAD><TITLE></TITLE></HEAD>
<BODY>
<%  Response.Redirect(Request.QueryString("url")) %>
</BODY>
</HTML>
```

Note that this file makes use of the `Request.QueryString` method to return the URL that is passed when the user clicks the ad. The `"url"` variable will be replaced with the correct URL for the company's home page or a page that deals directly with the advertised item.

Properties

Now that we have seen how the Ad Rotator works, it's time to look at the properties for this component. The Ad Rotator only has three properties associated with it.

Border

This property is used to determine whether there will be a border surrounding the ad or not. The only argument that it takes is the `size` argument.

Syntax

```
Border=size
```

`size` is an integer variable that determines the thickness of the border. This property is set in the rotator schedule file in the first section that sets up the ad image size.

Clickable

This is a Boolean value that accepts either TRUE or FALSE as a value. By setting the value to TRUE, you are indicating that the Ad Rotator can be used as a hyperlink to cause the client to be redirected to the URL for the ad.

By default, the `Clickable` property is set to TRUE.

Syntax

```
Clickable=value
```

`value` is either TRUE or FALSE.

If you wanted to prevent the Ad Rotator from being a hyperlink, you must specify this property in the same initialization section in which you create the object.

```
<% Set ad = Server.CreateObject("MSWC.AdRotator")
ad.Clickable = FALSE
%>
```

TargetFrame

If your pages make use of frames, you can use this property to place the ad into a specific frame on your page.

Syntax

TargetFrame=frame

frame specifies the name of the frame that you want the ad to appear in. You can use HTML frame-keywords as well for this variable, such as _TOP, _CHILD, and so on.

Example

```
<% Set ad = Server.CreateObject("MSWC.AdRotator")
ad.TargetFrame = _TOP
%>
```

By default, this property is set to NO FRAME.

GetAdvertisement

The Ad Rotator only has one method, GetAdvertisement, associated with it. This method is responsible for reading the schedule file and returning the HTML associated with it. It displays the next scheduled ad in the Ad Rotator component window when the page is loaded or refreshed.

Syntax

GetAdvertisement("schedule_file")

schedule_file is the relative path and filename of the schedule file that contains the ad image URLs.

Example

```
<%= ad.GetAdvertisement("/ads/adrot.txt") %>
```

The file *adrot.txt* is found in the /ads directory, which is under the Web's root directory.

Browser Capabilities Component

This component is used to determine a browser's capabilities and return that information in a BrowserType object. This object can then be used by your script code to determine the capabilities of a browser before sending content that might not function in it.

This functionality is possible through the use of the browscap.ini file. The HTTP User Agent header that is sent to the server when every Web client connects sends the browser version number and name. The server will compare this ASCII text string with the entries in the browscap.ini file to determine the browser's capabilities.

The Browser Capabilities component will search through the browscap.ini file for the entry that was supplied by the browser's header. If it finds a matching entry, it will apply the properties that pertain to that browser type.

The browscap.ini file is normally located in the %systemroot%\System32\inetsrv directory, wherein %systemroot% refers to the installation directory or Windows 2000. Listing 17.4 is an example of a browscap.ini file.

LISTING 17.4   A browscap.ini File

```
[IE 5.0]
browser=IE
Version=5.0
majorver=5
minorver=0
frames=True
tables=True
cookies=True
backgroundsounds=True
vbscript=True
javaapplets=True
javascript=True
ActiveXControls=True
Win16=False
beta=True
AK=False
SK=False
AOL=False
Update=False

[Mozilla/4.0 (compatible; MSIE 5.*; Windows 95*)]
parent=IE 5.0
platform=Win95
beta=True

[Mozilla/4.0 (compatible; MSIE 5.*; Windows 98*)]
parent=IE 5.0
platform=Win98
beta=True

[Mozilla/4.0 (compatible; MSIE 5.*; Windows NT*)]
parent=IE 5.0
platform=WinNT
beta=True
```

```
[Mozilla/4.0 (compatible; MSIE 5.*; Windows 2000*)]
parent=IE 5.0
platform=Win2000
beta=True

[Mozilla/4.0 (compatible; MSIE 5.*)]
parent=IE 5.0

[*]
browser=Default
Version=0.0
majorver=#0
minorver=#0
frames=False
tables=True
cookies=False
backgroundsounds=False
vbscript=False
javascript=False
javaapplets=False
activexcontrols=False
AK=False
SK=False
AOL=False
beta=False
Win16=False
Crawler=False
CDF=False
AuthenticodeUpdate=
```

For brevity's sake, I will not include a complete file here, but you can view the contents of the file in the directory mentioned previously. If no match is found in this file for a browser that connects to your site, the last section in the file offers settings or a default browser. The server will use these settings for that browser.

Syntax

Set BrowserType = Server.CreateObject("MSWC.BrowserType")

BrowserType is the name of the object that is created by the call to *Server.CreateObject*.

Example *(Not intended to be fully functional)*

```
<%@ LANGUAGE="VBScript" %>
<HTML>
<HEAD><TITLE>Browser Capabilities</TITLE></HEAD>
```

```
<BODY>
<%  Set bc = Server.CreateObject("MSWC.BrowserType") %>
<TABLE BORDER=1>
<TR><TD>Browser</TD><TD>   <%= bc.browser   %>
<TR><TD>Version</TD><TD>   <%= bc.version   %>   </TD></TR>
<TR><TD>Frames</TD><TD>
<%  if (bc.frames = TRUE) then  %>   TRUE
<%  else  %>  FALSE
<%  end if  %> </td></TR>
<TR><TD>Tables</TD><TD>
<%  if (bc.tables = TRUE) then  %>   TRUE
<%  else  %> FALSE
<%  end if  %> </TD></TR>
<TR><TD>BackgroundSounds</TD><TD>
<%  if (bc.BackgroundSounds = TRUE) then  %>   TRUE
<%  else  %> FALSE
<%  end if  %> </TD></TR>
<TR><TD>VBScript</TD><TD>
<%  if (bc.vbscript = TRUE) then  %>   TRUE
<%  else  %> FALSE
<%  end if  %> </TD></TR>
<TR><TD>JScript</TD><TD>
<%  if (bc.javascript = TRUE) then  %>   TRUE
<%  else  %> FALSE
<%  end if  %> </TD></TR>
</TABLE>
</BODY>
</HTML>
```

This sample code creates a Browser Capabilities component and then builds a table containing some of the data that it has determined the browsers can display.

The information is checked against the entries in the browscap.ini file and given the value of TRUE if the browser supports it or FALSE if it does not.

Content Linking Component

IIS includes the Content Linking component, which enables you to create the NextLink object for managing URLs and navigation on your site. You can use this component to automatically update a table of contents for your site or provide links for Next and Previous buttons for page navigation.

The component provides this functionality by accessing a Content Linking List file stored on the server.

17

Syntax

```
Set NextLink = Server.CreateObject("MSWC.NextLink")
```

Example *(Not intended to be functional)*

```
<OL>
<%
  Set NextLink = Server.CreateObject ("MSWC.NextLink")
  count = NextLink.GetListCount ("nextlink.txt")
  I = 1
%>

<UL>
<%  Do While (I <= count)  %>
<LI><A HREF=" <%= NextLink.GetNthURL ("/data/nextlink.txt", I) %>  ">
<%= NextLink.GetNthDescription ("/data/nextlink.txt", I) %>
</A>
<%
  I = (I + 1)
  Loop
%>
</UL>
```

Using the preceding code snippet, you can create a small sample table of contents using the
nextlink.txt file with a description of the links available.

The Content Linker component has a list of methods that perform the necessary functions to
make the component work. These methods are described in the following sections.

GetListCount

This method is responsible for determining the number of URLs that are listed in the Content
Linking text file.

Syntax

```
GetListCount(listURL)
```

listURL is the location and name of the Content Linking text file.

This method will return an integer value to use in your code as demonstrated in the preceding
table of contents code.

GetListIndex

This method will retrieve the index value of the current item. The Content List file acts like an
array in that the URLs entered in the file can be referenced by an index number.

Syntax

```
GetListIndex(listURL)
```

listURL is the name and location of the Content Linking text file.

You use this method to determine the index value of the current page within the Content Link text file.

GetNextDescription

You can use this method to get the description of the next URL in the list file.

Syntax

```
GetNextDescription(listURL)
```

Once again, *listURL* refers to the Content Linking text file.

This method will return an ASCII string value containing the descriptive text.

GetNextURL

This method will retrieve the next URL in the list file. In other words, it will cause the browser to navigate to the URL that is next in the list if used in an HREF statement.

Syntax

```
GetNextURL(listURL)
```

Example

```
<A HREF="<%= NextLink.GetNextURL ("/data/nextlink.txt") %>">Next Page </A>
```

GetNthDescription

This method will retrieve the description of the item specified by the index value placed in the call.

Syntax

```
GetNthDescription(listURL, i)
```

The *i* indicated in the parentheses is the index number that you want to retrieve. You can use a loop variable to fill in a value for *i*.

GetNthURL

This method returns the URL for the *N*th-specified URL in the Content Linking list file.

Syntax

```
GetNthURL(listURL, i)
```

listURL is the location of the Content Linking file and *i* is used to select the correct index for the value.

GetPreviousDescription

This method will retrieve the description of the previous item in the list file.

Syntax

```
GetPreviousDescription(listURL)
```

This method returns a string value from the Content list file.

GetPreviousURL

This will return the URL of the previous item in the Content list file.

Syntax

```
GetPreviousURL(listURL)
```

The value returned is a string value indicating the URL.

Each of these methods can be used in code to retrieve the necessary information to form the HTML that creates the pages.

Content Rotator Component

This component is used to rotate HTML content on a page based on information specified in a Content Schedule file. You could use this component to add a quote of the day section to a page by placing it in a frame, or you could use it to schedule the appearance of various images or any other legal HTML content.

In the same way as for the installable components, you need to instantiate the Content Rotator component before you can use it. The following line shows how to create a Content Rotator component:

```
<% Set crRot = Server.CreateObject("MSWC.ContentRotator") %>
```

Content Schedule File

After you have created the component, you will need to create a Content Schedule file before you can use the methods of this object. The schedule file takes on the following syntax:

```
%%[#weight][//comments]
Content String
```

The double percentage signs, `%%`, indicate the start of a section within the file. The next entry is optional and is known as the *weight* of the entry. This is similar in concept to the percentage indicator used in the Ad Rotator component and will determine the probability of that particular entry being displayed.

There is also an optional comments section that starts with the `//` comment indicators. You can use this section to provide a descriptive comment about the particular entry.

The `Content String` portion contains actual HTML content to be displayed by the Content Rotator component. The data can be one or more lines and can contain images, text, and sound. Anything between the first `%%` signs and the next `%%` signs is considered one content string. You can see an example of the Content Schedule file in the following three entries:

```
%% // The first section
Welcome to the first section of the Content Schedule File

%% #2 //Second section
<H1>HTML Heading 1 Text</H1>
<HR>

%% #2
<IMG SRC="images/picture.gif">
```

Here you can see an example of the Content Schedule file with three entries. The first entry just displays a single line of text. There is no weight defined, so it will use the default of 1. The second section uses some HTML tags to format the displayed text and inserts a horizontal rule. The third section uses a reference to an image. The second and third sections use a weight of 2, which means that this data will be displayed more often than that in section 1.

ChooseContent

This is a method of the Content Rotator component that retrieves an HTML content string from the Content Schedule file. Each time the page is loaded or refreshed, `ChooseContent` will retrieve a new content string that contains the component.

Syntax

```
ChooseContent(content schedule file)
```

Replace the `content schedule file` with the path and filename of your content schedule file.

Example

```
<%
Set TipofDay = Server.CreateObject("MSWC.ContentRotator")
TipofDay.ChooseContent("/contentrot/TipContent.txt")
%>
```

This example would create the component in your Web page, and then it would choose an entry from the `TipContent.txt` schedule file located in the `/contentrot` directory.

GetAllContent

As you might guess, this method will retrieve all the content from the Content Schedule file and display it on the page. Each section will be separated by a horizontal rule. The most common use for this is to enable proofreading of all of your content at once.

Syntax

```
GetAllContent(Content Schedule File)
```

In the same way as the `ChooseContent` method, `Content Schedule File` enters the path and filename of the schedule file.

Counters Component

The Counters component is used to create a counters object. You can create any number of counters, but it is recommended that you create only one counters object, which is capable of creating more than one counter.

After you have created a counter, it will persist until you decide to remove it. The counter will not increment automatically. You must use the methods of the counter to set its value or to increase it.

The counters object does not have a limited scope. Any page on the site can access the same counter and manipulate it. You do this by accessing a counter with its name. For example, if you are using a counter to indicate the number of hits that a page has received and you named it *PageHits*, you can set up a script that will increment the value each time the page is accessed. You can also increment that same counter from an ASP script located on another page by using the same name, *PageHits*.

All counters are stored in the same text file, `Counters.txt`. This file and the `counters.dll` file should reside in the same directory.

Normally, you need to add the counter object to a `Global.asa` file so that it is available to all pages in the site. The syntax for creating a counter object is

```
<OBJECT RUNAT=Server SCOPE=Application ID=PageHits PROGID="MSWC.Counters">
➥</OBJECT>
```

This example creates a counter object with an ID of PageHits. As mentioned before, you access the functionality of the counter's object through its methods, which are explained in the following sections.

Get

This method is used to return the current value of the counter. If no counter exists, this method will create a new one with the name given and set its value to 0.

Syntax

```
Counters.Get(countername)
```

countername is the name of the counter from which you want the value returned.

Example

```
There have been <% =Counters.Get(PageHits) %> hits on this page.
```

This sample code snippet would get the value of the *PageHits* counter and display it in the text string.

Increment

You use this method to increment the counter by a value of one. You can place this in the Session_OnStart procedure in a Global.asa file to have the page counter incremented each time the page is accessed. If no counter exists, a new one will be created, and the value is set to 1.

Syntax

```
Counters.Increment(countername)
```

countername is used to indicate the name of the counter increment.

Example

```
<% Counters.Increment("PageHits") %>
```

This code snippet will cause the counter named PageHits to increase by one.

Remove

You use this method to delete a counter from the Counters object. When you call this method, it will also remove the entry from the Counters.txt file.

Syntax

```
Counters.Remove(countername)
```

The *countername* variable is a string indicating the name of the counter to remove from the Counters object and the Counters.txt file.

Example

```
<% Counters.Remove("PageHits") %>
```

This code will cause the counter named PageHits to be removed from the Counters object and the Counters.txt file.

Set

This method is the only one of the four that takes two parameters. The first parameter is the name of the counter that will be affected, and the second is an integer value that sets the new value of the counter. You could use this method to set any integer value that you want for the counter. The main use of this method is to ensure that the counter restarts at the correct number should you make changes to the page and upload it to the server.

Syntax

```
Counters.Set(countername, int)
```

The *countername* is the same variable mentioned in the previous methods sections; it gives the name of the counter to use. The second parameter, *int*, indicates the new value for the counter.

Example

```
<% Counters.Set("PageHits, 5000") %>
```

You could use a line in your code similar to this to set the counter to start at 5000.

There are other ways of adding counters to your Web pages. FrontPage has a counter component that you can control with properties from FrontPage, and there are other freely available counters on the Internet as well. This component enables you to control the counter yourself and increment it when you want to.

Database Access Component

The Database Access Component uses the ADO model for accessing databases on the server. The ADO model is a high-level database access method that prevents the need to program low-level data access APIs.

The access methods of ADO make use of many constants, such as `adOpenStatic` or `adLockPessimistic`. These constants are used to indicate cursor types, recordset types, and locking mechanisms. See the documentation on ADO at `http://www.microsoft.com/data/ado/`.

In order to use this component, you must create a reference to ADO in the `Global.asa` file or include a file that contains the names of the constants. Microsoft recommends that you create a reference to the ADO library in the `Global.asa` file, as shown in this sample code snippet:

```
<!--METADATA TYPE="typelib" FILE="C:\Program Files\Common
➥Files\System\ADO\msado2x.dll" -->
```

You will notice that in the preceding example, I have called the DLL file `msado2x.dll`. This is because, at present, there are three different 2x versions of ADO, 2.0, 2.1, and 2.5. You will need to search the directory mentioned to ensure that you are using the version that is present on your server.

File Access Component

This component enables you to create a FileSystemObject on the server that provides access to the file system there. There are methods, properties, and collections that provide the necessary access to the file system through this object.

The FileSystemObject provides the following objects for working with the local file system:

- **Drive**—Enables you to access information to drives whether they are physical or logical, local or network.
- **Drives**—This is a collection that includes a list of drives connected to the system whether they are physical or logical. If you have removable media drives, the media does not need to be inserted for the drive to be included in the collection.
- **File**—An object that enables you to copy, create, delete, and move files. You can also query the system for the existence of a file.
- **Files**—A collection that contains a list of files that exist in a folder.
- **Folder**—An object that enables you to create, delete, or move folders in the file system. You can also query the system for the existence of a folder.
- **Folders**—A collection that provides a list of folders within a folder.
- **TextStream**—Using this object, you can create, read, and write text files on the server.

Care must be taken when using the FileSystemObject so that it doesn't present a security issue regarding access to the files on your server.

Logging Utility

You can allow your applications to read from an IIS log file by using the IIS Log component to create an IISLog Object. With this component, you can create scripts or applications that can read through your IIS logs and extract information. This can be a great time saver because you do not have to search through the log files manually.

> **NOTE**
>
> The client connecting to the server that attempts to run the IISLog component must be authenticated as an Administrator or Server Operator. Any other user—or an anonymous user attempting to use the component by connecting to the page that the component is on—will cause the component to fail.

Syntax

```
Set logOne = Server.CreateObject(MSWC.IISLOG)
```

logOne is the name that will be used to refer to the log object.

After you have created a log object, you can then proceed to call the methods and set the properties of the object. These methods and properties are described in the following sections.

AtEndOfLog

This method indicates whether all the records have been read. AtEndOfLog returns a Boolean value of TRUE if there are no more records to read.

Syntax

```
AtEndOfLog()
```

CloseLogFiles

This method will close all open log files.

Syntax

```
CloseLogFiles(IOMode)
```

IOMode takes one of three parameters to determine which file to close. These parameters are

- **1**—Uses a constant of ForReading and will close log files that have been opened for reading

- **2**—Has a constant of ForWriting and closes log files that have been opened for writing
- **32**—Uses a constant of AllOpenFiles and will close all open files regardless of how they were opened (by reading or writing)

OpenLogFile

This method opens a log file for reading from it or writing to it.

Syntax

```
OpenLogFile(filename, [IOmode], ServiceName, ServiceInstance, —
➥OutputLogFileFormat)
```

Parameters

- *filename*—The name of the log file that you want to open.
- *IOMode*—Determines how the file is to be opened: 1 for reading and 2 for writing. The default is open for reading.
- *ServiceName*—This parameter is optional and is used to indicate that the logging module should return only the records that match the service.
- *ServiceInstance*—This parameter is optional as well and indicates that the logging module should return only the records that match the service instance.
- *OutputLogFileFormat*—An optional parameter that can be used to indicate the format for the log file if it was opened for writing.

ReadFilter

This method specifies a start and end date as criteria for reading the logs.

Syntax

```
ReadFilter([startDateTime], [endDateTime])
```

Parameters

- *startDateTime*—Use this optional parameter to specify the date and time after which you want to read the log files.
- *endDateTime*—An optional parameter indicating the date and time before which you want to read the log files.

These parameters are optional, and you can include either one or both to generate the appropriate filter.

ReadLogRecord

Use this method to read the next available log record.

Syntax

```
ReadLogRecord()
```

There are no parameters for this method.

WriteLogRecord

Use this method to write records to a current log file.

Syntax

```
WriteLogRecord(IISLog)
```

The IISLog parameter is an object that indicates where the log files were read.

BytesReceived

This property returns the number of bytes that were received during the operation. This pertains to the current log file.

Syntax

```
bytes = BytesReceived
```

The variable *bytes* can be any name you choose; it will contain the number of bytes received.

BytesSent

This property returns the number of bytes that were sent during the operation referred to by the current log record.

Syntax

```
count=BytesSent
```

The *count* variable can also be named anything you want. It contains the number of bytes sent.

ClientIP

This property returns the client's IP address in reference to the current log record.

Syntax

```
var=ClientIP
```

The variable *var* holds the client's IP address that is returned.

Cookie

Use this property to examine the cookie from the client.

Syntax

var=cookie

The *var* variable holds the cookie that is returned.

CustomFields

This property is used to retrieve any special or extra HTTP headers that might have been included in the operation that was logged. These headers will be returned as a two-dimensional array consisting of a matching key and value.

Syntax

var=CustomFields

The *var* variable is a two-dimensional array that contains the key-value pair used to describe the header.

DateTime

Use this property to retrieve the date and time from the current log record object.

Syntax

var=DateTime

The *var* variable will contain the date and time that is returned from the log file.

Method

Use this property to retrieve or extract the HTTP operation from the log record.

Syntax

var=Method

The *var* variable is used to hold the method used by the HTTP operation. These are operations like GET and PUT.

ProtocolStatus

The HTTP protocol status code is returned in this property.

Syntax

var=ProtocolStatus

The *var* variable holds the returned status code. These status codes indicate the success and failure of events as recorded by the log.

ProtocolVersion

Using this property, you can retrieve the protocol version from the current log record.

Syntax

```
var=ProtocolVersion
```

The *var* variable will hold the return value indicating the version of the protocol that was used to access the resource when the log was recorded. This value is a string value.

Referer

If the log file recorded a visit that was the result of a referral, this property will return that URL.

Syntax

```
var=Referer
```

The *var* variable contains the URL that referred the client to the Web site.

ServerIP

This property returns the IP address of the server for the operation that was recorded.

Syntax

```
var=ServerIP
```

The *var* variable will contain the IP address of the server that was recorded at the time of the operation.

ServerName

Use this property to read the name of the server. ServerName is the same as the ServerIP property but returns the name instead of the IP address.

Syntax

```
var=ServerName
```

The *var* variable will contain the name of the server as string value.

ServerPort

Use this property to return the port number that was used during the operation.

Syntax

```
var=ServerPort
```

The *var* variable will contain the port number that was accessed at the time the operation was recorded in the log file.

ServiceName

Use this property to extract the name of the service that was accessed at the time of the action. This name will include the server instance as well.

Syntax

```
var=ServiceName
```

The *var* variable contains the name of the service and the server instance (such as MSFTPSVC1 to indicate the FTP service using the first FTP server).

TimeTaken

This property will return the total time that the process took to complete, as recorded in the log file.

Syntax

```
var=TimeTaken
```

The *var* variable will contain the total time that the process took.

URIQuery

If a client made a request to the server for a URL that contained parameters, such as a form POST or GET method would include, this property will return that information.

Syntax

```
var=URIQuery
```

The *var* variable will contain the parameters that were passed as a part of the URL, as recorded in the log file.

URIStem

Use this property to return the URL recorded in the log file at the time of the request.

Syntax

`var=URIStem`

The *var* variable will contain the target URL, minus any parameters that were passed.

UserAgent

Use this property to return the browser's user agent string.

Syntax

`var=UserAgent`

The *var* variable will contain the user agent string value recorded in the log file at the time of the request.

UserName

If you have clients who authenticate with a username and password, this property will return the username that was used at the time of the operation. This is only for nonanonymous connections.

Syntax

`var=UserName`

The *var* variable will contain the name of the user that connected to the server.

Win32Status

You use this property to return the Win32 status code that was issued at the time of the operation.

Syntax

`var=Win32Status`

The *var* variable will contain the Win32 status code.

As you can see, there are quite a few methods and properties that enable you to query the log files for just the information that you need.

> **CAUTION**
>
> Only the four log file formats that are included in IIS can be read. If you are using a third-party logging utility, this object might not work as indicated here. Be sure to read the documentation thoroughly for any third-party logging utility.

MyInfo Component

The MyInfo component enables you to create properties within a MyInfo object that contain information about you and your Web site. This component is mostly used with the Windows 9x versions of Personal Web Server (PWS).

The MyInfo component for PWS contains a number of properties that do not pertain to IIS, so they will not be covered here. You can view the properties in more depth in the online help file for IIS.

The important aspect of the MyInfo component for IIS is that you can create your own properties and populate them with values that pertain to your personal situation. In order to use the component, you first need to create an instance of it:

```
Set MyOwnInfoObject = Server.CreateObject("MSWC.MyInfo")
```

You can also create the component in a `Global.asa` file by using the `<OBJECT>` tags, as in the following example:

```
<OBJECT RUNAT=Server SCOPE=Session ID=MyOwnInfoObject
➥PROGID="MSWC.MyInfo"></OBJECT>
```

After you have created the object, you can add and access various properties to build the information you would like the object to contain.

```
<% MyOwnInfoObject.FavoriteColor = "Blue"
   MyOwnInfoObject.Car = "Chevy Malibu"
%>
```

This example creates two new properties for the MyOwnInfoObject object, called `FavoriteColor` and `Car`. It then assigns two values to these properties. These properties will persist throughout a Web site and can be called at anytime from within the script because the object was created in the `Global.asa` file previously.

Page Counter Component

This component is designed to keep track of how many times a specific page has been opened. This component is not available across an entire Web site as the Counters Component is. Page Counter pertains to one page only.

You can use the Page Counter component to determine which pages receive the most visits and which ones haven't been accessed. In this way, you can streamline your Web site by concentrating more effort on the busy pages and possibly removing the least-accessed pages or recreating them to make them more appealing.

After the Page Counter component has been created on your Web page, it will periodically save the count information to a text file on disk so that you will not lose the count data in the event of a server failure.

The Page Counter component makes use of an internal Central Management Object to perform the recording of the page hits. When the Page Counter component is created, it will query the hit count from the Central Management Object. You can then use the methods of the Page Counter component to manipulate it, as you will see later in this section.

To create the Page Counter component object on a Web page, use this code example:

```
<% Set ctr = Server.CreateObject("MSWC.PageCounter") %>
```

The `ctr` variable is the name that you will use to reference the object from within your script code.

A Registry key is created for the object, and it can be found in the following location:

```
HKEY_CLASSES_ROOT
    \MSWC.PageCounter
```

This key will contain two values:

- **File_Location**—A string value that indicates the path and filename of the Hit Count Data file. By default, this file is located in the WINNT directory and is named Hitcnt.cnt.
- **Save_Count**—This is a DWORD value and is used to indicate the number of hits before the hit count is saved to the count data file.

Three methods are associated with the Page Counter component:

- **Hits**—This method will display the number of times the page or URL has been opened.
- **PageHit**—This method increments the hit count by one.
- **Reset**—This method resets the hit count for a specific page to 0.

Permission Checker Component

If you use authentication on your Web sites to provide visitor access to sensitive material, you can make use of the Permission Checker component in your code. Permission Checker will customize Web page availability based on the user's access permissions.

For example, using a script, you could check a user's access level and display only the URLs which that access level has permission to use. In this way, the user will not even see any references to pages that he should not have access to.

In order to use this component, you need to create an instance of it on the server with the following code:

```
Set prmCheck = Server.CreateObject("MSWC.PermissionChecker")
```

You can then use the name prmCheck, or whatever name you choose, to access the object. The Permission Checker component only has one method, HasAccess. You use this method to determine whether the user has the necessary access to the requested file(s).

The following example shows how you might use this component to check for access to a file:

```
<% Set prmCheck = Server.CreateObject("MSWC.PermissionChecker") %>

File Access = <% =prmCheck.HasAccess("C:\InetPub\wwwroot\securedfile.htm") %>
```

You can check for the access permissions on physical files, or virtual files and paths as well.

In order for this component to work, you need to be aware of the way in which IIS authenticates users when you have Anonymous access enabled. When it is first enabled, IIS will authenticate all users using Anonymous access. This will prevent the authentication mechanisms from checking for user accounts.

If you use the Permission Checker component, you should disable Anonymous access and use the Basic or Integrate Windows Authentication method. In this way, IIS will check the appropriate user account for access permission, and the Permission Checker component will work.

If you need to use both Anonymous and password authentication on the same site, make sure that you prevent Anonymous access to any secure pages. This will cause IIS to use whatever other authentication method you have set up, and the Permission Checker will work on those restricted pages.

You can set the ACLs for a page to deny Anonymous access. You can also use ASP to determine whether the user is attempting to access the site without a username/password combination. Use the following code example:

```
<% If Request("USER_LOGON") = "" THEN
      Response.Status = "401 Unauthorized"
   End If
%>
```

This little code snippet will issue the 401 Unauthorized Status message if the user is attempting to gain access to the page without a username. This causes IIS to attempt the authorization by using one of the password-based authentication means.

> **TIP**
>
> I recommend that you use the Basic authentication method to ensure that you cover browsers other than IE. Netscape and other browsers do not support the Windows NT Lan Manager (NTLM) authentication method. Also, NTLM might not work correctly over a proxy connection.

Status Component

You can use this component to create a Status object for your site. You can then use the properties of the object to check the server status information

Syntax

```
Set Status = Server.CreateObject("MSWC.Status")
```

`Status` is the name to use to refer to the component in code. You can name the object whatever you like.

This component, in its present implementation, can return only the status for Personal Web Server for Macintosh. If you attempt to use this component on a Windows platform, all the status properties will return as "unavailable." To return server status for ASP scripts that were developed on a Macintosh computer, you can use the properties listed here:

- `VisitorsSinceStart`—The number of unique visitors since the server has started. The IP addresses must be unique.
- `RequestsSinceStart`—The number of requests since the server was started.
- `ActiveHTTPSessions`—The current number of connections.
- `HighHTTPSessions`—The highest number of connections since the server started.
- `ServerVersion`—The version number of the Personal Web Server.
- `StartTime`—The time when the server was started last.
- `StartDate`—The date the server was started.
- `FreeMem`—The amount of free memory on the computer.
- `FreeLowMem`—The lowest amount of free memory that was available since the server started.
- `VisitorsToday`—The number of unique visitors since midnight local time.
- `RequestsToday`—The number of requests since midnight local time.
- `BusyConnections`—The total of rejected connections because the server connection limit was reached.

- **RefusedConnections**—The number of connections refused because of invalid authentication.

- **TimedoutConnections**—The number of connections closed without the request having been received.

- **Ktransferred**—The number of kilobytes transferred since the server startup.

- **TotalRequests**—Total requests received since the counter was last reset using the admin tool.

- **CurrentThreads**—The sum of the active HTTP connections and number of threads in the thread pool that are not currently handling connections.

- **AvailableThreads**—The number of threads in the pool that are not currently handling connections.

- **RecentVisitors**—This is actually an HTML table that will contain the 32 most recent unique visitors, including their domain names or IP addresses and the number of requests they made.

- **PopularPages**—Another HTML table for the 32 most recently visited pages, including the URLs and number of requests.

Tools Component

This component creates a Tools object that contains five methods you can use to add extra-sophisticated functionality to the Web Server.

You create an object similar to all other objects discussed thus far:

```
Set Tool = Server.CreateObject("MSWC.Tools")
```

The following sections identify the methods of this object and uses for the methods.

FileExists

This method will check for the existence of a file and will return a -1 if the file exists or a 0 if it does not exist. You can use this method in an If...Then structure, as in the following example:

```
<% If Tool.FileExists("/images/logo.gif") Then %>
<img src="C:\InetPub\wwwroot\images\logo.gif">
<% End If %>
```

This code snippet first checks to see whether the logo.gif file exists in the /images subfolder before inserting it into the page.

Owner

Use this method to determine whether the current user is the site administrator. If the username and password match, this method will return -1; it returns 0, otherwise.

This method only works on PWS for Macintosh.

PluginExists

This method will return a -1 if a specified Macintosh Server plug-in is present on the system. You specify the plug-in name as a parameter to the method as in the following example:

```
Tool.PluginExists(PlugInName)
```

On Windows-based computers, this method will always return 0.

ProcessForm

This method will process form contents submitted by a visitor. The method takes three parameters:

- **OutputFileURL**—A string value that holds the URL of the file that the data was sent to.
- **TemplateURL**—The URL that contains the template for processing the data.
- **InsertionPoint**—This parameter is optional and indicates where the data should be inserted into the output file. Presently, this parameter is not implemented.

Random

This last method will return a random integer between the values of -32768 and 32767.

You can use two functions with Random to restrict or manipulate the output. For example, you can use the ABS function to return positive numbers. You can also use the Mod function to return a number below a specific value. Examples of each follow:

```
<% =Tools.Random %>    ' This will return a random integer in the range
➥mentioned earlier.
<% =(Abs(Tools.Random)) %>    ' This will return a positive integer
<% =(Abs(Tools.Random)) Mod 50 %>    'This will display a random positive
➥number between 0 and 49.
```

Summary

This chapter has shown the available components that are included with IIS for use in ASP scripts. Although not all of them are intended for the Windows platform, Microsoft might make them functional in future releases.

Some of these components, such as the Logging utility, can make life easier for an administrator by providing the tools necessary for looking at log files and generating reports based on the information contained in them. This prevents the need to export the information into a text file and then use a parsing application to pull the necessary information from the log.

Other components, such as the Content Rotator and Content Linking components, can help ease administrative tasks by offering automation capabilities.

Whatever your needs, I'm sure you will find that at least one of these components will make your day-to-day duties as an IIS administrator somewhat easier.

Administrator's Reference

IN THIS APPENDIX

This appendix will provide you, the administrator, with a reference to the Registry, the metabase, and the Windows Events for IIS. You will also find information pertaining to counters, timeouts, and logging properties. Each topic is referenced in its own section.

Registry

As you are already aware, the Windows Registry stores configuration information relating the operating system and the applications and services that run on it. You make changes to the Registry using the Control Panel, Windows Setup, IIS Admin snap-in or the two Registry editing tools, REGEDIT and REGEDT32.

> ### TIP
>
> If you are not familiar with the REGEDIT and REGEDT32 utilities, you should note that only REGEDIT would allow you to search the Registry for data and values. The REGEDT32 utility allows searching the Registry for keys only. You can find the search feature for REGEDT32 on the view menu called Find. REGEDIT uses the Edit menu and includes the Find and Find Next options.

Almost every reference to editing the Registry offers this caution: It is recommended that you use the Control Panel or, in our case, the IIS snap-in to make the necessary changes to the Registry configuration keys. This will prevent inadvertently making changes that can render the computer unbootable.

Global Entries

The global entries can be found in the following Registry path:

```
HKEY_LOCAL_MACHINE
    \SYSTEM
        \CurrentControlSet
            \Services
                \InetInfo
                    \Parameters
```

CacheSecurityDescriptor—Type **REG_DWORD**, Range **1,0**, and Default **1**

This entry is used to specify whether the security descriptors are cached for the file objects. When enabled, IIS will retrieve the security settings of the file and cache them, preventing the need to access the file-access permissions from the file object.

CheckCertRevocation—Type **REG_DWORD**, Range **0,1**, Default **0**

This entry will check for certificate revocation by IIS. Enabling this will cause a server performance penalty because of the resources required to check this over the Internet. Should only be enabled if you issue certificates from your server.

DisableMemoryCache—Type **REG_DWORD**, Range **0,1**, Default **0**

Disables the server caching. Note that this entry cannot be set using the IIS snap-in.

ListenBackLog—Type **REG_DWORD**, Range **1–250**, Default **25**

Use this entry to specify how many connections to hold in queue if the server is busy. If you have an extremely busy server, you can set this value to 50. If you need a higher setting, you need to look at server upgrades.

MaxConcurrency—Type **REG_DWORD**, Range **0–unlimited**, Default **0**

This is the amount of concurrency that you want the system to provide. It is used to specify the number of threads-per-processor that can run simultaneously for a pending I/O operation. The default setting allows the server to make the choice.

MaxPoolThreads—Type **REG_DWORD**, Range **0–unlimited**, Default **4**

The number of pool threads-per-processor to create. This does not include threads that are used by ISAPI applications.

PoolThreadLimit—Type **REG_DWORD**, Range **0–unlimited**, Default **2* #MB**

The maximum number of pool threads allowed to be created. This value limits all IIS threads and will always be greater than or equal to the MaxPoolThreads.

MinFileKbSec—Type **REG_DWORD**, Range **1–8192**, Default **1000**

This Registry entry is used in relation to the timeout value that is specified in IIS and the size of the file. When IIS sends a file, it will use the timeout value as a basis for how long IIS will let the transfer continue before stopping it. The timeout value is calculated as the sum of the maximum Connection Timeout value from IIS and the size of the file, divided by the value specified in this key.

A

ADMINISTRATOR'S REFERENCE

NOTE

The value in this key is actually measured in bytes and not kilobytes as the name suggests. I cannot offer an answer as to why Microsoft did this.

ObjectCacheTTL—Type **REG_DWORD**, Range **0–unlimited**, Default **30 seconds**

This entry controls the Time To Live (TTL) value pertaining to the length of time that objects are held in cache memory. You use this value to prevent objects that are not frequently used from taking up memory space. If an object has not been accessed in the determined amount or time, the object will be dumped from the cache to make room for a new object.

It is a good idea to set this value low if your server is low on memory resources. You can disable the object cache by setting the value in this key to 0xFFFFFFFF. Any cached objects will remain in the cache until they are overwritten. It is not recommended that you do this if your server does not have sufficient memory resources.

ThreadTimeout—Type **REG_DWORD**, Range **0–unlimited**, Default **24 hours**

This entry is used to indicate the amount of time that will be allotted to maintain an I/O thread even if no I/O activity is taking place.

UserTokenTTL—Type **REG_DWORD**, Range **0–0x7FFFFFFF**, Default **15*60(15 minutes)**

This entry is used in conjunction with the security aspects of the Web site. When a user connects to the server and is required to provide a username and password, the server will create an access token for that user. The server will then impersonate this token when accesses to resources needing it are attempted. In this way, the server will cache the token, which means that the logon only needs to take place once. This value will limit the amount of time that the token will live in cache and is measured in seconds.

Service-Specific Entries

You will find these entries in the following Registry path. Note that the *servicename* entry is replaced by the name of the specific service, which is either *MSFTPSVC* (FTP Service) or *W3SVC* (Web Service).

```
HKEY_LOCAL_MACHINE
    \SYSTEM
        \CurrentControlSet
            \Services
                \servicename
                    \Parameters
```

AllowGuestAccess—Type **REG_DWORD**, Range **1,0**, Default **1 (enabled)**

This value will determine if Guest logons are allowed for the Internet services running on the server. Normally, Guest access is enabled on the server, but most administrators turn it off to prevent unauthorized access to the resources on the server. It is therefore a good idea to set this value to 0 (disabled).

EnableSvcLoc—Type **REG_DWORD**, Range **1,0**, Default **1 (enabled)**

In order for a service to be discovered by the MMC, it must register itself with a service locator. By setting this value to 1 (enabled), you are telling that service to register itself.

There is another Registry key that does not get created automatically but that resides in the specific service key if needed. This is the **LanguageEngines** key, and it is used to indicate scripting languages other than the default VBScript and JScript.

This key is located in the following location:

```
HKEY_LOCAL_MACHINE
    \SYSTEM
        \CurrentControlSet
            \Services
                \W3SVC
                    \ASP
                        \LanguageEngines
                            \languagename
```

The *languagename* variable is used to specify the name of the chosen language. There are two value entries for this key.

```
Write REG_SZ:Response.WriteEquiv |
WriteBlock REG_SZ:Response.WriteBlockEquiv |
```

LanguageEngines—Type **REG_STRING**, Range **String**, Default **Not Applicable**

You use this parameter to specify a scripting language that does not support the Object.Method syntax. The two values mentioned previously are used to indicate the equivalent commands to the Response.Write and Response.WriteBlock commands. I recommend that you read the documentation for the scripting language that you are going to use to ensure that it will be compatible with IIS. If it is not, you should learn VBScript or JScript.

WWW Service Entries

The World Wide Web service contains the following entries in addition to the Service-Specific entries mentioned earlier.

```
HKEY_LOCAL_MACHINE
    \SYSTEM
        \CurrentControlSet
            \Services
                \W3SVC
                    \Parameters
```

A

ADMINISTRATOR'S REFERENCE

AcceptByteRanges—Type **REG_DWORD**, Range **1,0**, Default **1 (enabled)**

If you set this value to 1 (enabled), the server will process the "Range" header for the type "bytes:" This will be processed according to the Internet Draft pertaining to byte range extension to HTTP.

AllowSpecialCharsInShell—Type **REG_DWORD**, Range **0,1**, Default **0**

If you enable this value by setting it to 1, you are allowing the use of the special characters (|(,;%< >) to be used in the command line from CMD.exe when running batch files. It is highly recommended that you leave this value at the default setting of 0 (disabled) unless you have a very specific reason for enabling it. There is a serious security concern with allowing the use of these special characters because they can be used by an intruder to execute commands on the server.

DLCSupport—Type **REG_DWORD**, Range **0,1**, Default **0**

If you are using multiple virtual Web sites on your server that make use of host header names, you should enable this value by setting it to 1. This provides what is known as *downlevel support* for older browsers that do not include support for host header names.

DLCCookieNameString—Type **REG_STRING**, Range **String**, Default **Not Applicable**

You use this entry to specify the name of a cookie that will be sent to downlevel clients. This string value will serve as a "pseudo" host header that will allow the server to properly route the client's request to the correct site.

DLCHostNameString—Type **REG_STRING**, Range **String**, Default **Not Applicable**

This entry is used to indicate the name of the Web site that contains the downlevel host menu. This is stored in the **DLCCookieMenuDocumentString** entry that is covered next. The menu that is referred to here is an HTML or ASP file that lists all the Web sites on the server that share the same IP address. Users can choose the Web site they want from this menu.

DLCCookieMenuDocumentString—Type **REG_STRING**, Range **String**, Default **Not Applicable**

This is the string value that contains the name of the file that is the menu for the downlevel clients that support cookies but not host header names.

DLCMungeMenuDocumentString—Type **REG_STRING**, Range **String**, Default **Not Applicable**

For clients that do not support cookies either, you can use this key to enter the name of the file that contains the host menu. This file will be used to embed the host name into the URL sent from the client.

DLCMenuString—Type **REG_STRING**, Range **String**, Default **Not Applicable**

This string value is used to specify the special prefix of the URL that is requested by the downlevel clients. The server will check all the requests from the downlevel clients against this string.

LogSuccessfulRequests—Type **REG_DWORD**, Range **0,1**, Default **1**

This is used to tell the server whether to record successful events into the log file. By default, it is turned on. Specify 0 to turn it off.

SSIEnableCmdDirective—Type **REG_DWORD**, Range **0,1**, Default **0**

This value does not exist in the Registry and must be added if you want to use it. By creating this key and setting its value to 1 (enabled), you are allowing the use of the **#exec cmd** server-side directive to run on the server.

This is a potentially dangerous option to enable on a server that is open to the public Internet because a malicious user could copy a virus or Trojan horse application onto your server and use the cmd command to execute that application.

TryExceptDisable—Type **RED_DWORD**, Range **0,1**, Default **0**

The default setting is 0 for this key because an exception error that is caused by an ISAPI application will halt the server if this setting is enabled (1). The only good reason to set this value to 1 is if your developers are debugging their applications. It should be immediately disabled before going into production.

UploadReadAhead—Type **REG_DWORD**, Range **0–0x80000000**, Default **48KB**

You can use this entry to control how much data is read by the server before passing it on to the application. When this data is passed to the application, the server passes the responsibility of reading the remaining data to the application. The more you increase this value, the more RAM you might need on the server.

UsePoolThreadForCGI—Type **REG_DWORD**, Range **1,0**, Default **1**

CGI processing is normally done using a server pool thread. You can change this value to 0 (disabled). One reason for disabling this option is if your CGI processing is taking a long time. In this case, the CGI process will consume the server pool thread.

FTP Service Registry Entries

You will find that the FTP service contains extra entries in addition to those in the Service-Specific entry as well. These entries can be found in the following location.

A

ADMINISTRATOR'S REFERENCE

```
HKEY_LOCAL_MACHINE
    \SYSTEM
        \CurrentControlSet
            \Services
                \MSFTPSVC
                    \Parameters
```

AnnotateDirectories—Type **REG_DWORD**, Range **1,0**, Default **0**

The ability to annotate directories for the FTP service allows you to place a text-based file on the server that contains the annotation text. When an FTP CWD operation takes place and the file is located in the target directory, the server will respond with the contents of the file. In this way, you can place custom messages for specific directories.

This file is named ~ftpsvc~.ckm and needs to be placed in the directory that you want annotated. It is also a good idea to apply the hidden attribute to this file so that it will not show up in directory listings.

EnablePortAttack—Type **REG_DWORD**, Range **0,1**, Default **0**

Because the FTP Service specification allows passive connections based on port addresses given by the client, this setting is disabled by default. This can help to prevent any intruders executing malicious code in the FTP Service. The only reason you would want to enable this option is if you want your users to be able to connect to the FTP service using other ports.

LowercaseFiles—Type **REG_DWORD**, Range **0,1**, Default **0**

The FTP Service will use the case settings for filenames based on the settings in the operating system. This might cause problems if file comparisons are used with case-sensitive file systems such as UNIX or Linux. In this case, you can enable this feature to ensure that there is support for case-sensitive filename comparisons.

Metabase

IIS uses a hierarchical database known as the metabase for storing its configuration information. This allows for easier manipulation of the configuration values using scripting languages. The metabase sets up the configuration values as objects. These objects are automation enabled so that any automation-aware language can gain access to the objects.

> **CAUTION**
>
> Configuring the metabase directly is somewhat like editing the Registry directly. There are certain risks in that you can cause a service to fail by incorrectly making configuration changes. It is best to use the IIS snap-in or the HTML Administration tool to make the necessary changes to the metabase.

The locations of the metabase properties are specified in the namespace. This namespace takes on the following syntax.

```
LM/Service/Website/Root/virtual directory/dir/file
```

LM is the name of the local computer.

Service indicates either W3SVC or MSFTPSVC.

Website is the Web site name.

Root is the virtual root directory.

Virtual Directory is the virtual directory name.

Dir is the directory.

File is the name of the file.

An example of how this namespace works is shown here:

```
LM/W3SVC/Website1/Root
```

This namespace path could then be mapped to the local path of `C:\InetPub\wwwroot\Default.htm`.

If you have specified any metabase properties at the root level, the object below that root will also inherit those settings. You can make changes to the lower objects individually that will override these inherited settings.

Windows Events for IIS

IIS makes use of the Windows Event Viewer to provide information about the various events that are taking place with the service. You can view any messages in the Event Viewer that pertain to IIS for information, warning messages and error messages as well.

When the Write unsuccessful client requests to event log option is checked in the Process Options property sheet, all ASP errors are sent to the Windows Event Viewer and will be logged and displayed in the Application Log.

To reach this option, open the Internet Services Manager, right-click the computer icon in the Tree pane, and choose Properties. Ensure that the WWW Service is selected in the Master Properties drop-down combo box and click the Edit button. Select the Home Directory tab sheet and click the Configuration button in the Application Settings section. Select the Process Options tab on the Application Configuration dialog box and make sure that the Write unsuccessful option is checked.

Even though you have set this option, not all ASP errors will be sent to the Event log. If you want all the ASP errors to be sent, you will need to set the metabase property

AspErrorsToNTLog setting to TRUE. See Chapter 14, "Administering IIS Programmatically," for details about setting the metabase properties and IIS Admin Objects in Chapter 14 as well, for information on how to set this property.

Web Services Events

Table A.1 lists the events for the Web services, providing their ID and a description.

TABLE A.1 Web Services Events

ID	Description
	Authentication
1	Error loading map file %1, error %2.
2	Logon failed for user %1 : %2.
3	Digest authentication: invalid authentication for user "%1", realm "%2".
4	Digest authentication: unrecognized user "%1", realm "%2".
5	Digest authentication: stalled authentication for user "%1", realm "%2".
	Logging
1	IIS Logging for %1 has been shut down because a disk full error has been encountered.
2	IIS Logging was unable to create the directory %1. The data is the error.
3	IIS Logging was unable to create the file %1. The data is the error.
4	IIS Logging for %1 was resumed.
5	IIS ODBC Logging failed to connect to data source %1. Error text is [%2].
100	The server was unable to log on the Windows account '%1' because of the following error: %2. The data is the error code.
101	The server was unable to add the virtual root '%1' for the directory '%2' because of the following error: %3. The data is the error code.
102	The server was unable to load ODBC32.DLL for sql logging because of the following error: %1. The data is the error code.
103	The server was unable to open ODBC Data source %1, Table: %2, under UserName %3. The ODBC Error is %4. The data is the error code.
104	The parameters specified for logging are too long. Field: %1; Data Given: %2.
105	The server was unable to register the administration tool discovery information. The administration tool might not be able to see this server. The data is the error code.

ID	Description

Logging

106   The creation of InetLog Context failed. The data is the error code.

107   Logging information failed. The log object was never created possibly because of wrong configuration.

108   The server was unable to find the log file directory %1. The data is the error code.

109   The server has suspended request logging because an error occurred writing a log record. The data is the error code. The error code text is %1.

110   The server has resumed request logging.

111   The service could not initialize the socket library. The data is the error code.

112   The service could not find module %1. The data is the error code.

113   Instance %1 has invalid binding descriptor %2.

114   Instance %1 has invalid secure binding descriptor %2 (hostname ignored).

115   The service could not bind instance %1. The data is the error code.

116   The service metabase path '%1' could not be opened. The data is the error code.

Metabase

1   Can't access IIS metabase configuration for server %1 instance %2, error %3.

2   Server %1 instance %2 does not respond to HTTP query, error %3.

800   MetaData has not been initialized.

801   The specified metadata was not found.

802   The version specified in metadata storage was not recognized.

803   A specified metaobject path was not found. The metaobject and associated metadata was ignored.

804   A metaobject or metadata was specified more than once. The duplicate ignored.

805   Invalid metadata was specified. The invalid metadata was ignored.

806   A secure communications channel could not be established with the target server.

807   The path was not inserted into the string as requested. The probable cause is that the data is at an object at a higher level than the handle.

808   The METADATA_SECURE attribute cannot be removed from a data item via the GetData method. Use the DeleteData method to remove the secure data.

809   The metadata save_prior to backup failed. The previous version of the data was backed up.

A

ADMINISTRATOR'S REFERENCE

TABLE A.1 Continued

ID	Description

ODBC Logging

1	Unable to perform Query %1.
2	The form you just filled in requires the %1 entry to be filled in. Please fill in that entry in the form and resubmit the form.
3	The query file %1 could not be opened. The file might not exist, or you might have insufficient permission to open the file.
4	The template file %1 could not be opened. The file might not exist, or you might have insufficient permission to open the file.
5	The template file contains an else tag without a matching if tag.
6	The template file contains an endif tag without a matching if tag.
7	The template file contains an expression with parameters that are of different type. For example, an if tag comparing a string with a number would cause this error.
8	The template file contains an expression using the CONTAINS operator where one or both parameters are not strings. CONTAINS is only valid with string values.
9	The template file contains an expression that uses a quoted string, but the close quote is missing.
10	The template file contains an expression with an unrecognized operator. Valid operators are GT, LT, EQ, and CONTAINS.
11	The query file contains an unrecognized field %1.
12	The query file must contain a valid, non-empty Datasource: field and SQLStatement: field.
13	The library odbc32.dll could not be loaded to perform the query. Make sure ODBC has been properly installed on the server.
14	The specified HTTP method is not supported. Only POST and GET are supported.
15	Error Performing Query %1.
16	The maximum number of SQLStatement fields in the IDC file has been exceeded.

Server-Side Includes

1	Can't resolve virtual path '%1'.
2	Error processing SSI file '%1'.
3	Invalid SSI tag.
4	Cannot perform flastmod('%1'): Win32 Error Code = %2.
5	Cannot perform fsize('%1'): Win32 Error Code = %2.
6	Variable '%1' cannot be found.

ID	Description
	Server-Side Includes
7	Variable '%1' cannot be evaluated.
8	SSI feature not supported.
9	Error handling SSI File '%1': Win32 Error Code = %2.
10	Successfully processed SSI file '%1'.
11	Failed to process SSI file '%1'.
12	Failed to execute CMD '%1': Win32 Error Code = %2.
13	Failed to execute script '%1': Win32 Error Code = %2.
14	Failed to execute ISAPI extension '%1'.
16	This document has moved to this (URL) location.
17	Failed to set up child process environment: Win32 Error Code = %1.
18	Failed to set up child process pipes: Win32 Error Code = %1.
19	Failed to create process: Win32 Error Code = %1.
20	#EXEC command timed out.
21	Failed to #EXEC ISAPI Application: Win32 Error Code = %1.
22	ISAPI application tried to send this (URL) location.
23	Cannot #EXEC '%1' because of lack of EXECUTE permission.
24	Cannot process '%1' because of access denied.
25	A server-side include file has included itself, or the maximum depth of server-side includes has been exceeded.
26	Unsupported ServerSupportFunction() option used by ISA.
27	The CMD option is not enabled for #EXEC calls.
28	#EXEC calls have been disabled for this virtual path.
29	There is a recursive #INCLUDE chain with '%1'.
	Web Services
1	HTTP Server could not initialize its security. The data is the error.
3	HTTP Server could not initialize the socket library. The data is the error.
4	HTTP Server was unable to initialize because of a shortage of available memory. The data is the error.
6	HTTP Server could not create the main connection socket. The data is the error.
8	HTTP Server could not create a client connection object for user at host %1. The connection to this user is terminated. The data is the error.

A

ADMINISTRATOR'S
REFERENCE

TABLE A.1 Continued

ID	Description

Web Services

ID	Description
14	The HTTP Filter DLL %1 failed to load. The data is the error.
16	The script started from the URL '%1' with parameters '%2' has not responded within the configured timeout period. The HTTP server is terminating the script.
18	The HTTP server encountered an error processing the server-side include file '%1'. The error was '%2'.
19	The HTTP server encountered an unhandled exception while processing the ISAPI Application '%1'.
20	The HTTP server was unable to load the ISAPI Application '%1'. The data is the error.
21	A server-side include file has included itself or the maximum depth of server-side includes has been exceeded.
22	An attempt was made to load filter '%1' on a server instance, but it requires the SF_NOTIFY_READ_RAW_DATA filter notification so it must be loaded as a global filter.
23	For compatibility with previous versions of IIS, the filter '%1' was loaded as a global filter from the Registry. To control the filter with the Internet Services Manager, remove the filter from the Registry and add it as a global filter with Internet Services Manager. Filters in the Registry are stored at HKLM\System\CurrentControlSet\Services\W3Svc\Parameters\Filter DLLs.
26	The server was unable to read the file %1 due to a lack of access permissions.
27	The server was unable to acquire a license for an SSL connection.
28	The server stopped serving requests for application '%1' because the number of Out of Process component crashes exceeded a limit.
29	The server failed to shut down application '%1'. The error was '%2'.
30	The server was unable to read the file %1. The file does not exist.
31	The server was unable to read the file %1. The Windows 32 error returned from the attempt is %2.
32	The server was unable to read the file %1. The file exceeds the maximum allowable size of %2.
33	The server was unable to allocate a buffer to read the file %1.
34	The server was unable to PUT to the URL %1 (filename %2). This file might have been lost. A backup copy was saved as %3.
35	The server was unable to PUT to the URL %1 (filename %2).
36	The server failed to load application '%1'. The error was '%2'.
37	Out of process application '%1' terminated unexpectedly.

ID	Description
	Web Application Manager
201	WAM Instance started with `Process Id` %1.
202	WAM Instance failed to start in process %1. The data is the error.
203	WAM Instance in process %1 is shut down.
204	The HTTP server encountered an unhandled exception while processing the ISAPI Application '%1'.
205	The HTTP server was unable to load the ISAPI Application '%1'. The data is the error.

These error messages are displayed in the Event Properties window that you access by double-clicking the event in the details pane of the Event Viewer.

The % variables, such as %1 and %2 as well as the | variable in the previous tables, will be replaced with appropriate data in the error description within the Event Properties window description section.

FTP Services Events

The FTP services will also generate entries in the Event log, although not quite as many as the Web services. Table A.2 lists the event messages for the FTP service.

TABLE A.2   FTP Services Events

ID	Description
1	FTP Server could not initialize its security. The data is the error.
3	FTP Server could not initialize the socket library. The data is the error.
4	FTP Server was unable to initialize because of a shortage of available memory. The data is the error.
5	FTP Server could not locate the FTP/TCP service. The data is the error.
6	FTP Server could not create the main connection socket. The data is the error.
7	FTP Server could not create the main connection thread. The data is the error.
8	FTP Server could not create a client worker thread for user at host %1%1. The connection to this user is terminated. The data is the error.
9	A call to a system service failed unexpectedly. The data is the error.
10	User %1 at host %2 has timed-out after %3 seconds of inactivity.
11	Anonymous logon request received from %1 at host %2.

TABLE A.2 Continued

ID	Description
12	User logon request received from %1 at host %2.
13	User %1 failed to log on, could not access the home directory %2.
14	User %1 denied access to the current directory %2 because of a security change.
1000	Unable to collect the FTP performance statistics. The error code returned by the service is data DWORD 0.

The % variables, such as %1 and %2 as well as the | variable in the previous tables, will be replaced with appropriate data in the error description within the Event Properties window description section.

Active Server Pages Events

As mentioned in the introduction to this chapter, not all ASP events will get sent to the log file unless the AspErrorsToNTLog option is set in the metabase. Table A.3 lists ASP messages that make up the Active Server Pages events.

TABLE A.3 Active Server Pages Events Messages

ID	Description
100	Out of memory—Unable to allocate required memory.
101	Unexpected error—The function returned |.
102	Expecting string input—The function expects a string as input.
103	Expecting numeric input—The function expects a number as input.
104	Operation not Allowed.
105	Index out of range—An array index is out of range.
106	Type Mismatch—An unhandled data type was encountered.
107	Stack Overflow—The data being processed is over the allowed limit.
108	Create object failed—An error occurred while creating object '%s'.
109	Member not found.
110	Unknown name.
111	Unknown interface.
112	Missing parameter.
113	Script timed out—The maximum amount of time for a script to execute was exceeded. You can change this limit by specifying a new value for the property Server.ScriptTimeOut or by changing the value in the IIS administration tools.

ID	Description
114	Object not free threaded—The application object accepts only free threaded objects; object `'%s'` is not free threaded.
115	Unexpected error—A trappable error (`%X`) occurred in an external object. The script cannot continue running.
116	Missing close of script delimiter—The Script block lacks the close of script tag (`%>`).
117	Missing close of script tag—The Script block lacks the close of script tag (`</SCRIPT>`) or close of tag symbol (`>`).
118	Missing close of object tag—The Object block lacks the close of object tag (`</OBJECT>`) or close of tag symbol (`>`).
119	Missing `Classid` or `Progid` attribute—The object instance `'|'` requires a valid `Classid` or `Progid` in the object tag.
120	Invalid `Runat` attribute—The `Runat` attribute of the Script tag or Object tag can only have the value `'Server'`.
121	Invalid Scope in object tag—The object instance `'|'` cannot have Application or Session scope. To create the object instance with Session or Application scope, place the Object tag in the `Global.asa` file.
122	Invalid Scope in object tag—The object instance `'|'` must have Application or Session scope. This applies to all objects created in a `Global.asa` file.
123	Missing Id attribute—The required `Id` attribute of the Object tag is missing.
124	Missing Language attribute—The required `Language` attribute of the Script tag is missing.
125	Missing close of attribute—The value of the `'|'` attribute has no closing delimiter.
126	Include file not found—The `include` file `'|'` was not found.
127	Missing close of HTML comment—The HTML comment or server-side include lacks the close tag (`-->`).
128	Missing File or Virtual attribute—The `Include` filename must be specified using either the `File` or `Virtual` attribute.
129	Unknown scripting language—The scripting language `'|'` is not found on the server.
130	Invalid File attribute—File attribute `'|'` cannot start with forward slash or backslash.
131	Disallowed Parent Path—The `Include` file `'|'` cannot contain `'..'` to indicate the parent directory.
132	Compilation Error—The Active Server Page `'|'` could not be processed.

TABLE A.3   Continued

ID	Description
133	Invalid `ClassID` attribute—The object tag has an invalid `ClassID` of '|'.
134	Invalid `ProgID` attribute—The object has an invalid `ProgID` of '|'.
135	Cyclic Include—The file '|' is included by itself (perhaps indirectly). Please check `include` files for other `Include` statements.
136	Invalid object instance name—The object instance '|' is attempting to use a reserved name. This name is used by Active Server Pages intrinsic objects.
137	Invalid Global Script—Script blocks must be one of the allowed `Global.asa` procedures. Script directives within `<% ... %>` are not allowed within the `global.asa` file. The allowed procedure names are `Application_OnStart`, `Application_OnEnd`, `Session_OnStart`, or `Session_OnEnd`.
138	Nested Script Block—A script block cannot be placed inside another script block.
139	Nested Object—An object tag cannot be placed inside another object tag.
140	Page Command Out Of Order—The @ command must be the first command within the Active Server Page.
141	Page Command Repeated—The @ command can only be used once within the Active Server Page.
142	Thread token error—A thread token failed to open.
143	Invalid Application Name—A valid application name was not found.
144	Initialization Error—The page level objects list failed during initialization.
145	New Application Failed—The new Application could not be added.
146	New Session Failed—The new Session could not be added.
147	Server Error.
148	Server Too Busy.
149	Application Restarting—The request cannot be processed while the application is being restarted.
150	Application Directory Error—The Application directory could not be opened.
151	Change Notification Error—The change notification event could not be created.
152	Security Error—An error occurred while processing a user's security credentials.
153	Thread Error—A new thread request failed.
154	Write HTTP Header Error—The HTTP headers could not be written to the client browser.
155	Write Page Content Error—The page content could not be written to the client browser.

ID	Description
156	Header Error—The HTTP headers are already written to the client browser. Any HTTP header modifications must be made before writing page content.
157	Buffering On—Buffering cannot be turned off when it is already turned on.
158	Missing URL—A URL is required.
159	Buffering Off—Buffering must be on.
160	Logging Failure—Failure to write entry to log.
161	Data Type Error—The conversion of a Variant to a String variable failed.
162	Cannot Modify Cookie—The cookie `ASPSessionID` cannot be modified. It is a reserved cookie name.
163	Invalid Comma Use—Commas cannot be used within a log entry. Please select another delimiter.
164	Invalid TimeOut Value—An invalid TimeOut value was specified.
165	SessionID Error—A `SessionID` string cannot be created.
166	Uninitialized Object—An attempt was made to access an uninitialized object.
167	Session Initialization Error—An error occurred while initializing the Session object.
168	Disallowed object use—An intrinsic object cannot be stored within the Session object.
169	Missing object information—An object with missing information cannot be stored in the Session object. The threading model information for an object is required.
170	Delete Session Error—The Session did not delete properly.
171	Missing Path—The Path parameter must be specified for the `MapPath` method.
172	Invalid Path—The Path parameter for the `MapPath` method must be a virtual path. A physical path was used.
173	Invalid Path Character—An invalid character was specified in the Path parameter for the `MapPath` method.
174	Invalid Path Character(s)—An invalid `'/'` or `'\\'` was found in the Path parameter for the `MapPath` method.
175	Disallowed Path Characters—The `'..'` characters are not allowed in the Path parameter for the `MapPath` method.
176	Path Not Found—The `Path` parameter for the `MapPath` method did not correspond to a known path.
177	Server.CreateObject Failed.
178	Server.CreateObject Access Error—The call to `Server.CreateObject` failed while checking permissions. Access is denied to this object.

A

ADMINISTRATOR'S REFERENCE

TABLE A.3 Continued

ID	Description
179	Application Initialization Error—An error occurred while initializing the Application object.
180	Disallowed object use—An intrinsic object cannot be stored within the Application object.
181	Invalid threading model—An object using the apartment threading model cannot be stored within the Application object.
182	Missing object information—An object with missing information cannot be stored in the Application object. The threading model information for the object is required.
183	Empty Cookie Key—A cookie with an empty key cannot be stored.
184	Missing Cookie Name—A name must be specified for a cookie.
185	Missing Default Property—A default property was not found for the object.
186	Error parsing certificate.
187	Object addition conflict—Could not add object to application. Application was locked down by another request for adding an object.
188	Disallowed object use—Cannot add objects created using object tags to the session intrinsic.
189	Disallowed object use—Cannot add objects created using object tags to the application intrinsic.
190	Unexpected error—A trappable error occurred while releasing an external object.
191	Unexpected error—A trappable error occurred in the `OnStartPage` method of an external object.
192	Unexpected error—A trappable error occurred in the OnEndPage method of an external object.
193	`OnStartPage` Failed—An error occurred in the `OnStartPage` method of an external object.
194	`OnEndPage` Failed—An error occurred in the `OnEndPage` method of an external object.
195	Invalid Server Method Call—This method of the Server object cannot be called during `Session_OnEnd` and `Application_OnEnd`.
197	Disallowed object use—Cannot add object with apartment model behavior to the application intrinsic object.
198	Server shutting down. Cannot process request.
199	Disallowed object use—Cannot add JScript objects to the session.

ID	Description
200	Out of Range `'Expires'` attribute—The date and time given for `'Expires'` precedes Jan 1, 1980 or exceeds Jan 19, 2038, 3:14:07 GMT.
201	Unknown scripting language in Registry—The scripting language `'|'` specified in the Registry is not found on the server.
202	Missing Code Page—The code page attribute is missing.
203	Invalid Code Page—The specified code page attribute is invalid.
205	Change Notification—Failed to create event for change notification.
206	Cannot call `BinaryRead`—Cannot call `BinaryRead` after using `Request.Form` collection.
207	Cannot use `Request.Form`—Cannot use `Request.Form` collection after calling `BinaryRead`.
208	Cannot use generic `Request` collection—Cannot use the generic `Request` collection after calling `BinaryRead`.
209	Illegal value for `TRANSACTION` property—The `TRANSACTION` property can only be `REQUIRED`, `REQUIRES_NEW`, `SUPPORTED`, or `NOT_SUPPORTED`.
210	Method not implemented—This method has not yet been implemented.
211	Object out of scope—A built-in ASP object has been referenced, which is no longer valid.
212	Cannot Clear Buffer—`Response.Clear` is not allowed after a `Response.Flush` while Client Debugging is Enabled.
214	Invalid `Path` parameter—The `Path` parameter exceeds the maximum length allowed.
215	Illegal value for `SESSION` property—The `SESSION` property can only be `TRUE` or `FALSE`.
216	MSDTC Service not running—Transactional Web pages cannot be run if the MSDTC service is not running.
217	Invalid Scope in object tag—Object scope must be Page, Session, or Application.
218	Missing `LCID`—The `LCID` attribute is missing.
219	Invalid `LCID`—The specified `LCID` is not available.
220	Requests for `GLOBAL.ASA` Not Allowed—Requests with the URL pointing to `GLOBAL.ASA` are not allowed.
221	Invalid @ Command directive—The specified `'|'` option is unknown or invalid.
222	Invalid TypeLib Specification—`METADATA` tag contains an invalid Type Library specification.

A

ADMINISTRATOR'S REFERENCE

TABLE A.3 Continued

ID	Description
223	TypeLib Not Found—METADATA tag contains a Type Library specification that does not match any Registry entry.
224	Cannot load TypeLib—Cannot load Type Library specified in the METADATA tag.
225	Cannot wrap TypeLibs—Cannot create a Type Library Wrapper object from the Type Libraries specified in METADATA tags.
226	Cannot modify StaticObjects—StaticObjects collection cannot be modified at runtime.
227	Server.Execute Failed—The call to Server.Execute failed.
228	Server.Execute Error—The call to Server.Execute failed while loading the page.
229	Server.Transfer Failed—The call to Server.Transfer failed.
230	Server.Transfer Error—The call to Server.Transfer failed while loading the page.
231	Server.Execute Error—Invalid URL form or fully-qualified absolute URL was used. Use relative URLs.
232	Invalid Cookie Specification—METADATA tag contains an invalid cookie specification.
233	Cannot load cookie script source—Cannot load cookie script source file specified in the METADATA tag.
234	Invalid include directive—Server-side include directives might not be present in script blocks. Please use the SRC= attribute of the <SCRIPT> tag.
235	Server.Transfer Error—Invalid URL form or fully-qualified absolute URL was used. Use relative URLs.
236	Invalid Cookie Specification—METADATA tag contains an invalid or missing SRC parameter.
237	Invalid Cookie Specification—METADATA tag contains an invalid or missing NAME parameter.
238	Missing attribute value—No value was specified for the '|' attribute.
239	Cannot process file—UNICODE ASP files are not supported.
240	Script Engine Exception—A ScriptEngine threw exception '%X' in '%s' from '%s'.
241	CreateObject Exception—The CreateObject of '%s' caused exception %X.
242	Query OnStartPage Interface Exception—Querying Object '%s''s OnStartPage or OnEndPage method caused exception %X.

The variables used in the table, %1, %2, and |, will be replaced with the appropriate errors in the description text for the error when it occurs and is recorded.

Counters Reference

Counters can be broken down into eight different categories along with four areas of availability. They are based on the criteria shown in Tables A.4.

TABLE A.4 Counter Availability

Bandwidth Usage Counters	
Current Blocked Async I/O Request	Global, Web, FTP
Measured Async I/O Bandwidth Usage	Global, Web
Total Allowed Async I/O Requests	Global, Web
Total Blocked Async I/O Requests	Global, Web
Total Rejected Async I/O Requests	Global, Web
Throughput Counters	
Bytes Received/sec	Web, FTP
Bytes Sent/sec	Web, FTP
Bytes Total/sec	Web, FTP
Files/sec	Web
Files Received/sec	Web
Files Sent/sec	Web
Total Files Received	Web, FTP
Total Files Sent	Web, FTP
Total Files Transferred	Web, FTP
Specific Requests and Errors Counters	
CGI Requests/sec	Web
Current CGI Requests	Web
Current ISAPI Extension Requests	Web
Debugging Requests	ASP
Delete Requests/sec	Web
Errors During Script Runtime	ASP

A

ADMINISTRATOR'S REFERENCE

TABLE A.4   Continued

Specific Requests and Errors Counters

Errors From ASP Preprocessor	ASP
Errors From Script Compiler	ASP
Errors/sec	ASP
Get Requests/sec	Web
Head Requests/sec	Web
ISAPI Extension Requests/sec	Web
Maximum CGI Requests	Web
Maximum ISAPI Extension Requests	Web
Not Found Errors/sec	Web
Other Request Methods/sec	Web
Post Requests/sec	Web
Put Requests/sec	Web
Request Bytes In Total	ASP
Request Bytes Out Total	ASP
Request Execution Time	ASP
Request Wait Time	ASP
Requests Disconnected	ASP
Requests Executing	ASP
Requests Failed Total	ASP
Requests Not Authorized	ASP
Requests Not Found	ASP
Requests Queued	ASP
Requests Rejected	ASP
Requests Succeeded	ASP
Requests Timed Out	ASP
Requests Total	ASP
Requests/sec	ASP
Total CGI Requests	Web
Total Delete Requests	Web
Total Get Requests	Web
Total Head Requests	Web

Specific Requests and Errors Counters

Total ISAPI Extension Requests	Web
Total Method Requests	Web
Total Method Requests/sec	Web
Total Not Found Errors	Web
Total Other Request Methods	Web
Total Post Requests	Web
Total Put Requests	Web
Total Trace Requests	Web
Trace Requests/sec	Web

Connections and Users Counters

Anonymous Users/sec	Web
Connection Attempts/sec	Web
Current Anonymous Users	Web, FTP
Current Connections	Web, FTP
Current NonAnonymous Users	Web, FTP
Maximum Anonymous Users	Web, FTP
Maximum Connections	Web, FTP
Maximum NonAnonymous Users	Web, FTP
Total Anonymous Users	Web, FTP
Total Connection Attempts	Web, FTP
Total Logon Attempts	Web, FTP
Total NonAnonymous Users	Web, FTP

Caching and Memory Counters

Cache Flushes	Global
Cache Hits	Global
Cache Hits %	Global
Cache Misses	Global
Cached File Handles	Global
Directory Listings	Global
Memory Allocated	ASP
Objects	Global

TABLE A.4   Continued

Caching and Memory Counters

Script Engines Cached	ASP
Templates Cached	ASP
Template Cache Hit Rate	ASP
Template Notifications	ASP

Sessions Counters

Session Duration	ASP
Sessions Current	ASP
Sessions Timed Out	ASP
Sessions Total	ASP

Transaction Counters

Transactions Aborted	ASP
Transactions Committed	ASP
Transactions Pending	ASP
Transactions Total	ASP
Transactions/sec	ASP

There is one counter left and that relates to the restarts. It is named Service Uptime and is available for the Web and FTP services.

Descriptions of Counters

Current Blocked Async I/O Request—The current number of temporarily blocked requests because of bandwidth throttling.

Measured Async I/O Bandwidth Usage—The number of bytes sent and received by the server averaged over one minute.

Total Allowed Async I/O Requests—The number of requests allowed since service startup.

Total Blocked Async I/O Requests—The number of requests blocked temporarily because of bandwidth throttling since server startup.

Total Rejected Async I/O Requests—Total requests rejected because of bandwidth settings since server startup.

Bytes Received/sec—The rate at which the data bytes are received by the service. This does not include any headers on the packets.

Bytes Sent/sec—The rate at which the data bytes are sent from the server.

Bytes Total/sec—Total bytes transferred by the service.

Files/sec—The rate of file transfers of the Web service since server startup.

Files Received/sec—The rate of files uploaded to the service since server startup.

Files Sent/sec—The rate of files sent or downloaded from the service since server startup.

Total Files Received—The sum of the files sent and received by the service since server startup.

Total Files Sent—Total number of files sent by the Web service since server startup.

Total Files Transferred—The sum of the files sent and received since server startup of the Web service.

CGI Requests/sec—The rate of CGI requests being processed simultaneously.

Current CGI Requests—The current number of requests being simultaneously processed.

Current ISAPI Extension Requests—The current ISAPI requests being processed.

Debugging Requests—The number of debugging document requests.

Delete Requests/sec—The rate of HTTP DELETE method requests.

Errors During Script Runtime—The number of failed requests because of runtime errors.

Errors From ASP Preprocessor—The number of preprocessor failed requests.

Errors From Script Compiler—The number of failed requests because of script compilation errors.

Errors/sec—The number of errors per second.

Get Requests/sec—The rate of GET method requests.

Head Requests/sec—The rate of HEAD method requests.

ISAPI Extension Requests/sec—The rate of ISAPI extension requests being processed.

Maximum CGI Requests—The maximum number of CGI requests processed since server startup.

Maximum ISAPI Extension Requests—The maximum number of ISAPI requests processed since server startup.

A

ADMINISTRATOR'S
REFERENCE

Not Found Errors/sec—The rate of errors because of the 404 file not found message.

Other Request Methods/sec—The rate of HTTP method requests other than GET, PUT, POST, DELETE, TRACE, or HEAD.

Post Requests/sec—The rate of POST method requests.

Put Requests/sec—The rate of PUT method requests.

Request Bytes In Total—Total size of all requests in bytes.

Request Bytes Out Total —Total of all responses sent to clients measured in bytes.

Request Execution Time—Milliseconds required to complete the most recent request.

Request Wait Time—Amount of time the most recent request spent in queue in milliseconds.

Requests Disconnected—The number of disconnected requests because of communications errors.

Requests Executing—The number of currently executing requests.

Requests Failed Total—Total number of failed requests.

Requests Not Authorized—The number of failed authorization requests.

Requests Not Found—The number of failed file requests because of files not found.

Requests Queued—The number of requests in the queue.

Requests Rejected—The number of requests rejected because of insufficient resources.

Requests Succeeded—The number of successfully executed requests.

Requests Timed Out—The number of timed out requests.

Requests Total—Total of all requests since server startup.

Requests/sec—The number of requests executed per second.

Total CGI Requests—Total of CGI requests since server startup.

Total Delete Requests—Total number of DELETE method requests.

Total Get Requests—Total number of GET method requests.

Total Head Requests—Total number of HEAD method requests.

Total ISAPI Extension Requests—Total number of ISAPI extension requests.

Total Method Requests—Total number of GET, PUT, POST, DELETE, HEAD, and TRACE method requests.

Total Method Requests/sec—The rate at which the GET, PUT, POST, DELETE, HEAD, and TRACE methods were made.

Total Not Found Errors—Total number of requests not satisfied because of the file not being found.

Total Other Request Methods—Total number of method requests other than GET, PUT, POST, DELETE, HEAD, and TRACE.

Total Post Requests—Total number of POST method requests.

Total Put Requests—Total number of PUT method requests.

Total Trace Requests—Total number of TRACE method requests.

Trace Requests/sec—The rate of TRACE requests per second.

Anonymous Users/sec—The rate at which anonymous connections are being made.

Connection Attempts/sec—The rate of Web service connection attempts.

Current Anonymous Users—The number of anonymous users currently connected to the Web or FTP service.

Current Connections—The current number or Web and DTP connections.

Current NonAnonymous Users—The current number of nonanonymous users connected to the Web and FTP services.

Maximum Anonymous Users—The maximum number of concurrent anonymous connections since server startup.

Maximum Connections—The maximum number of simultaneous connections to the Web and FTP services.

Maximum NonAnonymous Users—The maximum number of nonanonymous concurrent connections.

Total Anonymous Users—Total number of anonymous connections since server startup.

Total Connection Attempts—Total number of connection attempts to the server since startup.

Total Logon Attempts—Total number of successful logon attempts since server startup.

Total NonAnonymous Users—Total number of nonanonymous users connected to the server since startup.

Cache Flushes—Total number of times that the cache has been flushed since server startup.

Cache Hits—Total number of times that a request was served from the cache since server startup.

Cache Hits %—The ratio of cache hits to cache requests.

Cache Misses—Total number of times that requests were not found in the cache since server startup.

Cached File Handles—The current number of cached file handles by all IIS services.

Directory Listings—The current number of directory listings cached by all IIS services.

Memory Allocated—Total amount of currently allocated memory in bytes for ASP usage.

Objects—The current number of all cached objects used by all IIS services.

Script Engines Cached—The number of script engines residing in the cache.

Templates Cached—The number of currently cached templates.

Template Cache Hit Rate—The percentage of templates hit in cache.

Template Notifications—The number of invalidate templates in cache as a result of a change in notification.

Session Duration—The number of milliseconds that the most recent session persisted.

Sessions Current—The number of current sessions.

Sessions Timed Out—The number of sessions that timed out.

Sessions Total—The number of sessions since server startup.

Transactions Aborted—The number of aborted transactions.

Transactions Committed—The number of committed transactions.

Transactions Pending—The number of pending transactions.

Transactions Total—Total transactions since server startup.

Transactions/sec—The number of transactions started per second.

Timeouts Reference

IIS provides timeout resources for allotting time frames to allow resource allocation to tasks. Table A.5 lists the available timeouts and where to set them. If the value of the Snap-In column is No, you will need to set the timeout in the metabase.

TABLE A.5 Timeouts for Resource Allocation

Timeout	Default Value (Seconds)	Set in Snap-In
AspScriptTimeout	90	Yes
AspSessionTimeout	1200	Yes
ConnectionTimeout	900	Yes
CGITimeout	300	Yes
ServerListenTimeout	120	No
PoolIdcTimeout	30	No
AspQueueTimeout	−1 (No timeout)	No
CpuLimitLogEvent	User defined percentage	Yes
CpuLimitPriority	150% of `CpuLimitLogEvent`	Yes
CpuLimitProcStop	200% of `CpuLimitLogEvent`	Yes
CpuLimitPause	0 (Unlimited)	No

There are also three IIS Restart timeouts, shown in Table A.6.

TABLE A.6 Restart Timeouts

Timeout	Default Value (Seconds)
Stop	60
Restart	20
Reboot	0

Logging Properties Reference

Table A.7 covers the logging properties definitions and their values. This only deals with the W3C Extended format.

TABLE A.7 Logging Properties Definitions for W3C Extended Format

Prefix	Meaning
s-	Server actions
c-	Client actions
cs-	Client-to-server actions
sc-	Server-to-client actions

TABLE A.7 Continued

Field	Appears As	Definition
Date	Date	Date the activity occurred
Time	Time	Time the activity occurred
Client IP	c-ip	IP address of connecting Client
User Name	c-username	Authenticated user's name
Service Name& Instance #	s-sitename	Internet service and instance number running on the client
Server Name	s-computername	Name of the server on which the log entry was generated
Server IP	s-ip	IP address of server on which the log entry was generated
Method	sc-method	Action the client was performing
URI Stem	cs-uri-stem	The accessed resource
URI Query	cs-uri-query	Query the client was performing
HTTP Status	sc-status	Status of the action
Win32 Status	sc-win32-status	Status of the action in Windows 2000 status
Bytes Sent	sc-bytes	The number of bytes sent by server
Bytes Received	cs-bytes	The number of bytes received
Server Port	s-port	Port number client is connected to
Time Taken	Time taken	Length of time the action took
Protocol Version	cs-protocol	Protocol version used by client
User Agent	cs(UserAgent)	Browser used by client
Cookie	cs(Cookie)	Content of the cookie
Referrer	cs(Referrer)	Previous site visited by user that referred user
Process Type	s-proctype	Type of process that triggered the event
Process Event	s-event	The event that was triggered
Total User Time	s-usertime	Total accumulated user time
Total Kernel Time	s-kerneltime	Total accumulated kernel mode time
Total Page Faults	s-pagefaults	Total number of page faults
Total Processes	s-total-Procs	Total of CGI and out-of-process applications during interval

Field	Appears As	Definition
Active Processes	s-active-procs	Total of CGI and out-of-process applications during log event
Total Terminated Process	s-stopped-total procs	Total of CGI and out-of-process applications stopped due to process throttling

Table A.8 displays events that only contain a value and a meaning in lieu of the Field and Appears As pair.

TABLE A.8 Events with Only a Value and Meaning

Value	Meaning
Site-Stop	The Web site was stopped.
Site-Start	The Web site was started or restarted.
Site-Pause	The Web site was paused.
Periodic-Log	A regular log entry that had an interval specified by an administrator.
Interval-Start	Reset interval has begun.
Interval-End	Reset interval end has been reached and reset.
Interval-Change	Reset interval was changed.
Log-Change Int/Start/Stop	One of the three events occurred.
Eventlog-Limit	An event log was made because a CGI or out-of-process application reached the event limit.
Priority-Limit	The site had a CGI application set to low priority.
Process-Stop-Limit	A CGI application stopped because it reached a process stop limit.
Site-Pause-Limit	The site paused because a CGI application reached the pause limit.
Eventlog-Limit-Reset	The reset level was reached or the Eventlog-Limit was reset manually.
Priority-Limit-Reset	The reset level was reached or the Priority-Limit was manually reset.
Process-Stop-Limit-Reset	The reset level was reached or the Process-Stop-Limit was manually reset.
Site-Pause-Limit-Reset	The reset interval was reset or the Site-Pause-Limit was manually reset.

A

ADMINISTRATOR'S REFERENCE

Redirect Reference

IIS offers the capability to redirect a user's request to another URL if the requested URL no longer exists, or for any other purposes for which you might want to use redirection. Table A.9 shows the six redirection variables used to pass portions of the original URL to the destination URL:

TABLE A.9   Redirection Variables

Variable	Description
$S	Passes the matched suffix of the requested URL. This suffix is the portion of the original URL that remains after the redirected URL is substituted.
$P	Passes the parameters that existed in the original URL.
$Q	Passes the parameters from the original URL but it also passes the question mark as well.
$V	Passes the requested URL minus the server name.
$0 to $9	Passes a portion of the URL that matches the indicated wildcard
!	Means to not redirect.

Examples

$S	If the original request was for `http://localhost/default.htm`, the suffix would be `default.htm`.
$P	With a URL of `www.gkcomput.com?username=gobrien`, the parameter `username=gobrien` would be passed.
$Q	Using the previous URL example, the parameter passed would be `?username=gobrien`.
$V	If the URL was `//localhost/scripts/adrot.asp`, this would pass `/scripts/adrot.asp`.

Administration Object Reference

IN THIS APPENDIX

This appendix will provide you with information on the IIS Administration Objects.

IIsCertMapper

This object is responsible for mapping client certificates to Windows user accounts. The IIsCertMapper is an ADSI Object.

ADsPath

`IIS://`*`computername`*`/W3SVC/`*`n`*`/IIsCertMapper`

There are two variables used in the `ADsPath`: *computername* is used to indicate the name of the computer on which the object resides, and the *n* is used to indicate the number of services to which you are referring.

Syntax

`varRetVal` `= IIsCertMapper.`*`Method`*

The *varRetVal* variable is used to hold the value returned from the method called.

Method is the method chosen.

The IIsCertMapper object is one of the objects that contain methods, listed in the following sections.

CreateMapping

This method is responsible for the actual mapping of the certificate to the Windows user account.

Syntax

`IIsCertMapper.`**`CreateMapping`** `vCert, strAcct, strPasswd, strName,`
`boolEnabled`

vCert is a string or byte array that contains the certificate.

strAcct is a string that contains the Windows account name.

strPasswd contains the password for the account as a string value.

StrName is used to specify a friendly name for the account.

boolEnabled is a Boolean `TRUE` or `FALSE` that indicates whether to enable or disable mapping.

Example

```
<%
Dim objCert, strCert
```

```
strCert = Request.ClientCertificate("CERTIFICATE")
Set objCert = GetObject("IIS://ADsPath../IIsCertMapper")
objCert.CreateMapping strCert, _ "MYACCT", "MYPASS", "My Name", True
%>
```

DeleteMapping

This method will delete an existing certificate mapping. You use one of four methods to search for the mapping, certificate, name, Windows account, or a numeric string index.

Syntax

IIsCertMapper.**DeleteMapping** *intMethod, strKey*

intMethod refers to the search method for the mapping. It contains four valid integer values indicating the search method:

- 1—Search by certificate
- 2—Search by name
- 3—Search by Windows account
- 4—Search by numeric string index

strKey specifies the string that will be used in the search indicated by the *intMethod* value. For example, if *intMethod* were searching on 2 (name), then *strKey* would contain the name for which you want to search.

Example

```
<%
Dim objCert
Set objCert = GetObject("IIS://ADsPath../IIsCertMapper")_
objCert.DeleteMapping 3, "MYACCT"
%>
```

GetMapping

This method will retrieve a certificate and its mapping data from an existing mapping. This method uses the four search methods. The method also provides the necessary variables to hold the returned values.

Syntax

IIsCertMapper.**GetMapping** intMethod, strKey, vCert, strAcct, strPasswd, strName, boolEnabled

intMethod contains four valid integer values indicating the search method:

B

- 1—Search by certificate
- 2—Search by name
- 3—Search by Windows account
- 4—Search by numeric string index

strKey specifies the string that will be used in the search indicated by the *intMethod* value.

vCert holds the returned certificate.

strAcct holds the return Windows account name.

strPasswd holds the returned password.

strName holds the name that is returned.

boolEnabled holds a Boolean TRUE or FALSE that is returned.

Example

```
<%
Dim objCert, strCert, strAcct, strPwd, strName, boolEnabled
Set objCert = GetObject("IIS://ADsPath../IIsCertMapper")_
objCert.GetMapping 3, "MYACCT", strCert, strAcct, strPwd,_ strName, boolEnabled
%>
```

SetAcct

The SetAcct method is used to change the Windows account name string for an existing certificate mapping. This method uses the four search methods:

- 1—Search by certificate
- 2—Search by name
- 3—Search by Windows account
- 4—Search by numeric string index

Syntax

IIsCertMapper.**SetAcct** *intMethod, strKey, strAcct*

intMethod specifies one of the four methods used for searching.

strKey specifies a string value that will be searched.

strAcct contains the new string value that will replace the existing account name.

Example

```
<%
Dim objCert
```

```
Set objCert = GetObject("IIS://ADsPath../IIsCertMapper")
objCert.SetAcct 3, "MYACCT", "NewAccount"
%>
```

SetEnabled

Use this method to enable or disable an existing certificate mapping.

Syntax

IIsCertMapper.**SetEnabled** *intMethod*, *strKey*, *boolEnabled*

intMethod indicates one of the four search methods available:

- 1—Search by certificate
- 2—Search by name
- 3—Search by Windows account
- 4—Search by numeric string index

strKey indicates the key to be used in the search method.

boolEnabled indicates TRUE or FALSE to enable or disable the mapping.

Example

```
<%
Dim objCert
Set objCert = GetObject("IIS://ADsPath../IIsCertMapper")_
objCert.SetEnabled 3, "MYACCT", True
%>
```

SetName

This method will change the name string of an existing certificate mapping.

Syntax

IIsCertMapper.**SetName** *intMethod*, *strKey*, *strName*

intMethod specifies one of four possible search methods:

- 1—Search by certificate
- 2—Search by name
- 3—Search by Windows account
- 4—Search by numeric string index

strKey specifies the key value that will be used to search on.

strName contains the new string value that will replace the existing name.

Example

```
<%
Dim objCert
Set objCert = GetObject("IIS://ADsPath../IIsCertMapper")_
objCert.SetName 3, "MYACCT", "NewName"
%>
```

SetPwd

The SetPwd method allows you to set a new password value for an existing certificate mapping.

Syntax

IIsCertMapper.**SetPwd** *intMethod, strKey, strPwd*

intMethod specifies the search method to use. There are four possible values:

- 1—Search by certificate
- 2—Search by name
- 3—Search by Windows account
- 4—Search by numeric string index

strKey specifies the key value to use in the search method.

strPwd specifies the new string value for the replacement password.

Example

```
<%
Dim objCert
Set objCert = GetObject("IIS://ADsPath../IIsCertMapper")_
objCert.SetPwd 3, "MYACCT", "NewPassword"
%>
```

IIsCompressionSchemes

IIsCompressionSchemes is an ADSI Container Object. It contains individual compression schemes based on the HTTP 1.1 protocol. Each of these schemes is represented by the IIsCompressionSchemes object. All global compression settings for your IIS installation are contained in this object.

ADsPath

IIS://*computername*/W3SVC/Filters/Compression/Parameters

computername can be any name or "LocalHost" for the local computer.

Syntax

```
RetVal = object.Method
RetVal = object.Property
```

RetVal holds the return value from the method.

object contains the IIsCompressionSchemes object returned from the GetObject method.

Method/Property is the method or property chosen.

Can Contain

IIsCompressionScheme

Properties

ADSI Object Properties, ADSI Container Object Properties

For information on these properties, see Appendix C, "ADSI Reference."

Metabase Properties

HcCacheControlHeader	HcCompressionBufferSize
HcCompressionDirectory	HcDoDiskSpaceLimiting
HcDoDynamicCompression	HcDoOnDemandCompression
HcDoStaticCompression	HcExpiresHeader
HcFilesDeletedPerDiskFree	HcIoBufferSize
HcMaxDiskSpaceUsage	HcMaxQueueLength
HcMinFileSizeForComp	HcNoCompressionForHttp10
HcNoCompressionForProxies	HcNoCompressionForRange
HcSendCacheHeaders	

Methods

ADSI Object Methods, ADSI Container Object Methods

For more information on these methods, see Appendix C.

IIsCompressionScheme

This is an ADSI object that contains information pertaining to an individual compression scheme. All IIsCompressionScheme objects are contained within the IIsCompressionSchemes container object.

ADsPath

IIS://*computername*/W3SVC/Filters/Compression/Scheme

computername can be any name or "LocalHost" for the local computer.

Syntax

```
RetVal = object.Method
RetVal = object.Property
```

RetVal holds the return value from the method.

object contains the IIsCompressionScheme object returned by the GetObject method.

Method/Property is the method or property chosen.

Properties

ADSI Object Properties

More information on these properties can be found in Appendix C.

Metabase Properties

HcCompressionDll	HcCreateFlags
HcDoDynamicCompression	HcDoStaticCompression
HcDoOnDemandCompression	HcDynamicCompressionLevel
HcFileExtensions	HcMimeType
HcOnDemandCompLevel	HcPriority
HcScriptFileExtensions	

Methods

ADSI Object Methods—Where this object is not a container object, ADSI Container Object Methods are not available. For more information on the ADSI Object Methods, see Appendix C.

IIsComputer

This object is used to set global metabase properties that will be used to determine how IIS will operate. It is a container object.

The IIsComputer Object contains four methods that you can use to back up and restore the metabase, to delete backups, and to enumerate backups.

ADsPath

IIS://*computername*

computername can be any name or "LocalHost" for the local computer.

Syntax

RetVal =.*Method*

RetVal holds the return value from the method.

object contains the IIsComputer object returned by the *GetObject* method

Method is the method chosen.

Can Contain

IIsFtpService, IIsMimeMap, IIsLogModules, IIsWebService

Properties

ADSI Object Properties

See Appendix C for more information on the ADSI Object Properties.

Metabase Properties

```
MaxBandwidth        MaxBandwidthBlocked
MimeMap
```

Backup

Backup is a method of the IISComputer object and is used to back up the metabase. This method will take a location of up to 100 characters. You can store multiple metabase backups in one backup location.

Syntax

IIsComputer.**Backup** *BackupLocation, BackupVersion, BackupFlags*

Parameters

BackupLocation is the backup location, consisting of 100 characters or less. IIS automatically determines the storage mechanism. If no string is specified for the backup location, IIS will store the backup in the default location.

BackupVersion specifies the version number to assign to the backup. This version number must be less than or equal to MD_BACKUP_MAX_VERSION. The following values can be used:

- MD_BACKUP_HIGHEST_VERSION—Causes the highest existing backup version in the specified backup location to be overwritten

- MD_BACKUP_NEXT_VERSION—Uses the next backup version number that is available in the specified backup location

BackupFlags are used to indicate how the backup is performed. The following values can be used:

- MD_BACKUP_FORCE_BACKUP—Forces backup, even if the SaveData operation that was specified by MD_BACKUP_SAVE_FIRST failed

- MD_BACKUP_OVERWRITE—Backs up to the specified location and overwrites any backup with the same name

- MD_BACKUP_SAVE_FIRST—Performs a SaveData operation before the backup

NOTE

If you are trying to locate the backup that you created, it is important to note that IIS determines the storage mechanism. This means that the backup location you specify does not necessarily map to valid directory path. IIS store all metabase backups in the system32\Inetsrv\MetaBack directory.

Example

```
<%
Dim objComputer, varFlags
Set objComputer = GetObject("IIS:// computername ")
varFlags = (MD_BACKUP_SAVE_FIRST)
objComputer.Backup "MyBackups", MD_BACKUP_NEXT_VERSION, varFlags
%>
```

DeleteBackup

This method is used to delete an existing metabase backup from a specified backup location.

Syntax

IIsComputer.**DeleteBackup** *BackupLocation, BackupVersion*

BackupLocation contains a string value, up to 100 characters, that specifies the location of the metabase backup file.

BackupVersion contains the version number of the backup file to delete that was specified in the backup location. This variable can also use the following constant.

The constant *MD_BACKUP_HIGHEST_VERSION* will cause the DeleteBackup method to delete the highest version number of a backup file found in the specified location when used in place of the BackupVersion parameter.

Example

```
<%
Dim objComputer
Set objComputer = GetObject("IIS:// computername ")
objComputer.DeleteBackup "MyBackups", 1
%>
```

EnumBackups

This method enumerates all the metabase backups specified in the location. This method will return the following values for each metabase backup:

- Location
- Version number
- Date of backup

Syntax

```
IIsComputer.EnumBackups strBkupLoc, intIndex, strBkupVer, strBkupLoc,
BkupDateTimeOut
```

strBkupLoc specifies the string value, 100 characters or less, for the location of the metabase backup file.

intIndex specifies the index value of the backup to enumerate. The index starts at 0 and is incremented by 1 until the end of the backup is reached. This is indicated by an MD_ERROR_DATA_NOT_FOUND returned value.

strBkupVer holds the returned version number of the enumerated backup.

strBkupLoc holds the returned value that specifies the location of the enumerated backup.

BkupDateTimeOut holds the returned date and time of the enumerated backup. This value is in Universal Time Convention (UTC).

Example

```
<%@ LANGUAGE=VBScript %>
<SCRIPT LANGUAGE = "JScript" RUNAT = SERVER>
 var TempDate = new Date();
TempDif = TempDate.getTimezoneOffset();
Session("sTempDif") = TempDif;
</SCRIPT>
```

```
<%
Dim objComp, Index, Version, Location, GMTDate, LocDate, MinDif
MinDif = Session("sTempDif")
On Error Resume Next
Set objComp = GetObject("IIS:// computername ")
Index = 0
Do While True
objComp.EnumBackups "", Index, Version, Location, GMTDate
If Err.Number <> 0 Then
     Exit Do
End If
Response.Write Version & ", "
Response.Write Location & ", "
Response.Write GMTDate & ", "
LocDate = DateAdd("n", (-MinDif), GMTDate)
Response.Write "(" & LocDate & ")"
Response.Write "<BR>"
Index = Index + 1
Loop
%>
```

Restore

This method is used to restore the metabase from backup. You must plan ahead before restoring a metabase backup as the Restore operation will cause all services dependent on the IISAdmin service to stop while the operation is in progress. Once the restore is complete, all services will be restarted.

You cannot run the restore in an ASP script that is running on the server where you will be restoring the metabase. You must run the script from another server and specify the name of that server in the method.

Syntax

IIsComputer.**Restore** *strBackupLocation, intBackupVersion, intBackupFlags*

strBackupLocation is a string variable used to indicate the location of the backup. Must be 100 characters or less.

intBackupVersion specifies the version number of the backup to restore. It can also contain the following constant.

This constant *MD_BACKUP_HIGHEST_VERSION* will cause the highest version number of backup to be restored from the specified location when used in place of the intBackupVersion parameter.

IntBackupFlags must have a value of 0 for the time being, as it is reserved.

Example

```
<%
Dim objComputer, ComputerName
ComputerName = "MyOtherComputer"
Set objComputer = GetObject("IIS://" & ComputerName)
objComputer.Restore "MyBackups", MD_BACKUP_HIGHEST_VERSION, 0
%>
```

This example illustrates how to run the method on another computer in an ASP script to prevent stopping the services on the computer where the script is running.

NOTE

You can run the Restore operation on the same computer by using the Cscript.exe scripting utility. For more information on this utility, refer to Chapter 13, "Administration Scripts."

CAUTION

Do not attempt to restore the metabase backup to a computer other than the one from which it was backed up. The Backup and Restore methods are not to be used for replication purposes. Restore will only work on the computer from which it was backed up.

IIsCustomLogModule

This method is used to configure custom logging information fields.

ADsPath

IIS://*computername*/Logging/CustomLogging

IIS://*computername*/Logging/CustomLogging/*Field*

IIS://*computername*/Logging/CustomLogging/*FieldGroup*

IIS://*computername*/Logging/CustomLogging/*FieldGroup*/*Field*

computername can be any name or "LocalHost" for the local computer.

Syntax

```
RetVal = object.method
```

RetVal holds the return value from the method.

object contains the name of the object returned from the `GetObject` method.

method is the method chosen.

Properties

ADSI Object Properties

Metabase Properties

LogCustomPropertyDataType	LogCustomPropertyHeader
LogCustomPropertyID	LogCustomPropertyMask
LogCustomPropertyName	LogCustomPropertyServicesString

Methods

ADSI Object Methods

IlsFilter

This object is used to set the metabase properties that will define the operation of ISAPI applications. These can be set at the Web service level or for individual Web Servers.

ADsPath

```
IIS://computername/W3SVC/Filters/FilterName
```

wherein computername can be any name or "LocalHost" for the local computer, or

```
IIS://computername /W3SVC/N/Filters/FilterName
```

wherein computername can be any name or "LocalHost," and *N* is the number of a Web Server.

Syntax

```
RetVal = Object.Method
```

RetVal holds the return value from the method.

Object contains the object returned by the `GetObject` method.

Method is the method chosen.

Properties

ADSI Object Properties

Metabase Properties

FilterDescription	FilterEnabled
FilterFlags	FilterPath
FilterState	NotifyAccessDenied
NotifyAuthentication	NotifyEndOfNetSession
NotifyEndOfRequest	NotifyLog
NotifyNonSecurePort	NotifyOrderHigh
NotifyOrderLow	NotifyOrderMedium
NotifyPreProcHeaders	NotifyReadRawData
NotifySecurePort	NotifySendRawData
NotifySendResponse	NotifyUrlMap

Methods

ADSI Object Methods

IIsFilters

This object is an ADSI Container Object that contains IIsFilter Objects. You can use this object to enumerate the IIsFilter Objects and to specify the sequence in which the filters will be loaded by using the `FilterLoadOrder` property.

This object can be set at the Web service level or at individual Web sites.

ADsPath

IIS://*computername*/W3SVC/Filters

wherein computername can be any name or "LocalHost" for the local computer, or

IIS:// *computername* /W3SVC/*N*/Filters

wherein computername can be any name or "LocalHost," and *N* is the number of a Web Server.

Syntax

RetVal = Object.Method

RetVal holds the return value from the method.

B

Object contains the object returned from the GetObject method.

Method is the method chosen.

Can Contain

IIsFilter

Properties

ADSI Object Properties

Metabase Properties

> FilterLoadOrder

Methods

ADSI Object Methods

ADSI Container Object Methods

IIsFtpInfo

This object is used to set the values for the FTP service; these values are stored in the Info sub-key of the MSFTPSVC Key.

ADsPath

IIS://*computername*/MSFTPSVC/Info

computername can be any name or "LocalHost" for the local computer.

Syntax

RetVal = *object.Method*

Parts

RetVal holds the return value from the method.

object contains the object returned from the GetObject operation.

Method is the method chosen.

Properties

ADSI Object Properties

Metabase Properties

> LogModuleList

Methods

ADSI Object Methods

IIsFtpServer

This object is used to set metabase properties for specific FTP servers. It also sets inheritable properties for FTP virtual directories.

You can use some methods to control the server operation. This object is an ADSI Container Object.

ADsPath

IIS://*computername*/MSFTPSVC/*N*

computername can be any name or "LocalHost" for the local computer.

Syntax

RetVal = object.Method

Parts

RetVal holds the return value from the method.

object contains the object returned from the GetObject operation.

Method is the method chosen.

Can Contain

IisFtpVirtualDir

Properties

ADSI Object Properties

Metabase Properties

AccessFlags	AccessRead
AccessWrite	AdminACL
AllowAnonymous	AnonymousOnly
AnonymousPasswordSync	AnonymousUserName
AnonymousUserPass	ConnectionTimeout
DefaultLogonDomain	DisableSocketPooling
DontLog	ExitMessage
FtpDirBrowseShowLongDate	GreetingMessage

B

IPSecurity

LogAnonymous

LogExtFileBytesRecv

LogExtFileBytesSent

LogExtFileClientIp

LogExtFileComputerName

LogExtFileCookie

LogExtFileDate

LogExtFileFlags

LogExtFileHttpStatus

LogExtFileMethod

LogExtFileProtocolVersion

LogExtFileReferer

LogExtFileServerIp

LogExtFileServerPort

LogExtFileSiteName

LogExtFileTime

LogExtFileTimeTaken

LogExtFileUriQuery

LogExtFileUriStem

LogExtFileUserAgent

LogExtFileUserName

LogExtFileWin32Status

LogFileDirectory

LogFileLocaltimeRollover

LogFilePeriod

LogFileTruncateSize

LogNonAnonymous

LogOdbcDataSource

LogOdbcPassword

LogOdbcTableName

LogOdbcUserName

LogPluginClsId

LogType

MaxClientsMessage

MaxConnections

MaxEndpointConnections

MSDOSDirOutput

Realm

ServerAutoStart

ServerBindings

ServerComment

ServerListenBacklog

ServerListenTimeout

ServerSize

ServerState

Continue

This method resumes the server after a pause.

Syntax

IIsFtpServer.**Continue**

Example

```
<%
Dim objServer
Set objServer = GetObject("IIS:// computername /MSFTPSVC/2")
objServer.Continue
%>
```

Pause

This method pauses the server.

Syntax

IIsFtpServer.**Pause**

Example

```
<%
Dim objServer
Set objServer = GetObject("IIS:// computername /MSFTPSVC/2")
objServer.Pause
%>
```

Start

This method starts the server.

Syntax

IIsFtpServer.**Start**

Example

```
<%
Dim objServer
Set objServer = GetObject("IIS:// computername /MSFTPSVC/2")
objServer.Start
%>
```

Stop

This method stops the server.

Syntax

IIsFtpServer.**Stop**

Example

```
<%
Dim objServer
Set objServer = GetObject("IIS:// computername /MSFTPSVC/2")
objServer.Stop
%>
```

Status

This method provides current status on the server by returning an integer value.

Syntax

`IIsFtpServer.`**`Status`**

Return Values

- 1—Starting
- 2—Started
- 3—Stopping
- 4—Stopped
- 5—Pausing
- 6—Paused
- 7—Continuing

IIsFtpService

This object allows you to set metabase properties for FTP sites and FTP Virtual directories.

ADsPath

`IIS://`*`computername`*`/MSFTPSVC`

computername can be any name or "LocalHost" for the local computer.

Syntax

`RetVal = Object.Method`

Parts

`RetVal` holds the return value from the method.

`object` contains the object returned from the `GetObject` operation.

`Method` is the method chosen.

Can Contain

IIsFtpServer, IIsFtpInfo

Properties

ADSI Object Properties

Metabase Properties

AccessFlags	AccessRead
AccessWrite	AdminACL

AllowAnonymous

AnonymousPasswordSync

AnonymousUserPass

DefaultLogonDomain

DisableSocketPooling

ExitMessage

GreetingMessage

LogAnonymous

LogExtFileBytesSent

LogExtFileComputerName

LogExtFileDate

LogExtFileHttpStatus

LogExtFileProtocolVersion

LogExtFileServerIp

LogExtFileSiteName

LogExtFileTimeTaken

LogExtFileUriStem

LogExtFileUserName

LogFileDirectory

LogFilePeriod

LogNonAnonymous

LogOdbcPassword

LogOdbcUserName

LogType

MaxConnections

MSDOSDirOutput

ServerAutoStart

ServerComment

ServerListenTimeout

AnonymousOnly

AnonymousUserName

ConnectionTimeout

DirectoryLevelsToScan

DontLog

FtpDirBrowseShowLongDate

IPSecurity

LogExtFileBytesRecv

LogExtFileClientIp

LogExtFileCookie

LogExtFileFlags

LogExtFileMethod

LogExtFileReferer

LogExtFileServerPort

LogExtFileTime

LogExtFileUriQuery

LogExtFileUserAgent

LogExtFileWin32Status

LogFileLocaltimeRollover

LogFileTruncateSize

LogOdbcDataSource

LogOdbcTableName

LogPluginClsId

MaxClientsMessage

MaxEndpointConnections

Realm

ServerBindings

ServerListenBacklog

ServerSize

Methods

ADSI Object Methods

ADSI Container Object Methods

IIsFtpVirtualDir

You can set and manipulate the metabase properties that apply to the FTP Server, or to the FTP Virtual Directories on the server, using this object.

Applying properties at the root level with this object will cause any children of the root to inherit these same settings unless the settings are specifically overridden at the individual virtual directory.

This object is an ADSI Container Object.

ADsPath

The path for the server's root virtual directory is

```
IIS://computername/MSFTPSVC/N/ROOT
```

computername can be any name or "LocalHost" for the local computer.

The path for a specific virtual directory is

```
IIS:// computername /MSFTPSVC/N/ROOT/vdirName
```

computername can be any name or "LocalHost" for the local computer.

Syntax

RetVal = Object.Method

Parts

RetVal holds the return value from the method.

object contains the IIsFtpVirtualDir object returned from the `GetObject` operation.

Method is the method chosen.

Can Contain

IIsFtpVirtualDir

Properties

ADSI Object Properties

Metabase Properties

AccessFlags	AccessRead
AccessWrite	DontLog
FtpDirBrowseShowLongDate	IPSecurity

Path   UNCPassword

UNCUserName

Methods

ADSI Object Methods

ADSI Container Object Methods

IIsIPSecurity

Use this object to set security settings based on IP addresses and domain addresses. You can
use the `GrantByDefault` Boolean property to determine if a user is granted or denied access by
default.

ADsPath

To specify the server's root virtual directory, use

`IIS://computername/W3SVVC/N/ROOT`

computername can be any name or "LocalHost" for the local computer.

To specify a virtual directory, use

`IIS://computername /W3SVC/N/ROOT/vdirName`

computername can be any name or "LocalHost" for the local computer.

Syntax

`RetVal = Object.Method`

Parts

`RetVal` holds the return value from the method.

object contains the IIsIPSecurity object returned from the `GetObject` operation.

`Method` is the method chosen.

Valid Locations

Key Type	Metabase Path
IIsWebService	/LM/W3SVC/
IIsWebServer	/LM/W3SVC/1
IIsWebFile	/LM/W3SVC/1/ROOT/*vdirName*/*text.htm*
IIsWebDirectory	/LM/W3SVC/1/ROOT/*vdirName*/*subdirectory*

B

Key Type	Metabase Path
IIsFtpVirtualDir	/LM/SMFTPSVC/1/ROOT/*vdirName*
IIsFtpService	/LM/SMFTPSVC/
IIsFtpServer	/LM/SMFTPSVC/1
IIsWebVirtualDir	/LM/W3SVC/1/ROOT/Samples

IIsIPSecurity Properties

- IPDeny—Uses a method to access an array of IP addresses that have been set to deny

- IPGrant—Uses a method to access an array of IP addresses that have been set to allow

- DomainDeny—Accesses an array of domains that are not allowed access to the server

- DomainGrant—Accesses an array of domains that are allowed access to the server

- GrantByDefault—A Boolean property that determines if access will be granted or denied by default

NOTE

If you have the GrantByDefault value set to TRUE, you can only make use of the IPDeny and DomainDeny properties. You need to set GrantByDefault to FALSE to use the IPGrant and DomainGrant properties.

Metabase Properties

    ADSI Object Properties

IPSecurity sets the IP address restrictions.

IPDeny

This property is used to edit an array or list of IP addresses that are not allowed access to the server.

Syntax

*objIPSec.***IPDeny** "*IPAddress,SubnetMask*"

Parameters

ObjIPSec is an IIS Admin Object of the type IIsIPSecurity.

IPAddress specifies the IP address that you want to deny access to the server.

SubnetMask is the subnet mask for the specified IP address.

Example

```
<%
Dim objIPSec, MyIPSec
Dim IPList, DomainList
Set objIPSec = GetObject("IIS:// computername /W3SVC/1")
Set MyIPSec = objIPSec.IPSecurity
DomainList = MyIPSec.DomainDeny
IPList = MyIPSec.IPDeny
Redim IPList (Ubound(IPList)+1)
IPList (Ubound(IPList)) = "142.166.17.1,255.255.255.0"
Redim DomainList (Ubound(DomainList)+1)
DomainList (Ubound(DomainList)) = "domain.com"
IPSec.DomainDeny = DomainList
IPSec.IPDeny = IPList
Set objIPSec.IPSecurity = MyIPSec
Ojb.Setinfo
%>
```

IPGrant

Use this property to edit an array of IP addresses that are allowed access to the server.

Syntax

objIPSec.**IPGrant** *"IPAddress,SubnetMask"*

Parameters

ObjIPSec is an IIS Admin Object of the type IIsIPSecurity.

IPAddress specifies the IP address that you want to grant access to the server.

SubnetMask is the subnet mask for the specified IP address.

Example

```
<%
Dim objIPSec, MyIPSec
Dim IPList, DomainList
Set objIPSec = GetObject("IIS:// computername /W3SVC/1")
Set MyIPSec = objIPSec.IPSecurity
DomainList = MyIPSec.DomainGrant
IPList = MyIPSec.IPGrant
Redim IPList (Ubound(IPList)+1)
IPList (Ubound(IPList)) = "142.166.17.1, 255.255.255.0"
Redim DomainList (Ubound(DomainList)+1)
DomainList (Ubound(DomainList)) = "domain.com"
IPSec.DomainGrant = DomainList
IPSec.IPGrant = IPList
```

```
Set objIPSec.IPSecurity = MyIPSec
Ojb.Setinfo
%>
```

DomainDeny

This property is used to access an array of domains you want denied access to the server.

Syntax

objIPSec.**DomainDeny** *Domain*

Parameters

objIPSec is an IIS Admin Object of type IIsIPSecurity.

Domain is the domain that you want denied access to the server.

Example

```
<%
Dim objIPSec, MyIPSec
Dim IPList, DomainList
Set objIPSec = GetObject("IIS:// computername /W3SVC/1")
Set MyIPSec = objIPSec.IPSecurity
DomainList = MyIPSec.DomainDeny
IPList = MyIPSec.IPDeny
Redim IPList (Ubound(IPList)+1)
IPList (Ubound(IPList)) = "123.0.0.1,255.255.255.0"
Redim DomainList (Ubound(DomainList)+1)
DomainList (Ubound(DomainList)) = "domain.com"
IPSec.DomainDeny = DomainList
IPSec.IPDeny = IPList
Set objIPSec.IPSecurity = MyIPSec
Ojb.Setinfo
%>
```

DomainGrant

This property is used to access an array of domains that you want to grant access to the server.

Syntax

objIPSec.**DomainGrant** *Domain*

Parameters

ObjIPSec is an IIS Admin Object of the type IIsIPSecurity.

Domain is the domain you want to grant access to the server.

Example

```
<% Dim objIPSec, Dim MyIPSec
Dim IPList, DomainList
Set objIPSec = GetObject("IIS:// computername /W3SVC/1")
Set MyIPSec = objIPSec.IPSecurity
DomainList = MyIPSec.DomainGrant
IPList = MyIPSec.IPGrant
Redim IPList (Ubound(IPList)+1)
IPList (Ubound(IPList)) = "142.166.17.1,255.255.255.0"
Redim DomainList (Ubound(DomainList)+1)
DomainList (Ubound(DomainList)) = "domain.com"
IPSec.DomainGrant = DomainList
IPSec.IPGrant = IPList
Set objIPSec.IPSecurity = MyIPSec
Ojb.Setinfo
%>
```

GrantByDefault

You can use the GrantByDefault Boolean property to determine if a user is granted access or denied access by default.

Syntax

objIPSec.**GrantByDefault** *Boolean*

Parameters

objIPSec is an IIS Admin Object of the type IIsIPSecurity.

Boolean is a Boolean value of TRUE or FALSE.

Example

```
<% Dim objIPSec
Set objIPSec = GetObject("IIS:// computername /W3SVC/1")
objIPSec.GrantByDefault=TRUE
objIPSec.SetInfo
%>
```

IIsLogModule

Use this object to manipulate the metabase properties that deal with the operation of logging modules. You can set these properties at the computer level, the Web or FTP service level, or at the individual Web or FTP Server.

ADsPath

`IIS://computername/LOGGING/LogModuleName`

computername can be any name or "LocalHost" for the local computer. The *LogModuleName* is the name of a log module.

Syntax

`RetVal = object.Method`

Parts

RetVal holds the return value from the method.

object contains the IIsLogModule object returned from the `GetObject` method.

Method is the method chosen.

Properties

ADSI Object Properties

Metabase Properties

> `LogModuleId`   `LogModuleUiId`

Methods

ADSI Object Methods

IIsLogModules

This is an ADSI Container object that holds a collection of IIsLogModule objects. Use the IIsLogModules container object to work with log modules at the computer level.

ADsPath

`IIS://computername/LOGGING`

computername can be any name or "LocalHost" for the local computer.

Syntax

`RetVal = object.Method`

Parts

RetVal holds the return value from the method.

object contains the IIsLogModules object returned from the `GetObject` operation.

Method is the method chosen.

Can Contain

IIsLogModule

Properties

ADSI Object Properties

Methods

ADSI Object Methods

ADSI Container Object Methods

Example

```
<%
Dim LoggingModules, objCurrent
Set objCurrent = GetObject("IIS:// computername /W3SVC/1")
Set LoggingModules = GetObject("IIS:// computername /logging")
If objCurrent.LogPluginClsid <> "" Then
    For Each LogModule in LoggingModules
        If LogModule.LogModuleID = objCurrent.LogPluginClsid Then
Response.Write LogModule.Name & "<BR>"
        End If
    Next
Response.Write objCurrent.LogFileDate
End If
%>
```

IIsMimeMap

The Multipurpose Internet Mail Extensions (MIME) mappings can be set using this object.

ADsPath

IIS://*computername*/MIMEMAP

computername can be any name or "LocalHost" is the local computer.

Syntax

RetVal = object.Method

Parts

RetVal holds the return value from the method.

object contains the IIsMimeMap object returned from the GetObject operation.

Method is the method chosen.

Properties

ADSI Object Properties

Metabase Properties

MimeMap

Methods

ADSI Object Methods

IIsMimeType

This object is found in an array of IIsMimeTypes that are contained within the MimeMap property.

In order to add an IIsMimeType object to the array, you need to first create the object, and then set its MimeType. You next need to create the extension and then add it to the array.

Syntax

```
varMimeMap = object.MimeMap
Set objMimeType = aMimeMap(0)
```

Parts

varMimeMap is the variable that will receive the list of IIsMimeType objects.

object is the variable that supports the MimeType property and is returned from the GetObject operation.

objMimeType is an object variable that will receive the IIsMimeType object.

Can Contain

This object cannot contain any other objects.

Properties

ADSI Object Properties

Metabase Properties

MimeMap (A list of filename extensions for the Mime mappings)

MimeType

This property is used to PUT and GET the MIME types.

Syntax

objDir.**MimeType**=*string*

Parameters

objDir is an IIS Admin Object of the type IIsMimeType.

string is a string that specifies the MIME type for the object.

Example

```
<%Dim objDir,  Dim MimeMapNode,   Dim MimeMapList,   Dim MimeMapEntry
Set objDir = GetObject("IIS:// computername /MimeMap")
MimeMapList = objDir.MimeMap
Redim preserve MimeMapList (Ubound(MimeMapList)+1)
Set MimeMapEntry = CreateObject ("IIsMimeTypeEntry")
MimeMapEntry.MimeType = "Text/Plain"
Mime.Extension = ".log"
Set MimeMapList (Ubound(MimeMapList)) = MimeMapEntry
objDir.MimeMap = MimeMapList
objDir.Setinfo
%>
```

Extension

This property is used to indicate the MIME type for the filename extension.

Syntax

objDir.**Extension** = *string*

Parameters

*objDir is a*n IIS Admin Object of the type IIsMimeType.

string is the specific filename extension that is associated with the MIME type specified in
the MimeType property.

Example

```
<% Dim objDir, Dim MimeMapNode,  Dim MimeMapList,  Dim MimeMapEntry
Set objDir = GetObject("IIS:// computername /MimeMap")
MimeMapList = objDir.MimeMap
Redim preserve MimeMapList (Ubound(MimeMapList)+1)
Set MimeMapEntry = CreateObject ("IIsMimeTyepEntry")
MimeMapEntry.MimeMap = "Text/Plain"
Mime.Extension = ".log"
Set MimeMapList (Ubound(MimeMapList)) = MimeMapEntry
objDir.MimeMap = MimeMapList
objDir.Setinfo
%>
```

B

ADMINISTRATION
OBJECT
REFERENCE

IIsWebDirectory

Use this object to set the metabase properties for Web directories on a Web Server. These properties will be inherited by the subdirectories and files.

You can use the methods available with the IIsWebDirectory object to create and manage the applications on your Web directories.

This object is an ADSI Container Object.

ADsPath

IIS://*computername*/W3SVC/N/ROOT/*vdirName*/*DirName*

computername can be any name or "LocalHost" for the local computer.

Syntax

RetVal = object.Method

Parts

RetVal holds the return value from the method.

object contains the IIsWebDirectory object returned from the GetObject operation.

Method is the method chosen.

Can Contain

IIsWebDirectory   IIsWebFile

Properties

ADSI Properties

Metabase Properties

AccessExecute	AccessFlags
AccessNoRemoteExecute	AccessNoRemoteRead
AccessNoRemoteScript	AccessNoRemoteWrite
AccessRead	AccessScript
AccessSSL	AccessSSL128
AccessSSLFlags	AccessSSLMapCert
AccessSSLNegotiateCert	AccessSSLRequireCert
AccessWrite	AnonymousPasswordSync
AnonymousUserName	AnonymousUserPass

AppAllowClientDebug

AppAllowDebugging

AppFriendlyName

AppIsolated

AppOopRecoverLimit

AppPackageID

AppPackageName

AppRoot

AppWamClsID

AspAllowOutOfProcComponents

AspAllowSessionState

AspBufferingOn

AspCodepage

AspEnableApplicationRestart

AspEnableAspHtmlFallback

AspEnableChunkedEncoding

AspEnableParentPaths

AspEnableTypelibCache

AspErrorsToNTLog

AspExceptionCatchEnable

AspLogErrorRequests

AspProcessorThreadMax

AspQueueConnectionTestTime

AspQueueTimeout

AspRequestQueueMax

AspScriptEngineCacheMax

AspScriptErrorMessage

AspScriptErrorSentToBrowser

AspScriptFileCacheSize

AspScriptLanguage

AspScriptTimeout

AspSessionMax

AspSessionTimeout

AspThreadGateEnabled

AspThreadGateLoadHigh

AspThreadGateLoadLow

AspThreadGateSleepDelay

AspThreadGateSleepMax

AspThreadGateTimeSlice

AspTrackThreadingModel

AuthAnonymous

AuthBasic

AuthFlags

AuthNTLM

AuthPersistence

AuthPersistSingleRequest

AuthPersistSingleRequestIfProxy

AuthPersistSingleRequestAlwaysIfProxy

CacheControlCustom

CacheControlMaxAge

CacheControlNoCache

CacheISAPI

ContentIndexed

CpuAppEnabled

CpuCgiEnabled

CreateCGIWithNewConsole

CreateProcessAsUser

DefaultDoc

DefaultDocFooter

DefaultLogonDomain

DirBrowseFlags

DirBrowseShowDate

DirBrowseShowExtension

DirBrowseShowLongDate

DirBrowseShowSize

DirBrowseShowTime

B

ADMINISTRATION
OBJECT
REFERENCE

DontLog	EnableDefaultDoc
EnableDirBrowsing	EnableDocFooter
EnableReverseDns	HttpCustomHeaders
HttpErrors	HttpExpires
HttpPics	HttpRedirect
IPSecurity	LogonMethod
MimeMap	PoolIDCTimeout
PutReadSize	Realm
RedirectHeaders	ScriptMaps
SSIExecDisable	UNCAuthenticationPassthrough
UploadReadAheadSize	

The methods are listed in the following sections.

AppCreate

This method is used to create a Web application definition. It takes one parameter that determines if the application is going to run in-process or out-of-process.

If the application already exists, you can use this method to change that behavior from in-process to out-of-process, or vice versa.

Syntax

objDir.**AppCreate** *InProcFlag*

Parameters

ObjDir is an IIS Admin Object of type IIsWebDirectory or IIsWebVirtualDir.

InProcFlag specifies whether the application being created is to run in-process (TRUE) or out-of-process (FALSE).

Example

```
<%
Dim objDir
Const INPROC = True
Const OUTPROC = False
Set objDir = GetObject("IIS:// computername /W3SVC/1/ROOT/AppDir")
objDir.AppCreate INPROC
%>
```

AppCreate2

This method is used to create a Web application definition. It takes one parameter that determines if the application is going to run in-process or out-of-process.

If the application already exists, you can use this method to change that behavior to whatever run method you like.

Syntax

objDir.**AppCreate2** *InProcFlag*

Parameters

objDir is an IIS Admin Object of type IIsWebDirectory or IIsWebVirtualDir.

InProcFlag is a binary value that indicates how the application will run: in-process (0), out-of-process (1), or in a pooled process (2). If the application already exists and is running, changing this value causes the definition to be deleted. A new application definition will be created to run in the specified process space.

Example

```
<%
Dim objDir
Const INPROC = 0
Const OUTPROC = 1
Const POOLED = 2
Set objDir = GetObject("IIS://computername/W3SVC/1/ROOT/AppDir")
objDir.AppCreate INPROC
%>
```

AppDelete

This method is used to delete an application definition from the metabase key. If the application is running when you call this method, it will shut down the application. If the application is in-process with the IIS service, then all resources in use by that application will be released.

> **CAUTION**
>
> Any deletion that you make with the AppDelete method cannot be undone later.

Syntax

objDir.**AppDelete**

B

Parameters

objDir is an IIS Admin Object of type IIsWebDirectory or IIsWebVirtualDir.

Example

```
<%
Dim objDir
Set objDir = GetObject("IIS://computername/W3SVC/1/ROOT/AppDir")
objDir.AppDelete
%>
```

AppDeleteRecursive

This method will act like the `AppDelete` method in that it will delete an application definition from the metabase key, but it will also delete all subkeys as well.

If the application is running when you call this method, it will shut down the application. If the application is in-process with the IIS service, then all resources in use by that application will be released.

CAUTION

Any deletion that you make with the `AppDeleteRecursive` method cannot be undone later.

Syntax

objDir.**AppDeleteRecursive**

Parameters

objDir is an IIS Admin Object of type IIsWebDirectory or IIsWebVirtualDir.

Example

```
<%
Dim objDir
Set objDir = GetObject("IIS://computername/W3SVC/1/ROOT/AppDir")
objDir.AppDeleteRecursive
%>
```

AppDisable

This method will disable an out-of-process application. Any resources used by the application are released, and the application process itself is terminated. Any attempts to access the application after this method has been executed will fail. You can re-enable the application by using the `AppEnable` method discussed later.

Syntax

objDir.**AppDisable**

Parameters

objDir is an IIS Admin Object of type IIsWebDirectory or IIsWebVirtualDir.

Example

```
<%
Dim objDir
Set objDir = GetObject("IIS://computername/W3SVC/1/ROOT/AppDir")
objDir.AppDisable
%>
```

AppDisableRecursive

This method will disable applications running out-of-process. Any applications running in sub-keys of the metabase key that you specify will also be disabled.

Any resources used by the application are released, and the application process itself is terminated. Any attempts to access the application after this method has been executed will fail. You can re-enable the application by using the `AppEnableRecursive` method discussed later.

This method has no effect on applications that are running as in-process applications.

Syntax

objDir.**AppDisableRecursive**

Parameters

objDir is an IIS Admin Object of type IIsWebDirectory or IIsWebVirtualDir.

Example

```
<%
Dim objDir
Set objDir = GetObject("IIS://computername/W3SVC/1/ROOT/AppDir")
objDir.AppDisableRecursive
%>
```

AppEnable

This method can re-enable a previously disabled application. If the application was not deleted, it will be re-registered with the COM services.

Syntax

objDir.`AppEnable`

Parameters

objDir is an IIS Admin Object of type IIsWebDirectory or IIsWebVirtualDir.

Example

```
<%
Dim objDir
Set objDir = GetObject("IIS://computername/W3SVC/1/ROOT/AppDir")
objDir.AppEnable
%>
```

AppEnableRecursive

This method is used to re-enable an application that was previously disabled with the `AppDisableRecursive` method.

Syntax

objDir.`AppEnableRecursive`

Parameters

objDir is an IIS Admin Object of type IIsWebDirectory or IIsWebVirtualDir.

Example

```
<%
Dim objDir
Set objDir = GetObject("IIS://computername/W3SVC/1/ROOT/AppDir")  objDir.
AppEnableRecursive
%>
```

AppGetStatus

This method can retrieve the current status of a Web application.

Syntax

RetVal = *objDir*.`AppGetStatus`

Parameters

RetVal is used to receive the status of the application.

objDir is an IIS Admin Object of type IIsWebDirectory or IIsWebVirtualDir.

Return Values

APPSTATUS_NOTDEFINED—There is no application defined in the specified path.

APPSTATUS_RUNNING—The application is currently running.

APPSTATUS_STOPPED—The application is currently stopped.

Example

```
<%
Dim objDir, RetVal
Set objDir = GetObject("IIS://computername/W3SVC/1/ROOT/AppDir")
RetVal = objDir.AppGetStatus
%>
```

AppUnload

This method will unload an out-of-process Web application. The resources that the application was using will be released, and then the applications process will be terminated. If the application is an in-process application, it will only be released if there are no other applications referencing it.

Syntax

objDir.**AppUnload**

Parameters

objDir is an IIS Admin Object of type IIsWebDirectory or IIsWebVirtualDir.

Example

```
<%
Dim objDir
Set objDir = GetObject("IIS://computername/W3SVC/1/ROOT/AppDir")
objDir.AppUnload
%>
```

AppUnloadRecursive

This acts like the AppUnload method with the exception that it will unload the application and any subkeys under the applications key.

Syntax

objDir.**AppUnloadRecursive**

Parameters

onjDir is an IIS Admin Object of type IIsWebDirectory or IIsWebVirtualDir.

Example

```
<%
Dim objDir
Set objDir = GetObject("IIS://computername/W3SVC/1/ROOT/AppDir")
objDir.AppUnloadRecursive
%>
```

AspAppRestart

This method restarts ASP applications without the need to access the global.asa file.

Syntax

objDir.**AspAppRestart**

Parameters

objDir is an ASP application object of type IIsWebDirectory or IIsWebVirtualDir.

IIsWebFile

This object can be used to set properties pertaining to files in a Web directory or virtual server. These properties will override any settings that may have been inherited from parent objects.

ADsPath

IIS://*computername*/W3SVC/*n*/Root/*vdirName*/*DirName*/*FileName*

computername can be any name or "LocalHost" for the local computer.

Syntax

RetVal = object.Method

Parts

RetVal holds the return value from the method.

object contains the **IIsWebFile** object, returned from the GetObject operation.

Method is the method chosen.

Properties

ADSI Object Properties

Metabase Properties

AccessExecute	AccessFlags
AccessNoRemoteExecute	AccessNoRemoteRead
AccessNoRemoteScript	AccessNoRemoteWrite
AccessRead	AccessSource
AccessScript	AccessSSL
AccessSSL128	AccessSSLFlags
AccessSSLMapCert	AccessSSLNegotiateCert
AccessSSLRequireCert	AccessWrite
AnonymousPasswordSync	AnonymousUserName
AnonymousUserPass	AuthAnonymous
AuthBasic	AuthFlags
AuthNTLM	AuthPersistence
AuthPersistSingleRequest	
AuthPersistSingleRequestIfProxy	
AuthPersistSingleRequestAlwaysIfProxy	
CacheControlCustom	CacheControlMaxAge
CacheControlNoCache	CpuAppEnabled
CpuCgiEnabled	CreateCGIWithNewConsole
CreateProcessAsUser	DefaultDocFooter
DefaultLogonDomain	DontLog
EnableDocFooter	EnableReverseDns
HttpCustomHeaders	HttpErrors
HttpExpires	HttpPics
HttpRedirect	IPSecurity
LogonMethod	MimeMap
PoolIDCTimeout	PutReadSize
Realm	RedirectHeaders
ScriptMaps	SSIExecDisable
UNCAuthenticationPassthrough	UploadReadAheadSize

Methods

ADSI Object Methods

IIsWebInfo

Use this object to set the values for properties relating to the Web service Info subkey.

ADsPath

IIS://*computername*/W3SVC/INFO

computername can be any name or "LocalHost" for the local computer.

Syntax

RetVal = object.Method

Parts

RetVal holds the return value from the method.

object contains the **IIsWebInfo** object returned from the GetObject operation.

Method is the method chosen.

Properties

ADSI Object Properties

Metabase Properties

AdminServer	CustomErrorDescriptions
LogModuleList	ServerConfigAutoPWSync
ServerConfigFlags	ServerConfigSSL128
ServerConfigSSL40	ServerConfigSSLAllowEncrypt

Methods

ADSI Object Methods

IIsWebServer

The IIsWebServer object is used to set the metabase properties for a specific Web virtual server. By setting these properties at the server level, you also set inheritable properties for the virtual directories and subdirectories under that Web site.

The object also includes methods that allow you to control the operation of the Web Server, such as starting and stopping it. These methods are covered later in this section.

The IIsWebServer object is an ADSI Container object.

ADsPath

IIS://*computername*/W3SVC/*N*

computername can be any computer name or "LocalHost" for the local computer.

Syntax

RetVal = ***objWebServer***.*Method*

Parts

RetVal holds the return value from the method.

ObjWebServer refers to the IIS Admin Object.

Method is the method called.

Can Contain

IIsCertMapper, IIsFilters, and IIsWebVirtualDir

Properties

ADSI Object Properties

Metabase Properties

AccessExecute	AccessFlags
AccessNoRemoteExecute	AccessNoRemoteRead
AccessNoRemoteScript	AccessNoRemoteWrite
AccessRead	AccessSource
AccessScript	AccessSSL
AccessSSL128	AccessSSLFlags
AccessSSLMapCert	AccessSSLNegotiateCert
AccessSSLRequireCert	AccessWrite
AdminACL	AllowKeepAlive
AllowPathInfoForScriptMappings	
AnonymousPasswordSync	AnonymousUserName
AnonymousUserPass	AppAllowClientDebug
AppAllowDebugging	AppFriendlyName
AppIsolated	AppOopRecoverLimit
AppPackageID	AppPackageName
AppRoot	AppWamClsID

AspAllowOutOfProcComponents

AspAllowSessionState

AspBufferingOn

AspCodepage

AspEnableApplicationRestart

AspEnableAspHtmlFallback

AspEnableChunkedEncoding

AspEnableParentPaths

AspEnableTypelibCache

AspErrorsToNTLog

AspExceptionCatchEnable

AspLogErrorRequests

AspProcessorThreadMax

AspQueueConnectionTestTime

AspQueueTimeout

AspRequestQueueMax

AspScriptEngineCacheMax

AspScriptErrorSentToBrowser

AspScriptFileCacheSize

AspScriptLanguage

AspSessionMax

AspScriptTimeout

AspSessionTimeout

AspThreadGateEnabled

AspThreadGateLoadHigh

AspThreadGateLoadLow

AspThreadGateSleepDelay

AspThreadGateSleepMax

AspThreadGateTimeSlice

AspTrackThreadingModel

AuthAnonymous

AuthBasic

AuthFlags

AuthNTLM

AuthPersistence

AuthPersistSingleRequest

AuthPersistSingleRequestIfProxy

AuthPersistSingleRequestAlwaysIfProxy

CacheControlCustom

CacheControlMaxAge

CacheControlNoCache

CacheISAPI

CGITimeout

ConnectionTimeout

CpuAppEnabled

CpuCgiEnabled

CpuEnableActiveProcs

CpuEnableAllProcLogging

CpuEnableAppLogging

CpuEnableCgiLogging

CpuEnableEvent

CpuEnableKernelTime

CpuEnableLogging

CpuEnablePageFaults

CpuEnableProcType

CpuEnableTerminatedProcs

CpuEnableTotalProcs

CpuEnableUserTime

CpuLimitLogEvent

CpuLimitPause

CpuLimitPriority

CpuLimitProcStop

CpuLimitsEnabled

CpuLoggingMask

CpuResetInterval

CreateProcessAsUser

DefaultDocFooter

DirBrowseFlags

DirBrowseShowExtension

DirBrowseShowSize

DisableSocketPooling

EnableDefaultDoc

EnableDocFooter

FrontPageWeb

HttpErrors

HttpPics

IPSecurity

LogExtFileBytesRecv

LogExtFileClientIp

LogExtFileCookie

LogExtFileFlags

LogExtFileMethod

LogExtFileReferer

LogExtFileServerPort

LogExtFileTime

LogExtFileUriQuery

LogExtFileUserAgent

LogExtFileWin32Status

LogFileLocaltimeRollover

LogFileTruncateSize

LogOdbcPassword

LogOdbcUserName

LogPluginClsId

MaxBandwidth

MaxConnections

MimeMap

CpuLoggingInterval

CpuLoggingOptions

CreateCGIWithNewConsole

DefaultDoc

DefaultLogonDomain

DirBrowseShowDate

DirBrowseShowLongDate

DirBrowseShowTime

DontLog

EnableDirBrowsing

EnableReverseDns

HttpCustomHeaders

HttpExpires

HttpRedirect

LogAnonymous

LogExtFileBytesSent

LogExtFileComputerName

LogExtFileDate

LogExtFileHttpStatus

LogExtFileProtocolVersion

LogExtFileServerIp

LogExtFileSiteName

LogExtFileTimeTaken

LogExtFileUriStem

LogExtFileUserName

LogFileDirectory

LogFilePeriod

LogOdbcDataSource

LogOdbcTableName

LogonMethod

LogType

MaxBandwidthBlocked

MaxEndpointConnections

NetLogonWorkstation

B

ADMINISTRATION OBJECT REFERENCE

NotDeletable

NTAuthenticationProviders

PasswordCacheTTL

PasswordChangeFlags

PasswordExpirePrenotifyDays

PoolIDCTimeout

ProcessNTCRIfLoggedOn

PutReadSize

Realm

RedirectHeaders

ScriptMaps

SecureBindings

ServerAutoStart

ServerBindings

ServerComment

ServerListenBacklog

ServerListenTimeout

ServerSize

ServerState

SSIExecDisable

UNCAuthenticationPassthrough

UploadReadAheadSize

UseHostName

Continue

This method returns a paused server to operation.

Syntax

IIsWebServer.**Continue**

Example

```
<%
Dim objServer
Set objServer = GetObject("IIS://computername/W3SVC/2")
objServer.Continue
%>
```

Pause

This method pauses the server.

Syntax

IIsWebServer.**Pause**

Example

```
<%
Dim objServer
Set objServer = GetObject("IIS://computername/W3SVC/2"
objServer.Pause
%>
```

Start

This method starts the server.

Syntax

```
IIsWebServer.Start
```

Example

```
<%
Dim objServer
Set objServer = GetObject("IIS://computername/W3SVC/2"
objServer.Start%>
```

Status

This method returns one of these integer values, which represents the current status of the server:

- 1—Starting
- 2—Started
- 3—Stopping
- 4—Stopped
- 5—Pausing
- 6—Paused
- 7—Continuing

Syntax

```
IIsWebServer.Status
```

Stop

This method stops the server.

Syntax

```
IIsWebServer.Stop
```

Example

```
<%
Dim objServer
Set objServer = GetObject("IIS://computername/W3SVC/2")
objServer.Stop
%>
```

IIsWebService

This object is an ADSI Container Object. You can use it to set inheritable metabase properties for Web sites and Virtual directories.

ADsPath

IIS://*computername*/W3SVC

computername can be any computer name or "LocalHost" for the local computer.

Syntax

RetVal = *object.Method*

Parts

RetVal holds the return value from the method.

object contains the **IIsWebServer** object returned from the GetObject operation.

Method is the method chosen.

Can Contain

IIsFilters, IIsWebInfo, IIsWebServer

Properties

ADSI Object Properties

Metabase Properties

AccessExecute	AccessFlags
AccessNoRemoteExecute	AccessNoRemoteRead
AccessNoRemoteScript	AccessNoRemoteWrite
AccessRead	AccessSource
AccessScript	AccessSSL
AccessSSL128	AccessSSLFlags
AccessSSLMapCert	AccessSSLNegotiateCert
AccessSSLRequireCert	AccessWrite
AdminACL	AllowKeepAlive
AllowPathInfoForScriptMappings	
AnonymousPasswordSync	AnonymousUserName
AnonymousUserPass	AppAllowClientDebug
AppAllowDebugging	AppFriendlyName

AppIsolated

AppPackageID   AppPackageName

AppRoot   AppWamClsID

AspAllowOutOfProcComponents   AspAllowSessionState

AspBufferingOn   AspCodepage

AspEnableApplicationRestart   AspEnableAspHtmlFallback

AspEnableChunkedEncoding   AspEnableParentPaths

AspEnableTypelibCache   AspErrorsToNTLog

AspExceptionCatchEnable   AspLogErrorRequests

AspProcessorThreadMax

AspQueueConnectionTestTime

AspQueueTimeout   AspRequestQueueMax

AspScriptEngineCacheMax   AspScriptErrorMessage

AspScriptErrorSentToBrowser

AspScriptFileCacheSize   AspScriptLanguage

AspSessionMax   AspScriptTimeout

AspSessionTimeout   AspThreadGateEnabled

AspThreadGateLoadHigh   AspThreadGateLoadLow

AspThreadGateSleepDelay   AspThreadGateSleepMax

AspThreadGateTimeSlice   AspTrackThreadingModel

AuthAnonymous   AuthBasic

AuthFlags   AuthNTLM

AuthPersistence   AuthPersistSingleRequest

AuthPersistSingleRequestIfProxy

AuthPersistSingleRequestAlwaysIfProxy

CacheControlCustom   CacheControlMaxAge

CacheControlNoCache   CacheISAPI

ContentIndexed   ConnectionTimeout

CpuAppEnabled   CpuCgiEnabled

CpuEnableActiveProcs   CpuEnableAllProcLogging

CpuEnableAppLogging   CpuEnableCgiLogging

CpuEnableEvent   CpuEnableKernelTime

CpuEnableLogging   CpuEnablePageFaults

CpuEnableProcType   CpuEnableTerminatedProcs

CpuEnableTotalProcs   CpuEnableUserTime
CpuLimitLogEvent   CpuLimitPause
CpuLimitPriority   CpuLimitProcStop
CpuLimitsEnabled   CpuLoggingInterval
CpuLoggingMask   CpuLoggingOptions
CpuResetInterval   CreateCGIWithNewConsole
CreateProcessAsUser   DefaultDoc
DefaultDocFooter   DefaultLogonDomain
DirBrowseFlags   DirBrowseShowDate
DirBrowseShowExtension   DirBrowseShowLongDate
DirBrowseShowSize   DirBrowseShowTime
DirectoryLevelsToScan   DisableSocketPooling
DontLog   DownlevelAdminInstance
EnableDefaultDoc   EnableDirBrowsing
EnableDocFooter   EnableReverseDns
HttpCustomHeaders   HttpErrors
HttpExpires   HttpPics
HttpRedirect   InProcessIsapiApps
IPSecurity

LogExtFileBytesRecv   LogExtFileBytesSent
LogExtFileClientIp   LogExtFileComputerName
LogExtFileCookie   LogExtFileDate
LogExtFileFlags   LogExtFileHttpStatus
LogExtFileMethod   LogExtFileProtocolVersion
LogExtFileReferer   LogExtFileServerIp
LogExtFileServerPort   LogExtFileSiteName
LogExtFileTime   LogExtFileTimeTaken
LogExtFileUriQuery   LogExtFileUriStem
LogExtFileUserAgent   LogExtFileUserName
LogExtFileWin32Status   LogFileDirectory
LogFileLocaltimeRollover   LogFilePeriod
LogFileTruncateSize   LogOdbcDataSource
LogOdbcPassword   LogOdbcTableName
LogOdbcUserName   LogonMethod

LogPluginClsId	LogType
MaxConnections	MaxEndpointConnections
MimeMap	NetLogonWorkstation
NTAuthenticationProviders	
PasswordCacheTTL	PasswordChangeFlags
PasswordExpirePrenotifyDays	PoolIDCTimeout
ProcessNTCRIfLoggedOn	PutReadSize
Realm	RedirectHeaders
ScriptMaps	ServerAutoStart
ServerBindings	ServerComment
ServerListenBacklog	ServerListenTimeout
ServerSize	SSIExecDisable
SSLUseDSMapper	UNCAuthenticationPassthrough
UploadReadAheadSize	UseHostName
WAMUserName	WAMUserPass

Methods

ADSI Object Methods

ADSI Container Object Methods

IIsWebVirtualDir

This object is used to set the metabase properties for the virtual directories on the Web Server. Setting these properties at the ROOT directory will allow the subdirectories to inherit the settings. You can override these settings at the individual virtual directory.

The IIsWebVirtualDir object is an ADSI Container Object.

ADsPath

To specify the server's root virtual directory, use

IIS://*computername*/W3SVC/*N*/ROOT

computername can be any name or "LocalHost" for the local computer.

To indicate a specific virtual directory, use

IIS://*computername* /W3SVC/*N*/ROOT/*vdirName*

computername can be any name or "LocalHost" for the local computer.

Syntax

RetVal = object.Method

Parts

RetVal holds the return value from the method.

object contains the IIsWebVirtualDir object returned from the GetObject operation.

Method is the method chosen.

Can Contain

IIsWebVirtualDir, IIsWebDirectory, IIsWebFile

Properties

ADSI Object Properties

Metabase Properties

AccessExecute	AccessFlags
AccessNoRemoteExecute	AccessNoRemoteRead
AccessNoRemoteScript	AccessNoRemoteWrite
AccessRead	AccessSource
AccessScript	AccessSSL
AccessSSL128	AccessSSLFlags
AccessSSLMapCert	AccessSSLNegotiateCert
AccessSSLRequireCert	AccessWrite
AnonymousPasswordSync	AnonymousUserName
AnonymousUserPass	AppAllowClientDebug
AppAllowDebugging	AppFriendlyName
AppIsolated	AppOopRecoverLimit
AppPackageID	AppPackageName
AppRoot	AppWamClsID
AspAllowOutOfProcComponents	AspAllowSessionState
AspBufferingOn	AspCodepage
AspEnableApplicationRestart	AspEnableAspHtmlFallback
AspEnableChunkedEncoding	AspEnableParentPaths
AspEnableTypelibCache	AspErrorsToNTLog
AspExceptionCatchEnable	AspLogErrorRequests

AspProcessorThreadMax

AspQueueConnectionTestTime

AspQueueTimeout   AspRequestQueueMax

AspScriptEngineCacheMax   AspScriptErrorMessage

AspScriptErrorSentToBrowser

AspScriptFileCacheSize   AspScriptLanguage

AspSessionMax   AspScriptTimeout

AspSessionTimeout   AspThreadGateEnabled

AspThreadGateLoadHigh   AspThreadGateLoadLow

AspThreadGateSleepDelay   AspThreadGateSleepMax

AspThreadGateTimeSlice   AspTrackThreadingModel

AuthAnonymous   AuthBasic

AuthFlags   AuthNTLM

AuthPersistence   AuthPersistSingleRequest

AuthPersistSingleRequestIfProxy

AuthPersistSingleRequestAlwaysIfProxy

CacheControlCustom   CacheControlMaxAge

CacheControlNoCache   CacheISAPI

ContentIndexed   CpuAppEnabled

CpuCgiEnabled   CreateCGIWithNewConsole

CreateProcessAsUser   DefaultDoc

DefaultDocFooter   DefaultLogonDomain

DirBrowseFlags   DirBrowseShowDate

DirBrowseShowExtension   DirBrowseShowLongDate

DirBrowseShowSize   DirBrowseShowTime

DontLog

EnableDefaultDoc   EnableDirBrowsing

EnableDocFooter   EnableReverseDns

HttpCustomHeaders   HttpErrors

HttpExpires   HttpPics

HttpRedirect

IPSecurity   LogonMethod

MimeMap   Path

PoolIDCTimeout   PutReadSize

B

Realm	RedirectHeaders
ScriptMaps	SSIExecDisable
UNCAuthenticationPassthrough	
UNCPassword	UNCUserName
UploadReadAheadSize	

Methods

The IIsWebVirtualDir object supports the following methods. For information on these methods, see the section on IIsWebDirectory.

- AppCreate
- AppCreate2
- AppDelete
- AppDeleteRecursive
- AppDisable
- AppDisableRecursive
- AppEnable
- AppEnableRecursive
- AppGetStatus
- AppUnload
- AppUnloadRecursive
- AspAppStart

Constants

The constants listed below are available for use with the methods and properties of the IIS Administration Objects.

```
Const ADS_PROPERTY_CLEAR = 1     'PutEx
Const ADS_PROPERTY_UPDATE = 2    'PutEx
Const APPSTATUS_NOTDEFINED = 4   'AppStatus
Const APPSTATUS_RUNNING = 2      'AppStatus
Const APPSTATUS_STOPPED = 3      'AppStatus
Const APPSTATUS_UNLOADED = 1     'AppStatus
Const IIS_ANY_PROPERTY = 0       'GetDataPaths
Const IIS_INHERITABLE_ONLY = 1   'GetDataPaths
Const MD_ERROR_DATA_NOT_FOUND = &H800CC801    'GetDataPaths
Const MD_ERROR_IISAO_INVALID_SCHEMA = &H8800CC810   'GetObject
Const MD_BACKUP_FORCE_BACKUP = 4     'Backup
```

```
Const MD_BACKUP_HIGHEST_VERSION = &HFFFFFFFE    'Backup, Delete, Restore
Const MD_BACKUP_MAX_VERSION = 9999    'Limit
Const MD_BACKUP_MAX_LEN = 100    'Limit
Const MD_BACKUP_NEXT_VERSION = &HFFFFFFFF    'Backup
Const MD_BACKUP_OVERWRITE = 1    'Backup
Const MD_BACKUP_SAVE_FIRST = 2    'Backup
Const MD_SERVER_STATE_CONTINUING = 7    'ServerState
Const MD_SERVER_STATE_PAUSING = 5    'ServerState
Const MD_SERVER_STATE_PAUSED = 6    'ServerState
Const MD_SERVER_STATE_STARTING = 1    'ServerState
Const MD_SERVER_STATE_STARTED = 2    'ServerState
Const MD_SERVER_STATE_STOPPING = 3    'ServerState
Const MD_SERVER_STATE_STOPPED = 4    'ServerState
Const NOT_A_VALID_PROPERTY = &H80005006    'Various methods
```

ADSI Reference

IN THIS APPENDIX

This appendix will offer explanations of the methods and objects that are exposed for use with the IIS Administration Objects.

ADSI Object Properties

The following list displays the six basic properties of the IIS Admin Objects that are required by all ADSI Objects. These properties are all string data types.

Property	Description
Name	The name of the object that will be used, such as W3SVC
ADsPath	The path that is used to uniquely identify the object, for example, IIS://computername/W3SVC
Class	The schema class name, for example, IISWebService
GUID	A globally unique identifier for the object, for example, {8B645678-7CF4-11CF-B24H-00AA006E1200}
Parent	Used for the ADsPath of the parent container object, for example, IIS://computername
Schema	The ADsPath of the object, for example, IIS://computername/schema/IIsWebService

ADSI Methods

In order to change the metabase properties of the IIS Admin Object, you use the ADSI methods, described in the following sections. First, open the object that you want to modify, make the changes, and then resave it back to the metabase.

Get

Use this method to retrieve values from an object and store them in a variable for use in your code.

Syntax

```
RetVal = object.Get(property)
```

or

```
RetVal = object.property
```

Parts

RetVal will receive the returned value of the property.

object contains an IIS Admin Object that is returned from the **GetObject** operation.

property is the property of the object that has been retrieved from the metabase.

Example

```
<%
Dim objIIs, varRead, varWrite
Set objIIs = GetObject("IIS://computername/W3SVC/1/Root")
varRead = objIIs.Get("AccessRead")
varWrite = objIIs.AccessWrite
varRead = True
varWrite = False
objIIs.Put "AccessRead", varRead
objIIs.AccessWrite = varWrite
objIIs.SetInfo
%>
```

GetDataPaths

Use this method to retrieve the paths for all the locations of a metabase property. These paths reside under the specified start path.

Syntax

varList = *object*.**GetDataPaths***(property, AttributeFlag)*

Parts

varList is used to hold the list of paths to occurrences of the specified property.

object contains an IIS Admin Object that is returned by the **GetObject** operation.

property is the name of the property whose paths you want to locate.

AttributeFlag is one of the following flags:

IIS_ANY_PROPERTY	Retrieve the paths whether the property is inheritable or not.
IIS_INHERITABLE_ONLY	Retrieve the paths only if the property is inheritable. This will return an MD_ERROR_DATA_NOT_FOUND if the property is not inheritable.

> **NOTE**
>
> The For each Path in varList…Next statement can be used to retrieve individual paths from *varList*.

Example

```
<%
Const IIS_ANY_PROPERTY = 0
Const IIS_INHERITABLE_ONLY = 1
Const MD_ERROR_DATA_NOT_FOUND = &H800CC801
```

C

ADSI REFERENCE

```
Dim objWebSvr, varList, varProperty
On Error Resume Next
Set objWebSvr = GetObject("IIS://computername/W3SVC/1")
varProperty = "AccessFlags"
varList = objWebSvr.GetDataPaths(varProperty, IIS_INHERITABLE_ONLY)
If Err.Number = 0 Then
    Response.Write "Paths for property " & varProperty & "<BR>"
    For each Path in varList
    Response.Write Path & "<BR>"
    Next
ElseIf Err.Number = MD_ERROR_DATA_NOT_FOUND Then
    Response.Write "Property is not inheritable.<BR>"
ElseIf Err.Number = &H80005006 Then
    Response.Write "Property does not exist.<BR>"
Else
    Response.Write "Error " & Err.Number & "  " & Err.Description
End If
%>
```

GetEx

This method will retrieve a value or values from a named property of the object. If the property contains only one value, that value is returned; if there are more, all values are returned.

Syntax

*RetVal = object.**GetEx***(property)*

Parts

RetVal will contain the returned property value from the method.

object contains an IIS Admin Object that is returned by the **GetObject** operation.

property is a property of the object that has been retrieved from the metabase.

Return Value

The value of the property.

Example

```
<%
Dim objIIs, varList
Set objIIs = GetObject("IIS://computername/W3SVC/Info")
varList = objIIs.GetEx("CustomErrorDescriptions")
objIIs.PutEx 2, "CustomErrorDescriptions", varList
objIIs.SetInfo
%>
```

GetInfo

This method will retrieve the object's values that exist in the metabase. It will reinitialize the object's properties with the returned information.

Syntax

object.**GetInfo**

Parts

object contains an IIS Admin Object that is returned by the **GetObject** operation.

Example

```
<%
Dim objIIs
Set objIIs = GetObject("IIS://computername/W3SVC/1/Root")
     ' place code here to change the properties
objIIs.GetInfo
%>
```

GetPropertyAttribObj

This method is used to retrieve the object that contains the properties' attributes. You can then use it to retrieve individual attributes.

Syntax

To initialize

objPropAtt = object.**GetPropertyAttribObj***(property)*

To use

boolRetVal = PropAttObj.Attribute

Parts

ObjPropAtt references an object that contains the property attributes for the *property*.

object contains an IIS Admin Object that is returned by the **GetObject** operation.

property is a string that contains the name of the property whose attributes you are requesting.

BoolRetVal is a Boolean value indicates whether the attribute specified by *Attribute* is enabled or disabled.

C

ADSI REFERENCE

Attribute indicates which of the attributes is being queried. The possible attributes are

Attribute	Description
Inherit	Indicates whether the property is inheritable
PartialPath	Indicates whether a partial path is present
Secure	Indicates whether the property is secure
Reference	Indicates whether the property was received by a reference
Volatile	Indicates whether the property is volatile
IsInherited	Indicates whether the property is inherited
InsertPath	Indicates whether a string in a property contains a special insert value
AllAttributes	Contains the attributes listed in this table in a Long value

Example

```
<%
Dim WebServerObj
Dim boolRetValue

'Open the object for the first virtual Web server root.
Set WebServerObj = GetObject("IIS://MyComputer/W3SVC/1/Root")

propAttribObj = WebServerObj.GetPropertyAttribObj("Name")
boolRetVal = propAttribObj.Inherit
%>
```

> **NOTE**
>
> This property attribute does not support the Get and Put methods. You must use the *object.property* syntax instead.

Put

Use this method to set a value for the property of an object.

Syntax

*object.**Put** property, value*

or

object.property = value

Parts

object contains an IIS Admin Object that is returned by the **GetObject** operation.

property is a property of the object that has been retrieved.

value is the value for the property.

Example

```
<%
Dim objIIs, varRead
Set objIIs = GetObject("IIS://computername/W3SVC/1/Root")
varRead = objIIs.Get("AccessRead")
varRead = True
objIIs.Put "AccessRead", varRead
objIIs.SetInfo
%>
```

PutEx

This method will set the value for a single property or multiple values for a property that contains more than one value.

Syntax

object.**PutEx** *controlcode, property, value*

Parts

object contains an IIS Admin Object that is returned by the **GetObject** operation.

controlcode specifies whether to update the property, or to remove the property from the object. This can be either ADS_PROPERTY_CLEAR (value 1) to remove the property, or ADS_PROPERTY_UPDATE (value 2) to update the property.

property is a property of the object that has been retrieved.

value is the value for the property. This is an empty string when removing the property (*controlcode* = ADS_PROPERTY_CLEAR).

Example

```
<%
Dim objIIs, varList
Set objIIs = GetObject("IIS://computername/W3SVC/Info")
varList = objIIs.GetEx("CustomErrorDescriptions")
objIIs.PutEx 2, "CustomErrorDescriptions", varList
objIIs.PutEx 1, "ObsoleteProperty", ""
objIIs.SetInfo
%>
```

C

ADSI REFERENCE

SetInfo

This method will write the property values to the metabase. You must call this method to write the changes to the metabase. Any changed values will be saved, and unchanged data will remain untouched.

Syntax

object.`SetInfo`

Parts

object contains an IIS Admin Object that is returned by the `GetObject` operation.

Example

```
<%
Dim objIIs
Set objIIs = GetObject("IIS://computername/W3SVC/1/Root")
      ' code to change properties
objIIs.SetInfo
%>
```

ADSI Container Object Properties

ADSI objects that can contain other ADSI objects are known as *ADSI Container Objects*. Any ADSI Container Object is able to implement ADSI container methods and properties. This section lists and describes two read-only ADSI container properties:

- **_NewEnum**—This property will return an enumerator object. This object can then be used to contain the objects that are retrieved. Using this object, any automation-enabled language, such as VBScript, can make use of the For…Each loop to iterate through the object collection and manipulate the objects.

- **Count**—This property represents the number of objects in the container object. Using this property, you can determine how many objects exist in the container, or you can use it in a For…Next loop to iterate the objects in the container object.

ADSI Container Object Methods

The five methods available to the ADSI Container Objects can be used to manipulate the objects in a container object.

> **NOTE**
>
> If the IIS Admin Object is a container object, it will retain its own ADSI object proper-
> ties and methods. It will also maintain any IIS-specific methods and associated
> metabase properties.

CopyHere

This method is used to copy an object into a container.

Syntax

```
Set objCopied = object.CopyHere(SourceName, NewName)
```

Parts

objCopied is used to access the object that was copied into the container.

object contains an IIS Admin Object that is returned by the **GetObject** operation.

SourceName is the name of the object to be copied.

NewName is the new name for the copied object.

> **NOTE**
>
> The *ObjCopied* variable only receives a pointer to the object. The object itself remains
> in the container. Anyone familiar with programming in C or C++ will understand this
> behavior.

Example

```
<%
Dim ToobjDir, FromobjDir, RootobjDir
Set RootobjDir = GetObject("IIS://computername/W3SVC/4/ROOT")
Set ToobjDir = RootVDirObj.CopyHere("VDir1", "VDir2")
RootobjDir.SetInfo
%>
```

Create

This method is used to create a new object in the container.

Syntax

```
Set objNewObj = object.Create(KeyType, Name)
```

Parts

objNewObj is used to access the new object that was created in the container.

object contains an IIS Admin Object that is returned by the **GetObject** operation.

KeyType is the type of IIS Admin Object to create.

Name is the name that will be given to the new object.

Example

```
<%
Dim objWebService, objServer
Set objWebService = GetObject("IIS://computername/W3SVC")
Set objServer = objWebService.Create("IIsWebServer", "3")
%>
```

Delete

This method is used to delete an object from a container.

Syntax

*Object.***Delete** *KeyType, Name*

Parts

object contains an IIS Admin Object that is returned by the **GetObject** operation.

KeyType is the type of IIS Admin Object that you want to delete.

Name is the name of the object to be deleted.

> **NOTE**
>
> If the contained object that will be deleted is a part of an application, the Delete method will remove the application definition first, and then it will delete the object.

Example

```
<%
Dim objWebService
Set objWebService = GetObject("IIS://computername/W3SVC")
objWebService.Delete "IIsWebServer", "4"
%>
```

GetObject

This method is used to access an object in a container and return it to a calling procedure.

Syntax

```
Set objChildObj = object.GetObject(Class, ChildName)
```

Parts

objChildObj is used to access the object. This method works the same way as the ASP **GetObject** function.

Object contains an IIS Admin Object that is returned by the **GetObject** operation.

Class specifies the class of the object that will be accessed.

ChildName is the name of the object to be accessed.

> **NOTE**
>
> The *ChildObj* variable will receive a pointer to the object. The object will remain in the container.

Example

```
<%
Dim objWebService, objServer
Set objWebService = GetObject("IIS://computername/W3SVC")
Set objServer = objWebService.GetObject("IIsWebServer", "3")
%>
```

MoveHere

This method is used to move an object into the container. It will also remove the object from its original container.

Syntax

```
Set objMoved = object.MoveHere(SourceName, NewName)
```

Parts

objMoved is used to access the object that is moved into the container.

object contains an IIS Admin Object that is returned by the **GetObject** operation.

SourceName is the name of the object that will be moved.

NewName is the new name for the moved object.

NOTE

The *objMoved* variable will receive a pointer to the object. The object itself will remain in the container.

Example

```
<%
Dim ToobjDir, FromobjDir, RootobjDir
Set RootobjDir = GetObject("IIS://computername/W3SVC/3/ROOT")
Set FromobjDir = GetObject("IIS://computername/W3SVC/3/ROOT/VDir1")
Set ToobjDir = RootobjDir.MoveHere("VDir1", "VDir2")
Set FromobjDir = nothing
%>
```

Changes in ADSI for IIS 5.0

This section will list the changes and additions in ADSI for IIS version 5.0.

IIS Performance Features

One of the issues in IIS 4.0 that caused some performance issues was the use of sockets for Web sites. Because each site had to be bound to its own IP address, it required its own socket to operate. This meant that every new Web site needed to open a socket for communication. These sockets used non-paged memory, and each socket opened would consume more memory.

With IIS 5.0, you can have Web sites bound to different IP addresses but sharing the same port number. In this way, the sites can also share the same socket. This prevents the need to open a socket for each Web site, thereby reducing the amount of memory resources required.

Some sites might still require a dedicated socket for security reasons. You can use the DisableSocketPooling property and set it to TRUE to cause the site to use its own socket. You should set this property at the site level and not at the computer level.

Properties Removed from IIS 5.0

Microsoft has removed the AspMemFreeFactor property from ADSI in IIS 5.0.

Properties Added to IIS 5.0

The following properties have been added to ADSI in IIS 5.0.

AccessSource	AspEnableApplicationRestart
AspEnableAspHtmlFallback	AspEnableChunkedEncoding
AspEnableTypeLibCache	AspErrorsToNTLog
AspProcessorThreadMax	AspQueueConnectionTestTime
AspRequestQueueMax	AspSessionMax
AspTrackThreadingModel	CPUAppEnabled
CPUCGIEnabled	CPUCGILimit
CPUEnableActiveProcs	CPUEnableAllProcLogging
CPUEnableAppLogging	CPUEnableCGILogging
CPUEnableEvent	CPUEnableKernelTime
CPUEnablePageFaults	CPUEnableProcType
CPUEnableTerminatedProcs	CPUEnableTotalProcs
CPUEnableUserTime	CPULimitLogEvent
CPULimitPause	CPULimitPriority
CPULimitProcStop	CPULimitsEnabled
CPULoggingInterval	CPULoggingMask
CPULoggingOptions	CPUResetInterval
DisableSocketPooling	HcCacheControlHeader
HcCompressionBufferSize	HcCompressionDirectory
HcCompressionDll	HcCreateFlags
HcDoDiskSpaceLimiting	HcDoDynamicCompression
HcDoOnDemandCompression	HcDoStaticCompression
HcDynamicCompressionLevel	HcExpiresHeader
HcFileExtensions	HcFilesDeletedPerDiskFree
HcIoBufferSize	HcMaxDiskSpaceUsage
HcMaxQueueLength	HcMimeType
HcMinFileSizeForComp	HcNoCompressionForHttp10
HcNoCompressionForProxies	HcNoCompressionForRange
HcOnDemandCompLevel	HcPriority
HcSendCacheHeaders	LogCustomPropertyDataType

LogCustomPropertyHeader	LogCustomPropertyID
LogCustomPropertyMask	LogCustomPropertyName
LogCustomPropertyServicesString	NotDeletable
SSLUseDSMapper	

Property Key Type Changes

The following four properties have had some changes in the key type from II 4.0. (These changes are described in Appendix D, "Script Reference.")

KeyType

FrontPageWeb

CacheISAPI

AspTrackThreadingModel

Changed Properties in IIS 5.0

There has been a syntax change implemented for the ScriptMaps property in the current release of IIS 5.0. Microsoft has made the change from verb exclusion to required verb inclusion. This means that verbs are now required in the property syntax.

For more information on verb inclusion, see Appendix D for the section on ScriptMaps.

Script Reference

D

IN THIS APPENDIX

In this section, you will find reference information regarding the @ directives included in IIS 5.0. There is also a reference section of the `Global.asa` file. Microsoft's MSDN Web site contains a rather large reference site pertaining to VBScript and JScript that can offer you information and tutorials on each of the languages. For other scripting language references, you will need to look to the specific Web sites pertaining to those languages.

@ Directives Reference

This appendix explains the @ processing directives that are used to send processing information to IIS in regards to your ASP scripts.

@CODEPAGE

This directive is used to set the codepage that will be used by your `.asp` file. The codepage will define what character set to use in the same way that a word processor uses a codepage.

Syntax

```
<%@ CODEPAGE = codepage %>
```

The `codepage` variable is used to indicate the valid codepage to be used by the page.

This value can be overridden by using the Session.Codepage property, but only for the current session. When the session ends, the codepage will fall back to the value set used during the previous procedure.

Some of the more common code pages are

437	United States (English)
850	Multilingual (Latin 1)
852	Slavic
855	Cyrillic (Russian)
857	Turkish
860	Portuguese
861	Icelandic
863	Canadian French
865	Nordic
866	Russian
869	Modern Greek
932	Japanese
936	Simplified Chinese
950	Traditional Chinese

These code pages are normally set using the Regional Settings on your Windows-based computer. If the code page definitions are not installed on the computer, you will get an ASP error.

@ENABLESESSIONSTATE

This directive is used to turn session state on or off. It is a Boolean value that accepts either TRUE or FALSE. If you are not using any sessions within your Web site, you should set this value to FALSE. Doing so can improve performance on the server because then IIS is not required to process session variables in the scripts.

Syntax

```
<%@ ENABLESESSIONSTATE=TRUE|FALSE %>
```

You specify TRUE to turn on session state management on the ASP page or FALSE to turn it off.

@LANGUAGE

This directive is used to specify the language that you will use on the ASP page. The specified language must be installed on the server. VBScript and JScript are installed with IIS.

VBScript is the default language specified in the properties of IIS and therefore does not need to be specified in the header of the ASP file.

Syntax

```
<%@ LANGUAGE=Jscript|VBScript|OtherScriptEngine %>
```

The OtherScriptEngine variable is the name of any other compatible scripting engine that you have installed.

You can change the default scripting engine programmatically using the IIS Admin Objects, using the AspScriptLanguage property. This property can be set at the Web Service, Web Server, Virtual Directory or directory level.

Alternatively, you can set the default scripting language by changing the properties for the Web site. Open the Properties sheet for the Web site on which you want to set the default language, choose the Home Directory tab, and click the Configuration button located in the Application Settings section at the bottom of the page. This displays the Application Configuration dialog box. Select the App Options tab sheet and change the Default ASP Language setting to reflect the scripting language you want for the default.

@LCID

LCID stands for *locale identifier*. You use this directive to set this value for the Web page based on the locales installed in the computer. This identifier is the standard international numeric abbreviation.

When you set this value, you are determining what will be used for number and currency formats as well as separators and date/time formats.

LCID uses two predefined values for the locale. LOCALE_SYSTEM_DEFAULT is used to indicate the local system's default locale. The second is the LOCALE_USER_DEFAULT that specifies the current user's locale.

Syntax

```
<%@ LCID=localeidentifier %>
```

The *localeidentifier* variable will contain a valid locale identifier entry.

@TRANSACTION

If you are concerned about the possibility of losing data during transmissions, you can make use of the COM capabilities of Windows 2000, IIS and VB, by specifying that you want to use transactions. Transactions help ensure that data transfer either completes successfully or not at all. A good example of this is the use of automatic teller machines. If your ATM transaction is interrupted in the middle for some reason, you don't want your account charged for a withdrawal when you didn't get the money. The use of transactions helps to solve this problem.

Using the @TRANSACTION directive will tell IIS that you want to use transactions for this script. In this case, the Component Services on the computer will create the necessary transaction to keep track of the processing and ensure that the necessary transaction takes place.

Syntax

```
<%@ TRANSACTION=value %>
```

The *value* variable can contain one of the following values.

- **Required**—This will cause the script to initiate a transaction.
- **Requires_New**—This also causes an initiation of a transaction.
- **Supported**—A transaction will not be initiated.
- **Not-Supported**—A transaction will not be initiated.

NOTE

The @TRANSACTION directive must be the first line of the page to prevent IIS from generating an error. You must also ensure that it is on every page that needs to use transactions.

global.asa Reference

The global.asa file is an optional file used to declare objects for your ASP pages that need to have Session or Application scope. This file must be located in the root directory of the application, and each application can have only one global.asa file.

The global.asa file is only permitted to contain the following items:

- **<OBJECT> Declarations**—These declarations are used to create objects on the server that are required for Session or Application scope. An example would look like this:

```
<OBJECT RUNAT=server SCOPE=Session ID=adHot
➥PROGID="MSWC.AdRotator"></OBJECT>
```

  This will create an Ad Rotator object that will run on the server with Session scope.

- **TypeLibrary Declarations**—Type libraries are files that contain information about objects supported by COM components. More information on TypeLibrary can be found later in this appendix in the section "TypeLibrary Declarations."

- **Application Events**—These are events such as Application_Onstart and Application_OnEnd. These are covered later in the section "Application Events."

- **Session Events**—There are two session events, Session_OnStart and Session_OnEnd. These are discussed in the section "Session Events."

You can write your scripts in any supported language for use in the global.asa file. Any script that is not enclosed by the <SCRIPT> tags will generate an error.

Any HTML in the global.asa file is ignored as are any tagged scripts that are not used by the application or session events.

If there are any active sessions or applications in use at the time you modify the global.asa file, the changes will not take place until all applications and sessions have ended. At this time, the server will end all sessions and applications, recompile the global.asa file and then save the changes.

> **NOTE**
>
> When you make changes to the global.asa file and save it, the server will continue to process existing sessions and applications until they end. However, it will not allow any new connections until the global.asa file has been recompiled.

When you are working with a global.asa file and procedures within your ASP code, it is important to remember that any procedure or function that is defined in the global.asa file is not available to the procedures in your ASP code. These procedures and functions in the `global.asa` file are only available to scripts that call the `Application_Onstart`, `Application_OnEnd`, `Session_OnStart`, and `Session_OnEnd` events. If you need to allow procedures or functions to be available to all applications or a group of applications, it is a better idea to create the procedure in a file and include that file in the pages that require the functionality that the procedure provides.

Application Events

When you create an application in ASP to run on IIS, the application and all its supporting files exist in a root directory and any subdirectories of that root that might be needed.

When a user accesses a Web page that contains the ASP code, he is starting that application. When the application first starts, the server will look for the `global.asa` file in the root directory of the application, and, if it exists, the server will process the `Application_OnStart` event script.

When the application ends, the server will then process the `Application_OnEnd` script.

Application_OnStart

This event is the first event that is processed when an application starts. The `Session_OnStart` event has not been processed yet, and any scripts within the `Session_OnStart` event are not available to your code. The only objects available to your code are the Application and Server objects. Any references to objects other than these two will generate an error.

Syntax

```
<SCRIPT LANGUAGE=scriptlanguage RUNAT=Server>
Sub Application_OnStart
    Code goes here
End Sub
</SCRIPT>
```

The *scriptlanguage* variable is used to indicate the scripting language used.

Example

```
Sub Application_OnStart

    Application("PageCounter") = 0

End Sub
```

This small sample code snippet demonstrates using the `Application_OnStart` event to reset a page counter to 0. You might want to use this to reset the page counter to 0 each time the application starts. You might use this to determine how many times within the same application session that the page is accessed.

There are other methods of the Application object that are used within your script code as well, such as `Application.Lock` or `Application.Unlock`. These two methods are used to prevent any changes to the Application object while a user is accessing a portion of it. These two methods are not required in the `Application_OnStart` event because the event is only called once.

Application_OnEnd

When all session code has ended and the `Session_OnEnd` event has been processed, the only available objects to your application are the Server and Application objects.

This is not a problem because normally you will be using the `Application OnEnd` event to set any application-level declared objects to nothing to clean up memory usage.

Syntax

```
<SCRIPT LANGUAGE=scriptlanguage RUNAT=Server >

Sub Application_OnEnd
    Code goes here
End Sub

</SCRIPT>
```

The `scriptlanguage` variable is used to hold the name of the scripting language that will be used. Multiple script languages can be used on the same page, and they can be combined in the same <SCRIPT> tags. For example

Example

```
<SCRIPT LANGUAGE=VBScript RUNAT=Server>
code goes here
</SCRIPT>
```

> **NOTE**
>
> You cannot call the `MapPath` method from the `Application_OnEnd` script.

Session Events

When a new client connects to the server and attempts to use an application, the server will start a new session for that user. This session will persist for that user until the timeout value is reached with no activity or the `Abandon` method is called.

There are two methods related to Sessions, **Session_OnStart** and **Session_OnEnd**. These methods can contain scripts that are executed in the *Global.asa* file when an application starts.

D

SCRIPT REFERENCE

NOTE

Session tracking is enabled by default and can be disabled by using the @ENABLESESSIONSTATE directive as discussed earlier in this appendix.

Session_OnStart

When a user makes a request for a Web page that contains an application, the Session_OnStart event is processed before the page is executed and returned to the user. For this reason, this event is a good place to put code that initializes and sets any systemwide variables.

The Application, ObjectContext, Response, Request, and Server objects are all available to this event.

Syntax

```
<SCRIPT LANGUAGE= scriptlanguage RUNAT=Server>
Sub Session_OnStart
    code goes here
End Sub
</SCRIPT>
```

The *scriptlanguage* variable indicates a valid scripting language that is installed on the computer.

Example

```
<SCRIPT RUNAT=Server LANGUAGE=VBScript>
Sub Session_OnStart
Dim startPage, currentPage
startPage = "/MyApp/StartPage.asp"
currentPage = Request.ServerVariables("SCRIPT_NAME")

If strcomp(currentPage,startPage,1) then
➥Response.Redirect(startPage)
End If
End Sub
</SCRIPT>
```

This code example will only work for browsers that support cookies because it makes use of the SessionID property. For those browsers that do not support cookies, a new session will be started for every page they visit.

Session_OnEnd

This event occurs if the session timeout value is reached or if the session has been abandoned. The only objects available to this event are the Application, Server, and Session objects.

Syntax

```
<SCRIPT LANGUAGE=scriptlanguage RUNAT=Server>
Sub Session_OnEnd

code goes here

End Sub
</SCRIPT>
```

The *scriptlanguage* variable indicates the scripting language that will be used on the page.

Example

```
<SCRIPT LANGUAGE=VBScript RUNAT=Server>
Sub Session_OnEnd

Set objSomeObject = Nothing

End Sub
</SCRIPT>
```

D

This event is a good place to locate any code that cleans up session variables.

<OBJECT> Declarations

The <OBJECT> tag is a self-contained tag that can reside outside of the <SCRIPT> tags. It can be used to create global objects that are available for application or session use.

When the scripts are processed in the `global.asa` file, the objects are created at that time.

Syntax

```
<OBJECT RUNAT=Server SCOPE=Scope ID=Id {PROGID="progid"|CLASSID="classid"}>

code goes here

</OBJECT>
```

Scope indicates the scope for the object. This value will be either Application or Session in the `global.asa` file.

Id gives the object a name that can be referenced in code.

progid is an identifier for the object that is associated with a class identifier. The format for this ID is normally *Vendor.Component.Version*.

classid specifies a unique ID for a COM class object.

> **NOTE**
>
> You must specify either a *progid* or a *classid* in the <OBJECT> tag.

Example

```
<OBJECT RUNAT=Server SCOPE=Session ID=dbConnection PROGID="ADODB.Connection">

code goes here

</OBJECT>
```

This example creates an ADODB database connection with a session scope. By declaring this variable here in the `global.asa` file, you can reference it from anywhere in your script code. This makes sense if you have more than one Web page that needs to gain access to the same database. By declaring the variable in the `global.asa` file, each page can make reference to the object there and doesn't need to declare an ADODB connection for each page.

TypeLibrary Declarations

You use a TypeLibrary declaration to specify information about objects and types that are supported by COM components. You can then refer to the data for the type from within your code using the type library name.

Syntax

```
<!--METADATA TYPE="TypeLib"
FILE="filepath"
UUID="typelibraryuuid"
VERSION="majorversionnumber.minorversionnumber"
LCID="localeid"
-->
```

The *filepath* variable specifies an absolute path to the type library.

typelibraryuuid is a universally unique identifier for the type library. Either this parameter or the *filepath* parameter must be provided.

majorversionnumber is an optional parameter that specifies the version to select. The most recent version will be selected if the requested version does not exist.

minorversionnumber is an optional parameter that specifies the version to select. The most recent version will be selected if the requested version does not exist.

localeid specifies a locale to use for the type library. If the requested locale ID is not found, then the default system locale will be used.

When working with type libraries, some errors can occur. The server will return the following error messages for the specified reasons:

- ASP 0222—Invalid type library specification. The METADATA tag contains an invalid type library specification.
- ASP 0223—Type library not found. The METADATA tag contains a type library specification that does not match any Registry entry.
- ASP 0224—Type library cannot be loaded. ASP cannot load the type library specified in the METADATA tag.
- ASP 0225—Type library cannot be wrapped. ASP cannot create a Type Library Wrapper object from the type libraries specified in the METADATA tag.

Example

```
<!--METADATA TYPE="TypeLib"
FILE="C:\wwwroot\gkcomput\typelibs\NewComponent.tlb"
VERSION="1.0"
LCID="localeid"
-->
```

Here you see the typelib declared for a component called NewComponent with the full pathname specified instead of a UUID. The version number is indicated along with the locale ID.

TIP

It is a good practice to place your type declarations at the top of the global.asa file. This makes it easier to determine the type libraries used in the code by just scanning the top of the file.

TIP

In much the same way as you get accustomed to using the object.method or object.property syntax, you can also use the same concept with type libraries. For example, ADODB.strConnection is easier to decipher than strConnection in code.

Programmatic Administration Examples

IN THIS APPENDIX

There are quite a few tasks that can take up some time with IIS using the snap-in or HTML-based tools. There are also some prebuilt scripts that can help you to perform some of these tasks more efficiently or automatically.

Microsoft provides some sample scripts to help you perform some common tasks. You can also use these scripts to learn how to write your own.

These scripts can be written in VBScript or JScript, whichever you are comfortable using. The scripts that are included with IIS 5.0 are meant to be executed using Windows Scripting Host (WSH) using the Wscript.exe or the Cscript.exe utility.

The Cscript utility is intended to be used at the command line and follows the syntax

```
Cscript.exe scriptname
```

wherein *scriptname* is the name of the script that you want to run.

You can run the Wscript.exe utility within a window using the same syntax as the Cscript.exe utility.

If you want to execute more than one script at a time, you can place the commands into a batch file.

> **NOTE**
>
> In order for these scripts to execute on the computer, WSH must be installed locally to interpret the commands.

Metabase Backup

This utility is perhaps one of the most important scripts that Microsoft could have supplied. Because the metabase contains so much important information regarding your IIS installation's configuration, it is important to ensure that it is backed up on a regular basis. This script can help you do that. In Listing E.1, I have reproduced the script that you will find in the \InetPub\iissamples\sdk\admin; it is called metaback.vbs. There is also a JScript backup script called metaback.js.

For those not familiar with the coding techniques of VBScript or Visual Basic in general, the underscore (_) indicated in lines 53, 92, 96, 102, 105, and 114 is used to indicate that the line of code is continued on the next line and should be written on one line if possible. The code is clipped here for space purposes of printing.

Also note that the line numbers are not entered in the code. They are only added here as a reference to help you when I discuss the script file.

LISTING E.1   *Metaback.vbs*

```
1  '''''''''''''''''''''''''''''''''''''''''''''''
2  '
3  '   Metabase Backup Utility
4  '
5  '''''''''''''''''''''''''''''''''''''''''''''''
6
7  ' Description:
8  ' ------------
9  ' This sample admin script allows you to create a backup of your
10 '  Metabase.
11 '
12 '  To Run:
13 '  -------
14 '  This is the format for this script:
15 '
16 '        cscript metaback.vbs
17 '
18 '  NOTE:   If you want to execute this script directly from Windows, 18
19 " ' use 'wscript' instead of 'cscript'.
20 '
21 '''''''''''''''''''''''''''''''''''''''''''''''
22
23 ' Initialize error checking
24 On Error Resume Next
25
26 ' Initialize variables
27 Dim ArgCount, BuName, BuVersion, BuFlags, CompObj, VersionMsg
28
29 ' Default values
30 ArgCount = 0
31 BuName= "SampleBackup"
32 BuVersion = &HFFFFFFFF    ' Use next available version number
33 BuFlags = 0    ' No special flags
34
35
36  ' ** Parse Command Line
37
38  ' Loop through arguments
39  While ArgCount < Wscript.Arguments.Count
40
41  ' Determine switches used
42    Select Case Wscript.Arguments(ArgCount)
43
44        Case "-v":    ' Designate backup version number
```

LISTING E.1   Continued

```
45            ' Move to next arg, which should be parameter
46            ArgCount =  ArgCount + 1
47            If ArgCount => Wscript.Arguments.Count Then
48                Call UsageMsg
49            Else
50                BuVersion = Wscript.Arguments(Argcount)
51            End If
52
53   Case "-F":   ' Force overwrite, even if name and version_
54 exists
55            BuFlags = 1
56
57        Case "-h", "-?", "/?":
58            Call UsageMsg
59        Case Else:
60            If BuName <> "SampleBackup" Then   ' Only one name allowed
61                Call UsageMsg
62            Else
63                BuName = Wscript.Arguments(ArgCount)
64            End If
65
66     End Select
67
68     ' Move pointer to next argument
69     ArgCount = ArgCount + 1
70
71   Wend
72
73
74
75 ' **Perform Backup:
76 ' First, create instance of computer object
77 Set CompObj = GetObject("IIS://Localhost")
78
79 ' Call Backup method, with appropriate parameters
80 CompObj.Backup BuName, BuVersion, BuFlags
81
82   ' Make pretty version string
83 If BuVersion = &HFFFFFFFF Then
84        VersionMsg = "next version"
85 Else
86        VersionMsg = "version " & BuVersion
87 End If
88
89   ' Check for error backing up Metabase
```

```
90  If Err <> 0 Then   'Errors!
91       If Err.Number = &H80070050 Then    ' Duplicate backup
92            Wscript.Echo "'" & BuName & "' (version " & BuVersion &_
93            ➥") already exists. -F switch will causes existing version to be
94            replaced."
95       Else    ' Something else went wrong
96            Wscript.Echo "Error backing up Metabase to '" & BuName &
97            ➥   "' (" & VersionMsg & ")."
98            Wscript.Echo "Error number:  " & Hex(Err.Number)
99       End If
100 Else    ' No errors!
101      If BuFlags = 1 Then   ' Forced creation
102           Wscript.Echo "Force created: Backup '" & BuName & "'
103           ➥("_ 103 & VersionMsg & ")."
104      Else
105           Wscript.Echo "Created: Backup '" & BuName & "'
106           ➥(" &         VersionMsg & ")."
107      End If
108 End If
109
110
111
112 ' Displays usage message, then QUITS
113 Sub UsageMsg
114   Wscript.Echo "Usage:  cscript metaback.vbs [<backupname>]
115   ➥[-v_ <versionnum>][-F (to force)]"
116   Wscript.Quit
117 End Sub
```

Listing E.1 is used to perform a backup of the metabase. When you first issue the script command to execute it, the code will first parse the command that you issued for any options specified in the command line. This code sequence starts on line 39 and continues to line 71. If any option switches are found, they will be applied.

Line 77 starts the backup sequence by requesting an object to fill the CompObj variable with a value returned by the GetObject method. This object will be used to access the metabase for the local computer as specified by Localhost. Replace Localhost with the name or IP address of the computer you will be working with.

Line 80 applies the command line option switches that the parse routine returned.

Lines 90 to 108 contain an error-checking routine. This is not the same as an error-handling routine for code errors. This routine checks the backup status to see if any errors are encountered during the backup. Any errors encountered are displayed by using the Echo command to display the content on the screen at the command prompt.

Lines 113 to 117 contain a little subroutine that will display the syntax for the command if a user doesn't enter the command correctly and then quits the script.

For the most part, you should not need to perform any modifications on this script to make it work on the local computer on which it resides.

Metabase Restore

It only makes sense that, if you can back up the Registry, you should also be able to restore it. The metabackrest.vbs script is used for this purpose.

You will find this script in the same location as the backup script. It is reproduced in Listing E.2 for your convenience and for discussion purposes.

LISTING E.2 Metabackrest.vbs

```
1  '''''''''''''''''''''''''''''''''''''''''''''''''''
2  '
3  '  Metabase Backup Restore Utility
4  '
5  '''''''''''''''''''''''''''''''''''''''''''''''''''
6
7  '  Description:
8  '  -----------
9  '  This sample admin script allows you to restore backups of your

10 ' metabase
11 '
12 '  To Run:
13 '  -------
14 '  This is the format for this script:
15 '
16 '      cscript metabackrest.vbs
17 '
18 '  NOTE:  If you want to execute this script directly from Windows,
19    use
20 '  'wscript' instead of 'cscript'.
21 '
22 '''''''''''''''''''''''''''''''''''''''''''''''''''
23
24 ' Initialize error checking
25 On Error Resume Next
26
27 ' Initialize variables
28 Dim ArgCount, BuName, BuVersion, BuFlags, CompObj, VersionMsg
29
```

```
30 ' Default values
31 ArgCount = 0
32 BuName= "SampleBackup"
33 BuVersion = &HFFFFFFFE    ' Use highest version number
34 BuFlags = 0    ' RESERVED, must stay 0
35
36
37   ' ** Parse Command Line
38
39   ' Loop through arguments
40   While ArgCount < Wscript.Arguments.Count
41
42     ' Determine switches used
43     Select Case Wscript.Arguments(ArgCount)
44
45       Case "-v":    ' Designate backup version number
46         ' Move to next arg, which should be parameter
47         ArgCount =  ArgCount + 1
48         If ArgCount => Wscript.Arguments.Count Then
49            Call UsageMsg
50         Else
51            BuVersion = Wscript.Arguments(Argcount)
52         End If
53
54       Case "-?", "-h", "/?":
55         Call UsageMsg
56
57       Case Else:
58         If BuName <> "SampleBackup" Then   ' Only one name allowed
59            Call UsageMsg
60         Else
61            BuName = Wscript.Arguments(ArgCount)
62         End If
63
64     End Select
65
66     ' Move pointer to next argument
67     ArgCount = ArgCount + 1
68
69   Wend
70
71
72 ' **Perform backup restore:
73 ' First, create instance of computer object
74 Set CompObj = GetObject("IIS://Localhost")
75
```

LISTING E.2   Continued

```
76  ' Call Restore method
77  ' NOTE:   ** All IIS services will be stopped by this method, then
78    restarted!
79  Wscript.Echo "All services stopping ..."
80  CompObj.Restore BuName, BuVersion, BuFlags  ' NOTE: for
81   restoration, BuFlags MUST be 0
82
83  ' Make pretty version string
84  If BuVersion = &HFFFFFFFE Then
85       VersionMsg = "highest version"
86  Else
87       VersionMsg = "version " & BuVersion
88  End If
89
90  ' Check for error backing up Metabase
91  If Err <> 0 Then   'Errors!
92       If Err.Number = 5 Then   ' Location name not available
93          Wscript.Echo "Error restoring Metabase: '" & BuName & "'
94  (" & VersionMsg & ") not available."
95       Else
96          Wscript.Echo "Error restoring Metabase from '" & BuName &
97   "' (" & VersionMsg & ")."
98          Wscript.Echo "Error number:  " & Hex(Err.Number)
99       End If
100      Wscript.Echo "Services restarting."
102 Else   ' No errors!
103      Wscript.Echo "Restored: Backup '" & BuName & "' (" &
104  VersionMsg & ")."
105      Wscript.Echo "Services restarted."
106 End If
107 ' Display usage messsage, then QUIT
108 Sub UsageMsg
109 Wscript.Echo "Usage:  cscript metabackrest.vbs <backupname> [-v
110 ➡ <versionnum>]"
111 Wscript.Quit
112   End Sub
```

Rather than going through this script as I did Listing E.1, I'll just point out the differences.

As I mentioned in Appendix B in the section on restoring the IIsComputer Object, the IIS services must be stopped before any restore operation is performed. This script will stop the services, as indicated on lines 76 to 80. There is no stop command, but the Restore command will stop the service.

Once the Restore is completed, the IIS services will be restarted.

Both the backup and restore scripts are available in VBScript and Jscript versions in the indicated directory. You can create your own scripts in a language of your choice, providing you install a valid, supported scripting engine.

Summary

This appendix provided information on the backup and restore scripts only as they are the two most important scripts for your IIS installation that are already included with the IIS product. They can be used as a guide to developing your own scripts or customized to suit your specific needs. Be sure to check out the admin samples that come with IIS in the directory mentioned in this appendix for more examples of administration scripts that can be executed from the command line.

INDEX

SYMBOLS

A

B

M